CHELSEA HOUSE PUBLISHERS
Modern Critical Views

HENRY ADAMS
EDWARD ALBEE
A. R. AMMONS
MATTHEW ARNOLD
JOHN ASHBERY
W. H. AUDEN
JANE AUSTEN
JAMES BALDWIN
CHARLES BAUDELAIRE
SAMUEL BECKETT
SAUL BELLOW
THE BIBLE
ELIZABETH BISHOP
WILLIAM BLAKE
JORGE LUIS BORGES
ELIZABETH BOWEN
BERTOLT BRECHT
THE BRONTËS
ROBERT BROWNING
ANTHONY BURGESS
GEORGE GORDON, LORD BYRON
THOMAS CARLYLE
LEWIS CARROLL
WILLA CATHER
CERVANTES
GEOFFREY CHAUCER
KATE CHOPIN
SAMUEL TAYLOR COLERIDGE
JOSEPH CONRAD
CONTEMPORARY POETS
HART CRANE
STEPHEN CRANE
DANTE
CHARLES DICKENS
EMILY DICKINSON
JOHN DONNE & THE
    17th-CENTURY POETS
ELIZABETHAN DRAMATISTS
THEODORE DREISER
JOHN DRYDEN
GEORGE ELIOT
T. S. ELIOT
RALPH ELLISON
RALPH WALDO EMERSON
WILLIAM FAULKNER
HENRY FIELDING
F. SCOTT FITZGERALD
GUSTAVE FLAUBERT
E. M. FORSTER
SIGMUND FREUD
ROBERT FROST

ROBERT GRAVES
GRAHAM GREENE
THOMAS HARDY
NATHANIEL HAWTHORNE
WILLIAM HAZLITT
SEAMUS HEANEY
ERNEST HEMINGWAY
GEOFFREY HILL
FRIEDRICH HÖLDERLIN
HOMER
GERARD MANLEY HOPKINS
WILLIAM DEAN HOWELLS
ZORA NEALE HURSTON
HENRY JAMES
SAMUEL JOHNSON
BEN JONSON
JAMES JOYCE
FRANZ KAFKA
JOHN KEATS
RUDYARD KIPLING
D. H. LAWRENCE
JOHN LE CARRÉ
URSULA K. LE GUIN
DORIS LESSING
SINCLAIR LEWIS
ROBERT LOWELL
NORMAN MAILER
BERNARD MALAMUD
THOMAS MANN
CHRISTOPHER MARLOWE
CARSON MCCULLERS
HERMAN MELVILLE
JAMES MERRILL
ARTHUR MILLER
JOHN MILTON
EUGENIO MONTALE
MARIANNE MOORE
IRIS MURDOCH
VLADIMIR NABOKOV
JOYCE CAROL OATES
SEAN O'CASEY
FLANNERY O'CONNOR
EUGENE O'NEILL
GEORGE ORWELL
CYNTHIA OZICK
WALTER PATER
WALKER PERCY
HAROLD PINTER
PLATO
EDGAR ALLAN POE

POETS OF SENSIBILITY &
    THE SUBLIME
ALEXANDER POPE
KATHERINE ANNE PORTER
EZRA POUND
PRE-RAPHAELITE POETS
MARCEL PROUST
THOMAS PYNCHON
ARTHUR RIMBAUD
THEODORE ROETHKE
PHILIP ROTH
JOHN RUSKIN
J. D. SALINGER
GERSHOM SCHOLEM
WILLIAM SHAKESPEARE (3 vols.)
    HISTORIES & POEMS
    COMEDIES
    TRAGEDIES
GEORGE BERNARD SHAW
MARY WOLLSTONECRAFT SHELLEY
PERCY BYSSHE SHELLEY
EDMUND SPENSER
GERTRUDE STEIN
JOHN STEINBECK
LAURENCE STERNE
WALLACE STEVENS
TOM STOPPARD
JONATHAN SWIFT
ALFRED LORD TENNYSON
WILLIAM MAKEPEACE THACKERAY
HENRY DAVID THOREAU
LEO TOLSTOI
ANTHONY TROLLOPE
MARK TWAIN
JOHN UPDIKE
GORE VIDAL
VIRGIL
ROBERT PENN WARREN
EVELYN WAUGH
EUDORA WELTY
NATHANAEL WEST
EDITH WHARTON
WALT WHITMAN
OSCAR WILDE
TENNESSEE WILLIAMS
WILLIAM CARLOS WILLIAMS
THOMAS WOLFE
VIRGINIA WOOLF
WILLIAM WORDSWORTH
RICHARD WRIGHT
WILLIAM BUTLER YEATS

Further titles in preparation.

Modern Critical Views

WILLIAM SHAKESPEARE
Histories & Poems

Modern Critical Views

WILLIAM SHAKESPEARE
Histories & Poems

Edited with an introduction by

Harold Bloom

Sterling Professor of the Humanities
Yale University

1986
CHELSEA HOUSE PUBLISHERS
New York
New Haven   Philadelphia

THE COVER:

The cover gives us a view of the Monarch of Wit, Sir John Falstaff, in his tavern world, preferring a wench and a bottle to politics and battle.—H.B.

PROJECT EDITORS: Emily Bestler, James Uebbing
EDITORIAL COORDINATOR: Karyn Gullen Browne
ASSOCIATE EDITOR: Maria Behan
EDITORIAL STAFF: Laura Ludwig, Linda Grossman, Perry King, Marena Fisher, Susan Laity
DESIGN: Susan Lusk

Cover illustration by Kye Carbone

Library of Congress Cataloging in Publication Data

William Shakespeare.
    (Modern critical views)
    Includes bibliographies and indexes.
    Contents: Pt. 1. The tragedies—pt. 2. The
histories and poems.
    1. Shakespeare, William, 1564–1616—Criticism
and interpretation—Addresses, essays, lectures.
I. Bloom, Harold. II. Series.
PR2976.W535   1986   822.3'3   85–3815

ISBN 0–87754–658–4

Chelsea House Publishers
Harold Steinberg, Chairman and Publisher
Susan Lusk, Vice President
A Division of Chelsea House Educational Communications, Inc.
133 Christopher Street, New York, NY 10014

Contents

Editor's Note

This volume is a representative selection of the best criticism devoted to Shakespeare's poems and history plays. It is arranged in the chronological order of publication, from 1930 to the present day.

My "Introduction" centers upon Falstaff as Shakespeare's largest single instance of original representation in the history plays. One of the purposes of this volume is to juxtapose several very different modern perspectives upon Falstaff, including my own, and the views of Goddard, Wyndham Lewis, Barber and Kernan, which together afford a fairly comprehensive vision of the only figure in Shakespeare who challenges Hamlet and Cleopatra in variety and profundity.

The chronological sequence begins with the late William Empson's two challenging exegeses of the sonnets. E. M. W. Tillyard's classic reading of *Richard II* prepares for the warmth and insight of Harold C. Goddard's loving account of Falstaff, and the shrewdness of Wyndham Lewis's portrait of the fat knight as shaman, proto-Machiavel, woman and child.

Two very different, but equally distinguished readings of Shakespeare's long poems, *Venus and Adonis* and *The Rape of Lucrece*, by Muriel C. Bradbrook and C. S. Lewis, provide another compelling contrast in modes of criticism.

We return to Falstaff with C. L. Barber's brilliant interpretation of *Henry IV* as a mingling of social order with ritual magic and public festivity. Again this is complemented by the unmatched reading of *Richard III* by A. P. Rossiter, where the "cruel-comic side" of Shakespeare's King Richard III is seen as opening perspectives upon Iago, Macbeth and even Coriolanus.

Stephen Booth's thorough and discriminating way of analyzing the sonnets provides an interlude of minute examination of Shakespeare's rhetorical art before we return to Falstaff, for a last time, with Alvin B. Kernan's reading of "The Henriad," the major cycle of the history plays. Kernan's Falstaff is marked by "quick opportunism, raw common sense, and cat-footed sense of survival." If my introduction and Goddard's essay are wholly on Falstaff's side, and Wyndham Lewis's and Barber's partly set against him, Kernan's portrait may be said to be the best balanced, being perhaps the worldliest.

With Frank Kermode's unmatched reading of the enigmatic "The Phoenix and the Turtle," we return to Shakespeare's poems. Anne Barton's dramatically informed interpretation of *Henry V* completes this volume's consideration of *The Henriad*. Finally, the essay by John Blanpied on *King John* ends this book. Blanpied's analysis of "strong possession" as a trope at once political, theatrical, and psychological opens yet another perspective not only upon *King John*, but upon the cosmos of Falstaff and all the history plays.

Introduction

I

Falstaff is to the world of the histories what Shylock is to the comedies, and Hamlet to the tragedies: *the* problematical representation. Falstaff, Shylock, Hamlet put to us the question: precisely how does Shakespearean representation differ from anything before it, and how has it overdetermined our expectations of representation ever since?

⸳   The fortunes of Falstaff in scholarship and criticism have been endlessly dismal, and I will not resume them here. I prefer Harold Goddard on Falstaff to any other commentator, and yet I am aware that Goddard appears to have sentimentalized and even idealized Falstaff. I would say better that than the endless litany absurdly patronizing Falstaff as Vice, Parasite, Fool, Braggart Soldier, Corrupt Glutton, Seducer of Youth, Cowardly Liar and everything else that would not earn the greatest wit in all literature an honorary degree at Yale or a place on the board of the Ford Foundation.

Falstaff, I will venture, in Shakespeare rather than in Verdi, is precisely what Nietzsche tragically attempted yet failed to represent in his Zarathustra: a person without a superego, or should I say, Socrates without the *daimon*? Perhaps even better, Falstaff is not the Sancho Panza of Cervantes, but the exemplary figure of Kafka's parable, "The Truth about Sancho Panza." Kafka's Sancho Panza, a free man, has diverted his *daimon* from him by many nightly feedings of chivalric romances (it would be science fiction, nowadays). Diverted from Sancho, his true object, the *daimon* becomes the harmless Don Quixote, whose mishaps prove edifying entertainment for the "philosophic" Sancho, who proceeds to follow his errant *daimon*, out of a sense of responsibility. Falstaff's "failure," if it can be termed that, is that he fell in love, not with his own *daimon*, but with his bad son, Hal, who all too truly is Bolingbroke's son. The witty knight should have diverted his own *daimon* with Shakespearean comedies, and philosophically have followed the *daimon* off to the forest of Arden.

Falstaff is neither good enough nor bad enough to flourish in the world of the histories. But then he is necessarily beyond, not only good and evil, but cause and effect as well. A greater monist than the young Milton, Falstaff plays at dualism partly in order to mock all dualisms, whether Christian, Platonic or even the Freudian dualism that he both anticipates and in some sense refutes.

Falstaff provoked the best of all critics, Dr. Johnson, into the judgment that "he has nothing in him that can be esteemed." George Bernard Shaw, perhaps out of envy, called Falstaff "a besotted and disgusting old wretch." Yet Falstaff's sole rival, in Shakespeare, is Hamlet; no one else, as Oscar Wilde noted, has so comprehensive a consciousness. Representation itself changed permanently because of Hamlet and Falstaff. I begin with my personal favorite among all of Falstaff's remarks, if only because I plagiarize it daily:

> O, thou hast damnable iteration, and art indeed able to corrupt a saint: thou hast done much harm upon me, Hal, God forgive thee for it: before I knew thee, Hal, I knew nothing, and now am I, if a man should speak truly, little better than one of the wicked.

W. H. Auden, whose Falstaff essentially was Verdi's, believed the knight to be "a comic symbol for the supernatural order of charity," and thus a displacement of Christ into the world of wit. The charm of this reading, though considerable, neglects Falstaff's grandest quality, his immanence. He is as immanent a representation as Hamlet is transcendent. Better than any formulation of Freud's, Falstaff perpetually shows us that the ego indeed is always a bodily ego. And the bodily ego is always vulnerable, and Hal indeed has done much harm upon it, and will do far worse, and will need forgiveness, though no sensitive audience ever will forgive him. Falstaff, like Hamlet, and like Lear's Fool, does speak truly, and Falstaff remains, despite Hal, rather better than one of the wicked, or the good.

For what is supreme immanence in what might be called the order of representation? This is another way of asking: is not Falstaff, like Hamlet, so original a representation that he originates much of what we know or expect about representation? We cannot see how original Falstaff is because Falstaff *contains* us; we do not contain him. And though we love Falstaff, he does not need our love, any more than Hamlet does. His sorrow is that he loves Hal rather more than Hamlet loves Ophelia, or even Gertrude. The Hamlet of Act V is past loving anyone, but that is a gift (if it is a gift) resulting from transcendence. If you dwell wholly in this world, and if you are, as Falstaff is, a *pervasive* entity, or as Freud would say, "a strong egoism," then you must begin to love, as Freud also says, in order that you may not fall ill. But what if your strong egoism is not afflicted by any ego-ideal, what if you are never watched, or watched over, by what is above the ego? Falstaff is *not* subject to a power that watches, discovers and criticizes all his intentions. Falstaff, except for his single and misplaced love, is free, is freedom itself, because he seems free of the superego.

II

Why does Falstaff (and not his parody in *The Merry Wives of Windsor*) pervade histories rather than comedies? To begin is to be free, and you cannot begin freshly in comedy, any more than you can in tragedy. Both genres are family romances, at least in Shakespeare. History, in Shakespeare, is hardly the genre of freedom for kings and nobles, but it is for Falstaff. How and why? Falstaff is of course his own mother and his own father, begotten out of wit by caprice. Ideally he wants nothing except the audience, which he always has; who could watch anyone else on stage when Ralph Richardson was playing Falstaff? Not so ideally, he evidently wants the love of a son, and invests in Hal, the impossible object. But primarily he has what he must have, the audience's fascination with the ultimate image of freedom. His precursor in Shakespeare is not Puck or Bottom, but Faulconbridge the Bastard in *The Life and Death of King John.* Each has a way of providing a daemonic chorus that renders silly all royal and noble squabbles and intrigues. The Bastard in *John*, forthright like his father, Richard the Lion Heart, is not a wicked wit, but his truthtelling brutally prophesies Falstaff's function.

There are very nearly as many Falstaffs as there are critics, which probably is as it should be. These proliferating Falstaffs tend either to be degraded or idealized, again perhaps inevitably. One of the most ambiguous Falstaffs was created by the late Sir William Empson: "he is the scandalous upper-class man whose behavior embarrasses his class and thereby pleases the lower class in the audience, as an 'exposure.' " To Empson, Falstaff also was both nationalist and Machiavel, "and he had a dangerous amount of power." Empson shared the hint of Wyndham Lewis that Falstaff was homosexual, and so presumably lusted (doubtless in vain) after Hal. To complete this portrait, Empson added that Falstaff, being both an aristocrat and a mob leader, was "a familiar dangerous type," a sort of Alcibiades, one presumes.

Confronted by so ambiguous a Falstaff, I return to the sublime knight's rhetoric, which I read very differently, since Falstaff's power seems to me not at all a matter of class, sexuality, politics, or nationalism. Power it is: sublime pathos, *potentia*, the drive for life, more life, at every and any cost. I will propose that Falstaff is neither a noble synecdoche nor a grand hyperbole, but rather a metalepsis or far-fetcher, to use Puttenham's term. To exist without a superego is to be a solar trajectory, an ever-early brightness, which Nietzsche's Zarathustra, in his bathos, failed to be. "Try to live as though it were morning," Nietzsche advises. Falstaff does not need the advice, as we discover when we first encounter him:

> FALSTAFF: Now, Hal, what time of day is it lad?
> PRINCE: Thou art so fat-witted with drinking of old sack, and unbuttoning thee after supper, and sleeping upon benches after noon, that thou hast forgotten to demand that truly which thou wouldst truly know. What a devil hast thou to do with the time of day? Unless hours were cups of sack, and minutes capons, and clocks the tongues of bawds, and dials the signs of leaping-houses, and the blessed sun himself a fair hot wench in flame-coloured taffeta, I see no reason why thou shouldst be so superfluous to demand the time of day.

I take it that wit here remains with Falstaff, who is not only witty in himself but the cause of wit in his ephebe, Prince Hal, who mocks his teacher, but in the teacher's own exuberant manner and mode. Perhaps there is a double meaning when Falstaff opens his reply with: "Indeed, you come near me now, Hal," since near is as close as the Prince is capable of, when he imitates the master. Master of what? is the crucial question, generally answered so badly. To take up the stance of most Shakespeare scholars is to associate Falstaff with: "such inordinate and low desires, /Such poore, such bare, such lewd, such mean attempts,/Such barren pleasures, rude society." I quote King Henry the Fourth, aggrieved usurper, whose description of Falstaff's aura is hardly recognizable to the audience. We recognize rather: "Counterfeit? I lie, I am no counterfeit; to die is to be a counterfeit, for he is but the counterfeit of a man, who hath not the life of a man: but to counterfeit dying, when a man thereby liveth, is to be no counterfeit, but the true and perfect image of life himself." As Falstaff rightly says, he has saved his life by counterfeiting death, and presumably the moralizing critics would be delighted had the unrespectable knight been butchered by Douglas, "that hot termagant Scot."

The true and perfect image of life, Falstaff, confirms his truth and perfection by counterfeiting dying and so evading death. Though he is given to parodying Puritan preachers, Falstaff has an authentic obsession with the dreadful parable of the rich man and Lazarus in Luke 16:19 ff. A certain rich man, a purple-clad glutton, is contrasted with the beggar Lazarus, who desired "to be fed with the crumbs which fell from the rich man's table: moreover the dogs came and licked his sores." Both glutton and beggar die, but Lazarus is carried into Abraham's bosom, and the purple glutton into hell, from which he cries vainly for Lazarus to come and cool his tongue. Falstaff stares at Bardolph, his Knight of the Burning Lamp, and affirms: "I never see thy face but I think upon hell-fire, and Dives that lived in purple: for there he is in his robes, burning, burning." Confronting his hundred and fifty tattered prodigals, as he marches them off to be food for powder, Falstaff calls them "slaves as ragged as Lazarus in the painted cloth, where the glutton's dogs licked his sores." In *Part II* of *Henry the Fourth*, Falstaff's first speech again returns to this fearful text, as he cries out against one who denies him credit: "Let him be damn'd like the glutton! Pray God his tongue be hotter!" Despite the ironies abounding in Falstaff the glutton invoking Dives, Shakespeare reverses the New Testament, and Falstaff ends, like Lazarus, in Abraham's bosom, according to the convincing testimony of Mistress Quickly in *Henry V*, where Arthur Britishly replaces Abraham:

> BARDOLPH: Would I were with him, wheresome'er he is, either in heaven or in hell!
> HOSTESS: Nay sure, he's not in hell; he's in Arthur's bosom, if ever man went to Arthur's bosom. 'A made a finer end, and went away and it had been any christom child.

In dying, Falstaff is a newly baptized child, innocent of all stain. The pattern of allusions to Luke suggests a crossing over, with the rejected Falstaff a poor Lazarus upon his knees in front of Dives wearing the royal purple of Henry V. To a moralizing critic, this is outrageous, but Shakespeare does stranger tricks with Biblical texts. Juxtapose the two moments:

> FALSTAFF: My King, My Jove! I speak to thee, my heart!
> KING: I know thee not, old man, fall to thy prayers. How ill white hairs becomes a fool and jester! I have long dreamt of such a kind of man, So surfeit-swell'd, so old, and so profane; But being awak'd, I do despise my dream.

And here is Abraham, refusing to let Lazarus come to comfort the "clothed in purple" Dives:

> And beside all this, between us and you there is a great gulf fixed: so that they which would pass from hence to you cannot: neither can they pass to us, that would come from thence.

Wherever Henry V is, he is not in Arthur's bosom, with the rejected Falstaff.

III

I suggest that Shakespearean representation, in the histories, indeed demands our understanding of what Shakespeare did to history, in contrast to what his contemporaries did. Standard scholarly views of literary history, and all Marxist reductions of literature and history alike, have the curious allied trait of working very well for, say, Thomas Dekker, but being absurdly irrelevant for Shakespeare. Falstaff and the Tudor theory of kingship? Falstaff and surplus value? I would prefer Falstaff and Nietzsche's vision of the use and abuse of history for life, if it were not that Falstaff triumphs precisely where the Overman fails. One can read Freud on our discomfort in culture backwards, and get somewhere close to Falstaff, but the problem again is that Falstaff triumphs precisely where Freud denies that triumph is possible. With Falstaff as with Hamlet (and, perhaps, with Cleopatra) Shakespearean representation is so self-begotten and so influential that we can apprehend it only by seeing that it originates us. We cannot judge a mode of representation that has overdetermined our ideas of representation. Like only a few other authors—the Yahwist, Chaucer, Cervantes, Tolstoi—Shakespeare calls recent critiques of literary representation severely into doubt. Jacob, the Pardoner, Sancho Panza, Hadji Murad: it seems absurd to call them figures of rhetoric, let alone to see Falstaff, Hamlet, Shylock, Cleopatra as tropes of ethos and/or of pathos. Falstaff is not language but diction, the product of Shakespeare's will over language, a will that changes characters through and by what they say. Most simply, Falstaff is not how meaning is renewed, but rather how meaning gets started.

Falstaff is so profoundly original a representation because most truly he represents the essence of invention, which is the essence of poetry. He is a perpetual catastrophe, a continuous transference, a universal family romance. If Hamlet is beyond us and beyond our need of him, so that we require our introjection of Horatio, so as to identify ourselves with Horatio's love for Hamlet, then Falstaff too is beyond us. But in the Falstaffian beyonding, as it were, in what I think we must call the Falstaffian sublimity, we are never permitted by Shakespeare to identify ourselves with the Prince's ambivalent affection for Falstaff. Future monarchs have no friends, only followers, and Falstaff, the man without a superego, is no one's follower. Freud never speculated as to what a person without a superego would be like, perhaps because that had been the dangerous prophecy of Nietzsche's Zarathustra. Is there not some sense in which Falstaff's whole being implicitly says to us: "The wisest among you is also merely a conflict and a hybrid between plant and phantom. But do I bid you become phantoms or plants?" Historical critics who call Falstaff a phantom, and moral critics who judge Falstaff to be a plant, can be left to be answered by Sir John himself. Even in his debased form, in *The Merry Wives of Windsor*, he crushes them thus:

> Have I liv'd to stand at the taunt of one that makes fritters of English? This is enough to be the decay of lust and late-walking through the realm.

But most of all Falstaff is a reproach to all critics who seek to demystify mimesis, whether by Marxist or deconstructionist dialectics. Like Hamlet, Falstaff is a super-mimesis, and so compels us to see aspects of reality we otherwise could never apprehend. Marx would teach us what he calls "the appropriation of human reality" and so the appropriation also of human suffering. Nietzsche and his deconstructionist descendants would teach us the necessary irony of failure in every attempt to represent human reality. Falstaff, being more of an original, teaches us himself: "No, that's certain, I am not a double man; but if I be not Jack Falstaff, then am I a Jack." A double man is either a phantom or two men, and a man who is two men might as well be a plant. Sir John is Jack Falstaff; it is the Prince who is a Jack or rascal, and so are Falstaff's moralizing critics. We are in no position then to judge Falstaff or to assess him as a representation of reality. Hamlet is too dispassionate even to *want* to contain us. Falstaff is passionate, and challenges us not to bore him, if he is to deign to represent us.

WILLIAM EMPSON

Some Types of Ambiguity
in Shakespeare's Sonnets

The fundamental situation, whether it deserves to be called ambiguous or not, is that a word or a grammatical structure is effective in several ways at once. [*First-type ambiguities arise when a detail is effective in several ways at once, e.g. by comparisons with several points of likeness, antitheses with several points of difference, "comparative" adjectives, subdued metaphors, and extra meanings suggested by rhythm.*] To take a famous example, there is no pun, double syntax, or dubiety of feeling, in

> Bare ruined choirs, where late the sweet birds sang,

but the comparison holds for many reasons; because ruined monastery choirs are places in which to sing, because they involve sitting in a row, because they are made of wood, are carved into knots and so forth, because they used to be surrounded by a sheltering building crystallised out of the likeness of a forest, and coloured with stained glass and painting like flowers and leaves, because they are now abandoned by all but the grey walls coloured like the skies of winter, because the cold and Narcissistic charm suggested by choir-boys suits well with Shakespeare's feeling for the object of the Sonnets, and for various sociological and historical reasons (the protestant destruction of monasteries; fear of puritanism), which it would be hard now to trace out in their proportions; these reasons, and many more relating the simile to its place in the Sonnet, must all combine to give the line its beauty, and there is a sort of

---

ambiguity in not knowing which of them to hold most clearly in mind. Clearly this is involved in all such richness and heightening of effect, and the machinations of ambiguity are among the very roots of poetry. . . .

[*In second-type ambiguities two or more alternative meanings are fully resolved into one.*]

. . . It is clear that ambiguity, not of word, but of grammar, though common enough in poetry, cannot be brought to this pitch without chaos, and must in general be used to produce a different effect. Where there is a single main meaning (the case we are now considering) the device is used, as in the following examples from Shakespeare Sonnets, to give an interpenetrating and, as it were, fluid unity, in which phrases will go either with the sentence before or after and there is no break in the movement of the thought.

> But heaven in thy creation did decree
> That in thy face sweet love should ever dwell,
> Whate'er thy thoughts or thy heart's workings be,
> Thy looks should nothing thence, but sweetness tell.
>
> (xciii)

You may put a full stop either before or after the third line.

> That tongue that tells the story of thy days
> (Making lascivious comments on thy sport)
> Cannot dispraise, but in a kind of praise,
> Naming thy name, blesses all ill report.
>
> (xcv)

The subject of *blesses* is either *tongue* or *naming*, and *but in a kind of praise* qualifies either *blesses* or *dispraise*. These devices are particularly useful in managing the sonnet form because they help it to combine variety of argumentation and the close-knit rhythmical unity of a single thought.

There is in the following Sonnet one of those important and frequent subtleties of punctuation, which in general only convey rhythm, but here it amounts to a point of grammar.

> If thou survive my well contented daye
> When that churle death my bones with dust shall cover
> And shalt by fortune once more re-survey:
> These poor rude lines of thy deceased Lover:
> Compare them with the bettering of the time, . . .
>
> (xxxii)

Line 4 is isolated between colons, carries the whole weight of the pathos, and is a pivot round which the rest of the Sonnet turns. *Re-survey* might conceivably be thought of as intransitive, so that line 4 could go with line 5 in apposition to *them*, but the point is not that either line 3 or line 5 could stand without line 4, it is in fact next to both of them, and yet it stands out from either, as if the Sonnet had become more conscious of itself, or was making a quotation from a tombstone.

> Thou doost love her, because thou knowest I love her,
> And for my sake even so doth she abuse me,
> Suffering my friend for my sake to approve her,
> If I loose thee, my loss is my love's gaine,
> And loosing her, my friend hath found that losse. . . .
>
> (xlii)

According as line 3 goes backwards or forwards, the subject of *suffering* is either *she* or *I*. The device is not here merely a rhythmic one, but it carries no great depth of meaning; the Elizabethans were trained to use lines that went both ways, for example in those chains of Sonnets, such as the *Corona* of Donne, in which each began with the last line of the one before.

Donne, indeed, uses these methods with vehemence; I shall break this series from the Sonnets for a moment to quote an example from the *Epithalamion for Valentine's Day*.

> Thou mak'st a Taper see
> What the sunne never saw, and what the Arke
> (Which was of Soules, and beasts, the cage, and park)
> Did not containe, one bed containes, through thee,
> Two Phoenixes, whose joyned breasts . . .

"You make a taper see what the ark did not contain. Through you one bed contains two phoenixes." "You make a taper see what the sun never saw. Through you one bed contains what the ark did not contain, that is, two phoenixes." The renewal of energy gained from starting a new sentence is continually obtained here without the effect of repose given by letting a sentence stop.

> Who lets so fair a house fall to decay,
> Which husbandry in honour might uphold
> Against the stormy gusts of winter's day
> And barren rage of death's eternal cold?
> O none but unthrifts, *dear my love you know,*
> You had a Father, let your Son say so.
>
> (xiii)

The phrase in italics is equally suited to the sentences before and after it; taking it as the former, a third meaning shows itself faintly, that *you know unthrifts;* "the company you keep may be riotous or ascetic, but is not matrimonial." Having quoted this for a comparatively trivial point of grammar, it seems worth pointing out that its beauty depends first on the puns, *house* and *husbandry,* and secondly on the shift of feeling from *winter's day,* winter is short, like its days; "your child will grow up after you and your house will survive to see another summer," to *death's eternal cold;* "if the house does not survive this winter it falls for ever"; there is a contrast between these two opposite ideas and the two open, similarly vowelled, Marlowan lines that contain them, which claim by their struc-ture to be merely repeating the same thought, so that the two notions are dissolved into both of them, and form a regress of echoes.

Sometimes the ambiguous phrase is a relative clause, with "that" omitted, which is able to appear for a moment as an independent sentence on its own, before it is fitted into the grammar.

> Their images I lov'd, I view in thee,
> And thou (all they) has all the all of me.
>
> (xxxi)

There is some suggestion that the first clause may be wholly independent, and that *I view in thee* means "I look for them in you"; but on the whole the device merely puts "which I loved" into special prominence.

> My life hath in this line some interest,
> Which for memorial still with thee shall stay.
> When thou reviewest this, thou dost review,
> The very part was consecrate to thee,
>
> (ixxiv)

Passing over the comma at the end of the third line, the object of *review* is *part;* stressing the comma, it says tautologically, with the emphasis on the second *thou,* "it is enough immortality for me to be remembered by you," and the fourth line becomes a separate sentence.

This fluidity of grammar is partly given by rhetorical balance, because since the lines are opposed to one another in regular pairs you still get some sort of opposition by opposing the wrong pair. Sonnet lxxxi. runs this principle to death:

> Or shall I live your Epitaph to make,
> Or you survive when I in earth am rotten,
> From hence your memory death cannot take,
> Although in me each part will be forgotten.
> Your name from hence immortall life shall have,
> Though I (once gone) to all the world must dye,
> The earth can yeeld me but a common grave,

> When you entombed in men's eyes shall lye,
> Your monument shall be my gentle verse,
> Which eyes not yet created shall ore-read,
> And toungs to be, your beeing shall rehearse,
> When all the breathers of this world are dead,
> > You still shall live (such vertue hath my Pen)
> > Where breath most breathes, even in the mouths of men.

Any two consecutive lines in this, except 2–3 and 10–11 for accidental reasons, make a complete sentence when separated from their context; I do not say that this makes it a good sonnet, or that I know how it ought to be read aloud.

Tongues can *over-read* as well as *eyes*, and this would leave either *being* the subject of *rehearse*, or both *tongues* and *eyes*. However, *tongues* is particularly connected with *rehearse*, because the contrast of *your being* with *to be* ("in order to be") shows the transient tongues *rehearsing* your ideal *being*, lapping up your blood as it were, and thus implies a sort of timeless Platonic existence for Mr. W. H., informing the examples of his type, but in no way dependent on them. These shadows of his perfection were once to have been his children, but Shakespeare's partly scoptophile desire to see him settled in love has by now been with a painful irony thwarted or over-satisfied, and they are now no more than those who read his praise.

The following Sonnet is more two-faced in idea ("a complaint in the form of an assertion that he has no right to complain"), but can be put in the second type so far as concerns the ambiguity of syntax, as it reduces to a single meaning:

> O let me suffer (being at your beck)
> The imprisoned absence of your liberty,
> And patience tame, to sufferance bide each check,
> Without accusing you of injury.
> Be where you list, your charter is so strong
> That you yourself may privilege your time
> To what you will, to you it doth belong,
> Yourself to pardon of self-doing crime.
>
> > > > > > > (lviii)

And patience tame expresses petulance by its contraction of meaning ("suffer tame patience"; "be patience-tame," is in iron-hard; and "tame patience," as in *bide each check*) followed by a rush of equivocal words, clinched with *belong,* which has for subject both *your time* and *to pardon,* and implies, still with sweetness and pathos (it is an extraordinary balance of feeling), "that is all I could have expected of you."

> But wherefore do not you a mightier waie
> Make warre vppon this bloudie tirant time?
> And fortifie your selfe in your decay
> With meanes more blessed than my barren rime?
> Now stand you on the top of happie houres,
> And many maiden gardens yet unset,
> With vertuous wish would beare your liuing flowers,
> Much liker then your painted counterfeit:
> So should the lines of life that life repaire
> Which this (Times pencil or my pupil pen)
> Neither in inward worth nor outward faire
> Can make you liue your selfe in eyes of men,
>   To give away your selfe, keeps your selfe still,
>   And you must liue drawn by your owne sweet skill.
>
> (xvi)

Lines of life refers to the form of a personal appearance, in the young man himself or repeated in his descendants (as one speaks of the lines of some one's figure); time's wrinkles on that face (suggested only to be feared); the young man's line or lineage—his descendants; lines drawn with a pencil—a portrait; lines drawn with a pen, in writing; the lines of a poem (the kind a Sonnet has fourteen of); and destiny, as in the lifeline of palmistry—Merchant of Venice, II. ii. 163.

This variety of meaning is rooted more effectively in the context because lines of life and that life may either of them be taken as subject of repair; taking the most prominent meanings, "lineage" and "the features of yourself and your children," lines is subject, and this is also insisted upon by rhythm and the usual sentence order; that life means "life such as your present one." But that life (repair) is given a secondary claim to the position by this (. . . make), which follows evidently in contrast, as subject in the next line. (Punctuations designed to simplify the passage all spoil the anthithesis.) This has a bracket expanding its meanings: time, bringing old age that will pencil you with wrinkles, or a riper manhood that will complete your beauty; this Times pencil, firstly, the style of painting, or average level of achievement, of Elizabethan portrait-painters; secondly, the frame and "atmosphere" given to beauty by that age of masques and gorgeous clothing and the lust of the eye (so that we must look back to the second line of the Sonnet, where the same double meaning is hinting that beautiful courtiers in the wake of Essex came to bad ends); my pen that describes you, pupil as immature and unskillful: as pupil of that time whose sonnet tradition I am imitating; or of Time which matures me. A natural way to take it is that life, "your life," and this, "my life" (devoted to describing you), but the meaning of this opens out into all the transient effects which are contrasted with the solid eternity of reproduction, and by reflection backwards *that life* is made subject of its sentence, meaning "the new way of life I propose to you," that is, of matrimony, or of the larger extra-human life in your lineage as a whole.

Independently of whether *lines of life* or *that life* is subject and whether *that life* is "your present way of life" or "the way of life I propose to you," there is a double syntax for lines 11 and 12. Taking them together there is a main reading, "the age of Elizabeth is not competent to express you, either in your appearance or character" (of the two pairs one would naturally associate the artist's pencil with *outward fair*, and the playwright's pen with *inward worth*, but the order is the other way round, so that each works with either, or "I try to write about your beauty, but the hand of time, graving the lines of character on your face, tries to show your inward worth"). This, the main grammar, involves a rather clumsy change from *life* to *you* in the object, and this greater directness of address, needed after the sagging of grammar in the extraordinary complexity of the intervening two lines, leaves room for an alternative syntax. For, taking line 11 with 10 (and preferably *that life* as subject), it is *this* which is not fair either in inward or outward worth; *make*, of the present age, which has produced out of its worthlessness such a beauty as yours, is opposed to *repair* of the vegetable life, capable of producing many such flowers, which I propose to you; as if the greater durability given to a type by making it repeatable, giving it to a noble house rather than a single person, was compared to making it anew, as "risen a heavenly body," in the next world, or to the placing of it timelessly among Platonic ideas, so that it need not be anxious about its particular patterns on earth; *live* of line 12 then becomes an adjective, and the force of so many words in apposition, *you, live, yourself,* is to express wonder at the production of such a thing out of the dull world of line 11, and make the young man, by contrast, ideal, heavenly, or worthy of being made into a general type. Line 13, separated from lines 12 and 14 equally by commas, is as a main meaning cut off into the final couplet, "you are not less yourself because you have had children," but in the minor sense has for subject *this*, "your present life of pleasure and brilliance carries in it no eternity, and keeps you only to give you away." *Drawn* of line 14 then may take an additional echo of meaning, as "drawing back," dragging yourself out of your present way of life, which your lover has not power to do for you.

Ambiguities of this sort may be divided into those which, once understood, remain an intelligible unit in the mind; those in which the pleasure belongs to the act of working out and understanding, which must at each reading, though with less labour, be repeated; and those in which the ambiguity works best if it is never discovered. Which class any particular poem belongs to depends in part on your mental habits and critical opinions, and I am afraid that for many readers who have the patience to follow out this last analysis, it will merely spoil what they had taken for a beautiful Sonnet by showing it to be much more muddled than they had realised. This is a pity, but however wise the view may be that poetry cannot safely be analysed, it seems to me to remain ignoble; and in so far as people are sure that their pleasure will not bear thinking about, I am surprised that they have the patience not to submit them to so easy a destruction. The fact is, if analysis gets in your way, it is easy enough to forget it; I do not think that all these meanings should pass through the mind in an appreciative reading of this Sonnet; what is gathered is the main sense, the main form and rhythm, and a general sense of compacted intellectual wealth, of an elaborate balance of variously associated feeling. . . .

[*In the fourth type the alternative meanings combine to make clear a complicated state of mind in the author.*]

An ambiguity of the fourth type occurs when two or more meanings of a statement do not agree among themselves, but combine to make clear a more complicated state of mind in the author. Evidently this is a vague enough definition which would cover much of the third type, and almost everything in the types which follow; I shall only consider here its difference from the third type. [*The condition for third-type ambiguity is that two apparently unconnected meanings are given simultaneously.*]

One is conscious of the most important aspect of a thing, not the most complicated; the subsidiary complexities, once they have been understood, merely leave an impression in the mind that they were to such-and-such an effect and they are within reach if you wish to examine them. I put into the third type cases where one was intended to be mainly conscious of a verbal subtlety; in the fourth type the subtlety may be as great, the pun as distinct, the mixture of modes of judgment as puzzling, but they are not in the main focus of consciousness because the stress of the situation absorbs them, and they are felt to be natural under the circumstances. Of course, different readers apply their consciousness in different ways, and a line which taken alone would be of the third type may become of the fourth type in its setting; but the distinction, I think, is usually clear.

> I never saw that you did painting need,
> And therefore to your fair no painting set,
> I found (or thought I found) you did exceed,
> The barren tender of a Poet's debt:

And therefore have I slept in your report,
That you yourself being extant well might show,
How far a modern quill doth come too short,
Speaking of worth, what worth in you doth grow,
This silence for my sin you did impute,
Which shall be most my glory being dumb,
For I impair not beauty being mute,
When others would give life, and bring a tomb.
   There lives more life in one of your fair eyes,
   Than both your Poets can in praise devise.

                       (lxxxiii)

Shakespeare is the writer upon whom ingenuity has most often been misapplied; and if his syntax appears ambiguous, it may be because the Elizabethan rules of punctuation trusted to the reader's intelligence and were more interested in rhetoric than in grammar. One must pause before shadowing with irony this noble compound of eulogy and apology. But one may notice its position in the sequence (Shakespeare seems to have been taunted for his inferiority, and is being abandoned for the rival poet); the mixture of extraordinary claims and bitter humility with which it is surrounded; and that the two adjacent Sonnets say: "Thou truly fair were truly sympathised/In true plain words by thy truth-telling friend," and "You to your beauteous blessings add a curse, Being fond on praise, which makes your praises worse." It is not true that the feeling must be simple because it is deep; irony is similar to this kind of lyrical self-abandonment, or they relieve similar situations; by the energy with which such an adoration springs forward one can measure the objections which it is overriding, by the sharpness of what is treated as an ecstasy one may guess that it would otherwise have been pain.

Line 2, then, goes both with line 1 and line 3. Taking it with line 1, Shakespeare was only concerned for the young man's best interests: "I did not praise you in verse because I could not see that your reputation could be set any higher by my praise." Even for this, the primary, meaning there are two implications; either *never* "until you told me to praise you," an order accepted humbly but with some echo of *being fond on praise*, or *never* "until I found you out"; "At one time I had not yet discovered that your cheeks needed rouge, and your character white-wash"; "When I first loved you I did not realise that you had this simple and touching desire for flattery."

The first line may also stand alone, as an introduction, with these meanings, so that line 2 goes with line 3; for this version one would put a comma after *therefore*; "And so, when no painting had been set to your fairness" (paint to your cheeks or to a portrait, praise to your beauty or to your virtue, apology to your vices), "I found that you exceeded" (in beauty, in virtue, or in wildness of life); "And so, judging you simply, not foreseeing the defences I should have to build up against feeling harshly of you, it came to me as a shock to know you as you are." The first version is much the stronger, both because *I found* is parallel to *I never saw* and because *exceed* wants to pass over the comma and take the fourth line as its object; indeed, I put the second version down less from conviction than because I cannot now read the line without thinking of it.

For the various senses of line 4 we must first consider the meaning of *tender*, which is almost wholly limited into its legal sense by *debt;* "offered payment of what is due." This is coloured, however, by "tender regard" (I *Henry IV.*, v. iv. 49); also the meaning "person who looks after" may be fancied in the background. Taking the word as object of *exceed*, we have: "I found you were worth more than the normal compliments due from a poet hired to write eulogies of you," "I found that you exceeded what I could express of beauty in verse," "I found your tenderness towards me exceeded the barren tenderness I owed you as your tame poet," "I found that you were more to me than the person who would see to it that the hired poet wrote adequate praises." These assume the *poet's debt* is a debt owed *by* a poet. Taking it as owed *to* a poet, we have: "I have found that you gave me more than you need have done," "I found that you treated me more as a friend than as a hired poet," and "I found you felt for me more generously than I felt for you, when I merely looked after my job and wrote eulogies of you." I am being verbose here to show the complexity of the material; the resultant ideas from all these permutations are only two: "You were treating me as a friend, not as a poet," and "You were more than I could describe." Here *tender* is the object of *exceed*, but, stressing the comma after *exceed, tender* may be either, as a mere echo, a second object of *found*, "I found only the barren tender," "You did *not* treat me more as a friend than as a poet, so I stopped writing" (*or thought I found* is now a more generous doubt), or may be a comment in apposition to the whole first three lines: "This was merely my business; I thought your beauty and virtue so excessive because that was the proper thing; to be expected from a poet in love; to be expected from a professional poet trying to win favour at Court." Most people in reading the line only recognise the meaning, "You were more than I could describe," but they are made to feel also in the word *barren* a more dreary and more petty way of feeling about the matter, they know there is some bitterness which this wave of generosity has submerged.

Therefore in line 5 seems parallel to *therefore* in line 2, so that it could refer to *found* or *saw*. Or with a larger rhythm, the fifth line refers to the whole first quatrain and starts a new one. Alternatively, *therefore* may refer forward to line 6: "for this reason . . . in order that." *Report* is either what people in general say or what Shakespeare says, or what Shakespeare writes, about him; thus *I have slept in your report* means either "I have stopped writing about you," or "I have stopped contradicting rumours about you," or "I have bolstered up my faith in you by accepting the public's good opinion of you." *That* means "in order that" (you might show well), "the fact that" (I have slept, which your being extant well shows), or "for fear that" (your being extant might show how far a modern quill comes too short). *Extant* means visible, or successful and respected, or the subject of scandal. *How* and *what* follow *show* and *speaking* respectively, but for variations of grammar which leave them detached they may be regarded as introducing an exclamation and a question. The last line of the quatrain evidently refers backwards as its main meaning: "A modern quill comes too short when attempting to write of as much worth as is in you"; it can also refer forwards, but in trying to regard it in this way one is bothered by a modern usage which could take it alone; "and, talking of worth, *are* you worth anything, now, frankly?" This is not an Elizabethan idiom and was certainly not intended, but its coarseness is hard to keep out of one's mind, because the version which takes line 8 with line 9 is very similar to it: "I was describing all the worth I could find in you without the effort of flattery, and this amounted to the silences of which you, being fond of praise, have been complaining." If you like you may call his version ridiculous, and hurriedly place a colon at the end of the second quatrain; but please notice that the line may still be read as: "I was afraid that a modern quill might come short of a high standard of worth in describing all the worth that it can find in you."

This seems to me a good illustration of the difference between the third type of ambiguity and the fourth. Shakespeare was exquisitely conscious of such subsidiary uses of grammar and the jokes that could be made out of bad stops (if example is needed, consider Quince in Act v., scene i. of the *Dream*); but I do not think he was conscious of these alternatives (certainly I do not think that the reader who is apprehending the result as poetry should be conscious of these alternatives) in a clear-cut way as if they were jokes. They do not need to be separated out to give their curious and harrowing overtone to the quatrain; and once they have been separated out, they can only be connected with the mood of the poem if you hold clearly in mind the third quatrain which is their reconciliation. I might first paraphrase the second. "I have not written or talked about you fully, as the absence, or the particular kind, or the excess of scandal about you shows; *either* because your reality was already a sufficient expression of your beauty and virtue, *or* in order that you might still make a good show in the eyes of the world, as you might not if I were to describe you as I now know you, *or* for fear that the contrast between you and your description might be bad for the literary reputation of the Elizabethans, *or* for fear that the contrast between what this time and previous times could produce in the way of beauty and virtue might be bad for the Elizabethan reputation as a whole."

It would be possible to regard line 12, which clinches the third quatrain, as an antithesis: "When others would bring life, I in fact bring a tomb." This might be Shakespeare's *tomb*; "I do not flatter you but I bring you the devotion of a lifetime." More probably it is W. H.'s; "I do not attempt to flatter you at the moment; I bring you the sad and reserved gift of an eternal praise." We may extract from this some such meaning as: "I do not describe your beauty or your faithlessness, but my love for you." However, there are two other ways of taking the syntax which destroy this antithesis: "When others would bring life, I, if I wrote about you, would bring a tomb," and "When others would try to write about you, would try to give you life, and thereby bring you a tomb"; for both these the *tomb* must imply some action which would *impair beauty*. The normal meaning is given by Sonnet xvii.:

> Who will beleeve my verse in time to come
> If it were fild with your most high deserts?
> Though yet Heaven knowes it is but as a tombe
> Which hides your life, and shows not halfe your parts.

This first use of the word has no doubt that it is eulogy; the Sonnet is glowing and dancing with his certitude. But when the metaphor is re-peated, this time without being explained, it has grown dark with an incipient double meaning; "I should fail you, now that you have behaved so badly to me, if I tried to express you in poetry; I should give you myself, and draw from my readers, a cold and limited judgment, praise you without sincerity, or blame you without thinking of the living man." ("Simply the thing I am Shall make me live"; Shakespeare continually draws on a generosity of this kind. It is not "tout comprendre," in his view, it is merely to feel how a man comes to be a working system, which necessarily excites a degree of sympathy.)

A literary conundrum is tedious, and these meanings are only worth detaching in so far as they are dissolved into the single mood of the poem. Many people would say that they cannot all be dissolved, that an evidently delicate and slender Sonnet ought not to take so much explaining, whatever its wealth of reference and feeling, that Shakespeare, if all this is true, wrote without properly clarifying his mind. One might protest *via* the epithet "natural," which has stuck to Shakespeare through so many literary fashions; that he had a wide rather than a sharp focus to his mind; that he snatched ideas almost at random from its balanced but multitudinous activity; that this is likely to be more so rather than less in his personal poetry; and that in short (as Macaulay said in a very different connection) the reader must take such grammar as he can get and be thankful. One might apologise by saying that people have always read obscure meanings into Shakespeare, secure in the feeling, "If it means less, why is it so beautiful?" and that this analysis can only be offered as another mode of approaching so mysterious a totality, another glance at the effects of language. Or it may boldly be said that the composition of feeling, which never falls apart among these ambiguities (it is, on any interpretation, pained, bitter, tender and admiring: Shakespeare is being abandoned by W. H., and stiffly apologising for not having been servile to him), rises and is clinched plainly in the final couplet; we are reminded of the references to the roving eye glancing round for new conquests; Shakespeare includes the whole ambiguity in his enthusiasm; the worth and sin, the beauty and painting, are all delightful to him, and too subtle to be grasped. . . .

WILLIAM EMPSON

They That Have Power

It is agreed that *They that have power to hurt and will do none* is a piece of grave irony, but there the matter is generally left; you can work through all the notes in the Variorum without finding out whether flower, lily, 'owner,' and person addressed are alike or opposed. One would like to say that the poem has all possible such meanings, digested into some order, and then try to show how this is done, but the mere number of possible interpretations is amusingly too great. Taking the simplest view (that any two may be alike in some one property) any one of the four either is or is not and either should or should not be like each of the others; this yields 4096 possible movements of thought, with other possibilities. The niggler is routed here; one has honestly to consider what seems important.

'The best people are indifferent to temptation and detached from the world; nor is this state selfish, because they do good by unconscious influence, like the flower. You must be like them; you are quite like them already. But even the best people must be continually on their guard, because they become the worst, just as the pure and detached lily smells worst, once they fall from their perfection'—('one's prejudice against them is only one's consciousness of this fact'—the hint of irony in the poem might be covered by this). It is a coherent enough Confucian sentiment, and there is no very clear hint as to irony in the words. No doubt *as stone* goes intentionally too far for sympathy, and there is a suggestive gap in the argument between octet and sestet, but one would not feel this if it was Shakespeare's only surviving work.

There is no reason why the subtlety of the irony in so complex a material must be capable of being pegged out into verbal explanations. The vague and generalised language of the descriptions, which might be talking about so many sorts of people as well as feeling so many things about them, somehow makes a unity like a cross-roads, which analysis does not deal with by exploring down the roads; makes a solid flute on which you can play a multitude of tunes, whose solidity no list of all possible tunes would go far to explain. The balance of feeling is both very complex and very fertile; experiences are recorded, and metaphors invented, in the Sonnets, which he went on 'applying' as a dramatist, taking particular cases of them as if they were wide generalisations, for the rest of his life. One can't expect, in writing about such a process, to say anything very tidy and complete.

But one does not start interpreting out of the void, even though the poem once partly interpreted seems to stand on its own. If this was Shakespeare's only surviving work it would still be clear, supposing one knew about the other Elizabethans, that it involves somehow their feelings about the Machiavellian, the wicked plotter who is exciting and civilised and in some way right about life; which seems an important though rather secret element in the romance that Shakespeare extracted from his patron. In any case one has only to look at the sonnets before and after it to be sure that it has some kind of irony. The one before is full of fear and horror at the hypocrisy he is so soon to recommend; and yet it is already somehow cuddled, as if in fascination or out of a refusal to admit that it was there.

> So shall I liue, supposing thou art true,
> Like a deceiued husband, . . .
> For ther can liue no hatred in thine eye
> Therefore in that I cannot know thy change, . . .
> How like *Eaues* apple doth thy beauty grow,
> If thy sweet vertue answere not thy show.

So the *summer's flower* may be its apple-blossom. His virtue is still sweet, whether he has any or not; the clash of fact with platonic idealism is too fearful to be faced directly. In the sonnet after, with a blank and exhausted humility, it has been faced; there remains for the expression of his love, in the least flaunting of poetry, the voice of caution.

> How sweet and louely dost thou make the shame, . . .
> Take heed (deare heart) of this large privilege.

The praise of hypocrisy is in a crucial and precarious condition of balance between these two states of mind.

The root of the ambivalence, I think, is that W. H. is loved as an arriviste, for an impudent worldliness that Shakespeare finds shocking and delightful. The reasons why he treated his poet badly are the same as the reasons why he was fascinating, which gives its immediate point to the profound ambivalence about the selfishness of the flower. Perhaps he is like the cold person in his hardness and worldly judgment, not in his sensuality and generosity of occasional impulse; like the flower in its beauty, vulnerability, tendency to excite thoughts about the shortness of life, self-centredness, and power in spite of it to give pleasure, not in its innocence and fertility; but the irony may make any of these change over. Both owner and flower seem self-centred and inscrutable, and the cold person is at least like the lily in that it is symbolically chaste, but the summer's flower, unlike the lily, seems to stand for the full life of instinct. It is not certain that the owner is liable to fester as the lily is—Angelo did, but W. H. is usually urged to acquire the virtues of Angelo. Clearly there is a jump from octet to sestet; the flower is not like the owner in its solitude and its incapacity to hurt or simulate; it might be because of this that it is of a summer only and may fester; yet we seem chiefly meant to hold W. H. in mind and take them as parallel. As for punctuation, the only full stop is at the end; all lines have commas after them except the fourth, eighth, and twelfth, which have colons.

> They that haue powre to hurt, and will doe none,
> That doe not do the thing, they most do showe,
> Who mouing others, are themselves as stone,
> Vnmoued, could, and to temptation slow:

They may *show*, while hiding the alternative, for the first couplet, the power to hurt or the determination not to hurt—cruelty or mercy, for the second, the strength due to chastity or to sensual experience, for either, a reckless or cautious will, and the desire for love or for control; all whether they are stealers of hearts or of public power. They are a very widespread group; we are only sure at the end that some kind of hypocrisy has been advised and threatened.

> They rightly do inherit heavens graces,
> And husband natures ritches from expence,

Either 'inherit, they alone, by right' or 'inherit what all men inherit and use it rightly'; these correspond to the opposed views of W. H. as aristocrat and vulgar careerist. There is a similar range of idea, half hidden by the pretence of easy filling of the form, in the pun on *graces* and shift to *riches*. *Heaven's graces* may be prevenient grace (strength from God to do well), personal graces which seem to imply heavenly virtues (the charm by which you deceive people), or merely God's gracious gift of *nature's riches*; which again may be the personal graces, or the strength and taste which make him capable either of 'upholding his house' or of taking his pleasure, or merely the actual wealth of which he is an *owner*. Clearly this gives plenty of room for irony in the statement that the cold people, with their fine claims, do well all round; it also conveys 'I am seeing you as a whole; I am seeing these things as necessary rather than as your fault.'

> They are the Lords and owners of their faces,
> Others, but stewards of their excellence:

It may be their beauty they put to their own uses, high or low, or they may just have poker-faces; this gives the same range of statement. The capital which tends to isolate *lords* from its phrase suggests 'they are the only true aristocrats; if you are not like them you should not pretend to be one.' *Others* may be stewards of their own excellence (in contrast with *faces*—'though they are enslaved they may be better and less superficial than the cold people') or of the cold people's excellence (with a suggestion of 'Their Excellencies'); the less plausible sense is insisted on by the comma after *others*. This repeats the doubt about how far the cold people are really excellent, and there may be a hint of a doubt about how far the individual is isolated, which anticipates the metaphor of the flower. And 'stewards of their own excellence' may be like 'stewards of the buttery' or like 'stewards of a certain lord'; either 'the good things they have do good to others, not to them' (they are too generous; I cannot ask you to aim so high in virtue, because I desire your welfare, not other people's, and indeed because you wouldn't do it anyway) or 'they are under the power of their own impulses, which are good things so long as they are not in power' (they are deceived; acts caused by weakness are not really generous at all). Yet this may be the condition of the flower and the condition for fullness of life; you cannot know beforehand what life will bring you if you open yourself to it, and certainly the flower does not; it is because they are unnatural and unlike flowers that the cold people rule nature, and the cost may be too great. Or the flower and the cold person may be two unlike examples of the limitation necessary to success, one experienced in its own nature, the other in the world; both, the irony would imply, are in fact *stewards*.

There is a Christian parable at work in both octet and sestet; in the octet that of the talents. You will not be forgiven for hoarding your talents; some sort of success is demanded; you must at least use your powers to the full even if for your own squalid purpose. The pain and wit and solemnity of *rightly*, its air of summing up a long argument, depend on the fact that these metaphors have been used to recommend things to W. H. before.

> Natures bequest giues nothing but doth lend,
> And being franck she lends to those are free:

> Who lets so faire a house fall to decay,
> Which husbandry in honour might uphold,

Rightly to be free with yourself, in the first simple paradox, was the best saving of yourself (you should put your money into marriage and a son); it is too late now to advise that, or to say it without being sure to be understood wrongly (this is 94; the first sonnet about his taking Shakespeare's mistress is 40); the advice to be generous as natural has become the richer but more contorted advice to be like the flower. Rightly to husband nature's riches, earlier in the sequence, was to accept the fact that one is only steward of them;

> Thou that art now the worlds fresh ornament,
> And only herauld to the gaudy spring,
> Within thine owne bud buriest thy content,
> And tender chorle makst waste in niggarding:

the flower was wrong to live to itself alone, and would become a tottered weed (2) whether it met with infection or not.

Though indeed *husbandry* is still recommended; it is not the change of opinion that has so much effect but the use of the same metaphors with a shift of feeling in them. The legal metaphors (debts to nature and so forth) used for the loving complaint that the man's chastity was selfish are still used when he becomes selfish in his debauchery; Shakespeare's own notation here seems to teach him; the more curiously because the metaphors were used so flatly in the earliest sonnets (1, 2, 4, 6, then 13; not again till now), only formally urging marriage, and perhaps written to order. It is like using a mathematical identity which implies a proof about a particular curve and then finding that it has a quite new meaning if you take the old constants as variables. It is these metaphors that have grown, till they involve relations between a man's powers and their use, his nature and his will, the individual and the society, which could be applied afterwards to all human circumstances.

> The sommers flowre is to the sommer sweet,
> Though to it selfe, it onely liue and die,

The use of *the* summer's flower about a human being is enough to put it at us that the flower will die by the end of summer, that the man's life is not much longer, and that the pleasures of the creature therefore cannot be despised for what they are. *Sweet to the summer* (said of the flower), since the summer is omnipresent and in a way Nature herself, may mean 'sweet to God' (said of the man); or may mean 'adding to the general sweetness; sweet to everybody that comes across it in its time.' It may do good to others though not by effort or may simply be a good end in itself (or combining these, may only be able to do good by concentrating on itself as an end); a preparatory evasion of the central issue about egotism.

Either 'though it lives only for itself' or 'though, in its own opinion, so far as it can see, it does no more than live and die.' In the first it is a rose, extravagant and doing good because the public likes to see it flaunting; in the second a violet, humble and doing good in private through an odour of sanctity. It is the less plausible sense which is insisted on by the comma after *itself.* Or you may well say that the flower is neither, but the final lily; the whole passage is hinting at the lilies of the field like whom Solomon was not arrayed.

This parable itself combines what the poem so ingeniously keeps on combining; the personal power of beauty and the political power of wisdom; so as to imply that the political power has in itself a sort of beauty and the personal beauty, however hollow it may be, a sort of moral grandeur through power. But in England 'consider the lilies of the field,' were we not at once told of their glory, would suggest lilies-of-the-valley; that name indeed occurs in the Song of Solomon, in surprising correspondence to the obviously grandiose Rose of Sharon. Shakespeare, I think, had done what the inventor of the name must have done, had read into the random flower-names of the Bible the same rich clash of suggestion—an implied mutual comparison that elevates both parties—as he makes here between the garden flower and the wild flower. The first sense (the rose) gives the root idea—'a brilliant aristocrat like you gives great pleasure by living as he likes; for such a person the issue of selfishness does not arise'; this makes W. H. a Renaissance Magnificent Man, combining all the virtues with a manysidedness like that of these phrases about him. The unlikeness of the cold people and the flowers, if you accept them as like, then implies 'man is not placed like flowers and though he had best imitate them may be misled in doing so; the Machiavellian is much more really like the flower than the Swain is.' And yet there is a suggestion in the comparison to the flower (since only beauty is demanded of it—Sonnet 54 made an odd and impermanent attempt at quelling this doubt by equating truth with scent) that W. H. has only power to keep up an air of reconciling in himself the inconsistent virtues, or even of being a

Machiavellian about the matter, and that it is this that puts him in danger like the flower. Or however genuine he may be he is pathetic; such a man is all too 'natural'; there is no need to prop up our ideas about him with an aristocratic 'artificial' flower. So this class-centred praise is then careful half to hide itself by adding the second sense and the humble flower, and this leads it to a generalisation: 'all men do most good to others by fulfilling their own natures.' Full as they are of Christian echoes, the Sonnets are concerned with an idea strong enough to be balanced against Christianity; they state the opposite to the idea of self-sacrifice.

But the machinery of the statement is peculiar; its clash of admiration and contempt seems dependent on a clash of feeling about the classes. One might connect it with that curious trick of pastoral which for extreme courtly flattery—perhaps to give self-respect to both poet and patron, to show that the poet is not ignorantly easy to impress, nor the patron to flatter—writes about the poorest people; and with those jazz songs which give an intense effect of luxury and silk underwear by pretending to be about slaves naked in the fields. To those who care chiefly about biography this trick must seem monstrously tantalising; Wilde built the paradox of his essay on it, and it is true that Shakespeare might have set the whole thing to work from the other end about a highly trained mudlark brought in to act his princesses. But it is the very queerness of the trick that makes it so often useful in building models of the human mind; and yet the power no less than the universality of this poem depends on generalising the trick so completely as to seem independent of it.

> But if that flowre with base infection meete,
> The basest weed out-braues his dignity:
>> For sweetest things turn sowrest by their deedes,
>> Lilies that fester, smell far worse than weeds.

It is not clear how the metaphor from 'meet' acts; it may be like 'meet with disaster'—'if it catches infection, which would be bad luck,' or like meeting someone in the street, as most men do safely—'*any* contact with infection is fatal to so peculiarly placed a creature.' The first applies to the natural and unprotected flower, the second to the lily that has the hubris and fate of greatness. They are not of course firmly separated, but *lilies* are separated from the *flower* by a colon and an intervening generalisation, whereas the flower is only separated from the cold people (not all of whom need be lilies) by a colon; certainly the flower as well as the lily is in danger, but this does not make them identical and equal to W. H. The neighbouring sonnets continually say that his deeds can do nothing to destroy his sweetness, and this seems to make the terrible last line point at him somewhat less directly. One may indeed take it as 'Though so debauched, you keep your looks. Only mean people who never give themselves heartily to anything can do that. But the best hypocrite is found out in the end, and shown as the worst.' But Shakespeare may also be congratulating W. H. on an imperfection which acts as a preservative; he is a son of the world and can protect himself, like the cold people, or a spontaneous and therefore fresh sinner, like the flower; he may safely stain, as heaven's sun, the kisser of carrion, staineth. At any rate it is not of virginity, at this stage, that he can be accused. The smell of a big lily is so lush and insolent, suggests so powerfully both incense and pampered flesh—the traditional metaphor about it is so perfect—that its festering can only be that due to the hubris of spirituality; it is ironically generous to apply it to the careerist to whom hypocrisy is recommended; and yet in the fact that we seem meant to apply it to him there is a glance backwards, as if to justify him, at the ambition involved in even the most genuine attempt on heaven. You may say that Shakespeare dragged in the last line as a quotation from *Edward III* that doesn't quite fit; it is also possible that (as often happens to poets, who tend to make in their lives a situation they have already written about) he did not till now see the full width of its application.

In a sense the total effect is an evasion of Shakespeare's problem; it gives him a way of praising W. H. in spite of anything. In the flower the oppositions are transcended; it is because it is self-concentrated that it has so much to give and because it is undesigning that it is more grandiose in beauty than Solomon. But it is held in mind chiefly for comfort; none of the people suggested to us are able to imitate it very successfully; nor if they could would they be safe. Yet if W. H. has festered, that at least makes him a lily, and at least not a stone; if he is not a lily, he is in the less danger of festering.

I must try to sum up the effect of so complex an irony, half by trying to follow it through a gradation. 'I am praising to you the contemptible things you admire, you little plotter; this is how the others try to betray you through flattery; yet it is your little generosity, though it show only as lewdness, which will betray you; for it is wise to be cold, both because you are too inflammable and because I have been so much hurt by you who are heartless; yet I can the better forgive you through that argument from our common isolation; I must praise to you your very faults, especially your selfishness, because you can only now be safe by cultivating them further; yet this is the most dangerous of necessities; people are greedy for your fall as for that of any of the great; indeed no one can rise above common life, as you have done so fully, without in the same degree sinking below it; you have made this advice real to me, because I cannot despise it for your sake; I am only sure that you are valuable and in danger.'

II

One may point out that the reason so little can be deduced about W. H., the reason why Butler and Wilde (though he had so much sympathy for snobbery) could make a plausible case for his being not a patron but an actor, is that this process of interaction between metaphors, which acts like a generalisation, is always carried so far; the contradictory elements in the relation are brought out and opposed absolutely, so that we cannot know their proportions in real life. It is hard not to go off down one of the roads at the crossing, and get one plain meaning for the poem from that, because Shakespeare himself did that so very effectively afterwards; a part of the situation of the Sonnets, the actual phrases designed for it, are given to Prince Henry, to Angelo, to Troilus, to the Greek army; getting further from the original as time went on. I shall look at the first two. It is only partly true that this untidy process, if successful, might tell one more about the original situation; discoveries of language and feeling made from a personal situation may develop themselves so that they can be applied to quite different dramatic situations; but to know about these might tell one more about the original discoveries. The fact that the feelings in this sonnet could be used for such different people as Angelo and Prince Henry, different both in their power and their coldness, is an essential part of its breadth.

The crucial first soliloquy of Prince Henry was put in to save his reputation with the audience; it is a wilful destruction of his claims to generosity, indeed to honesty, if only in Falstaff's sense; but this is not to say that it was a mere job with no feeling behind it. It was a concession to normal and decent opinion rather than to the groundlings; the man who was to write *Henry V* could feel the force of that as well as take care of his plot; on the other hand, it cannot have been written without bitterness against the prince. It was probably written about two years after the second, more intimate dedication to Southampton, and is almost a cento from the Sonnets.

We would probably find the prince less puzzling if Shakespeare had re-written *Henry VI* in his prime. The theme at the back of the series, after all, is that the Henries are usurpers; however great the virtues of

Henry V may be, however rightly the nation may glory in his deeds, there is something fishy about him and the justice of Heaven will overtake his son. In having some sort of double attitude to the prince Shakespeare was merely doing his work as a history-writer. For the critic to drag in a personal situation from the Sonnets is neither an attack nor a justification; it claims only to show where the feelings the play needed were obtained.

Sir Walter Raleigh said that the play was written when Shakespeare was becoming successful and buying New Place, so that he became interested in the problems of successful people like Henries IV and V rather than in poetical failures like Richard II. On this view we are to see in Prince Henry the Swan himself; he has made low friends only to get local colour out of them, and now drops them with a bang because he has made money and grand friends. It is possible enough, though I don't know why it was thought pleasant; anyway such a personal association is far at the back of the mind and one would expect several to be at work together. Henry might carry a grim externalisation of self-contempt as well as a still half-delighted reverberation of Southampton; Falstaff an attack on some rival playwright or on Florio as tutor of Southampton as well as a savage and joyous externalisation of self-contempt. But I think only the second of these alternatives fits in with the language and echoes a serious personal situation. Henry's soliloquy demands from us just the sonnets' mood of bitter complaisance; the young man must still be praised and loved, however he betrays his intimates, because we see him all shining with the virtues of success. So I shall now fancy Falstaff as Shakespeare (he has obviously some great forces behind him) and Henry as the patron who has recently betrayed him.

> I know you all, and will a-while vphold
> The vnyoak'd humor of your idlenesse:
> Yet heerein will I imitate the Sunne,
> Who doth permit the base contagious cloudes
> To smother vp his Beauty from the world,
> That when he please again to be himselfe,
> Being wanted, he may be more wondred at,
> By breaking through the foule and vgly mists
> Of vapours, that did seeme to strangle him.

This seems quite certainly drawn from the earliest and most pathetic of the attempts to justify W. H.

> Fvll many a glorious morning haue I seene, . . .
> Anon permit the *basest cloudes* to ride, . . .
> With *ougly* rack on his celestiall face, . . .
> *Suns* of the world may staine, when heauens sun staineth.

But it is turned backwards; the sun is now to free itself from the clouds by the very act of betrayal. 'Oh that you were yourself' (13) and 'have eyes to wonder' (106) are given the same twist into humility; Shakespeare admits, with Falstaff in front of him, that the patron would be better off without friends in low life. The next four lines, developing the idea that you make the best impression on people by only treating them well at rare intervals, are a prosaic re-hash of 'Therefore are feasts so solemn and so rare,' etc. (52); what was said of the policy of the friend is now used for the policy of the politician, though in both play and sonnet they are opposed. The connection in the next lines is more doubtful.

> So when this loose behaviour I throw off
> And pay the debt I never promised
> By so much better than my word I am
> By so much shall I falsify men's hopes

(He does indeed, by just so much.) This *debt* looks like an echo of the debt to nature there was so much doubt about W. H.'s method of paying; it has turned into a debt to society. At any rate in the sonnet-like final couplet

> I'll so offend, to make offence a skill

('The tongue that tells the story of thy days . . . Cannot dispraise but in a kind of praise') we have the central theme of all the sonnets of apology; the only difference, though it is a big one, is that this man says it about himself.

One element at least in this seems to reflect a further doubt on to the sonnet I have considered; the prince may be showing by this soliloquy that he can avoid infection, or may be an example of how sour a lord and owner can turn in his deeds on Coronation Day. The last irony and most contorted generosity one can extract from the sonnet is in the view that Shakespeare himself is the basest weed, that to meet him is to meet infection, that the result of being faithful to his friendship would be to be outbraved even by him, that the advice to be a cold person and avoid the fate of the lily is advice to abandon Shakespeare once for all.

This interpretation is more than once as firmly contradicted by Falstaff as it will be by my readers. He first comes on in a great fuss about his good name; he has been rated in the streets for leading astray Harry. At the end of the scene we find that this was unfair to him; the prince makes clear by the soliloquy that he is well able to look after himself. Meanwhile Falstaff amuses himself by turning the accusation the other way round.

> O, thou hast damnable iteration, and art indeede able to corrupt a Saint.
> Thou hast done much harme unto me *Hal*, God forgiue thee for it.
> Before I knew thee *Hal*, I knew nothing: and now I am (if a man shold
> speake truly) little better than one of the wicked. I must giue ouer this
> life, and I will giue it over: and I do not, I am a Villaine. Ile be damn'd
> for never a Kings sonne in Christendome.
> PRIN: Where shall we take a purse to morrow, Iacke?

The audience was not expected to believe this aspect of the matter, but there may well be some truth in it if applied to the situation Shakespeare had at the back of his mind. The other aspect is also preserved for us in the Sonnets.

> I may not euer-more acknowledge thee,
> Least my bewailed guilt should do thee shame,
> Nor thou with publike kindnesse honour me,
> Unlesse thou take that honour from thy name:

'I only warn you against bad company; I admit I am part of it.' One could throw in here that letter about Southampton wasting his time at the playhouse and out of favour with the Queen.

There are two sums of a thousand pounds concerned, so that the phrase is kept echoing through both parts of the history; it seems to become a symbol of Falstaff's hopes and his betrayal. The first he got by the robbery at Gadshill, and the prince at once robbed him of it; supposedly to give back to its owner, if you take his reluctance to steal seriously (he does give it back later, but one is free to suspect only under threat of exposure). He says he will give it to Francis the drawer, and Falstaff pacifies the hostess by saying he will get it back.

> HOSTESS: . . . and sayde this other day, You ought him a thousand
> pound.
> PRINCE: Sirrah, do I owe you a thousand pound?
> FALSTAFF: A thousand pound *Hal*? A Million. Thy loue is worth a
> Million: thou owe'st me thy loue.
>
> (Part I, III. iii.)

He will pay neither. But Falstaff gets another thousand pounds from Shallow, and the phrase is all he clings to in the riddling sentence at his final discomfiture: 'Master Shallow, I owe you a thousand pound.' This is necessary, to seem calm and reassure Shallow; it is either a sweeping gesture of renunciation ('What use to me now is the money I need never have repaid to this fool?') or a comfort since it reminds him that he has got the money and certainly won't repay it; but it is meant also for the king to hear and remember ('I class you with Shallow and the rest of my friends'). I cannot help fancying an obscure connection between this sum and the thousand pounds which, we are told, Southampton once gave Shakespeare, to go through with a purchase that he had a mind to.

It is as well to look at Falstaff in general for a moment, to show what this tender attitude to him has to fit in with. The plot treats him as a simple Punch, whom you laugh at with good-humour, though he is wicked, because he is always knocked down and always bobs up again. (Our attitude to him as a Character entirely depends on the Plot, and yet he is a Character who very nearly destroyed the Plot as a whole.) People sometimes take advantage of this to view him as a lovable old dear; a notion which one can best refute by considering him as an officer.

> Part I. v. iii.
>
> I haue led my rag of Muffins where they are pepper'd; there's not three of my 150 left alive, and they for the Townes end, to beg during life.

We saw him levy a tax in bribes on the men he left; he now kills all the weaklings he conscripted, in order to keep their pay. A large proportion of the groundlings consisted of disbanded soldiers who had suffered under such a system; the laughter was a roar of hatred here; he is 'comic' like a Miracle Play Herod. (Whereas Harry has no qualities that are obviously not W. H.'s.) And yet it is out of his defence against this, the least popularisable charge against him, that he makes his most unanswerable retort to the prince.

> PRINCE: Tell me, Jack, whose fellows are these that come after?
> FAL: Mine, Hal, mine.
> PRINCE: I never did see such pitiful rascals.
> FAL: Tut, tut; good enough to toss; food for powder, food for powder; they'll fill a pit as well as better; tush, man, mortal men, mortal men.

Mortal conveys both 'all men are in the same boat, all equal before God' and 'all you want is slaughter.' No one in the audience was tempted to think Harry as wicked as his enemy Hotspur, who deserved death as much as Lear for wanting to divide England. But this remark needed to be an impudent cover for villainy if the strength of mind and heart in it were not to be too strong, to make the squabbles of ambitious and usurping persons too contemptible.

On the other hand, Falstaff's love for the prince is certainly meant as a gap in his armour; one statement (out of so many) of this comes where the prince is putting his life in danger and robbing him of the (stolen) thousand pounds.

> I haue foresworne his company hourely any time this two and twenty
> yeares, and yet I am bewitcht with the Rogues company. If the Rascal
> haue not giuen me medecines to make me loue him, Ile be hang'd; it
> could not be else; I haue drunke Medecines.

He could continually be made to say such things without stopping the
laugh at him, partly because one thinks he is pretending love to the prince
for his own interest; 'never any man's thought keeps the roadway' as well
as those of the groundlings who think him a hypocrite about it, but this
phrase of mockery at them is used only to dignify the prince; the more
serious Falstaff's expression of love becomes the more comic it is, whether
as hopeless or as hypocrisy. But to stretch one's mind round the whole
character (as is generally admitted) one must take him, though as
the supreme expression of the cult of mockery as strength and the
comic idealisation of freedom, yet as both villainous and tragically
ill-used.

　　Angelo is further from the sonnets than Henry both in date and
situation; he is merely an extreme, perhaps not very credible, example
of the cold person and the lily; both simply as chaste and as claiming
to be more than human, which involves being at least liable to be as
much less. He has odd connections with this sonnet through *Edward III*,
which may help to show that there is a real connection of ideas. In the
following lines he is recoiling with horror from the idea that Isabella
has been using her virtue as a temptation for him, which was just what
her brother expected her to do (I. ii. 185—she is a cold person but can
'move men').

> II. ii. 165–8.
>
> Not she: nor doth she tempt; but it is I,
> That, lying by the Violet in the Sunne,
> Doe as the Carrion do's, not as the flowre,
> Corrupt with vertuous season:

Edward III is also a man in authority tempting a chaste woman, and he
too uses the notion that her qualities are a temptation, so that it is half
her fault.

> II. i. 58
>
> 　the queen of beauty's queens shall see
> Herself the ground of my infirmity.

Both Angelo's metaphor and the chief line of this sonnet come from a
speech by the lady's father, which contains the germ of most of the ideas
we are dealing with.

II. i. 430–457.

> The greater man, the greater is the thing,
> Be it good or bad, that he shall undertake . . .
> The freshest summer's day doth soonest taint
> The loathed carrion that it seems to kiss . . .
> Lilies that fester smell far worse than weeds;
> And every glory that inclines to sin,
> The shame is treble by the opposite.

The freshest summer's day is always likely to kiss carrion, and the suggestion from this is that the great man is always likely to do great harm as well as great good. The sun kissing carrion is brought out again both for Falstaff and by Hamlet (I *Henry IV*, II. iv. 113; *Hamlet*, II. ii. 158); it is clear that the complex of metaphor in this speech, whether Shakespeare wrote it or not, developed afterwards as a whole in his mind.

The obvious uses of the language of the Sonnets about Angelo all come in the first definition of his character by the Duke; once started like this he goes off on his own. The fascination of the irony of the passage is that it applies to Angelo's incorruptible virtues, associated with his chastity, the arguments and metaphors which had been used to urge abrogation of chastity on W. H.; nor is this irrelevant to the play. As in *virtues, torches,* and *fine touches,* its language, here and throughout, is always perversely on the edge of a bawdy meaning; even *belongings* may have a suggestion, helped out by 'longings,' of nature's gift of desire. It seems impossible even to praise the good qualities of Angelo without bringing into the hearer's mind those other good qualities that Angelo refuses to recognise. The most brilliant example of this trick in the play is the continual pun on *sense,* for sensuality, sensibleness (which implies the claim of Lucio) and sensibility (which implies a further claim of the poet). The first use may be unequivocal, as if to force the sexual meaning on our notice.

I. iv. 59: The wanton stings, and motions of the sence.

II. ii. 141. ANGELO: Shee speakes, and 'tis such sence
    That my sence breeds with it; fare you well.

II. ii. 168: Can it be
    That Modesty may more betray our Sence
    Than womans lightnesse?

II. iv. 73: Nay, but heare me,
    Your sence pursues not mine: either you are ignorant,
    Or seeme so craft(il)y; and that's not good.

IV.iv.27: He should haue liu'd,
    Save that his riotous youth with dangerous sence,
    Might in the times to come have ta'en revenge.
V.i.225.MARIANA: As there is sence in truth, and truth in vertue,
    I am affianced this man's wife, as strongly
    As words could make vp vowes:

But this sort of thing does not depend on echoes from the Sonnets, and I think those that occur have a further effect.

> Thy selfe, and thy belongings
> Are not thine owne so proper, as to waste
> Thy selfe upon thy vertues; they on thee:
> Heauen doth with us, as we, with Torches doe,
> Not light them for themselves: For if our vertues
> Did not goe forth of us, 'twere all alike
> As if we had them not: Spirits are not finely touch'd,
> But to fine issues: nor nature never lends
> The smallest scruple of her excellence,
> But like a thrifty goddesse, she determines
> Her selfe the glory of a creditour,
> Both thanks, and vse;

'All are but stewards of her excellence'—indeed *their* in the sonnet might refer back to *nature's riches*. Even Angelo is wrong to think he can be a lord and owner, though he seems the extreme case of those capable of reserve and power. He is a *torch* whom nature tricks because she destroys it by making it brilliant; it was because he accepted office and prepared to use his virtues that she could trick him all but disastrously into using more of them than he intended. For 'virtues' mean both 'good qualities' and 'capacities' ('a dormitive virtue') whether for good or ill; the same ambivalent attitude both towards worldly goods and towards what claim to be spiritual goods is conveyed by this as by the clash between *heaven's graces* and *nature's riches*. The same pun and irony on it, with a hint of a similar movement of thought about *honour*, are used when Isabella takes leave of Angelo after her first interviews.

II.ii.162–4. ISAB: Saue your Honour.
    ANG: From thee: euen from thy vertue.
        What's this? what's this? is this her fault, or mine?
        The Tempter, or the Tempted, who sins most?

It is his virtues and Isabella's between them that both trick him and nearly destroy Claudio. Not of course that this is straightforward satire against virtue in the sense of chastity; the first great speech of Claudio about 'too much liberty' has all the weight and horror of the lust sonnet (129) from which it is drawn; only the still greater mockery of Claudio could so drag the play back to its attack on Puritanism.

The issue indeed is more general than the sexual one; it is 'liberty, my Lucio, liberty,' as Claudio makes clear at once; which runs through pastoral and is at the heart of the clowns. (Lawrence too seems to make sex the type of liberty; Shaw's Don Juan liberty the type of sex.) 'Nature in general is a cheat, and all those who think themselves owners are pathetic.' Yet we seem here to transfer to Nature the tone of bitter complaisance taken up towards W. H. when he seemed an owner; she now, as he was, must be given the benefit of the doubt inseparable from these shifting phrases; she too must be let rob you by tricks and still be worshipped. There is the same suggestion with the same metaphors in that splendid lecture to Achilles to make him use his virtues as a fighter further; whether rightly to *thank* her is to view yourself as an owner or a steward, you must still in the end pay her the compound interest on her gifts, and still keep up the pretence that they are free. This tone of generous distaste for the conditions of life, which gives the play one of its few suggestions of sympathy for Angelo, I think usually goes with a suggestion of the Sonnets. For instance, it is the whole point about Bassanio; more than any other suitor he is an arriviste loved only for success and seeming; his one merit, and it is enough, is to recognise this truth with Christian humility. His speech before the caskets about the falsity of seeming is full of phrases from the Sonnets (*e.g.* 68, about hair) and may even have a dim reference to the Dark Lady. It is not surprising that this sentiment should make Shakespeare's mind hark back to the Sonnets, because it was there so essential; these poems of idealisation of a patron and careerist depend upon it for their strength and dignity. 'Man is so placed that the sort of thing you do is in degree all that any one can do; success does not come from mere virtue, and without some external success a virtue is not real even to itself. One must not look elsewhere; success of the same nature as yours is all that the dignity, whether of life or poetry, can be based upon.' This queer sort of realism, indeed, is one of the main things he had to say.

The feeling that life is essentially inadequate to the human spirit, and yet that a good life must avoid saying so, is naturally at home with most versions of pastoral; in pastoral you take a limited life and pretend it is the full and normal one, and a suggestion that one must do this with all life, because the normal is itself limited, is easily put into the trick though not necessary to its power. Conversely any expression of the idea that all life is limited may be regarded as only a trick of pastoral, perhaps chiefly intended to hold all our attention and sympathy for some limited life, though again this is not necessary to it either on grounds of truth or beauty; in fact the suggestion of pastoral may be only a protection for the idea which must at last be taken alone. The business of interpretation is obviously very complicated. Literary uses of the problem of free-will and necessity, for example, may be noticed to give curiously bad arguments and I should think get their strength from keeping you in doubt between the two methods. Thus Hardy is fond of showing us an unusually stupid person subjected to very unusually bad luck, and then a moral is drawn, not merely by inference but by solemn assertion, that we are all in the same boat as this person whose story is striking precisely because it is unusual. The effect may be very grand, but to make an otherwise logical reader accept the process must depend on giving him obscure reasons for wishing it so. It is clear at any rate that this grand notion of the inadequacy of life, so various in its means of expression, so reliable a bass note in the arts, needs to be counted as a possible territory of pastoral.

E.M.W. TILLYARD

"Richard II"

Richard II is imperfectly executed, and yet, that imperfection granted, perfectly planned as part of a great structure. It is sharply contrasted, in its extreme formality of shape and style, with the subtler and more fluid nature of *Henry IV*; but it is a necessary and deliberate contrast; resembling a stiff recitative composed to introduce a varied and flexible *aria*. Coming after *King John* the play would appear the strangest relapse into the official self which Shakespeare had been shedding; taken with *Henry IV* it shows that Shakespeare, while retaining and using this official self, could develop with brilliant success the new qualities of character and style manifested in the Bastard. *Richard II* therefore betokens no relapse but is an organic part of one of Shakespeare's major achievements. . . .

Of all Shakespeare's plays *Richard II* is the most formal and ceremonial. It is not only that Richard himself is a true king in appearance, in his command of the trappings of royalty, while being deficient in the solid virtues of the ruler; that is a commonplace: the ceremonial character of the play extends much wider than Richard's own nature or the exquisite patterns of his poetic speech.

First, the very actions tend to be symbolic rather than real. There is all the pomp of a tournament without the physical meeting of the two armed knights. There is a great army of Welshmen assembled to support Richard, but they never fight. Bolingbroke before Flint Castle speaks of the terrible clash there should be when he and Richard meet:

> Methinks King Richard and myself should meet
> With no less terror than the elements
> Of fire and water, when their thundering shock
> At meeting tears the cloudy cheeks of heaven.

From *Shakespeare's History Plays.* Copyright © 1944, 1956 by Chatto & Windus, Ltd.

But instead of a clash there is a highly ceremonious encounter leading to the effortless submission of Richard. There are violent challenges before Henry in Westminster Hall, but the issue is postponed. The climax of the play is the ceremony of Richard's deposition. And finally Richard, imprisoned at Pomfret, erects his own lonely state and his own griefs into a gigantic ceremony. He arranges his own thoughts into classes corresponding with men's estates in real life; king and beggar, divine, soldier, and middle man. His own sighs keep a ceremonial order like a clock:

> Now, sir, the sound that tells what hour it is
> Are clamorous groans, which strike upon my heart,
> Which is the bell: so sighs and tears and groans
> Show minutes, times, and hours.

Second, in places where emotion rises, where there is strong mental action, Shakespeare evades direct or naturalistic presentation and resorts to convention and conceit. He had done the same when Arthur pleaded with Hubert for his eyes in *King John,* but that was exceptional to a play which contained the agonies of Constance and the Bastard's perplexities over Arthur's body. Emotionally Richard's parting from his queen could have been a great thing in the play: actually it is an exchange of frigidly ingenious couplets.

> RICH.: Go, count thy way with sighs; I mine with groans.
> QU.: So longest way shall have the longest moans.
> RICH.: Twice for one step I'll groan, the way being short,
>   And piece the way out with a heavy heart.

This is indeed the language of ceremony, not of passion. Exactly the same happens when the Duchess of York pleads with Henry against her husband for her son Aumerle's life. Before the climax, when York gives the news of his son's treachery, there had been a show of feeling; but with the entry of the Duchess, when emotion should culminate, all is changed to prettiness and formal antiphony. This is how the Duchess compares her own quality of pleading with her husband's:

> Pleads he in earnest? Look upon his face;
> His eyes do drop no tears, his prayers are jest;
> His words come from his mouth, ours from our breast:
> He prays but faintly and would be denied;
> We pray with heart and soul and all beside:
> His weary joints would gladly rise, I know;
> Our knees shall kneel till to the ground they grow:
> His prayers are full of false hypocrisy;
> Ours of true zeal and deep integrity.

And to "frame" the scene, to make it unmistakably a piece of deliberate ceremonial, Bolingbroke falls into the normal language of drama when, having forgiven Aumerle, he vows to punish the other conspirators:

> But for our trusty brother-in-law and the abbot,
> And all the rest of that consorted crew,
> Destruction straight shall dog them at the heels.

The cause of Gaunt is different but more complicated. When he has the state of England in mind and reproves Richard, though he can be rhetorical and play on words, he speaks the language of passion:

> Now He that made me knows I see thee ill.
> Thy death-bed is no lesser than thy land
> Wherein thou liest in reputation sick.
> And thou, too careless patient as thou art,
> Commit'st thy anointed body to the cure
> Of those physicians that first wounded thee.
> A thousand flatterers sit within thy crown,
> Whose compass is no bigger than thy hand.

But in the scene of private feeling, when he parts from his banished son, both speakers, ceasing to be specifically themselves, exchange the most exquisitely formal commonplaces traditionally deemed appropriate to such a situation.

> Go, say I sent thee for to purchase honour
> And not the king exil'd thee; or suppose
> Devouring pestilence hangs in our air
> And thou art flying to a fresher clime.
> Look, what thy soul holds dear, imagine it
> To lie that way thou go'st, not whence thou com'st.
> Suppose the singing birds musicians,
> The grass whereon thou tread'st the presence strew'd,
> The flowers fair ladies, and thy steps no more
> Than a delightful measure or a dance;
> For gnarling sorrow hath less power to bite
> The man that mocks at it and sets it light.

Superficially this may be maturer verse than the couplets quoted, but it is just as formal, just as mindful of propriety and as unmindful of nature as Richard and his queen taking leave. Richard's sudden start into action when attacked by his murderers is exceptional, serving to set off by contrast the lack of action that has prevailed and to link the play with the next of the series. His groom, who appears in the same scene, is a realistic character alien to the rest of the play and serves the same function as Richard in action.

Thirdly, there is an elaboration and a formality in the cosmic references, scarcely to be matched in Shakespeare. These are usually brief and incidental, showing indeed how intimate a part they were of the things accepted and familiar in Shakespeare's mind. But in *Richard II* they are positively paraded. The great speech of Richard in Pomfret Castle is a tissue of them: first the peopling of his prison room with his thoughts, making its microcosm correspond with the orders of the body politic; then the doctrine of the universe as a musical harmony; then the fantasy of his own griefs arranged in a pattern like the working of a clock, symbol of regularity opposed to discord; and finally madness as the counterpart in man's mental kingdom of discord or chaos. Throughout the play the great commonplace of the king on earth duplicating the sun in heaven is exploited with a persistence unmatched anywhere else in Shakespeare. Finally (for I omit minor references to cosmic lore) there is the scene (III.4) of the gardeners, with the elaborate comparison of the state to the botanical microcosm of the garden. But this is a scene so typical of the whole trend of the play that I will speak of it generally and not merely as another illustration of the traditional correspondences.

The scene begins with a few exquisitely musical lines of dialogue between the queen and two ladies. She refines her grief in a vein of high ceremony and sophistication. She begins by asking what sport they can devise in this garden to drive away care. But to every sport proposed there is a witty objection.

> LADY: Madam, we'll tell tales.
> QUEEN: Of sorrow or of joy?
> LADY: Of either, madam.
> QUEEN: Of neither, girl:
> It doth remember me the more of sorrow;
> Or if of grief, being altogether had,
> It adds more sorrow to my want of joy.
> For what I have I need not to repeat,
> And what I want it boots not to complain.

Shakespeare uses language here like a very accomplished musician doing exercises over the whole compass of the violin. Then there enter a gardener and two servants: clearly to balance the queen and her ladies and through that balance to suggest that the gardener within the walls of his little plot of land is a king. Nothing could illustrate better the different expectations of a modern and of an Elizabethan audience than the way they would take the gardener's opening words:

> Go, bind thou up yon dangling apricocks,
> Which, like unruly children, make their sire
> Stoop with oppression of their prodigal weight.

The first thought of a modern audience is: what a ridiculous way for a gardener to talk. The first thought of an Elizabethan would have been: what is the symbolic meaning of those words, spoken by this king of the garden, and how does it bear on the play? And it would very quickly conclude that the apricots had grown inflated and overweening in the sun of the royal favour; that oppression was used with a political as well as a physical meaning; and that the apricots threatened, unless restrained, to upset the proper relation between parent and offspring, to offend against the great principle of order. And the rest of the gardener's speech would bear out this interpretation.

> Go thou, and like an executioner
> Cut off the heads of too fast growing sprays,
> That look too lofty in our commonwealth.
> All must be even in our government.
> You thus employ'd, I will go root away
> The noisome weeds, which without profit suck
> The soil's fertility from wholesome flowers.

In fact the scene turns out to be an elaborate political allegory, with the Earl of Wiltshire, Bushy, and Green standing for the noxious weeds which Richard, the bad gardener, allowed to flourish and which Henry, the new gardener, has rooted up. It ends with the queen coming forward and joining in the talk. She confirms the gardener's regal and moral function by calling him "old Adam's likeness," but curses him for his ill news about Richard and Bolingbroke. The intensively symbolic character of the scene is confirmed when the gardener at the end proposes to plant a bank with rue where the queen let fall her tears, as a memorial:

> Rue, even for ruth, here shortly shall be seen
> In the remembrance of a weeping queen.

. . . The one close Shakespearean analogy with this gardener is Iden, the unambitious squire in his Kentish garden, who stands for "degree" in 2 Henry VI. But he comes in as an obvious foil to the realistic disorder just exhibited in Cade's rebellion. Why was it that in Richard II, when he was so much more mature, when his brilliant realism in King John showed him capable of making his gardeners as human and as amusing as the gravediggers in *Hamlet*, Shakespeare chose to present them with a degree of formality unequalled in any play he wrote? It is, in a different form, the same question as that which was implied by my discussion of the other formal or ceremonial features of the play: namely, why did Shakespeare in *Richard II* make the ceremonial or ritual form of writing, found in differing quantities in the *Henry VI* plays and in *Richard III*, not merely one of the principal means of expression but the very essence of the play?

These are the first questions we must answer if we are to understand the true nature of *Richard II*. And here let me repeat that though Richard himself is a very important part of the play's ceremonial content, that content is larger and more important than Richard. With that caution, I will try to explain how the ritual or ceremonial element in *Richard II* differs from that in the earlier History Plays, and through such an explanation to conjecture a new interpretation of the play. There is no finer instance of ceremonial writing than the scene of the ghosts at the end of *Richard III*. But it is subservient to a piece of action, to the Battle of Bosworth with the overthrow of a tyrant and the triumph of a righteous prince. Its duty is to make that action a matter of high, mysterious, religious import. We are not invited to dwell on the ritual happenings as on a resting-place, to deduce from them the ideas into which the mind settles when the action of the play is over. But in *Richard II*, with all the emphasis and the point taken out of the action, we are invited, again and again, to dwell on the sheer ceremony of the various situations. The main point of the tournament between Bolingbroke and Mowbray is the way it is conducted; the point of Gaunt's parting with Bolingbroke is the sheer propriety of the sentiments they utter; the portents, put so fittingly into the mouth of a Welshman, are more exciting because they are appropriate than because they precipitate an event; Richard is ever more concerned with how he behaves, with the fitness of his conduct to the occasion, than with what he actually does; the gardener may foretell the deposition of Richard yet he is far more interesting as representing a static principle of order; when Richard is deposed, it is the precise manner that comes before all—

> With mine own tears I wash away my balm,
> With mine own hands I give away my crown,
> With mine own tongue deny my sacred state,
> With mine own breath release all duty's rites.

We are in fact in a world where means matter more than ends, where it is more important to keep strictly the rules of an elaborate game than either to win or to lose it. . . .

I noted above that at the end of *2 Henry VI* Clifford and York, though enemies, do utter some of the chivalric sentiments proper to medieval warfare. Such sentiments do not recur in *3 Henry VI*, where we have instead the full barbarities of Wakefield and Towton. Shakespeare is probably recording the historical fact that the decencies of the knightly code went down under the stress of civil carnage. But the really convincing analogy with *Richard II* is the play of *Julius Caesar*. There, however slender Shakespeare's equipment as historian and however much of his own time he slips in, he does succeed in giving his picture of antique Rome, of the dignity of its government and of the stoic creed of its great men. T. S. Eliot has rightly noted how much essential history Shakespeare extracted from Plutarch. And if from Plutarch, why not from Froissart likewise?

Till recently Shakespeare's debt to Berners's translation of Froissart's Chronicle has been almost passed over, but now it is rightly agreed that it was considerable. To recognise the debt helps one to understand the play. For instance, one of the minor puzzles of the play is plain if we grant Shakespeare's acquaintance with Froissart. When York, horrified at Richard's confiscating Gaunt's property the moment he died, goes on to enumerate all Richard's crimes, he mentions "the prevention of poor Bolingbroke about his marriage." There is nothing more about this in the play, but there is a great deal about it in Froissart—Richard had brought charges against the exile Bolingbroke which induced the French king to break off Bolingbroke's engagement with the daughter of the Duke of Berry, the king's cousin. If Shakespeare had been full of Froissart when writing *Richard II* he could easily have slipped in this isolated reference. But quite apart from any tangible signs of imitation it is scarcely conceivable that Shakespeare should not have read so famous a book as Berners's Froissart, or that having read it he should not have been impressed by the bright pictures of chivalric life in those pages. Now among Shakespeare's History Plays *Richard II* is the only one that falls within the period of time covered by Froissart. All the more reason why on this unique occasion he should heed this great original. Now though Froissart is greatly interested in motives, he also writes with an eye unmatched among chroniclers for its eager observation of external things and with a mind similarly unmatched for the high value it placed on the proper disposition of those things. In fact he showed a lively belief in ceremony and in the proprieties of heraldry akin to Elizabethan belief yet altogether more firmly attached to the general scheme of ideas that prevailed at the time. Shakepeare's brilliant wit must have grasped this; and *Richard II* may be his intuitive rendering of Froissart's medievalism.

But there were other reasons why the reign of Richard II should be notable. A. B. Steel, his most recent historian, begins his study by noting that Richard was the last king of the old medieval order:

> the last king ruling by hereditary right, direct and undisputed, from the Conqueror. The kings of the next hundred and ten years . . . were essentially kings *de facto* not *de jure*, successful usurpers recognised after the event, upon conditions, by their fellow-magnates or by parliament.

Shakespeare, deeply interested in titles as he had showed himself to be in his early History Plays, must have known this very well; and Gaunt's famous speech on England cannot be fully understood without this knowledge. He calls England

> This nurse, this teeming womb of royal kings,
> Fear'd by their breed and famous by their birth,
> Renowned for their deeds as far from home,
> For Christian service and true chivalry,
> As is the sepulchre in stubborn Jewry
> Of the world's ransom, blessed Mary's son.

Richard was no crusader, but he was authentic heir of the crusading Plantagenets. Henry was different, a usurper; and it is with reference to this passage that we must read the lines in *Richard II* and *Henry IV* which recount his desire and his failure to go to Palestine. That honour was reserved for the authentic Plantagenet kings. Richard then had the full sanctity of medieval kingship and the strong pathos of being the last king to possess it. Shakespeare probably realised that however powerful the Tudors were and however undisputed their hold over their country's church, they had not the same sanctity as the medieval kings. He was therefore ready to draw from certain French treatises, anti-Lancastrian in tone, that made Richard a martyr and compared him to Christ and his accusers to so many Pilates giving him over to the wishes of the London mob. Shakespeare's Richard says at his deposition:

> Though some of you with Pilate wash your hands,
> Showing an outward pity; yet you Pilates
> Have here deliver'd me to my sour cross,
> And water cannot wash away your sin.

Holy and virtuous as the Earl of Richmond is in *Richard III*, he does not pretend to the same kingly sanctity as Richard II. Such sanctity belongs to a more antique, more exotically ritual world; and Shakespeare composed his play accordingly.

Not only did Richard in himself hold a position unique among English kings, he maintained a court of excessive splendour. . . . In an age that was both passionately admiring of royal magnificence and far more retentive of tradition than our own the glories of Richard's court must have persisted as a legend. Anyhow that Shakespeare was aware of them is plain from Richard's address to his own likeness in the mirror:

> Was this face the face
> That every day under his household roof
> Did keep ten thousand men?

The legend must have persisted of this court's continental elegance, of the curiosities of its dress, of such a thing as Anne of Bohemia introducing the custom of riding side-saddle, of Richard's invention of the handkerchief for nasal use. Then there were the poets. Shakespeare must have associated the beginnings of English poetry with Chaucer and Gower; and they wrote mainly in Richard's reign. There must have been much medieval art, far more than now survives, visible in the great houses of Elizabeth's day, illuminated books and tapestry; and it would be generally associated with the most brilliant reign of the Middle Ages. Finally in Richard's reign there was the glamour of a still intact nobility: a very powerful glamour in an age still devoted to heraldry and yet possessing an aristocracy who, compared with the great men of Richard's day, were upstarts.

All these facts would have a strong, if unconscious, effect on Shakespeare's mind and induce him to present the age of Richard in a brilliant yet remote and unrealistic manner. He was already master of a certain antique lore and of a certain kind of ceremonial writing: it was natural that he should use them, but with a different turn, to do this particular work. Thus he makes more solemn and elaborates the inherited notions of cosmic correspondences and chivalric procedure and he makes his ritual style a central and not peripheral concern. Hence the portentous solemnity of the moralising gardeners, the powerful emphasis on the isolated symbol of the rue-tree, the elaborate circumstances of the tournament between Bolingbroke and Mowbray, and the unique artifice of Richard's great speeches: speeches which are the true centre of the play but central with a far wider reference than to the mere character of Richard.

In speaking of medieval illuminated books and tapestry I do not wish to imply anything too literal: that Shakespeare had actual examples of such things in mind when he wrote *Richard II*. But it is true that many passages in this play call them up and that unconscious memory of them *might* have given Shakespeare help. Take a passage from one of Richard's best known speeches.

> For God's sake, let us sit upon the ground
> And tell sad stories of the death of kings:

> How some have been depos'd, some slain in war,
> Some haunted by the ghosts they have depos'd,
> Some poison'd by their wives, some sleeping kill'd;
> All murder'd: for within the hollow crown
> That rounds the mortal temples of a king
> Keeps Death his court, and there the antic sits,
> Scoffing his state and grinning at his pomp,
> Allowing him a breath, a little scene,
> To monarchise, be fear'd, and kill with looks,
> Infusing him with self and vain conceit,
> As if this flesh which walls about our life
> Were brass impregnable, and, humour'd thus,
> Comes at the last and with a little pin
> Bores through his castle walls, and farewell king!

Critics have seen a reference here to the *Mirror for Magistrates*, but Chaucer's *Monk's Tale* would suit much better. Death, keeping his court, is a pure medieval motive. Still, these motives were inherited and need imply nothing unusual. But Death the skeleton watching and mocking the king in his trappings is a clear and concrete image that reminds one of the visual arts: and above all the exquisiteness, the very remoteness from what could have happened in an actual physical attempt, of someone boring through the castle wall with a little pin precisely recaptures the technique of medieval illumination. Before the tournament Bolingbroke prays God:

> And with thy blessings steel my lance's point
> That it may enter Mowbray's waxen coat.

That again is just like medieval illumination. When a wound is given in medieval art there is no fusion of thing striking with thing stricken; the blow simply rests in a pre-existing hole, while any blood that spouts out had pre-existed just as surely. This is the kind of picture called up by Mowbray's "waxen coat." Or take this comparison. If anywhere in *Henry IV* we might expect medievalism it is in the description of the Prince performing the most spectacular of chivalric actions: vaulting onto his horse in full armour.

> I saw young Harry, with his beaver on,
> His cuisses on his thighs, gallantly arm'd,
> Rise from the ground like feather'd Mercury,
> And vaulted with such ease into his seat,
> As if an angel dropp'd down from the clouds,
> To turn and wind a fiery Pegasus
> And witch the world with noble horsemanship.

There is nothing medieval here. It is a description recalling the art of the
high Renaissance with fused colours and subtle transitions. Set beside it
Gaunt's advice to Bolingbroke about to go into exile:

> Suppose the singing birds musicians,
> The grass whereon thou tread'st the presence strew'd,
> The flowers fair ladies, and thy steps no more
> Than a delightful measure or a dance.

Here each item is distinct, and the lines evoke the mincing figures of a
medieval tapestry in a setting of birds and flowers.

The case for the essential medievalism of *Richard II* is even stronger
when it is seen that the conspirators, working as such, do not share the
ceremonial style used to represent Richard and his court. Once again the
usual explanation of such a contrast is too narrow. It has been the habit
to contrast the "poetry" of Richard with the practical common sense of
Bolingbroke. But the "poetry" of Richard is all part of a world of gorgeous
tournaments, conventionally mournful queens, and impossibly sententious
gardeners, while Bolingbroke's common sense extends to his backers, in
particular to that most important character, Northumberland. We have in
fact the contrast not only of two characters but of two ways of life.

One example of the two different ways of life has occurred already:
in the contrast noted between the mannered pleading of the Duchess of
York for Aumerle's life and Henry's vigorous resolve immediately after to
punish the conspirators. The Duchess and her family belong to the old
order where the means, the style, the embroidery matter more than what
they further or express. Henry belongs to a new order, where action is
quick and leads somewhere. But other examples are needed to back up
what to many readers will doubtless seem a dangerous and forced theory of
the play's significance. First, a new kind of vigour, the vigour of strong
and swift action, enters the verse of the play at II. I. 224, when, after
Richard has seized Gaunt's property and announced his coming journey to
Ireland, Northumberland, Ross, and Willoughby remain behind and hatch
their conspiracy. Northumberland's last speech especially has a different
vigour from any vigorous writing that has gone before: from the vigour of
the jousters' mutual defiance or York's moral indignation at the king's
excesses. After enumerating Bolingbroke's supporters in Brittany, he goes
on:

> All these well furnish'd by the Duke of Brittain
> With eight tall ships, three thousand men of war,
> Are making hither with all due expedience
> And shortly mean to touch our northern shore:

> Perhaps they had ere this, but that they stay
> The first departing of the king for Ireland.
> If then we shall shake off our slavish yoke,
> Imp out our drooping country's broken wing,
> Redeem from broken pawn the blemish'd crown,
> Wipe off the dust that hides our sceptre's gift
> And make high majesty look like itself,
> Away with me in post to Ravenspurgh.

The four lines describing by different metaphors how the land is to be restored are not in a ritual manner but in Shakepeare's normal idiom of Elizabethan exuberance. It is not for nothing that the next scene shows the Queen exchanging elegant conceits about her sorrow for Richard's absence with Bushy and Green. But the largest contrast comes at the beginning of the third act. It begins with a very fine speech of Bolingbroke recounting to Bushy and Green all their crimes, before they are executed. It has the full accent of the world of action, where people want to get things and are roused to passion in their attempts:

> Bring forth these men.
> Bushy and Green, I will not vex your souls
> (Since presently your souls must part your bodies)
> With too much urging your pernicious lives,
> For 'twere no charity.

That is the beginning, and the speech goes on to things themselves not to the way they are done or are embroidered. And when at the end Bolingbroke recounts his own injuries it is with plain and understandable passion:

> Myself a prince by fortune of my birth,
> Near to the king in blood, and near in love
> Till you did make him misinterpret me,
> Have stoop'd my neck under your injuries
> And sigh'd my English breath in foreign clouds,
> Eating the bitter bread of banishment.

The scene is followed by Richard's landing in Wales, his pitiful inability to act, and his wonderful self-dramatisation. As a display of externals, as an exaltation of means over ends (here carried to a frivolous excess), it is wonderful; yet it contains no lines that for the weight of unaffected passion come near Bolingbroke's single line,

> Eating the bitter bread of banishment.

The world for which Bolingbroke stands, though it is a usurping world, displays a greater sincerity of personal emotion.

Thus *Richard II*, although reputed so simple and homogeneous a play, is built on a contrast. The world of medieval refinement is indeed the main object of presentation but it is threatened and in the end superseded by the more familiar world of the present.

In carrying out his object Shakespeare shows the greatest skill in keeping the emphasis sufficiently on Richard, while hinting that in Bolingbroke's world there is the probability of development. In other words he makes the world of Bolingbroke not so much defective as embryonic. It is not allowed to compete with Richard's but it is ready to grow to its proper fulness in the next plays. This is especially true of the conspirators' characters. Hotspur, for instance, is faintly drawn yet in one place he speaks with a hearty abruptness that shows his creator had conceived the whole character already. It is when Hotspur first meets Bolingbroke, near Berkeley Castle. Northumberland asks him if he has forgotten the Duke of Hereford, and Hotspur replies:

> No, my good lord, for that is not forgot
> Which ne'er I did remember: to my knowledge
> I never in my life did look on him.

At the beginning of the same scene Northumberland's elaborate compliments to Bolingbroke show his politic nature: it is the same man who at the beginning of *2 Henry IV* lies "crafty-sick." Bolingbroke too is consistent with his later self, though we are shown only certain elements in his character. What marks out the later Bolingbroke and makes him a rather pathetic figure is his bewilderment. For all his political acumen he does not know himself completely or his way about the world. And the reason is that he has relied in large part on fortune. Dover Wilson remarked truly of him in *Richard II* that though he acts forcibly he appears to be borne upward by a power beyond his volition. He is made the first mover of trouble in the matter of the tournament and he wants to do something about Woodstock's murder. But he has no steady policy and having once set events in motion is the servant of fortune. As such, he is not in control of events, though by his adroitness he may deal with the unpredictable as it occurs. Now a man who, lacking a steady policy, begins a course of action will be led into those "by-paths and indirect crook'd ways" of which Henry speaks to his son in *2 Henry IV*. Shakespeare says nothing of them in *Richard II*, but they are yet the inevitable result of Henry's character as shown in that play. It is worth anticipating and saying that Prince Hal differs from his father in having perfect knowledge both of himself and of the world around him. Of all types of men he is the least subject to the sway of fortune.

Another quality shown only in embryo is humour. It is nearly absent but there is just a touch: sufficient to assure us that Shakespeare has it there all the time in readiness. It occurs in the scene where Aumerle describes to Richard his parting from Bolingbroke.

> RICH.: And say, what store of parting tears were shed?
> AUM.: Faith, none for me: except the north-east wind
> Which then blew bitterly against our faces,
> Awak'd the sleeping rheum, and so by chance
> Did grace our hollow parting with a tear.

Richard II thus at once possesses a dominant theme and contains within itself the elements of those different things that are to be the theme of its successors. . . .

Richard II does its work in proclaiming the great theme of the whole cycle of Shakespeare's History Plays: the beginning in prosperity, the distortion of prosperity by a crime, civil war, and ultimate renewal of prosperity. The last stage falls outside the play's scope, but the second scene with the Duchess of Gloucester's enumeration of Edward III's seven sons, her account of Gloucester's death, and her call for vengeance is a worthy exordium of the whole cycle. The speeches of the Bishop of Carlisle and of Richard to Northumberland . . . are worthy statements of the disorder that follows the deposition of the rightful king. In doctrine the play is entirely orthodox. Shakespeare knows that Richard's crimes never amounted to tyranny and hence that outright rebellion against him was a crime. He leaves uncertain the question of who murdered Woodstock and never says that Richard was personally responsible. The king's uncles hold perfectly correct opinions. Gaunt refuses the Duchess of Gloucester's request for vengeance, the matter being for God's decision alone. Even on his deathbed, when lamenting the state of the realm and calling Richard the landlord and not the king of England, he never preaches rebellion. And he mentions deposition only in the sense that Richard by his own conduct is deposing himself. York utters the most correct sentiments. Like the Bastard, he is for supporting the existing government. And though he changes allegiance he is never for rebellion. As stated above, the gardener was against the deposition of Richard.

As well as being a study of medievalism, Richard takes his place among Shakespeare's many studies of the kingly nature. He is a king by unquestioned title and by his external graces alone. But others have written so well on Richard's character that I need say no more.

Lastly, for political motives, there is the old Morality theme of Respublica. One of Shakespeare's debts in *Richard II* is to *Woodstock*; and this play is constructed very plainly on the Morality pattern, with the king's three uncles led by Woodstock inducing him to virtue, and Tressilian, Bushy and Green to vice. There are traces of this motive in Shakespeare's play, but with Woodstock dead before the action begins and Gaunt dying early in it the balance of good and evil influences is destroyed. Bushy, Green and Bagot, however, remain very plainly Morality figures and were probably marked in some way by their dress as abstract vices. If Shakespeare really confused Bagot with the Earl of Wiltshire (according to a conjecture of Dover Wilson) he need not be following an old play heedlessly: he would in any case look on them all as a gang of bad characters, far more important as a gang than as individuals, hence not worth being careful over separately. Once again, as in the earlier tetralogy, England herself, and not the protagonist, is the main concern. Gaunt speaks her praises, the gardener in describing his own symbolic garden has her in mind. As part of the great cycle of English history covered by Hall's chronicle the events of the reign of Richard II take their proper place. But here something fresh has happened. The early tetralogy had as its concern the fortunes of England in that exciting and instructive stretch of her history. *Richard II* has this concern too, but it also deals with England herself, the nature and not merely the fortunes of England. In *Richard II* it is the old brilliant medieval England of the last Plantagenet in the authentic succession; in *Henry IV* it will be the England not of the Middle Ages but of Shakespeare himself. We can now see how the epic comes in and how *Richard II* contributes to an epic effect. Those works which we honour by the epic title always, among other things, express the feelings or the habits of a large group of men, often of a nation. However centrally human, however powerful, a work may be, we shall not give it the epic title for these qualities alone. It is not the parting of Hector and Andromache or the ransoming of Hector's body that make the *Iliad* an epic; it is that the *Iliad* expresses a whole way of life. Shakespeare, it seems, as well as exploiting the most central human affairs, as he was to do in his tragedies, was also impelled to fulfil through the drama that peculiarly epic function which is usually fulfilled through the narrative. Inspired partly perhaps by the example of Daniel and certainly by his own genius, he combined with the grim didactic exposition of the fortunes of England during her terrible ordeal of civil war his epic version of what England was.

     This new turn given to the History Play is a great stroke of Shakespeare's genius. Through it he goes beyond anything in Hall or Daniel or even Spenser. Hall and Daniel see English history in a solemn and moral light and they are impressive writers. Spenser is a great philosophical poet and epitomises the ethos of the Elizabethan age. But none of these can truly picture England. Of the epic writers Sidney in *Arcadia* comes nearest to doing this. It is indeed only in patches that authentic England appears through mythical Arcadia, but that it can this description of Kalander's house in the second chapter of the book is sufficient proof:

> The house itself was built of fair and strong stone, not affecting so much of any extraordinary kind of fineness as an honourable representing of a firm stateliness: the lights doors and stairs rather directed to the use of the guest than to the eye of the artificer, and yet, as the one chiefly heeded, so the other not neglected; each place handsome without curiosity and homely without loathsomeness; not so dainty as not to be trod on nor yet slubbered up with good fellowship; all more lasting than beautiful but that the consideration of the exceeding lastingness made the eye believe it was exceedingly beautiful.

This expresses the authentic genius of English domestic architecture.

Of this great new epic attempt *Richard II* is only the prelude. What of England it pictures is not only antique but partial: the confined world of a medieval courtly class. In his next plays Shakespeare was to picture (with much else) the whole land, as he knew it, in his own day, with its multifarious layers of society and manners of living.

HAROLD C. GODDARD

"Henry IV"

The two parts of *King Henry IV* are really a single drama in ten acts. Indeed the best things in Part II are invisible when it stands by itself, more proof, if any were needed, that Shakepeare did not think in purely theatrical terms, for staging the two parts as one play must always have been impracticable, and the second part has seldom been produced in our day.

The richness and complexity of this double drama may be seen in the fact that any one of three men may with reason be regarded as its central figure. If we think of it as a continuation of the story of Henry Bolingbroke who deposed and murdered Richard II, then King Henry IV, as the title implies, is the protagonist. If we conceive it as background and preface to *Henry V*, Prince Hal is central. But if we just give ourselves to it spontaneously as the spectator or naïve reader does, the chances are that the comic element will overbalance the historical. Sir John runs away with us as some critics think he did with the author. In that case these are "the Falstaff plays," and Falstaff himself the most important as he certainly is the most captivating figure in them. By stretching a point we might even find a fourth "hero": there have been productions of Part I in which Hotspur has outshone the other three. But that must have been a chance of casting, or miscasting.

II

In *Richard II* Shakespeare interred the doctrine of the divine right of kings. In *Henry IV* he tries out what can be said for the opposing theory.

From *The Meaning of Shakespeare*. Copyright © 1951 by The University of Chicago Press.

The twentieth century has fought two wars at enormous cost of life and treasure to avert the threat of the "strong" man. It is a pity that it could not have paid more attention in advance to Shakespeare's analysis and annihilation of this type and theory in his History Plays, particularly to the story of King Henry IV. Richard III was a "strong man" melodramatically represented. Pandulph, arch-power-politician of *King John*, was another, done closer to life. But compared with Henry IV either of these was a stage Machiavel with the label "Villain" on his sleeve. Henry, whatever he became, was natively neither cruel nor tyrannical, but a man of intelligence and insight and not devoid of a sense of justice. His story for that reason approximates tragedy.

The hypocrite has always been a favorite subject of satire. Henry IV is one of the most subtly drawn and effective hypocrites in literature, in no small measure because the author keeps his portrayal free of any satirical note. But not of any ironical note. Richard II had done Henry an injustice in banishing him and confiscating his inheritance. Coming back, the exile discovers that the opportunity to right his personal wrongs coincides with the chance to rid his native land of a weak king. So he finds himself ascending the throne almost before he knows it. Or so at least he protests later.

> Though then, God knows, I had no such intent,
> But that necessity so bow'd the state
> That I and greatness were compell'd to kiss.

"Necessity, the tyrant's plea." As previously in *The Rape of Lucrece*, as later in *Macbeth*, as so often in all literature from Aeschylus to Dostoevsky, opportunity is here made the mother of crime. And the punishment, though delayed outwardly, inwardly is immediate. It comes in the form of fear. Confirming a change that had long been in incubation, on the day when Henry deposed Richard he became a double man, one thing to the world, another to his own conscience. Force gives birth to fear. Fear gives birth to lies. And fear and lies together give birth to more force. Richard, symbol of Henry's own unjust act, had to be put out of the way. From the moment Henry gave the hint that ended in Richard's death to the moment of his own death at the end of *II Henry IV*, his life became a continuous embodiment of the strange law whereby we come to resemble what we fear. The basis of that law is plain. What we are afraid of we keep in mind. What we keep in mind we grow like unto.

Already at the conclusion of the play that bears Richard's name that nemesis had begun to work. Near its beginning Richard banished two men, Henry and Mowbray, who were symbols of his own fear and guilt.

He wanted them out of his sight. At the end of the same play Henry does the same thing. He banishes Carlisle and Exton. He wants them out of his sight—Carlisle because he is a symbol of truth and loyalty to Richard, Exton because he has been his instrument in Richard's murder.

Shakespeare dramatizes these ideas with impressive brevity and power. Unknown to Henry, the coffin containing Richard's body is at the door. It is as if the victim's ghost rises then and there from the dead and as if Henry, sensing its nearness, spares Carlisle's life in hope of indulgence. But to grant the Bishop a full pardon is beyond his power, for he could not endure the perpetual accusation and conviction of his presence. So he tells him to

> Choose out some secret place, some reverend room,

in which to spend the rest of his life. (It is like a prophecy of the Jerusalem Chamber in which Henry's own life was to end.) At that moment Exton enters, *"with Attendants bearing a coffin,"* and announces:

> Great king, within this coffin I present
> Thy buried fear.

By "buried fear" Exton of course means "the body of the man you feared." But the future reads into those three words another and more fearful meaning. It was indeed a buried fear, a fear buried deep in Henry's breast, that that coffin contained, a fear that was to shape every act and almost every thought of that "great king" henceforth. The spirit of the man who had once banished him and whom he had deposed enters his body and deposes and banishes his own spirit. When Henry bids Exton

> With Cain go wander through the shades of night,

it is to his own soul that, unaware, he issues that order. The later soliloquy on sleep shows through what shades of night that soul was destined to wander. From the moment he mentions the name of Cain, Henry's story is the story of the buried Richard within him:

> Lords, I protest, my soul is full of woe,
> That blood should sprinkle me to make me grow.

We do not need to wait for *Hamlet* to know that Henry "doth protest too much." It is not a protest but a confession. And to compensate for his crime in the eyes of the world, he decrees

> . . . a voyage to the Holy Land,
> To wash this blood off from my guilty hand.

III

1 *Henry IV* opens with a proclamation of peace and a definite proposal of the promised crusade to the sepulcher of Christ:

> To chase these pagans in those holy fields
> Over whose acres walk'd those blessed feet
> Which fourteen hundred years ago were nail'd
> For our advantage on the bitter cross.

It must have seemed to the pagans an odd way of instituting peace. But pagans of course did not count as human beings to Henry. There sounds, however, a note of something like genuine contrition in the reference to Christ. Yet, on his deathbed, Henry was to confess explicitly that this crusade was a purely political move to distract attention from civil unrest!

For the usual thing had happened. The men who helped Henry to the throne (the Percys) grew envious of the power they did not share and of his friendship:

> The king will always think him in our debt,
> And think we think ourselves unsatisfied,
> Till he hath found a time to pay us home.

This suspicion, reciprocated, led to acts on both sides that put foundations under it with the result that Henry's reign, where it was not open war, was incessant dissension.

Henry has no sooner declared the end of "civil butchery" in the opening speech of the play than a messenger from Wales enters announcing a thousand men "butcher'd" by the wild and irregular Glendower. And on the heels of this, news from Scotland: Hotspur has met and defeated the Scots. Ten thousand of them slain, and prisoners taken. But their captor refuses to hand them over to the King! This must be looked into. The pilgrimage to Jerusalem must be postponed.

A bit later the King confronts the Percys: father, son, and uncle. He declares that he has been too forbearing in the past, "smooth as oil, soft as young down," and implies that from now on he will demand the respect due him. Worcester bids him remember who helped him to his throne. To which the King retorts:

> Worcester, get thee gone; for I do see
> Danger and disobedience in thine eye.

The ghost of Richard again! Henry solving a problem by pushing it out of sight, doing to his enemy exactly what Richard did to him! The "buried fear" is stirring in its grave.

And the King's self-control is in for an even more severe jolt. Hotspur refuses to give up his prisoners unless his brother-in-law, Mortimer, who has been captured by the Welshman Glendower, shall be ransomed. At the mention of Mortimer something seems to explode inside the King:

> Let me not hear you speak of Mortimer;
> Send me your prisoners with the speediest means
> Or you shall hear in such a kind from me
> As will displease you.

Can this be Henry? The tone, so unlike him, shows that the name of Mortimer has touched something at the very foundation of his nature. When the King, in high dudgeon, has gone out, Worcester explains. Mortimer is legal heir to the throne: so by right, and so proclaimed by Richard. Of what avail to have had Richard murdered if his title transmigrated into a living man?

This is news to Hotspur. Mortimer! With the diabolic insight of a small boy who has hit on a scheme for teasing his sister, he dances about in an ecstasy and cries:

> I will find him when he lies asleep,
> And in his ear I'll holla "Mortimer!"
> Nay,
> I'll have a starling shall be taught to speak
> Nothing but "Mortimer," and give it him,
> To keep his anger still in motion.

Henry stands revealed to him for the hypocrite he is: a "vile politician," a "fawning greyhound," a "king of smiles."

Forthwith the three Percys hatch a plot to unite under themselves the Scots, the Welsh, and the Archbishop of York and, with Mortimer as the cutting edge, to defy the King. I said that three men, or even four, contend for the primacy in this play. And now we have a fifth. Mortimer is on the stage in only one scene. But he is the play's mainspring as certainly as is the Ghost in *Hamlet*. Shakespeare grew more and more fond of quietly suggesting the immense dramatic importance of figures partly or wholly behind the action, of making the absent present.

IV

These Percys, who having made a king now plan to unmake him, are an interesting group. They take up, both singly and together, the theme that Richard II introduced and Henry IV continued, and play their variations

of it, the theme of fear and lies—and the violence to which they inevitably give rise. Shakespeare seems as bent on getting together every known
type of duplicity, counterfeit, and deceit in this play as a boy is on
collecting every kind of bird's egg.

The elder Henry, Earl of Northumberland, the main factor in
Bolingbroke's elevation to the throne, is remembered as the man who in
the abdication scene kicked Richard when he was down. Confirming the
old proverb about the bully, he is the archcoward of *Henry IV*. He ruins
the cause of the rebellion against the King by his fears, his delays, his
faking of illness, his running away. While his son is fighting and dying at
Shrewsbury, he lies "crafty-sick" in his castle. When his party rallies after
its defeat, he starts north for Scotland.

Thomas Percy, Henry's brother, Earl of Worcester, is hardly more
attractive. He is a sour, dour, suspicious, and jealous man, envious himself
and therefore counting on and helping to create envy in Henry. His
concealment from Hotspur of the King's offer of peace before the battle of
Shrewsbury is characteristic of him. If his brother is the coward, he is the
liar.

And finally there is the younger Henry, "the Hotspur of the
North; he that kills me some six or seven dozen of Scots at a breakfast,
washes his hands, and says to his wife, 'Fie upon this quiet life! I want
work.' " The colorful Hotspur at any rate, it will be said, is in another
world from his father and uncle. In one sense he is indeed their utter
antithesis. But in another he is more like them than he seems. One
cannot help loving Hotspur for his blunt honesty. It seems almost his
central quality. And yet his very honesty is based on a lie, a degenerate
form of the medieval conception of "honour." The fact that Hotspur talks
so incessantly and extravagantly about "honour" shows that he distrusts
his own faith in it. He is another who "doth protest too much." This fact
is clinched by his uneasy sleep, which his wife reveals. He fights all night
long in his dreams. We are reminded of Richard III's "timorous dreams,"
which *his* wife reveals. Far as the noble Hotspur is from the villainous
Richard, the psychology is the same. It is fear begotten by falsehood.

The undegenerate chivalric conception of honor was a lofty one.
Under it trial by battle, and war, became religious affairs. Courage and
morale were given a religious ground. God was in the right arm of the
man whose cause was righteous, and to win under his sanction was to
cover oneself with glory, the glory of God himself. But the line between
war for God's sake and war for war's sake can become a very thin one to
one who enjoys fighting. It does in Hotspur's case. He rationalizes his
inborn pugnacity into a creed. War to him is the natural state of man, the

noble as well as the royal occupation. It is what art for art's sake is to the
artist. He is the extreme antitype of that "certain lord," that "popinjay,"
who, fresh as a bridegroom, accosted him, when he was breathless and
faint from fighting, with the declaration

> . . . that it was great pity, so it was,
> This villanous saltpetre should be digg'd
> Out of the bowels of the harmless earth,
> Which many a good tall fellow had destroy'd
> So cowardly; and but for these vile guns,
> He would himself have been a soldier.

Militarism and pacifism have always had a strange family resemblance,
and Hotspur and his popinjay are equally deluded. To put Hotspur beside
that other picturesque talker and valiant fighter, Faulconbridge, is to put
the "idealism" of war beside its realism, to the immense disadvantage of
the former.

But we must be fair to Hotspur. There are plenty of echoes in him
of the great tradition from which he comes. When he hears that his father
has failed them on the eve of battle, and cries,

> It lends a lustre and more great opinion,
> A larger dare to our great enterprise,

he anticipates the Winston Churchill of 1940. Even finer is his

> . . . the time of life is short;
> To spend that shortness basely were too long.

And when he bids them on the field of Shrewsbury

> Sound all the lofty instruments of war,
> And by that music let us all embrace,

it is as intoxicating as fife and drum to a small boy. But that is the trouble.
Hotspur intoxicates himself with "honour," and when "the morning after"
comes he is capable of saying, for example, that he would have Prince Hal
poisoned with a pot of ale if he weren't afraid that it would please the
King, his father. When honor has come to that pass, it is ready to be
debunked. Falstaff is on the horizon. When the play is done, there is about
as much left of "honour" as there was of the divine right of kings at the
end of *Richard II*. In fact the sentimental Richard and the pugnacious
Hotspur are closer to each other than they look. They are both the
victims of words.

V

And this brings us to the fourth and last of the Henrys in what are sometimes appropriately called these "Henry" plays: Henry, Prince of Wales, *alias* Harry, *alias* Hal, companion of Falstaff and heir apparent to the throne. His father first introduces us to him in the last act of *Richard II* when he asks,

> Can no man tell me of my unthrifty son?

and goes on to confess the low resorts that he haunts with a crew of dissolute companions, even the robberies he commits in their company. So at least the reports have it that have come to him. And Hotspur, who has recently talked with the Prince, more than confirms them. He tells specifically of Hal's intention to burlesque the spirit of chivalry in the spirit of the brothel.

With this glimpse of the heir to the throne added to what we have seen of the other three Henry's, the political pattern of these plays becomes clear. Henry IV, by deposing his legitimate sovereign, Richard, has committed himself to the best-man theory of kingship, which, in practice, is equivalent to the strong-man theory. Between himself and Richard, in his own opinion and in that of many others, there could be no question of relative merit. But here is Hotspur, the incarnation of valor (and brother-in-law incidentally of Mortimer, legal heir to the throne). And here is his own good-for-nothing son. What about the succession in this case, on the King's own theory?

Plainly Henry's revised version of the divine right of kings is in for trouble. He is caught in his own trap. And the nemesis is personal as well as political. "What the father hath hid cometh out in the son," says Nietzsche, "and often have I found the son a father's revealed secret." There was never a better illustration of this truth. In his concentration on power the elder Henry has suppressed both the playful and the passionate tendencies of his nature.

> My blood hath been too cold and temperate.

What he has kept under comes out in Hal, who leads a life of abandon under the tutelage of Falstaff. We are told little of the early life of the King. But what he says of his son is sufficient:

> Most subject is the fattest soil to weeds;
> And he, the noble image of my youth,
> Is overspread with them: therefore my grief
> Stretches itself beyond the hour of death.

Evidently Henry had had his fling too. His "grief" is partly unconscious envy—regret for his own lost youth, like that of that other hypocrite, Polonius, when he sent his son to Paris. But the important point is that the King recognizes his earlier self in his son.

Though it comes later, it is Henry's great soliloquy on sleep that confirms all this. It is the nocturnal part of a man that receives what he puts behind his back or under his feet in the daytime. In the apostrophe to sleep this victim of insomnia reveals the unrealized half of his soul. The lines have been called out of character. They are Shakespeare the poet, we are told, running away with Shakespeare the dramatist; Henry was incapable of anything so imaginative. On the contrary, the soliloquy is a measure of the amount of imagination that must be repressed before nature will permit one of her own creatures to be transformed into a worldling. It defines the distance Henry has travelled from innocence, and, in contrast with his diurnal aspect, the thickness of the mask that rank imposes.

> The king hath many marching in his coats,

cries Hotspur at Shrewsbury, referring to the counterfeit "kings" sent into the battle line in royal costume to lessen the chances of the real King's death. The device is a symbol of the man—as he became. The soliloquy on sleep tells us what he might have become.

When it is a question of the Prince, his father is honest and intelligent enough to perceive that he is himself trying to eat his cake and have it. The doctrine of the strong man and the doctrine of hereditary succession, he sees, do not cohere when the son is unworthy of the father. He catches the deadly parallel between the unkingly Richard and his own unkingly son and puts it in so many words to Hal:

> For all the world
> As thou art to this hour was Richard then
> When I from France set foot at Ravenspurgh,
> And even as I was then is Percy now.
> Now, by my sceptre and my soul to boot,
> He hath more worthy interest to the state
> Than thou the shadow of succession.

As Henry was to Richard, so is Hotspur now to Hal. There it is in a sentence. Hal gets the point and promises to be more himself in the future—at Hotspur's expense. The latter has been busy storing up glorious deeds all his life. Now Hal will make him exchange those deeds for his own "indignities."

> This, in the name of God, I promise here. . . .
> And I will die a hundred thousand deaths
> Ere break the smallest parcel of this vow.

To which boast his delighted father replies:

> A hundred thousand rebels die in this.

The Prodigal Son has returned and the Father has forgiven him! So at any rate it seems to those who make this play a fresh version of the biblical story. It is temptingly simple. But it leaves several things out of account.

To begin with, long before the Prince made to his father the promise to reform, he made it to himself. Left alone at the end of the scene in which we first see him, he breaks out into the memorable words which, though they have been quoted so often, must be quoted once more:

> I know you all, and will awhile uphold
> The unyok'd humour of your idleness:
> Yet herein will I imitate the sun,
> Who doth permit the base contagious clouds
> To smother up his beauty from the world,
> That, when he please again to be himself,
> Being wanted, he may be more wonder'd at,
> By breaking through the foul and ugly mists
> Of vapours that did seem to strangle him.
> If all the year were playing holidays,
> To sport would be as tedious as to work;
> But when they seldom come, they wish'd for come,
> And nothing pleaseth but rare accidents.
> So, when this loose behaviour I throw off
> And pay the debt I never promised,
> By how much better than my word I am,
> By so much shall I falsify men's hopes;
> And like bright metal on a sullen ground,
> My reformation, glittering o'er my fault,
> Shall show more goodly and attract more eyes
> Than that which hath no foil to set it off.
> I'll so offend, to make offence a skill;
> Redeeming time when men think least I will.

On top of our first glimpse of the carefree Hal, these lines come with a painful shock, casting both backward and forward, as they do, a shadow of insincerity. At a first reading or witnessing of the play the soliloquy is soon forgotten. But when we return to the text, there it is! So all this unaffected fun was not unaffected after all. Affected, according to Hal, is precisely what it was, put on for a purpose—only perhaps, deep down, it was just the other way around, perhaps it was the fun that was unaffected and it was the desire to make a dramatic impression on the world that was put on.

The speech just doesn't cohere with the Hal we love, his admirers protest. It is out of character. It is Shakespeare speaking, not Henry. And in support of them, the historical critics point out that the poet was merely following a familiar Elizabethan convention of tipping off the audence that they might be in the secret. It is odd, however, if it is just Shakespeare, that he made the speech so long and detailed and chose to base it on a metaphor that was forever running through Henry's mind. The playwright could have given the necessary information in a quarter of the space.

It is true that the soliloquy is unlike Hal. Yet there is not a speech in the role more strictly in character. How can that be? It can be for the simple reason that it is not Hal, primarily, who makes the speech at all. The Prince makes it. There are two Henrys. This is no quibble; it is the inmost heart of the matter. We saw that there were two elder Henrys. The King who had Richard murdered bears little resemblance to the man who utters the soliloquy on sleep. There are two younger Henrys who resemble each other just as little. If we need authority for what page after page of the play drives home, we have it in Falstaff, who makes just this distinction:

PRINCE: Darest thou be as good as thy word now?
FALSTAFF: Why, Hal, thou knowest, as thou art but man, I dare; but as
   thou art Prince, I fear thee as I fear the roaring of the lion's whelp.

Hal and the Prince: we shall never get anything straight about this story if we confuse them or fail to mark the differences, the connections, and the interplay of the two. Talk about the Prodigal Son! There is indeed more than a touch of him in Hal; but in the deliberately and coldly ambitious Prince not a spark. In him the Prodigal was reformed before he ever came into existence.

The Henry who is the Prince is, appropriately, like the Henry who is the King, the son like the father. And Shakespeare takes the utmost pains to point this out. The theme of the famous soliloquy is the function of the foil. The Prince says he will imitate the sun and suddenly appear from behind clouds at the theatrical moment to dazzle all beholders. Well, turn to that heart-to-heart talk between the King and his heir that ends in the latter's promise to amend his ways, and straight from the father's mouth we have the son's philosophy. The elder Henry tells how in earlier days he kept himself from the public gaze and dressed himself in humility in contrast with Richard, so that

> By being seldom seen, I could not stir
> But like a comet I was wonder'd at;
> That men would tell their children, "This is he";
> Others would say, "Where, which is Bolingbroke?"

Whereas Richard (and Hal of course catches the point)

> Grew a companion to the common streets . . .
> So when he had occasion to be seen,
> He was but as the cuckoo is in June,
> Heard, not regarded; seen, but with such eyes
> As, sick and blunted with community,
> Afford no extraordinary gaze,
> Such as is bent on sun-like majesty
> When it shines seldom in admiring eyes.

Not only the Prince's idea. His very metaphor! The young man has already bettered his adviser in advance. His opening soliloquy was nothing but a variation on his father's theme: the uses of contrast. But the father kept himself rare, it will be said, while the son made himself common, acting like Richard instead of following his father's example. That was indeed the ground of the King's complaint. But he got the truth there exactly upside down. He did not see that his son was acting far more like himself than he was like Richard. The Prince was doing precisely what his father had done, only in a wilier way. The King had kept himself literally hidden and then suddenly appeared. The Prince was keeping himself figuratively hidden by his wild ways in order to emerge all at once as a self-disciplined king. As between the two, who can question which was the more dramatic and effective? But we like neither father nor son for his tricks, no matter how well contrived or brilliantly executed. The better the worse, in fact, in both cases. "A great act has no subordinate mean ones," says Thoreau. In view of the elder Henry's abortive attempt to disprove this truth, we wonder whether the younger Henry will have better success.

Yet even after hearing his confession that his escapades are a political experiment in which his heart is not enlisted, we go on to the tavern scenes with unaffected delight. Hal seems to throw himself into them with a zest that gives the lie to the idea that he is holding anything back. Like ourselves, he seems to have forgotten his own words and plunges into the fun for its own sake quite in Falstaff's spirit. Not only does he appear to, he does—Hal does, that is. But the Prince is there in the background and occasionally intrudes. Then Hal will return and only the alertest sense can detect the Prince's presence. This is in accord with common experience. Who has not found himself so changed today from what he was yesterday that he could easily believe that other fellow was another man? He was. These vaunted modern discoveries about dual and multiple personalities are not discoveries at all. Shakespeare understood all about them in the concrete. I have quoted Falstaff. Let me quote a more recent and not less profound psychologist, Dostoevsky.

The second chapter of Dostoevsky's *The Devils* (wrongly called in England *The Possessed*) is entitled "Prince Harry." In it we are given an account of the youth of Nikolay Vsyevolodovitch Stavrogin. Utterly neglected by his father, Nikolay is initiated at his mother's request into the military life, just as some higher aspirations are being awakened in him by his tutor. Soon strange rumors come home. The young man has suddenly taken to riotous living. He is indulging in all sorts of outrageous conduct. His mother is naturally alarmed. But the tutor reassures her. It is only the first effervescence of a too richly endowed nature. The storm will subside. It is "like the youth of Prince Harry, who caroused with Falstaff, Poins, and Mrs. Quickly, as described by Shakespeare." The mother listens eagerly and asks the tutor to explain his theory. She even, in the words of the author, "took up Shakespeare herself and with great attention read the immortal chronicle. But it did not comfort her, and indeed she did not find the resemblance very striking." Neither may we, though we do not have the excuse of mother love to blind us. The resemblance is there just the same: the same charm, the same neglect, the same plunge into dissipation, the same outrageous pranks, the same contact with military life, the same impossibility of reconciling what seem like two different men. "I had expected to see a dirty ragamuffin, sodden with drink and debauchery," says the narrator of Nikolay's story. "He was, on the contrary, the most elegant gentleman I had ever met." One anecdote in particular clinches the parallelism. Leaning down to whisper something to the Governor of the province, Nikolay, on one occasion, suddenly takes his ear between his teeth. The exact, if exaggerated, counterpart of Hal's striking the Chief Justice.

Henry IV gives us an analysis of his son's temperament in advising Hal's brother how to handle him. It would fit Nikolay nearly as well.

> . . . blunt not his love,
> Nor lose the good advantage of his grace
> By seeming cold or careless of his will;
> For he is gracious, if he be observ'd:
> He hath a tear for pity and a hand

> Open as day for melting charity;
> Yet notwithstanding, being incens'd, he's flint,
> As humorous as winter, and as sudden
> As flaws congealed in the spring of day.
> His temper, therefore, must be well observ'd:
> Chide him for faults, and do it reverently,
> When you perceive his blood inclin'd to mirth;
> But, being moody, give him line and scope,
> Till that his passions, like a whale on ground,
> Confound themselves with working.

What in Henry's case is deep variation in mood amounts in Nikolay's to a pathological split in personality. If Nikolay's place in the world had been more comparable with Henry's, their histories might have been more alike than they were. Even so, the violence and tragedy that came from this division within the soul of Stavrogin are a profounder comment than any criticism could be on the gradual fading of the carefree Hal and the slow emergence of the formidable victor of Agincourt. Dostoevsky understood Shakespeare better than did either the tutor or the mother in his novel. His chapter title "Prince Harry" was no mistake.

But now comes the most remarkable fact: Falstaff diagnoses Hal precisely as Dostoevsky does Stavrogin! "Dost thou hear, Hal?" he cries, just after the ominous "knocking from within" which proves to be the Sheriff. "Dost thou hear, Hal? never call a true piece of gold a counterfeit: thou art essentially mad without seeming so." "Mad" appears to be just about the last word to apply to the self-controlled and cold-blooded Henry. He certainly does not seem mad. But that is precisely what Falstaff says. "Oh, but Falstaff was only joking!" it will be objected. Of course he was; but it is the very genius of Falstaff to utter truth in jest. There is madness and madness.

The moment we follow Falstaff's lead and cease thinking of Henry as Henry and conceive him as Hal-and-the-Prince we see how right Shakespeare was to build this play on an alternation of "tavern" scenes and political-military ones. Instead of being just chronicle play relieved by comedy (as historians of the drama are bound to see it), what we have is a genuine integration, both psychological and dramatic, the alternating character of the scenes corresponding to the two sides of a dual personality.

VI

And now we come to the third candidate for the role of "hero" in these plays.

Who at this late date can hope to say a fresh word about Falstaff?

Long since, his admirers and detractors have drained language dry in their efforts to characterize him, to give expression to their fascination or detestation. Glutton, drunkard, coward, liar, lecher, boaster, cheat, thief, rogue, ruffian, villain are a few of the terms that have been used to describe a man whom others find the very incarnation of charm, one of the liberators of the human spirit, the greatest comic figure in the history of literature. "A besotted and disgusting old wretch," Bernard Shaw calls him. And isn't he?—this man who held up unprotected travelers for pastime, betrayed innocence in the person of his page, cheated a trusting and hard-working hostess, borrowed a thousand pounds from an old friend with no intention of repaying it, abused his commission by taking cash in lieu of military service, and insinuated his way into the graces of the heir apparent with an eye to later favor. And yet after three centuries there the old sinner sits, more invulnerable and full of smiles than ever, his sagging paunch shaking like a jelly, dodging or receiving full on, unperturbed, the missiles his enemies hurl at him. Which is he? A colossus of sack, sensuality, and sweat—or a wit and humorist so great that he can be compared only with his creator, a figure, to use one of Shakeseare's own great phrases, livelier than life? One might think there were two Falstaffs.

The trouble with the "besotted and disgusting old wretch" theory is that Shakespeare has given us that old wretch exactly, and he is another man: the Falstaff of *The Merry Wives of Windsor*. The disparagers of Falstaff generally make him out a mixture, in varying proportions, of this other Falstaff, Sir Toby Belch, and Parolles, each of whom was an incalculably inferior person. But to assert that Falstaff is another man is not saying that he does not have many or even all of the vices of the "old wretch" for whom his defamers mistake him. Salt is not sodium, but that is not saying that sodium is not a component of salt. The truth is that there *are* two Falstaffs, just as there are two Henrys, the Immortal Falstaff and the Immoral Falstaff, and the dissension about the man comes from a failure to recognize that fact. That the two could inhabit one body would not be believed if Shakespeare had not proved that they could. That may be one reason why he made it so huge.

Curiously, there is no more convincing testimony to this double nature of the man than that offered by those who are most persistent in pointing out his depravity. In the very process of committing the old sinner to perdition they reveal that they have been unable to resist his seductiveness. Professor Stoll, for instance, dedicates twenty-six sections of a long and learned essay to the annihilation of the Falstaff that his congenital lovers love. And then he begins his twenty-seventh and last section with the words: "And yet people like Falstaff"! And before his first paragraph is done, all his previous labor is obliterated as we find him asserting that Falstaff is "supremely poetic" (even his most ardent admirers would hardly venture that "supremely") and that "his is in many ways the most marvelous prose ever penned." (It is, but how did the old sot, we wonder, ever acquire it?) Before his next paragraph is over, Stoll has called Falstaff "the very spirit of comradeship," "the king of companions," and "the prince of good fellows." "We, too, after all, like Prince Hal and Mrs. Quickly," he goes on, "take to a man because of his charm, if it be big enough, not because of his virtue; and as for Falstaff, we are bewitched with the rogue's company." (A Falstaff idolater could scarcely ask for more than that.) "Under the spell of his presence and speech," Stoll concludes, we should forget, as she does, the wrong he has done Mrs. Quickly, "did we not stop to think."

"Stop to think"! One may determine the orbit of the moon, or make an atomic bomb, by stopping to think, but when since the beginning of time did one man ever get at the secret of another by means of the intellect? It is all right to stop to think after we have taken a character to our hearts, but to do so before we have is fatal. Dr. Johnson stopped to think about Falstaff and as a result he decided that "he has nothing in him that can be esteemed." A child would be ashamed of such a judgment. But a child would never be guilty of it. "As for *Henry IV*," wrote one of the most imaginatively gifted young women I have ever known, "I love it. And I must have an utterly vulgar nature, for I simply adore Falstaff. He is perfectly delightful—not a fault in his nature, and the Prince is a DEVIL to reject him." That young woman evidently did not "stop to think." When she does, she will moderate that "not a fault in his nature," for that is the function of thinking—to hold our imagination within bounds and cut down its excrescences. Meanwhile, Falstaff has captured her, and she has captured Falstaff, for, as Blake said, enthusiastic admiration is the first principle of knowledge, and the last. Those who think about Falstaff before they fall in love with him may say some just things about him but they will never enter into his secret. "Would I were with him, wheresome'er he is, either in heaven or in hell!" Those words of poor Bardolph on hearing the account of Falstaff's death remain the highest tribute he ever did or ever could receive. In their stark sincerity they are worthy (irreverent as the suggestion will seem to some) to be put beside Dante's sublime incarnation of the same idea in the Paolo and Francesca incident in *The Inferno,* or even beside the words addressed to the thief who repented on the cross.

The scholars have attempted to explain Falstaff by tracing his origins. He has been found, variously, to have developed from the Devil of the miracle plays, the Vice of the morality plays, the boasting soldier of Plautine comedy, and so on. Now roots, up to a certain point, are interesting, but it takes the sun to make them grow and to illuminate the flower. And I think in this case we can find both roots and sun without going outside Shakespeare. If so, it is one of the most striking confirmations to be found of the embryological nature of his development.

If I were seeking the embryo of Falstaff in Shakespeare's imagination, I should consider the claims of Bottom—of Bottom and another character in A Midsummer-Night's Dream. "What!" it will be said, "the dull realistic Bottom and the lively witty Falstaff? They are nearer opposites." But embryos, it must be remembered, seldom resemble what they are destined to develop into. Bottom, like the physical Falstaff at least, is compact of the heaviness, the materiality, the reality of earth; and the ass's head that Puck bestows on him is abundantly deserved, not only in special reference to his brains but in its general implication of animality. But instead of letting himself be humiliated by it, Bottom sings, and Titania, Queen of the Fairies, her eyes anointed by the magic flower, awakening, mistakes him for an angel, and taking him in her arms, lulls him to sleep. The obvious meaning of the incident of course is that love is blind. Look at the asinine thing an infatuated woman will fall in love with! But whoever stops there, though he may have gotten the fun, has missed the beauty. The moment when Bottom emerges from his dream, as we pointed out when discussing A Midsummer-Night's Dream, is Shakespeare at one of his pinnacles. By a stroke of genius he turns a purely farcical incident into nothing less than a parable of the Awakening of Imagination within Gross Matter. It is the poet's way of saying that even within the head of this foolish plebeian weaver a divine light can be kindled. Bottom is conscious of transcendent things when he comes to himself. A creation has taken place within him. He struggles, in vain, to express it, and in his very failure, succeeds:

> God's my life! . . . I have had a most rare vision. I have had a dream, past the wit of man to say what dream it was. Man is but an ass, if he go about to expound this dream. Methought I was—there is no man can tell what. Methought I was,—and methought I had,—but man is but a patch'd fool, if he will offer to say what methought I had. The eye of man hath not heard, the ear of man hath not seen, man's hand is not able to taste, his tongue to conceive, nor his heart to report, what my dream was. I will get Peter Quince to write a ballad of this dream. It shall be called "Bottom's Dream," because it hath no bottom.

The dreamer may still be Bottom. But the dream itself is Puck. For one moment the two are one. Ass or angel? Perhaps Titania was not so deluded after all.

Do not misunderstand me. I am not suggesting that Shakespeare ever consciously connected Puck and Bottom with Falstaff in his own mind. But having achieved this inconceivable integration of the two, how easily his genius would be tempted to repeat the miracle on a grander scale: to create a perfect mountain of flesh and show how the same wonder could occur within it, not momentarily, but, humanly speaking, perpetually. That at any rate is what Falstaff is: Imagination conquering matter, spirit subduing flesh. Bottom was a weaver—a weaver of threads. "I would I were a weaver," Falstaff once exclaimed. He was a weaver—a weaver of spells. Here, if ever, is the embryology of the imagination. "Man is but a patch'd fool, if he will offer to say. . . ." Who cannot catch the very accent of Falstaff in that?

> I'll put a girdle round about the earth
> In forty minutes.

It might have been said of Falstaff's wit. His Bottom-like body is continually being dragged down, but his Puck-like spirit can hide in a thimble or pass through a keyhole as nimbly as any fairy's. What wonder that this contradictory being—as deminatured as a satyr or a mermaid—who is forever repeating within himself the original miracle of creation, has taken on the proportions of a mythological figure. He seems at times more like a god than a man. His very solidity is solar, his rotundity cosmic. To estimate the refining power we must know the grossness of what is to be refined. To be astounded by what lifts we must know the weight of what is to be lifted. Falstaff is levitation overcoming gravitation. At his wittiest and most aerial, he is Ariel tossing the terrestrial globe in the air as if it were a ball. And yet—as we must never forget—he is also that fat old sinner fast asleep and snoring behind the arras. The sins, in fact, are the very things that make the miracle astonishing, as the chains and ropes do a Houdini's escape.

To grasp Falstaff thus *sub specie aeternitatis* we must see him, as Titania did Bottom, with our imagination, not with our senses. And that is why we shall never see Falstaff on the stage. On the stage there the monster of flesh stands—made, we know, mainly of pillows—with all his sheer material bulk and greasy beefiness, a palpable candidate for perdition. It takes rare acting to rescue him from being physically repulsive. And as for the miracle—it just refuses to happen in a theater. It would take a child to melt this too too solid flesh into spirit. It would take

Falstaff himself to act Falstaff. But in a book! On the stage of our imagination! That is another matter. There the miracle can occur—and does for thousands of readers. Falstaff is a touch-stone to tell whether the juice of the magic flower has been squeezed into our eyes. If it has not, we will see only his animality. To the vulgar, Falstaff will be forever just vulgar.

The problem of Falstaff himself cannot be separated from the problem of the fascination he exercises over us. Critics have long since put their fingers on the negative side of that secret. Half his charm resides in the fact that he is what we long to be and are not: *free.* Hence our delight in projecting on him our frustrated longing for emancipation. It is right here that those who do not like Falstaff score a cheap victory over those who do. The latter, say the former, are repressed or sedentary souls who go on a vicarious spree in the presence of one who commits all the sins they would like to commit but do not dare to. Like some of Falstaff's own hypotheses, the idea has an air of plausibility. But it involves a pitifully superficial view of Falstaff—as if his essence lay in his love of sack! No! it is for liberation from what all men want to be rid of, not just the bloodless few, that Falstaff stands: liberation from the tyranny of things as they are. Falstaff is immortal because he is a symbol of the supremacy of imagination over fact. He forecasts man's final victory over Fate itself. Facts stand in our way. Facts melt before Falstaff like ice before a summer sun—dissolve in the *aqua regia* of his resourcefulness and wit. He realizes the age-old dream of all men: to awaken in the morning and to know that no master, no employer, no bodily need or sense of duty calls, no fear or obstacle stands in the way—only a fresh beckoning day that is wholly ours.

But we have all awakened that way on rare occasions without becoming Falstaffs. Some men often do. An untrammeled day is not enough; we must have something to fill it with—besides lying in bed. Freedom is only the negative side of Falstaff. Possessing it, he perpetually does something creative with it. It is not enough for him to be the sworn enemy of facts. Any lazy man or fool is that. He is the sworn enemy of the factual spirit itself, of whatever is dull, inert, banal. Facts merely exist—and so do most men. Falstaff lives. And where he is, life becomes bright, active, enthralling.

Who has not been a member of some listless group on whom time has been hanging heavy when in the twinkling of an eye a newcomer has altered the face of everything as utterly as the sun, breaking through clouds, transforms the surface of a gray lake? Boredom is banished. Gaiety is restored. The most apathetic member of the company is laughing and alert and will shortly be contributing his share to the flow of good spirits. What has done it? At bottom, of course, the mysterious fluid of an infectious personality. But so far as it can be analyzed, some tall tale or personal adventure wherein a grain of fact has been worked up with a pound of fiction, some impudent assumption about the host or absurd charge against somebody present rendered plausible by a precarious resemblance to the truth. Always *something made out of nothing*, with power, when added to the facts, to get the better of them. Never an unadulterated lie, but always some monstrous perversion, some scandalous interpretation, of what actually happened. An invention, yes, but an invention attached to reality by a thread of truth—the slenderer the better, so long as it does not break. What is Falstaff but an aggrandized, universalized, individualized version of this familiar phenomenon? He makes life again worth living.

And so, whether we approach Falstaff from the mythological or the psychological angle, we reach the same goal.

But alas! we have been neglecting the other Falstaff, the old sot. Unluckily—or perhaps luckily—there is another side to the story. Having fallen in love with Falstaff, we may now "stop to think" about him without compunction. And on examining more closely this symbol of man's supremacy over nature we preceive that he is not invulnerable. He has his Achilles heel. I do not refer to his love of Hal. That is his Achilles heel in another and lovelier sense. I refer to a tiny fact, two tiny facts, that he forgets and that we would like to: the fact that his imagination is stimulated by immense potations of sack and that his victories are purchased, if necessary, at the price of an utter disregard for the rights of others. We do not remember this until we stop to think. And we do not want to stop to think. We want to identify ourselves with the Immortal Falstaff. Yet there the Immoral Falstaff is all the while. And he must be reckoned with. Shakespeare was too much of a realist to leave him out.

The Greeks incarnated in their god Dionysus the paradox of wine, its combined power to inspire and degrade. *The Bacchae* of Euripides is the profoundest treatment of this theme in Hellenic if not in any literature. "No one can hate drunkenness more than I do," says Samuel Butler, "but I am confident the human intellect owes its superiority over that of the lower animals in great measure to the stimulus which alcohol has given to imagination—imagination being little else than another name for illusion." "The sway of alcohol over mankind," says William James, "is unquestionably due to its power to stimulate the mystical faculties of human nature [the imagination, that is, in its quintessence], usually crushed to earth by the cold facts and dry criticisms of the sober hour.

Sobriety diminishes, discriminates, and says no; drunkenness expands, unites, and says yes. It is in fact the great exciter of the *Yes* function in man . . . it is part of the deeper mystery and tragedy of life that whiffs and gleams of something that we immediately recognize as excellent should be vouchsafed to so many of us only in the fleeting earlier phases of what in its totality is so degrading a poisoning."

James's contrast between the earlier and the later phases of alcoholic intoxication inevitably suggests the degeneration that Falstaff undergoes in the second part of *Henry IV*. That degeneration is an actual one, though several recent critics have tended to exaggerate it. Dover Wilson thinks that Shakespeare is deliberately trying to make us fall out of love with Falstaff so that we may accept with good grace his rejection by the new king. If so, for many readers he did not succeed very well. (Of that in its place.)

It is significant that we never see Falstaff drunk. His wit still scintillates practically unabated throughout the second part of the play, though some critics seem set on not admitting it. He is in top form, for instance, in his interview with the Chief Justice, and, to pick a single example from many, the reply he gives to John of Lancaster's reproach,

When everything is ended, then you come,

is one of his pinnacles: "Do you think me a swallow, an arrow, or a bullet?" No, the degeneration of Falstaff is not so much in his wit or even in his imagination as in his moral sensibility. The company he keeps grows more continuously low, and his treatment of Shallow and of his recruits shows an increasing hardness of heart. Shakespeare inserts too many little realistic touches to let us take these scenes as pure farce, and while no one in his senses would want to turn this aspect of the play into a temperance tract it seems at times like an almost scientifically faithful account of the effect of an excess of alcohol on the moral nature. In view of what Shakespeare was at this time on the verge of saying about drunkenness in *Hamlet* and of what he was to say about it later in *Othello*, *Antony and Cleopatra*, and *The Tempest*, it is certain that he was profoundly interested in the subject; and it is not far-fetched to suppose that he had in the back of his mind in portraying the "degeneration" of Falstaff the nemesis that awaits the artificially stimulated mind. If so, the fat knight is Shakespeare's contribution, in a different key, to the same problem that is treated in *The Bacchae*, and his conclusions are close to those at which Euripides arrives.

VII

And then there is *The Merry Wives of Windsor*. (Here appears to be the right place for a brief interlude on that play.) Criticism has been much concerned over the connection, if any, between the Falstaff of *The Merry Wives* and the Falstaff of *Henry IV*—with something like a consensus that with the exception of a few dying sparks of the original one this is another man. Yet one link between the two Falstaffs cannot be denied: with respect to wit and resourcefulness they are exact opposites. The Falstaff we admire is an incarnation of readiness; this one of helplessness. Nothing is too much for the former. Anything is too much for the latter. They are, respectively, presence and absence of mind. Such an utter antithesis is itself a connection. Shakespeare must have meant something by it.

Nearly everyone is acquainted with the tradition that *The Merry Wives of Windsor* was written in a fortnight at the command of Queen Elizabeth, who wished to see the fat man in love. Shakespeare does appear to have "tossed off" this sparkling farce-comedy, his one play of purely contemporary life and of almost pure prose, and, along with *The Comedy of Errors*, his most inconsequential and merely theatrical one. Several hypotheses, or some combination of them, may account for the Falstaff of this play.

Poets, as distinct from poets laureate, do not like commissions. It would be quite like Shakespeare, ordered by the Queen to write another play about Falstaff, to have his playful revenge by writing one about another man entirely, under the same name. That was precisely the sort of thing that Chaucer did when commanded by another Queen to write a *Legend of Good Women*. It is fun to make a fool of royalty. Then, too, the conditions under which the play was written, if the tradition is true, practically compelled it to keep close to farce. And farce is the very atmosphere in which parody thrives. This Falstaff is a kind of parody of the other one. But the closer Shakespeare gets to farce, fancy, or nonsense, as he proves over and over, the more certain he is to have some serious underintention. On that principle, what better place than *The Merry Wives of Windsor* in which to insert an oblique comment on the Falstaff of *Henry IV*? Be that as it may, the Falstaff of this play is, as we said, an almost perfect picture, in exaggerated form and in a farcical key, of the Immoral Falstaff of the other plays, the old wretch of Bernard Shaw. Only the light tone of the piece keeps him from being "besotted and disgusting" also. Critics have seriously tried to determine at what spot chronologically this play should be inserted in the Henry series. Such an attempt betrays a curious ignorance of the ways of the imagination. But, after all due discount for the farce and fooling, the Falstaff of *The Merry Wives* looks like pretty good natural history of the latter end of an "old soak." From him it is a relief to get back, after our interlude, to the Immortal Falstaff, who, however entangled with the Immoral Falstaff, as the soul is with the body, breathes another and more transcendental air.

VIII

Is there any activity of man that involves the same factors that we find present in this Falstaff: complete freedom, an all-consuming zest for life, an utter subjugation of facts to imagination, and an entire absence of moral responsibility? Obviously there is. That activity is play.

Except for that little item of moral responsibility, "play" expresses as nearly as one word can the highest conception of life we are capable of forming: life for its own sake, life as it looks in the morning to a boy with

> . . . no more behind
> But such a day to-morrow as to-day,
> And to be boy eternal,

life for the fun of it, as against life for what you can get out of it—or whom you can knock out of it. "Play" says what the word "peace" tries to say and doesn't. "Play" brings down to the level of everyone's understanding what "imagination" conveys to more sophisticated minds. For the element of imagination is indispensable to true play. Play is not sport. The confusion of the two is a major tragedy of our time. A crowd of fifteen-year-old schoolboys "playing" football on a back lot are indulging in sport. They are rarely playing. The one who is playing is the child of five, all alone, pretending that a dirty rag doll is the rich mother of a dozen infants—invisible to the naked eye. Even boys playing war, if they are harmonious and happy, are conducting an experiment in peace. Play is the erection of an illusion into a reality. It is not an escape from life. It is the realization of life in something like its fulness. What it *is* an escape from is the boredom and friction of existence. Like poetry, to which it is the prelude, it stands for a converting or winning-over of facts on a basis of friendship, the dissolving of them in a spirit of love, in contrast with science (at least the science of our day), which, somewhat illogically, stands first for a recognition of the absolute autonomy of facts and then for their impressment and subjection to human demands by a kind of military conquest.

Now Falstaff goes through life playing. He coins everything he encounters into play, often even into *a* play. He would rather have the joke on himself and make the imaginative most of it than to have it on the other fellow and let the fun stop there. Whenever he seems to be taken in because he does not realize the situation, it is safer to assume that he does realize it but keeps quiet because the imaginative possibilities are greater in that case.

Watching him, we who in dead earnest have been attending to business or doing what we are pleased to call our duty suddenly realize what we have been missing. "The object of a man's life," says Robert Henri, "should be to play as a little child plays." If that is so we have missed the object of life, while Falstaff has attained it, or at least not missed it completely, as we have. It is his glory that, like Peter Pan, he never grew up, and that glory is the greater because he is an old man. As his immense size and weight were utilized by Shakespeare as a foil for the lightness of his spirit, so his age is used to stress its youthfulness. "You that are old," he says to the Chief Justice, who has been berating him for misleading the Prince, "consider not the capacities of us that are young." The Chief Justice replies that Falstaff is in every part "blasted with antiquity," his belly increasing in size, his voice broken, "and will you yet call yourself young? Fie, fie, fie, Sir John!" Falstaff retorts that as for his belly, he was born with a round one; as for his voice, he has lost it hollaing and singing of anthems; and as for his age, he is old only in judgment and understanding. Though the Lord Chief Justice has all the facts on his side, Falstaff has the victory. There has seldom been a more delicious interview.

As this scene suggests, the right way to take the Falstaff whom we love is to take him as a child. Mrs. Quickly did that in her immortal account of his death: he went away, she said, "an it had been any christom child." To call him a liar and let it go at that is like being the hardheaded father of a poetic little son who punishes him for falsehood when he has only been relating genuine imaginative experiences—as Blake's father thrashed him for saying he had seen angels in a tree. And to call him a coward and let it go at *that* is being no profounder.

But if it is the glory of the Immortal Falstaff that he remained a child, it is the shame of the Immoral Falstaff that he never became a man—for it is a child's duty to become a man no less than it is a man's duty to become a child. Falstaff detoured manhood instead of passing through it into a higher childhood. He is like the character in *The Pilgrim's Progress* who tried to steal into Paradise by climbing over the wall near its entrance instead of passing through the wicket gate and undergoing the trials that it is the lot of man to endure. He wanted the victory without paying the price. He wanted to be an individual regardless of the social consequences, to persist in the prerogatives of youth without undertaking the responsibilities of maturity. But if his virtues are those of a child rather than those of a man, that does not prevent him from being immensely superior to those in these plays who possess the virtues of neither man nor child, or from giving us gleams of a life beyond good and evil.

Dover Wilson would have us take *Henry IV* as a morality play wherein a madcap prince grows up into an ideal king. Falstaff is the devil who tempts the Prince to Riot. Hotspur and especially the Lord Chief Justice are the good angels representing Chivalry and Justice or the Rule of Law. It is a struggle between Vanity and Government for the possession of the Royal Prodigal.

The scheme is superbly simple and as moral as a Sunday-school lesson. But it calmly leaves the Immortal Falstaff quite out of account! If Falstaff were indeed just the immoral creature that in part he admittedly is, Wilson's parable would be more plausible, though even then the words he picks to characterize Falstaff are singularly unfortunate. "Vanity" by derivation means emptiness or absence of substance, and "riot" quarrelsomeness. Imagine calling even the Immoral Falstaff empty or lacking in substance—or quarrelsome! He had his vices but they were not these. For either vanity or riot there is not a single good word to be said. To equate Falstaff with them is to assert that not a single good word can be said for him—a preposterous proposition. Wit, humor, laughter, good-fellowship, insatiable zest for life: are these vanity or does Falstaff *not* embody them? That is the dilemma in which Mr. Wilson puts himself. And as for the Lord Chief Justice, he is indeed an admirable man; a more incorruptible one in high position is not to be found in Shakespeare. But if the poet had intended to assign him any such crucial role as Mr. Wilson thinks, he certainly would have presented him more fully and would have hesitated to let Falstaff make him look so foolish. For the Chief Justice's sense of justice was better developed than his sense of humor. And even justice is not all.

Henry IV does have a certain resemblance to a morality play. The two, however, between whom the younger Henry stands and who are in a sense contending for the possession of his soul are not Falstaff and the Chief Justice, but Falstaff and the King. It is between Falstaff and the Father—to see that word in its generic sense—that Henry finds himself.

Now in the abstract this is indeed Youth between Revelry and Responsibility. But the abstract has nothing to do with it. Where Henry really stands is between this particular companion, Falstaff, and this particular father and king, Henry IV. Of the two, which was the better man?

Concede the utmost—that is, take Falstaff at his worst. He was a drunkard, a glutton, a profligate, a thief, even a liar if you insist, but withal a fundamentally honest man. He had two sides like a coin, but he was not a counterfeit. And Henry? He was a king, a man of "honour," of brains and ability, of good intentions, but withal a "vile politician" and respectable hypocrite. He *was* a counterfeit. Which, if it comes to the choice, is the better influence on a young man? Shakespeare, for one, gives no evidence of having an iota of doubt.

But if even Falstaff at his worst comes off better than Henry, how about Falstaff at his best? In that case, what we have is Youth standing between Imagination and Authority, between Freedom and Force, between Play and War. My insistence that Falstaff is a double man, and that the abstract has nothing to do with it, will acquit me of implying that this is the whole of the story. But it is a highly suggestive part of it.

The opposite of war is not "peace" in the debased sense in which we are in the habit of using the latter word. Peace ought to mean far more, but what it has come to mean on our lips is just the absence of war. The opposite of war is creative activity, play in its loftier implications. All through these dramas the finer Falstaff symbolizes the opposite of force. When anything military enters his presence, it instantly looks ridiculous and begins to shrink. Many methods have been proposed for getting rid of war. Falstaff's is one of the simplest: laugh it out of existence. For war is almost as foolish as it is criminal. "Laugh it out of existence"? If only we could! Which is the equivalent of saying: if only more of us were like Falstaff! These plays should be required reading in all military academies. Even the "cannon-fodder" scenes of Falstaff with his recruits have their serious implications and anticipate our present convictions on the uneugenic nature of war.

How far did Shakespeare sympathize with Falstaff's attitude in this matter? No one is entitled to say. But much further, I am inclined to think, than he would have had his audience suspect or than the world since his time has been willing to admit. For consider the conditions under which Falstaff finds himself:

Henry has dethroned and murdered the rightful king of England. The Percys have helped him to obtain the crown, but a mutual sense of guilt engenders distrust between the two parties, and the Percys decide to dethrone the dethroner. Falstaff is summoned to take part in his defense. "Life is given but once." Why should Falstaff risk his one life on earth, which he is enjoying as not one man in a hundred million does, to support or to oppose the cause of either of two equally selfish and equally damnable seekers after power and glory? What good would the sacrifice of his life accomplish comparable to the boon that he confers daily and hourly on the world, to say nothing of himself, by merely being? This is no case of tyranny on one side and democracy on the other, with the liberty or slavery of a world at stake. This is a strictly dynastic quarrel. When two gangs of gunmen begin shooting it out on the streets of a great city, the discreet citizen will step behind a post or into a doorway. The analogy may not be an exact one, but it enables us to understand Falstaff's point of view. And there is plenty of Shakespearean warrant for it.

> See the coast clear'd, and then we will depart,

says the Mayor of London when caught, in *I Henry IV*, between similar brawling factions,

> Good God! these nobles should such stomachs bear;
> I myself fight not once in forty year.

And Mercutio's "A plague o' both your houses!" comes to mind. Shakespeare meant more by that phrase than the dying man who coined it could have comprehended.

"But how about Falstaff's honor?" it will be asked. "Thou owest God a death," says the Prince to him before the battle of Shrewsbury. " 'Tis not due yet," Falstaff answers as Hal goes out.

> I would be loath to pay him before his day. What need I be so forward with him that calls not on me? Well, 'tis no matter; honour pricks me on. Yea, but how if honour prick me off when I came on? how then? Can honour set to a leg? No. Or an arm? No. Or take away the grief of a wound? No. Honour hath no skill in surgery, then? No. What is honour? A word. What is in that word honour? What is that honour? Air; a trim reckoning! Who hath it? He that died o' Wednesday. Doth he feel it? No. Doth he hear it? No. 'Tis insensible, then? Yea, to the dead. But will it not live with the living? No. Why? Detraction will not suffer it. Therefore I'll none of it. Honour is a mere scutcheon: and so ends my catechism.

"You must be honorable to talk of honor," says a character in *A Raw Youth*, "or, if not, all you say is a lie." The word "honor," as that sentence of Dostoevsky's shows, is still an honorable word. It can still mean, and could in Shakespeare's day, the integrity of the soul before God. The Chief Justice had honor in that sense. But "honour" in its decayed feudal sense of glory, fame, even reputation, as page after page of these Chronicle Plays records, had outlived its usefulness and the time had come to expose its hollowness. The soul, lifted up, declared Saint Teresa (who died in 1582), sees in the word "honor" "nothing more than an immense lie of which the world remains a victim. . . . She laughs when she sees grave persons, persons of orison, caring for points of honor for which she now feels profoundest contempt. . . . With what friendship we would all treat each other if our interest in honor and in money could but disappear from the earth! For my own part, I feel as if it would be a remedy for all our ills."

Saint Teresa and Sir John Falstaff! an odd pair to find in agreement—about honor if not about money. In the saint's case no ambiguity is attached to the doctrine that honor is a lie. In the sinner's, there remains something equivocal and double-edged. Here, if ever, the two Falstaffs meet. The grosser Falstaff is himself a parasite and a dishonorable man, and coming from him the speech is the creed of Commodity and the height of irony. But that does not prevent the man who loved Hal and babbled of green fields at his death from revealing in the same words, as clearly as Saint Teresa, that life was given for something greater than glory or than the gain that can be gotten out of it.

"Give me life," cries Falstaff on the field of Shrewsbury. "Die all, die merrily," cries Hotspur. That is the gist of it. The Prince killed Hotspur in the battle, and Falstaff, with one of his most inspired lies, claimed the deed as his own. But Falstaff's lies, scrutinized, often turn out to be truth in disguise. So here. Falstaff, not Prince Henry, did kill Hotspur. He ended the outworn conception of honor for which Hotspur stood. The Prince killed his body, but Falstaff killed his soul—or rather what passed for his soul.

The dying Hotspur himself sees the truth. The verdict of his final breath is that life is "time's fool" and he himself dust. And the Prince, gazing down at his dead victim, sees it too, if only for a moment.

> Ill-weav'd ambition, how much art thou shrunk!
> When that this body did contain a spirit,
> A kingdom for it was too small a bound,

he exclaims, and, turning, he catches sight of another body from which life has also apparently departed:

> What, old acquaintance! could not all this flesh
> Keep in a little life? Poor Jack, farewell!
> I could have better spar'd a better man.

But nobody was ever more mistaken on this subject of life and flesh than was Henry on this occasion, as the shamming Falstaff proves a moment later, when the Prince goes out, by rising from the dead. " 'Sblood." he cries.

> 'twas time to counterfeit, or that hot termagant Scot had paid me scot
> and lot too. Counterfeit? I lie, I am no counterfeit. To die is to be a
> counterfeit; for he is but the counterfeit of a man who hath not the life
> of a man; but to counterfeit dying, when a man thereby liveth, is to be
> no counterfeit, but the true and perfect image of life indeed. The better
> part of valour is discretion.

> I fear thou art another counterfeit,

Douglas had cried, coming on Henry IV on the field of Shrewsbury,

> Another king! they grow like Hydra's heads.
> I am the Douglas, fatal to all those
> That wear those colours on them. What art thou,
> That counterfeit'st the person of a king?

The literal reference of course is to the knights, disguised to represent the King, that Henry had sent into the battle to divert the enemy from his own person. "The better part of valour is discretion." This, and that repeated word "counterfeit," is Shakespeare's sign that he intends the contrast, and the deeper unconscious meaning of Douglas'

> What art thou,
> That counterfeit'st the person of a king?

(a king, notice, not the king) is just one of the poet's judgments upon Henry. For all his "discretion," the Douglas would have killed this counterfeit king who tries to save his skin by the death of others if the Prince had not come to his rescue in the nick of time.

But that was earlier in the battle. At the point we had reached the Prince comes back with his brother John and discovers the "dead" Falstaff staggering along with the dead Hotspur on his back—a symbolic picture if there ever was one.

> Did you not tell me this fat man was dead?

cries Lancaster.

> I did; saw him dead,
> Breathless and bleeding on the ground,

replies Henry. He has underrated the vitality of the Imagination, and even now thinks he sees a ghost:

> Art thou alive?
> Or is it fantasy that plays upon our eyesight?
> I prithee, speak; we will not trust our eyes
> Without our ears. Thou art not what thou seem'st.

"No: that's certain," retorts Falstaff, "I am not a double man." And to prove it, he throws down the body of Hotspur he is carrying. But beyond this obvious meaning, who can doubt that Falstaff, in the phrase "double man," is also having a thrust at the dual role of the man he is addressing, or that Shakespeare, in letting Falstaff deny his own doubleness, is thereby calling our attention to it? At the very least the expression proves that the world did not have to wait for Dostoevsky before it heard of the double man.

Truth has made it necessary to say some harsh things about Prince Henry; so it is a pleasure to recognize the character of his conduct on the field of Shrewsbury: his valor in his encounter with Hotspur, his courage and loyalty in rescuing his father from Douglas, and his generosity in letting Falstaff take credit for Hotspur's death. Dover Wilson makes much of this last point—too much, I think, for the good of his own case—declaring that it proves the Prince thought nothing of renown, of "the outward show of honour in the eyes of men, so long as he has proved himself worthy of its inner substance in his own." But if he was as self-effacing as all that, why did he cry at the moment he met Hotspur?—

> . . . all the budding honours on thy crest
> I'll crop, to make a garland for my head.

Those words flatly contradict the "grace" he does Falstaff in surrendering to him so easily the greatest honor of his life. The paradox arises, I think, from the presence of those conflicting personalities, Hal and the Prince. Touched momentarily at the sight of what he believes to be his old companion dead at his feet, the fast-disappearing Hal returns and survives long enough after the surprise and joy of finding him still alive to accept Falstaff's lie for truth. But we wonder how much longer. Wilson's assumption that the Prince would or could have kept up the fiction permanently is refuted by the fact that Morton had observed the death of Hotspur at Henry's hands and reports the event correctly:

> . . . these mine eyes saw him in bloody state,
> Rendering faint quittance, wearied and outbreath'd,
> To Harry Monmouth; whose swift wrath beat down
> The never-daunted Percy to the earth,
> From whence with life he never more sprung up.

Everything, from the famous first soliloquy on, proves that the Prince not only craved renown but craved it in its most theatrical form.

IX

In the fourth scene of the fourth act of the second part of the play, King Henry, surrounded by his lords, returns to his earlier proposal of a crusade to Jerusalem. If God crowns our arms with success in our present quarrel, he promises,

> We will our youth lead on to higher fields
> And draw no swords but what are sanctified,

a way of phrasing it that suggests a buried doubt about the sanctity of the sword he has drawn against the Percys. The scene is the Jerusalem Chamber in Westminster. As the King's confession,

> Only, we want a little personal strength,

reveals, the hand of death is already on him.

Meanwhile, things have been happening in Yorkshire. John of Lancaster, a younger brother of Hal, has been guilty of the most despicable piece of treachery recorded anywhere in these plays. Just after berating the Archbishop of York for misusing his office.

> As a false favourite doth his prince's name,
> In deeds dishonourable,

he proceeds, in the King's name, to an act of dishonor of exactly the same kind. By a cold-blooded lie, a promise he makes and breaks in a breath, he tricks the leaders of the rebellion into laying down their arms, condemns them to the block as traitors, and gives credit for the fraud to God:

> God, and not we, hath safely fought today.

Safely, indeed! One more example of "honour."

News of this "victory" is brought to the King in the ironical line,

> Peace puts forth her olive everywhere.

But the good tidings are too much for Henry. He is stricken with sudden illness and we next see him in another room to which he has been borne, lying in bed listening to music. He calls for his crown. It is placed beside him on his pillow. Music, a dying king, and a crown: it is a symbolic picture.

Prince Henry enters. And then comes one of those little scenes, that seem at a first reading utterly superfluous, wherein Shakespeare was so fond of dropping the clue to what is coming. Whoever would understand the critical crown scene that is to follow must attend to its preface in these eleven apparently casual lines.

"Who saw the Duke of Clarence?" the Prince demands as he comes in. The Duke, his brother, is in the room at the moment, but overcome with grief at his father's illness has apparently withdrawn into a corner. He is weeping.

> How now! rain within doors and none abroad!

exclaims the Prince, catching sight of him. The jest in the circumstance is poor enough and is not much improved even if the King is too weak to hear it. Henry inquires for his father and, being told that he is "exceeding ill," declares that he will recover without medicine if he is sick with joy over the good news. Warwick reprimands him for speaking too loudly:

> Sweet prince, speak low;
> The king your father is dispos'd to sleep.

Clarence suggests that they all retire into another room. The Prince says he will remain and watch by the King. Such is Shakespeare's introduction to one of the most critical scenes of the play.

Left alone with the sick man, the Prince immediately spies the crown upon the pillow and breaks into an apostrophe to it. In the midst of it he notices that a feather near his father's lips does not stir and concludes that the King has suddenly expired.

> My gracious lord! my father!
> This sleep is sound indeed; this is a sleep
> That from this golden rigol hath divorc'd
> So many English kings. Thy due from me
> Is tears and heavy sorrows of the blood,
> Which nature, love, and filial tenderness
> Shall, O dear father, pay thee plenteously:
> My due from thee is this imperial crown,
> Which, as immediate from thy place and blood,
> Derives itself to me. Lo, here it sits,
> *(Putting it on his head)*
> Which God shall guard: and put the world's whole strength
> Into one giant arm, it shall not force
> This lineal honour from me. This from thee
> Will I to mine leave, as 'tis left to me.

We wonder why Henry, on the discovery of his father's death, did not instantly recall his brother and the nobles who have just gone out. Yet even after his address to the dead man is done, the Prince, now self-crowned king, does not do so, but passes into an adjoining chamber with the symbol of his new power still on his head.

But his assumption of the crown turns out to have been premature. His father is not dead, and waking at the moment and missing the crown, calls out in dismay, "Warwick! Gloucester! Clarence!" They come, and when they tell him that they left the Prince watching him, he realizes that it is he who has taken the crown and breaks into lamentations over what he is convinced is the Prince's craving for his death:

> Is he so hasty that he doth suppose
> My sleep my death?

Warwick, who has gone in search of the missing heir, returns to report that he found him weeping in the next room,

> Washing with kindly tears his gentle cheeks.

(Whether he was, or not, we shall never know.) But the King, unsatisfied, asks again:

> But wherefore did he take away the crown?
>
> I never thought to hear you speak again,

protests the Prince. He has entered at the moment and overheard.

> Thy wish was father, Harry, to that thought.
> . . . O foolish youth!
> Thou seek'st the greatness that will overwhelm thee,

cries the disillusioned servant of Commodity.

> Thou hast stol'n that which after some few hours
> Were thine without offence. . . .
> What! canst thou not forbear me half an hour?
> Then get thee gone and dig my grave thyself,

and he goes on to forecast the undoing of the realm under his son's coming reign when "apes of idleness," ruffians and the scum of the earth will

> . . . commit
> The oldest sins the newest kind of ways,

until England is finally reduced to a wilderness, peopled with wolves, its old inhabitants. The self-pity of the speech has the exact accent of

Richard II. The wheel has come full circle. Henry has become the image of the man he injured.

Under his father's indictment the Prince has stood speechless. What can he say? His conduct in putting on the crown at such a moment is indefensible. And so he does what anyone is likely to do in such a predicament: he swears, he promises, he exaggerates, he lies, he calls God to witness, and, in general, "doth protest too much." Now we see why Shakespeare was at pains to contrast the conduct of the Prince's younger brother with the Prince's. Clarence melts into tears and near silence at the sight of his father's illness. Henry, at the sight of what he supposes his death, is dry-eyed (we cannot but infer) and able to make a perfectly self-controlled speech (I almost said oration) in which he declares that his father's due from him is tears which he "shall" weep, while his due from his father is the crown that "sits" by his own immediate act on his head. Why the careful discrimination in tenses? Why the postponement of the emotion? Why the question in our minds whether Warwick *did* find Hal in tears in the next room—whether his report that he did may not be an exaggeration, or even a lie, to comfort the dying man? That there are tears in Henry's eyes when he comes back and finds his father still alive we need not go so far as to question. There must have been mixed emotions back of them, however, vexation at himself being one of them. But the culminating proof of the Prince's duplicity is the account he gives his father of his apostrophe to the crown while he was watching by the bedside. His father did not hear his words. But we did. It is revealing to put what he said beside what he says he said.

Here is what he said:

> Why doth the crown lie there upon his pillow,
> Being so troublesome a bedfellow?
> O polish'd perturbation! golden care!
> That keep'st the ports of slumber open wide
> To many a watchful night! Sleep with it now!
> Yet not so sound and half so deeply sweet
> As he whose brow with homely biggen bound
> Snores out the watch of night. O majesty!
> When thou dost pinch thy bearer, thou dost sit
> Like a rich armour worn in heat of day,
> That scalds with safety. By his gates of breath
> There lies a downy feather which stirs not:
> Did he suspire, that light and weightless down
> Perforce must move. My gracious lord! my father!
> *Etc.*

And here is what he says he said:

> I spake unto the crown as having sense,
> And thus upbraided it: "The care on thee depending
> Hath fed upon the body of my father;
> Therefore, thou best of gold art worst of gold:
> Other, less fine in carat, is more precious,
> Preserving life in medicine potable;
> But thou, most fine, most honour'd, most renown'd,
> Hast eat thy bearer up." Thus, my most royal liege,
> Accusing it, I put on my head,
> To try with it, as with an enemy
> That had before my face murder'd my father,
> The quarrel of a true inheritor.

The changes Henry quietly slips into his account of his own humiliating blunder are quite human and understandable. But if we want to understand Henry we cannot overlook them. Actually the address to the crown is half over before he discovers the supposed death of his father. But he tells the King he realized he was dead as soon as he came into the chamber and *for that reason* denounced the crown:

> God witness with me, when I here came in,
> And found no course of breath within your majesty,
> How cold it struck my heart!

Bringing God into the matter is in itself suspicious, and when a moment later he repeats what he has just said, we know that a bad conscience is back of the double protestation:

> Coming to look on you, thinking you dead,
> And dead almost, my liege, to think you were,
> I spake unto the crown. . . .

The theme of the actual apostrophe is the crown as a disturber of slumber—of royalty in general it might almost seem. Its theme, as Henry recounts it, is the crown as murderer—specifically of "my father." The tone of the real speech is meditative and reflective—not unlike that of Henry IV's own address to sleep. The tone of the supposed one is that of an upbraiding or accusation (the Prince's own words), and the act of putting the crown on his head a trial with an enemy.

> That had before my face murder'd my father.

He even inserts new details. Where, for instance, in the original is the reference to potable gold that he says he made? No, the revised version is doubtless what Henry now wishes he had said. What he did say was something quite different. And the vehemence with which he denies at the end—for we interrupted him—that he had any selfish motive in what he said or did is enough in itself to convict him. If he were innocent, words like these would be superfluous:

> But if it did infect my blood with joy,
> Or swell my thoughts to any strain of pride;
> If any rebel or vain spirit of mine
> Did with the least affection of a welcome
> Give entertainment to the might of it,
> Let God forever keep it from my head
> And make me as the poorest vassal is
> That doth with awe and terror kneel to it!

"I didn't take any cake," the guilty child protests even before he is accused, putting the hand that holds the cake behind him. Quite as boldly, if not quite so naïvely, the Prince puts behind him the words he spoke but a moment before. What he expressly declares he did not say or feel fits what he did say and obviously did feel with a damning neatness. In substance, he protests: "I, Prince Harry, feel any pride or offer the least welcome to the might of the crown! God keep it from me if I did." Yet this is what he said:

> . . . put the world's whole strength
> Into one giant arm, it shall not force
> This lineal honour from me. This from thee
> Will I to mine leave, as 'tis left to me.

If that is not dynastic pride and the poison of power, what is it? *Infection*: we have the Prince himself to thank for the one word that describes it best. And there comes to mind by way of contrast, as Shakespeare must have specifically intended that it should, the vow of Faulconbridge with which *King John* concludes:

> Come the three corners of the world in arms,
> And we shall shock them. Naught shall make us rue,
> If England to itself do rest but true.

So similar, yet so antipodal! Such is the difference, Shakespeare seems to say, between love of country and family pride, between an uncrowned and a self-crowned king. . . . Years afterward the poet passed judgment on Prince Henry's conduct in this scene in a singular and possibly unconscious way. The feather! Every lover of Shakespeare will instantly think of another feather that did not stir, the one King Lear held to the lips of

Cordelia. The depth and genuineness of the emotion there become a measure of its absence here.

But the Prince's explanation and apology (to come back to the scene) assuage the dying King. Begging his son to sit by him on the bed, he tells him of the "indirect crook'd ways" by which he came by the crown, of the disillusionment of power and the futility of his reign. He even admits that the long-planned crusade to the Holy Land was a political blind designed to distract the attention of the overinquisitive:

> Lest rest and lying still might make them look
> Too near unto my state.

So the long and pious address on peace with which the first of these two dramas opens turns out to have been a piece of political-religious duplicity. If ever the end of a work of art altered its beginning, it is this one. (Yet there are those who tell us that Shakespeare was concerned only with what the ordinary Elizabethan playgoer could take in at a first performance!)

But whatever his former words were, the King's present ones sound like a deathbed repentance, with entreaties from the father to the son to make *his* reign as different from his own as possible. But no! men generally die as they have lived, and just as we are ready for a miracle Henry reverts to his normal selfish self and concludes:

> Therefore, my Harry,
> Be it thy course to busy giddy minds
> With foreign quarrels; that action, hence borne out,
> May waste the memory of the former days.
> More would I, but my lungs are wasted so
> That strength of speech is utterly denied me.
> How I came by the crown, O God, forgive!
> And grant it may with thee in true peace live.

Was there ever such a "therefore"? "My reign was a futile one: therefore, go thou and do likewise. Use the trick I planned to use." Or to put it even more cynically: "Make war, dear boy, and God grant your reign may be a peaceful one." It sounds so incredible, so like a parody, that it is necessary to requote the text to substantiate its meticulous accuracy:

> Therefore, my Harry,
> Be it thy course to busy giddy minds
> With foreign quarrels. . . .
> How I came by the crown, O God, forgive!
> And grant it may with thee in true peace live.

The end forgets the beginning. Such is the level to which a fine brain may be reduced by a life of lies. Such is a king's idea of peace. And the new king, standing where his father formerly did, gives no sign that he so much as notices this typical piece of monarchical hypocrisy, but calmly replies:

> My gracious liege,
> You won it, wore it, kept it, gave it me;
> Then plain and right must my possession be:
> Which I with more than with a common pain
> 'Gainst all the world will rightfully maintain.

The son's "then" is like an antiphony to his father's "therefore." And immediately the stage direction reads: *"Enter John of Lancaster."* *"Enter the Prince of Liars,"* it might as well have been, *"fresh from the blackest act of treachery on record."* It is one of those symbolic entrances that are better than pages of criticism.

> Thou bring'st me happiness and peace, son John,

whispers the dying King. This entire family seems to have a curious conception of peace.

Turning to Warwick, the King asks the name of the chamber in which he was stricken.

> 'Tis call'd Jerusalem, my noble lord,

and the fast-failing monarch at his own request is carried into it that the prophecy may be fulfilled that he should die in Jerusalem. His crusade has at last begun—and ended—in a bitterly ironical sense. We are reminded of Tolstoy's story of *The Two Old Men* who set out for Jerusalem. They both arrived, one literally but not spiritually, the other spiritually but not literally. Henry IV arrived neither literally nor spiritually.

X

The two scenes that follow the King's death were made to go together. In them we see justice, first under its mundane, then under something more nearly resembling its eternal aspect.

We are taken to Gloucestershire and see Master Robert Shallow, rural justice of the peace, planning to keep Sir John Falstaff, "the man of war" as Shallow's servant Davy calls him, overnight at his home. The scene might be called *Peace and War Preparing to Swallow Each Other,* and the result is a foregone conclusion, for Shallow is as thin and spare a man as Falstaff is fat, and his wits and spirit as starved as Falstaff's are well fed. The news of the old king's death has not yet come, but Master Robert knows that Sir John is close to the man who will soon rule England. He lends him a thousand pounds on that security a little later. "A friend i' the court is better than a penny in purse," he declares, and accordingly nothing is too good for the man of war. Davy perceives that this is the moment to put in a plea for a friend of his, one William Visor. "Visor is an arrant knave, on my knowledge," says Shallow. "I grant your worship," Davy admits, "but yet, God forbid, sir, but a knave should have some countenance at his friend's request. . . . I have served your worship truly, sir, this eight years; and if I cannot once or twice in a quarter bear out a knave against an honest man, I have but a very little credit with your worship." "He shall have no wrong," declares the Justice.

The scene shifts to Westminster and we see the Lord Chief Justice of England awaiting the entrance of the new king. He awaits it with no illusions, for this new king is no other than the Prince Hal whom in his father's time he sent to prison for striking him in his "very seat of judgment." The power is now Henry's and the Chief Justice expects him to take revenge. And sure enough the new monarch has little more than entered than he reminds the Justice of the great indignities he once heaped upon him:

> What! rate, rebuke, and roughly send to prison
> The immediate heir of England!

But the Chief Justice, whose character proves that honor in its true sense is not obsolete, defends himself with such cogency and dignity that the King, quite won, replies:

> You are right, justice; and you weigh this well.

He reappoints him to his office and begs him to go on administering the laws of his kingdom in this "bold, just, and impartial spirit." Offering him his hand, Henry declares (in lines that call for the very closest scrutiny):

> You shall be as a father to my youth;
> My voice shall sound as you do prompt mine ear,
> And I will stoop and humble my intents
> To your well-practis'd wise directions.
> And, princes all, believe me, I beseech you:
> My father is gone wild into his grave,
> For in his tomb lie my affections;
> And with his spirit sadly I survive,
> To mock the expectation of the world,
> To frustrate prophecies and to raze out

Rotten opinion, who hath writ me down
After my seeming. The tide of blood in me
Hath proudly flow'd in vanity till now:
Now doth it turn and ebb back to the sea,
Where it shall mingle with the state of floods
And flow henceforth in formal majesty.
Now call we our high court of parliament:
And let us choose such limbs of noble counsel,
That the great body of our state may go
In equal rank with the best govern'd nation;
That war, or peace, or both at once, may be
As things acquainted and familiar to us;
In which you, father, shall have foremost hand.
Our coronation done, we will accite,
As I before remember'd, all our state:
And, God consigning to my good intents,
No prince nor peer shall have just cause to say,
God shorten Harry's happy life one day!

Here is Henry at his finest, it will be said. Here is the first fruit of the great reversal he has been keeping in reserve ever since that first soliloquy. Here is the sun about to emerge from the clouds. Here is the Prodigal Son putting off Vanity and adopting Justice as his father and guide. It is just as Dover Wilson said. His theory of the morality play is vindicated in this scene.

It would be churlish indeed to suggest that Henry did not mean, or at least think he meant, what he said to the Chief Justice. But that does not excuse our overlooking the fact that both his words and his attitude also happen to be the most expedient ones he could conceivably have uttered and adopted at a moment when a decorous impression was so imperative to his success, when the unexpected was the indispensable. (Even Richard III stood up to be seen of all men between two bishops.) It was Henry's luck on this occasion that the most generous action was also the most politic. In such cases the judging of motives becomes ticklish.

Whether Henry did at this moment turn from Vanity to Justice depends not at all on what he promised his future "father" at the moment, but on what he did during the days and months to come. It depends, that is, on what he did in the little that is left of this play and on what he did throughout the succeeding one. Except in the matter of the rejection of Falstaff, then, it would seem as if judgment must be suspended until we have taken the next play into account.

But, as we have seen over and over, Shakespeare is in the habit of revealing the embryo of the future in the present, and Henry's preview of his own reign in the last half of his apology to the Chief Justice will bear examination from this point of view. What a man thinks he is saying is often at odds with what he is really saying. Shakespeare is a master at giving us both at once, the one in the thought, the other in the imagery and accent. Prosaic men like Henry use metaphors at their peril.

The sense of Henry's speech seems plain enough. "Here is my promise." he says in effect to the Chief Justice, "to subject my inexperience to your experience, to bow my will to yours. My father is dead, but I survive to surprise the world by defeating its ominous expectations concerning my reign. Hitherto I have given my life to vanity; henceforth I will give it to good counsel to the end that England may be as well governed as any nation on earth. You, My Lord Chief Justice, shall be my foremost adviser in both war and peace. With God's help, no one will wish my reign abbreviated by a single day."

Here, apparently, is a complete subjection of himself on Henry's part to the wisdom of the Chief Justice. But examine it more closely and it bears every mark of being, actually, an abject surrender to the spirit of his father. Henry himself supplies the metaphor that proves it. Just as his own word "infect" gave the clue to the effect upon him of putting on the crown, so his own word "ebb" shows what is happening here. Hitherto I have flowed, he says, now I will ebb. An ominous figure! And one that utterly reverses all he has previously vowed. His carousing with Falstaff, he told us (if under a different metaphor) was to be just a temporary ebbing—a little eddy—in the main stream of his life, which thereafter would flow steadily forward. Now it is the other way around. He has been flowing with Falstaff; now he will "turn and ebb back to the sea." What he means, of course, is that his vanity has increased and now will decrease. But it is not superficial things like vanity that ebb and flow. It is elemental things like the tide and the blood of man. *The tide of my blood now turns and ebbs back to the sea*, he declares. He thinks that thereby he is saying that from now on he will control his passions. But what are those passions but that very sea? The word "sea" is older and Henry's imagination is wiser than he is, and what it describes, in spite of him, is precisely the process that psychologists today call a regression into The Father, the sacrifice to ancestral forces and the past of freedom to control the present and to be a unique individual. The formal and dignified accent and movement of the verse confirm the reactionary state of mind of the speaker. And so does his vocabulary with its insistence on such words as "state," "rank," "formal," "majesty," "governed." This is not the language of moral emancipation. It is just the opposite. What practically clinches the matter is an obviously intentional ambiguity on Shakespeare's part in the line,

In which you, father, shall have foremost hand.

Ostensibly this is addressed to the Chief Justice whom Henry has chosen as his father and counselor in war and peace. But, in its context, it fits far better that dead father with whose spirit he expressly says he survives:

> My father is gone wild into his grave,
> For in his tomb lie my affections;
> And with his spirit sadly I survive. . . .

These Delphic lines permit at least three interpretations. At a casual reading they mean no more than: my father is no longer living, but my love is still with him in the grave. But that leaves the word "wild" out of account. My father and I have executed an exchange, is what Henry says: my wild youth lies buried forever in his tomb, while his spirit has transmigrated into me (or, if that seems too strong, attends me as a guardian). And the lines will bear still another construction: my father is in his tomb and buried with him lie my powers to feel (the usual Elizabethan use of the word "affections"), while I survive with his spirit (which, the reader of these plays knows, was one lacking in human warmth). Henry, naturally, did not intend this. Shakespeare, I am convinced, did. In fact, the rejection of Falstaff, I should say, is specifically inserted to confirm it. But it is confirmed by something less debatable than that famous scene.

The final test of Henry's sincerity in his words to the Chief Justice depends neither on them nor on anything we may find under their surface, but, as I said, on what Henry does in the time to come. If we find that he did make the Chief Justice his political guide and counselor in war and peace, and if justice was the dominating note of his reign, then the promise was kept and the moral is unexceptionable. If not, not. We see Henry and the Chief Justice together just once more in *II Henry IV*, and on that occasion, instead of asking the Justice's advice, the King issues him an order. Then, except for three or four brief sentences not in Henry's presence, the Chief Justice passes out of the story forever, and at the beginning of the next play we find the King seeking counsel of an Archbishop and a Bishop who are morally at the opposite pole from the man who is supposed to be the symbol of his own regeneration. The characters who are absent from Shakespeare's plays are often as significant as those who are present. What became of the Chief Justice in *Henry V?*

The unconscious hypocrisy of Henry's ostentatious promises to him confirms the King's regression into the spirit of his father (the archhypocrite) just as the buried fears of that father confirm in turn *his* regression into the spirit of Richard II (the archvictim of fear). The Prince's insincerity to his

father in the crown scene is the promise of the King's insincerity to the
Chief Justice in the "father" scene. The one interpretation supports the
other. But we must await the next play for the crowning evidence (in all
senses) on this point.

Both the older and the younger Henry illustrate in extreme degree
the law of moral compensation which anyone with any power of intro-
spection may observe in himself. Whenever they say or do anything
unwontedly frank or generous it becomes necessary to ask what they may
just have done or are just about to do that is disingenuous or ungenerous.
If Falstaff had overheard Henry's words to the Chief Justice, he might
have guessed what was in store for him.

XI

Pistol brings word of the King's death to Falstaff in Shallow's garden. The
fat man's hour has come—or so he believes:

> Away, Bardolph! saddle my horse. Master Robert Shallow, choose what
> office thou wilt in the land, 'tis thine. . . . We'll ride all night. . . . I
> know the young king is sick for me. Let us take any man's horses; the
> laws of England are at my commandment. Blessed are they that have
> been my friends; and woe to my Lord Chief Justice!

When we next greet Falstaff, he is standing in the street near
Westminster Abbey waiting for the King to ride by. He comes and Falstaff
hails him. "God save thy grace, King Hal! my royal Hal! . . . God save
thee, my sweet boy!"

"I know thee not, old man," the King replies—and amplifies those
half-dozen words into twenty-five lines. It is the Rejection of Falstaff, one
of the three or four most debated scenes in Shakespeare. To have them
before us, the familiar lines must be quoted once more:

> I know thee not, old man: fall to thy prayers;
> How ill white hairs become a fool and jester!
> I have long dream'd of such a kind of man,
> So surfeit-swell'd, so old, and so profane;
> But, being awak'd, I do despise my dream.
> Make less thy body hence, and more thy grace;
> Leave gormandizing; know the grave doth gape
> For thee thrice wider than for other men.
> Reply not to me with a fool-born jest:
> Presume not that I am the thing I was;
> For God doth know, so shall the world perceive,
> That I have turn'd away my former self;

> So will I those that kept me company.
> When thou dost hear I am as I have been,
> Approach me, and thou shalt be as thou wast,
> The tutor and the feeder of my riots.
> Till then, I banish thee, on pain of death,
> As I have done the rest of my misleaders,
> Not to come near our person by ten mile.
> For competence of life I will allow you,
> That lack of means enforce you not to evil;
> And, as we hear you do reform yourselves,
> We will, according to your strengths and qualities,
> Give you advancement. Be it your charge, my lord,
> To see perform'd the tenour of our word.
> Set on.

The sun has come out from behind the clouds.

But what strange sun! It is the function of a sun to illuminate. But whoever heard of a sun that sermonized, or that refused to shine on the just and the unjust alike, particularly on one of its satellites, however ancient? Who, we ask, is this new king, to adopt this top-lofty manner toward an old man whom he could so easily have passed by in silence and rebuked, if he must, in private? "As we hear you do reform yourselves"! How long, in decency's name, has he been reformed himself? It is not Henry's rejection of tavern life with which we quarrel. That, naturally, had to go. It is not with his new sense of responsibility. That we welcome. What we inevitably remember is the beam and the mote (not to imply that "mote" does justice to Falstaff's vices).

The best we can say for Henry is that it is an outburst of that temper of which his father told us he was a victim ("being incens'd, he's flint"), sudden anger at Falstaff's highly untactful appearance at such a time and place. The worst we can say is that the King had deliberately planned to rebuke Falstaff publicly at the first opportunity for the sake of the moral contrast with his own past and in fulfilment of the promise of his first soliloquy. Unfortunately for Henry, however much anger he may have felt at the moment, Falstaff's explanation of the calamity to Shallow: "He must seem thus to the world," seems the most psychologically plausible account of what happened. But in what a different sense from that intended for Shallow! And we remember how Henry's father publicly pardoned Carlisle with his right hand, so to speak, while he was secretly murdering Richard with his left. Henry's vow to let his father "have foremost hand" in all his doings was being fulfilled, whomever he thought he was choosing as his guide. If it is a wise child that knows his own father, Henry was acquiring wisdom.

What did Shakespeare think?

Anyone is free to conjecture. And, however we take it, there is plenty of evidence.

This much at any rate is certain: we cannot imagine Shakespeare, no matter how high he might have risen in worldly place or esteem, rejecting a former friend by preaching him a sermon in public, no matter how low his friend might have fallen. So unthinkable is it that it seems almost silly to reduce the idea to words.

> "A new commandment," said the smiling Muse.
> "I give my darling son, Thou shalt not preach";—
> Luther, Fox, Behmen, Swedenborg, grew pale,
> And, on the instant, rosier clouds upbore
> Hafiz and Shakespeare with their shining choirs.

Surely in those lines "Shakespeare's younger brother"—as John Jay Chapman called Emerson—gave utterance to the innermost spirit of Shakespeare. It has become a commonplace that the poet rated ingratitude among the deadliest of the sins. What would he have thought of ingratitude supplemented by preaching?

Nor can we imagine Falstaff himself doing what Henry did, if, in some inconceivable way, their roles had been reversed. And we love him for that incapacity. I wonder if Shakespeare has not been at pains to point this out. In the very first scene in which we see Hal and Falstaff together the latter tells of a casual incident that takes on an entirely fresh meaning in the light of this very last scene in which we see them together, "together" now in what a different sense.

> FALSTAFF: An old lord of the council rated me the other day in the street
> about you, sir, but I marked him not; and yet he talked very wisely,
> but I regarded him not; and yet he talked wisely, and in the street
> too.
> PRINCE: Thou didst well; for wisdom cries out in the streets, and no man
> regards it.

Wisdom does indeed cry out in the streets, but generally without opening her mouth, and certainly not in the form of moral diatribe. It is Morality that indulges in moral indignation. Wisdom, like Shakespeare, speaks in more oblique fashion, as she does, if I am not mistaken, in this very scene.

When Falstaff has been rebuffed, and he and his followers have been carried off to the Fleet, the play is a dozen lines from its end. Those lines (except for six significantly terse and reticent words from the Chief Justice) are all spoken by John of Lancaster. Why does Shakespeare, who is so fond of remarking that "the end crowns the whole," give the crowning speeches of this play to a person whose sole distinction lies in the fact that he is the most dastardly character in it? Why does he permit him, and him alone, to pass judgment on his brother's act in rejecting Falstaff?

> I like this fair proceeding of the king's.

If you know the devil's opinion, you can infer the angels'. The safest way to vote is to find out how the most "intelligently" selfish man in the community is voting and then vote the other way. It is in recognition of this principle, I believe, that Shakespeare reserved the most emphatic place in his play for the judgment on the King's rejection of Falstaff by the man whom Falstaff, in just six words, caused *us* to cast forth into everlasting darkness: "a man cannot make him laugh." Dostoevsky declares that a man's character can be read by the way he laughs. By that token John of Lancaster had no character. He "doth not love me," said laughing John of sober John. And so when sober John welcomes the humiliation and degradation of laughing John by saying,

> I like this fair proceeding of the king's,

it sounds like a statement straight from Shakespeare that the proceeding was not fair and that he did not like it.

XII

But there is more evidence than this (not counting that in the next play). In Shakespeare, as in life, things do not happen unprepared for. If we look back, we find a little scene in which the rejection of Falstaff was specifically forecast. More than forecast, rehearsed.

The place is the Boar's Head Tavern in Eastcheap, and the time just after the "discomfiture" of Falstaff in the matter of the robbery. Mistress Quickly, the hostess, enters to announce that a nobleman of the court has a message for the Prince from his father. Falstaff goes to the door to send the interloper packing, but comes back with news that the Percys are in revolt and civil war is on in the North. The Prince must be at court in the morning.

> FALSTAFF: Tell me, Hal, art thou not horribly afeard? thou being heir apparent, could the world pick thee out three such enemies again as that fiend Douglas, that spirit Percy, and that devil Glendower? Art thou not horribly afraid? doth not thy blood thrill at it?

PRINCE: Not a whit, i' faith; I lack some of thy instinct.
FALSTAFF: Well, thou wilt be horribly chid to-morrow when thou comest
to thy father: if thou love me, practise an answer.
PRINCE: Do thou stand for my father, and examine me upon the particu-
lars of my life.
FALSTAFF: Shall I? content.

And Sir John instantly arranges the properties in a manner that reveals
equally deep insight into the affairs of the state and of the stage, anticipating Goethe's principle that nothing is right in the theater that is not a
symbol to the eye. "This chair shall be my state," he says, "this dagger my
sceptre, and this cushion my crown"—a treatise on political science in a
sentence—and he proceeds to impersonate King Henry with a perfection
that wrings tears of ecstasy from Mrs. Quickly:

O Jesu, this is excellent sport, i' faith! . . . O, the father, how he holds
his countenance! . . . he doth it as like one of these harlotry players as
ever I see!

This "harlotry" King Henry chides his son for defiling himself with pitch
by consorting with such loose companions—always excepting one "goodly
portly man, i' faith, and a corpulent," in whose looks he perceives virtue.
"Him keep with, the rest banish."

Whereupon the roles are reversed. "Do thou stand for me," says
Hal, "and I'll play my father."

"Depose me?" cries Falstaff.

And then, if ever, we behold the future in the instant. It is as if something in the air and accent of the Prince, merely playing as he is, enables
Falstaff to catch as in a magic mirror the bearing and voice of King Henry V
as he was to pause near the Abbey on that fateful day and call out for
all to hear, "I know thee not, old man." "If thou dost it half so gravely, so
majestically, both in word and matter," Falstaff goes on, laying aside his
role for a moment, "hang me up by the heels for a rabbit-sucker or a
poulter's hare." But Henry *was* to do it gravely and majestically, and
Falstaff *was*, figuratively, to be hung up by the heels. That one sentence
should be enough to show that what Shakespeare is giving us here is a
rehearsal of the rejection of Falstaff. But the little scene it introduces is
such a masterpiece in its own right that it throws us off the track of its
connection with what has come before, and what is to follow, in the main
play. Poetry, like the sun, can blind as well as illuminate.

When in a gay moment we are off guard, we give utterance under
the shield of wit to convictions and intentions from the bottom of our
hearts that in any other mood we wouldn't for the world reveal. This

principle is the key to this little scene. *Playing the part of his father,* Henry proceeds to castigate "that villanous abominable misleader of youth, Falstaff, that old white-bearded Satan," to which Falstaff, *playing the part of Hal,* retorts with a defense of himself that ends in a revelation of deep acquaintance with his own soul and with Henry's: "but for sweet Jack Falstaff, kind Jack Falstaff, true Jack Falstaff, valiant Jack Falstaff, and therefore more valiant, being, as he is, old Jack Falstaff, banish not him thy Harry's company, banish not him thy Harry's company: banish plump Jack, and banish all the world." To which the Prince in turn, *playing the King,* replies with unconscious divination of the future: "I do, I will." He will indeed. Now he pretends to be his father and *does* banish Falstaff. A little later he will become like his father and *will* banish him. Now he plays king. Then he will be king. Beware of what you play—it will come true. "Rehearsal" is not too strong a term for this scene.

Instantly following the Player-King's "I do, I will," the stage direction reads: *"A knocking is heard."* It is one of Shakespeare's earliest uses of the device he employs so subtly in *Julius Caesar,* and, as everyone knows, so tremendously in *Macbeth,* to betoken at a fateful moment the knocking of the inner mentor. . . . But no, it is only the sheriff at the door, just as it was only Macduff; and Hal, though he stands on the inside, does not heed, nor even hear, the warning from within. Yet there it is, saying plainly, if he could only hear it: "Banish sweet Jack Falstaff and banish all the world." (The sweet Jack Falstaff, be it most particularly noted, not the malodorous one.) The difference in tone between this scene and the one in *Macbeth* should not mislead us. Even in a tavern, life may be lived well.

This little play within a play, two plays within a play, each with its player-king, may well warn us that *Hamlet* itself is barely around the corner. Indeed, this mousetrap catches not only the conscience of a king but the conscience of a king-to-be. The play scene in Shakespeare's tragic masterpiece to come scarcely surpasses this one in the subtlety of its psychology or the intricacy of its interwoven meanings. Here, if anywhere, here, if ever, the truth is brought home that we are not single personalities, nor even double ones, but bundles rather of actual and potential, emerging and expiring selves, as many as there are people who love or hate us, or whom we love or hate. Each one out there evokes a different one in here. The relation between two individuals is itself an individual relation, and, when it is set up, something that never was before on sea or land is created. Within the confines of this brief scene, to the success of which Mrs. Quickly, as audience, makes a memorable if mainly silent contribution, half-a-dozen Falstaffs and Henrys jostle and elbow, come in and go out, split, disintegrate, and recombine, a veritable phantasmagoria of spiritual entities. Who would undertake even to enumerate, let alone characterize them? When Falstaff plays Hal's father, for instance, he is partly King Henry rebuking the Prince for his wildness and partly the Falstaff who loves Hal as if he were his own son, and who longs to have Hal love him as if he were his father and consequently pictures himself as the sort of ideal father he would actually like to be to him. When, the parts exchanged, Falstaff plays Hal, he is first the subdued and respectful Prince in the presence of authority, and then the Hal whom Falstaff loved, and who, as Falstaff acts him, loved him as the real Falstaff longed to have the real Hal love him, and as, alas, he never did. When Hal acts himself, he is modest and reticent, not to say a bit scared, speaking scarcely a dozen words, but when he becomes his father he grows dominating and forbidding, and evokes in his description of his son's dissolute misleader the drunken debauched Falstaff who, it is especially worth noting, is otherwise totally and conspicuously absent from the scene. The Prince, *as his father,* says exactly what Sir John's bitterest enemies among critics and readers have been saying of him ever since:

> That bolting-hutch of beastliness. . . . Wherein is he good, but to taste sack and drink it? wherein neat and cleanly, but to carve a capon and eat it? wherein cunning, but in craft? wherein crafty, but in villainy? Wherein villanous, but in all things? wherein worthy, but in nothing?

—while Hal, *impersonated by Falstaff,* describes the sweet, kind, true, valiant Jack that all the world loves, except the above-mentioned dissenters. It is all wonderful fun and we laugh. Yet underneath the mirth, how beautiful and tragic the implications, how beyond comparison the miracle by which so much is compressed into so little! And hovering over it all, over all these subordinate personalities that glide in and glide out like ghosts, is the evoker and master of them all (for it is only in his presence that Hal ever rises to such imaginative height), the Immortal Falstaff, the sweet Jack Falstaff whom Henry should never have rejected to the end of his days.

XIII

If anyone asks how Henry could have rejected one Falstaff and kept the other, there is both a general and a specific answer.

The first may be put in the form of another question: In what do love and friendship consist if not in a perpetual acceptance of the angels and rejection of the devils that we discover in everyone with whom we are brought into intimate contact? Here is merely an extreme instance of this truth.

Falstaff had been both Henry's tempter and his tutor. Tempter may seem the wrong word when we remember that Henry entered on his dissipations with both eyes open; but, like some of the critics of these plays, perhaps he was more seduced by Falstaff than he was willing to admit. At any rate he abandoned himself along with him to dissolute courses and moral irresponsibility. But this does not alter the fact that Falstaff gave him unconscious instruction in wit, humor, good-fellowship, understanding of human nature, and above all in imaginative love of life for its own sake. Even Mr. Stoll, remember, admits that Falstaff is "supremely poetic."

Practically all teachers have their good points, and even teachers of genius have their weaknesses. It is the art of the pupil to profit by the good points, to let himself be taken captive by the genius, and to overlook or reject the weaknesses.

> There is some soul of goodness in things evil,
> Would men observingly distil it out.

It was Henry himself who said that (in a moment of unusual insight), and it fits the case of himself and Falstaff so perfectly that one could think Shakespeare had him say it for that reason. Falstaff was a teacher of genius with lamentable weaknesses. Henry should have rejected those weaknesses and turned the genius to account in his position as king. Instead of distilling out the soul of goodness and throwing away what was left, he carefully kept what was left and threw away the soul of goodness. It is a strong statement, but the text of the next play, if not of this one, amply justifies it.

Consider what Henry might have done. The true pupil perpetuates the genius of his teacher not by adopting his ideas or imitating his conduct but by carrying on and living out his spirit under the peculiar conditions of his own life.

There is something like critical agreement that Shakespeare's three greatest achievements in character portrayal are Falstaff, Hamlet, and Cleopatra, to whom Iago is sometimes added as a diabolic fourth. Now Falstaff, Hamlet, and Cleopatra, different as they are in a hundred ways, have this in common: they are all endowed with imagination, and especially with dramatic and histrionic power, to something like the highest degree. Each is a genius of play. (Even Iago is in his perverted way.) In a word, they all are in this respect like their creator, a kind of proof that even Shakespeare could draw people better who resembled himself than he could others. Who would not like to have had Shakespeare as a teacher? Prince Henry did. A huge slice of him at least. And then he went and threw away his education.

Having glanced at Henry's teacher, consider next his opportunity. War is not the supreme tragedy of men and nations. The supreme tragedy of men and nations is that the moment war ceases they give themselves over to the pursuit of pleasure or power: either to idleness, amusement, diversions, dissipation, or sport: or to money, business, intrigue, politics, domination in some one of its diverse aspects—either, that is, to "peace" in that soft sense which indirectly makes more war inevitable, or to the hard selfishness that is nothing but war in its slumbering form. A third way that is neither pleasure nor power is humanity's supreme desideratum. What that third way is is no secret. How to get humanity to take it is the problem. The way itself is that of the imagination: of the love of life for its own sake, of human friendship or the good family on a social scale, of play in its adult estate. Shakespeare himself is an example of one who took that way. He taught us all to play. Think of the thousands who have "played" him in a dozen senses and perpetuated his spirit among tens of thousands of others who never or scarcely ever heard his name. Plato held that humanity will be saved only when philosophers become kings or kings philosophers. Falstaff-Hamlet-Cleopatra-Shakespeare go Plato one better. They cast their vote for the poet-and-player-king.

Now Henry had a marvelous chance to begin being such an ideal ruler. He was obviously endowed by nature with a spirit of good-fellowship. He had an imaginative genius for a teacher. He had the opportunity of a king. He ought to have taught all England to play. But what did he do? Instead of leading his kingdom first to justice under the spirit of the Chief Justice and then to good-fellowship under the spirit of Falstaff, he led it to war under the ghost of his father. He accepted his father's advice to "busy giddy minds with foreign quarrels" and *in precise imitation of his father* went out, as the next play shows, to appropriate a throne that did not belong to him. Shakespeare did not invent this colossal irony. He merely perceived it.

But it was not only the ghost of his father that Henry was obeying; he was following in the footsteps of the very Immoral Falstaff whom he thought he had rejected. From snatching travelers' purses in pure fun, Henry goes on to annexing crowns that do not belong to him in dead earnest. He goes Falstaff many times better. An amateur retail robber becomes a professional wholesale one. "Leave gormandizing," he says to Falstaff, and turns to his attempt to swallow France. As usual, moral indignation against others indicates more often than not that the man who feels it is guilty in some subtler or symbolic form of the very sin he is castigating. Remember Antonio and Shylock.

And so the pattern of this supposed morality play of the reformed prodigal grows more and more demoralized. As we get the four plays that begin with *Richard II* in perspective, we see that from the moment when Henry Bolingbroke usurped a throne, stealing has been a main theme of the tetralogy. So taken, the two parts of *Henry IV* are not an alternation of historical scenes and comic relief. The history and the comedy are concerned with the same thing. It is no longer necessary to say that Falstaff runs away with the author or "steals the show." (Even if he does, what could be more appropriate?) The poet was beginning to perceive that history has no significance until it is seen as comedy—and tragedy. Imagination was beginning to assert its mastery of fact.

Prince Hal's first soliloquy now becomes clear. It was spoken by two persons. "Someday I shall be king. And then good-by to fun. Let me have some while I can," was the nonchalant Hal's innocent version of it. "I'll sow some wild oats for a year or two, and then I'll reap a harvest of wheat—and market it at the highest price," was the cold calculating heir-apparent's version. "I'll eat my cake and have it." It is a fascinating theory. But it never works. We do *not* have what we have eaten. And we reap what we sow, except that we reap rather more than we sow, and if we sow the wind we sometimes reap the whirlwind. "I won't count this year" is not a whit sounder than "I won't count this drink." Life counts every minute. How she does so is most minutely and convincingly set down in this dramatic biography of Henry, Prince of Wales, later King Henry V, by William Shakespeare. So much profounder is the truth than a moral.

To recognize that here is the truth we need make no dusty study of history. The story of Prince Hal is the usual one. It is as contemporary as this morning's sun. It can be duplicated in its essential features in any American university, college, or private school:

The charming and talented son of an able and ambitious father (the basis of whose business success had better not be scrutinized too closely), foreseeing the career the paternal fortune has cut out for him, decides to enjoy himself while he can. Though he is at college, he will see a bit of life (which after all is a better teacher than books), have a taste of gaiety before the responsibilities of his inheritance compel him to settle down. He does. He has a "royal" time, and he is not guilty of anything particularly bad, though some of his companions, on the strength of his allowance, go a bit further than he does. Relying on his native wit, he neglects his college work rather scandalously and his stock falls pretty low in official quarters. Everyone knows, however, the high quality of the work he could do if he only wanted to, and with the help of those who are willing to count this as an asset, he manages to scrape through. When he is graduated he has lost his boyish bloom and something seems to have tarnished his charm, yet he is still a delightful youth and everyone expects great things of him—all but a few keen observers who have seen the same thing too often. He travels for a year or so and then goes into the business in which his father has been too deeply buried to notice much about his son one way or the other, except to half-smile and half-frown at certain rumors about wild oats, and to observe with regret that his interest in his father's business (and incidentally his scholastic record) is not to be compared with that of the promising son of one of his associates.

And then the young man goes back to his tenth class reunion and his friends are gratified—and the few discerning ones are shocked. Our Prince Charming has settled down—no more fast living for him—in fact he is well on the road to becoming a Successful Man. His delightful modesty has given way to an air of command. His eyes have lost their roguish twinkle. He has put on more flesh. People begin to remark his resemblance to his father, who, by the way, is now dead. (Whether the son took a look into the paternal ledgers just before he died under the impression that he had already expired is not recorded.) Those with insight have a pretty accurate picture of him in mind as he will be at his twenty-fifth reunion, and, if he is still alive, at his fortieth.

Put your American college youth back five centuries, make him heir to the throne, and give him as boon companion one of the greatest wits and humorists that ever lived, and you have the case of Hal–Prince Henry–King Henry V in its main outlines.

Why, then, is it not all perfectly obvious? For the same reason that most of his friends and classmates go on taking our American hero for a Successful Man. He is, in their sense. And maybe in that sense Henry is destined to be an ideal king. Moreover, we loved him in his youth, and love is notoriously unconscious of changes for the worse in its object—like the mother who goes on treating the cynical worldling of thirty-five as if he were still the innocent boy of ten. So we do not notice the gradations by which Henry ceases to be Hal.

> Crumbling is not an instant's act,
> A fundamental pause;
> Dilapidation's processes
> Are organized decays.
>
> 'Tis first a cobweb on the soul,
> A cuticle of dust,

> A borer in the axis,
> An elemental rust.
>
> Ruin is formal, devil's work,
> Consecutive and slow—
> Fail in an instant no man did,
> Slipping is crash's law.

Those lines of Emily Dickinson put in succinct form the truth that these dramas about Henry document in such detail. Hal had said that the sun would rise clouded and then suddenly burst forth in all his glory. It was just the other way around. The sun rose clear and was gradually obscured. Is it any wonder Shakespeare stresses that metaphor?

If the evidence so far presented for this view of Henry seems insufficient, more, in abundance, is found in the next play.

XIV

Undoubtedly the profoundest study of the father-son relationship since Shakespeare—possibly the profoundest in all literature—is Dostoevsky's in *The Brothers Karamazov*. That book, from one angle, is just an exhaustive contrast between natural and spiritual fatherhood. In it we see the sons of Fyodor Karamazov standing between him, their natural, and Zossima, their spiritual, father. This pure and saintlike man seems at the opposite pole from the debauched Falstaff. (To mention them in the same sentence will be an offense to some.) And so he is—from the *debauched* Falstaff, who indeed resembles in not a few respects the debauched Fyodor Karamazov. Yet Zossima's role in the story is in a way like the role of the finer Falstaff. Opposite as are their terminologies—that of religion and that of play— their creeds, in spirit, are startlingly alike. Zossima's is life for the joy of it as against Fyodor's pursuit of sensual pleasure. Falstaff's is life for the fun of it as against Henry IV's belief in power. The differences are, admittedly, abysmal, but the affinity is clear. And so when we see the sons (one son in particular) in the one case and the son in the other, standing between the racial father and the imaginative father, we recognize the same situation. And the conclusion reached by the two supreme geniuses who brought them into being is an identical one: namely, that in proportion as the child fails to be himself he falls back into the likeness of the racial father, while in proportion as he finds an imaginative father he rises, not into that father's image, but into his own soul's image, into himself. The negative side of this truth is clearly demonstrated in these History Plays; its positive aspect has to await the Tragedies for complete clarification.

WYNDHAM LEWIS

Falstaff and Don Quixote

"The wound that phantom gave me!"
is an exclamation illustrating the quixotic attitude to the environing
world, which, if it lends qualities to things they do not possess, restores in
a sense the balance by not bestowing on any existence quite the harshness
of the analytic eye of common sense. Don Quixote is of course one of the
many demented characters inhabiting the region of great fiction. Hamlet,
Lear, Othello, Timon are all demented or hallucinated, as so many of the
celebrated figures in nineteenth-century russian fiction were. It is the
supreme liberty that it is possible to take with your material. That it
should be so often taken in the case of the great characters of dramatic
fiction is the most evident testimony to the dependence on *untruth*, in
every sense, in which our human nature and human environment put us.
In the case of Muishkin, Dostoieffsky had to call in express and abnormal
physiological conditions to help him incarnate his saint. And the natural
heightening everywhere in Shakespeare is by way of madness. Since it is
mad to behave in the way the hero does, he has to be maddened by some
means or other more often than not in order to make him at all probable.

"The defeat of the hero" to see "the splendid triumph of his
heroism" is in accord with the definitely tragic nature of the jest, and the
movement of thought beneath the symbolization. That Don Quixote has
not a ceremonious *pathos,* and that he only fights with *phantoms* which we
know under homely shapes, does not make him any less a hero. Though
Persiles and Sigismunda, for instance, could easily be confounded with the
conventional heroes of Heliodorus—similarly connected with Thessaly—
Don Quixote is, in literature, a lonely hero, and even in that responds to

From *The Lion and the Fox.* Copyright © 1951, 1955 by Methuen & Co.

one of the chief requirements of tragedy, approximating at the same time to one of the conditions of madness.

The effect of Cervantes on the german romantics—G. Schlegel Tieck and Schelling—produced some interesting results. Some of their conclusions appear to me to correspond to the truth of the figure of Don Quixote.

"Schelling put into definite shape the formula of the new interpretation: he saw in *Don Quixote* the philosophical novel par excellence, in the great adventure of Quixote the universal conflict of the ideal and the real, and in the defeat of the hero the triumph of his heroism."

"For the rest, *Don Quixote*, interpreted from the romantic point of view, was in no way opposed to the spirit of adventure and mystical dreams, rather it exalted sacrifice and devotion to the Idea, and thus favoured every kind of religious and political initiative. And, on the other hand, romantic irony found in the spectacle of the eternal duality suggested by Don Quixote the justification of its smile and of its lofty detachment" (J. J. Bertrand).

You must not, the german romantics said, see in *Don Quixote* simply a good after-dinner laugh, a *bambocciata*.

"In the theory of universal discord, the principle [of the interpretation] is to be found. Schiller had adopted the hypothesis of the primordial disunity of the world, the result of which is the tragic antithesis in which we are struggling. Fichte opposed still more violently the self and not-self, and made familiar to contemporary thought this system of antagonism between life and the dream, the trivial and the ideal. Don Quixote is the symbol of this duality."

Such "romantic" explanations appear to be the only ones compatible with the great beauty of this book.

It was perhaps the long stay Cervantes made in Italy that enabled him to look at spanish life with detached and foreign eyes: but being an artist can alone have produced this condition in Shakespeare. And I think there is nothing in Shakespeare's work that makes him so *national* as Cervantes was. Shakespeare's laborious—and in a small business way successful—life was not a fierce and youthful episode, like Marlowe's. But he had his share of hardness and effectiveness: which again, if you regard it as the most exterior thing, and if you wished to trace it to the influence of an environment, would be natural to people living in a great and noisy town, in the midst of affairs, and of a rapidly changing life. Whereas Cervantes had the idyllic peace of the grave landscapes of his country as a background, and had round him the gentler agricultural life of a "backward" people.

According to Kyd, Marlowe was "irreligious . . . intemperate, and of a cruel heart." He was involved in seditious movements, was considered hostile to religion and died in a brawl. Raleigh's departure in search of El Dorado followed religious persecution and espionage. Marlowe was caught up in the atmosphere of plots and heroics of which that is an example. Kyd attributes to Marlowe a document for which he, Kyd, was arrested, and which is described as a "libell that concerned the State." It was apparently the text of a placard (described by the register of the Privy Council as *a lewd and mutinous libell*) of which some had been stuck upon the wall of the dutch churchyard. It is as well to remember on all counts that Shakespeare was very much influenced by Marlowe, and shared probably some, at least, of his habits and opinions.

Whether Falstaff (Shakespeare's "knight," as Don Quixote was Cervantes') was only a whimsical invention to amuse; or how far certain more fundamental things—and what things—were involved, has, like most of the matters connected with this very rich and complex work—overcrowded with startlingly real figures—been much discussed. Ulrici, for example, thinks that *The Merry Wives* is a satire, from the bourgeois point of view, on chivalry—Falstaff representing chivalry:

"The burgher class avenges itself pretty severely upon Falstaff's knighthood, and his knighthood does not anywhere appear more miserable and unknightly than when thrown into a basket among dirty clothes, when beaten as an old woman and tormented and pinched as a *fantastic satyr*. In fact, it seems to me that these three features might be found to contain as many metaphorico-satirical thrusts at the chivalry of the day."

Possibly every class—as it is supposed that every type of man— found its expression in this universal poet, and the new *magnificos* of London and the italianized courtier, and even the many-headed beast, could find something to please them. But with that mechanical type of criticism that could see in a figure like Falstaff the expression of a class it is difficult to agree.

Where Ulrici says that Falstaff is the "impersonification of the whole of this refined and artificial civilization"—and more closely still that he is a *child*, a *naif*—he has, I think, established one of the important things about him. To this I will presently return.

This passage of Ulrici on Falstaff is, in full, as follows:

"He is, so to say, the symbol, the personification of that general state of human frailty which, without being actually wicked—that is, without doing evil for the sake of evil, in order to find satisfaction in it—nevertheless perpetually does evil (to a certain extent against his will) simply because it happens to be the most direct means of attaining what he calls life and happiness; this, he believes, is not only actually arrived at by everyone, but ought to be allowed to be the aim of everyone. In so far Falstaff is a pure child of nature, and it cannot be denied that in *Henry IV.*, at least, he shows some sparks of that *naïveté*, gay humour and innocent good-nature, which is generally peculiar to the so-called children of nature; but he is a child of nature who not only stands in the midst of, on many sides, an advanced state of civilization, but who—owing to the refined luxury of his enjoyments, the variety of his dissolute appetites, and the manifold devices he makes use of to gratify them—is, at the same time, the impersonification of the whole of this refined and artificial civilization."

If you imagine Shakespeare taking Falstaff all through his plays—or through as many more as possible—then we should have, still more, a central and great figure (which would also be an *idea*) to place beside Cervantes' knight.

"These scenes [the comic falstaffian ones in *Henry IV.*] fill almost one half of the whole play. In no other historical drama of Shakespeare's do we find such a total disregard of the subject. Here . . . the comic and unhistorical portions are so surprisingly elaborate, that the question as to their justification becomes a vital point. . . ."

It was not, according to Ulrici, "Shakespeare's intention merely to give a broader foil to the character of Prince Henry." Nor can it have been "Shakespeare's intention in *Henry IV.* merely to give a representation of the return of honour and of man's different ideas and positions in regard to it; and he has assuredly not introduced the Falstaff episode merely in order to contrast the representatives of the idea of honour—the Prince and Percy—with Falstaff, the negative counterpart, the caricature of honour and knighthood" (Ulrici, Book VI., chap. vii.).

Ulrici's solution is that the comic is set to dog the historic in *Henry IV.* on purpose to show up its influence: "It is intended to parody the hollow pathos of the political history [*i.e.* of Henry IV.'s reign]. . . . Irony is to hold up its concave mirror to that mere semblance of history which is so frequently mistaken for history itself, as being considered great and important only when it parades about in its purple mantle with crown and sceptre, haggles about kingdoms, or lays about it with the scourge of war. For all that which in the present drama appears outwardly to be historical action—rebellion, dissension and war, victory and defeat, the critics of political cunning, treaties and negotiations with their high-sounding speeches about right and wrong—all this was in truth a mere show, the mere *mark* of history. The reign was of historical importance only as a transition stage in the further development of the great historical tragedy, and accordingly could not be passed over."

So "to give a clear exhibition of this unreality [that of the proceedings of the 'born actor' Bolingbroke and his playful barons] this semblance, this histrionic parade, was—conveniently or inconveniently—the poet's intention in placing the comic scenes so immediately by the side of the historical action, and in allowing them step by step to accompany the course of the latter."

Ulrici thinks that the contrast was necessary only because of the emptiness of this *particular* history, in short. It is very easy, in view of the so-called enigmatical play of *Troilus and Cressida,* and in the view upheld here of a great many other points in all the plays, to *extend* this estimate of Ulrici to the whole of Shakespeare's works.

II

I will now show how all these various questions we have passed in review during the last few chapters can be combined, and how they each contribute to the fixing a psychical centre of control which is responsible for all of them. First of all, what I named *shamanization* must be reverted to: its effects will be found a necessary ingredient of one of the most celebrated attributes of Shakespeare—namely, his humour. How "worldliness"—which we have discussed—comes in always on the feminine tide of feeling is evident; and how scepticism is not incompatible with courage, any more than it is with feminineness—indeed the contrary, since the female animal is very brave, but on account of different things to the male.

For those who are not familiar with the phenomenon of *shamanization,* still universally prevalent among the subarctic tribes, I will briefly describe it.

A *shaman* is a person following the calling of a magician or priest: and the word *shamanization* that I have employed would refer to a shaman (the most typical of them) who had in addition transformed himself. This phenomenon—that of sex-transformation—in our life to-day is so evident, and so widespread, that (unless we are never to refer at all to a thing that exercises such great social influence, and whose prevalence in one manner or another, principally by way of social suggestion, affects the general outlook on life) we should find some cliché that does not smell of the laboratory, or some word that does not belong to those latinizing vulgarities of speech depended on for popular discussion. On behalf of the word employed I have no ambitious views: it is only an inoffensive and convenient counter for my personal use; and because around the figure of the shaman I have elsewhere gathered a number of observations on this subject, and it has naturally suggested itself to me in the course of use.

As to the phenomenon itself, of sexual perversion, I am not one of those people who regard it as insignificant, or harmless as a widespread fashion: though it is so very much involved with other things (which on the surface seem to have little to do with it) that it is meaningless to discuss it by itself. Its manifestations and effects are extremely different in different ages and countries: successful in Sparta, in Lesbos it might be an offence, and in Chicago a useless and unornamental one, where it would probably take on a curious mechanical intensity, and an earnest scientific air. It might add charm to the south of Russia, but make the arctic rigours of the north still more unendurable. In Rome, for example, its effects were coarse and disagreeable, whereas in Athens they even had the intellect as an ally, recommending them. These general reflections on the nature of perversion do not concern us here very much, except that it seemed advisable to record that partiality for its numerous adepts, and its effects as revealed in current social life, cannot be attributed to me.

Shamanism, then, returning to the custom prevalent throughout the north of Asia and America, consists generally in the reversal of sex: a man, feeling himself unsuited for his sex, dresses himself as a woman, behaves as a woman (usually adopting the woman's rôle also where some man is concerned), or by means of this sexual abnegation prepares himself for the duties of a magician. Women similarly abandon the outward attributes of sex and become men. (This is more rare, because it is obviously a less attractive proposition—and this does not take with it properly an enhancement of the powers of "mystery," as the other trans-formation does.)

Generally speaking, the process of shamanizing himself confers on a man the feminine advantages. It signifies either a desire to experience the sensual delights peculiar to the female organization; or else an ambi-tion to identify himself with occult powers. But it is further a withdrawal from masculine responsibilities in every sense, and an adoption of the spectator's rôle of the woman (freed further, in his case, from the cares of motherhood). That this is a very radical and even inversely heroic, or heroically inverse, proceeding is evident. If we now turn to a figure with which we have already dealt—namely, the "man of the world" (a figure with whom by implication Shakespeare is compromised, but from identifi-cation with whom this analysis should, in effect, rescue him)—we shall find that there is nothing that exactly corresponds to the transformed shaman. Like the latter, as it is his strategy to include among his numerous advantages those possessed by the woman, he has a tincture of the *shaman* in him. Hotspur (one of Shakespeare's lesser heroes) tells in a famous speech how he meets on the battlefield a shamanizing sprig of nobility, whom he describes as chiding soldiers carrying dead bodies near him "for bringing a slovenly unhandsome corpse between the wind and his nobility." This exquisite was not necessarily a wholly shamanized man, but possibly only a macaroni of the time. He would in that case be a "man of the world" of a very extravagant type, very extravagantly *shamanized.* He would have on the field of battle all the privileges of a woman, only frowned at—and perhaps hustled—by the blustering Percy.

It is at this point that, fully prepared, we can address ourselves to the subject that can be regarded as the centre one in Shakespeare—that of his *humour.*

The *humour* of Falstaff achieves the same magical result as Don Quixote's chivalrous delusion—namely, it makes him immune from its accidents. The battles he finds himself engaged in are jokes; his opponents, the Douglas, Colevile of the dale, are "phantoms" (of a different sort, it is true), just as Don Quixote's are. The contrast of these two knights is a contrast in two unrealities—two specifics to turn the world by enchantment into something else. One is the sense of humour, the other is the mysticism of chivalry; the first a negation, the latter a positive inspiration. The one, the magic of being *wide awake* (very wide awake— beyond normal common sense): the other of having your eyes naturally sealed up, and of *dreaming.*

The "sense of humour," again, provides us with an exceptionally english or american attribute of worldliness.

In Falstaff, Shakespeare has given us a very interesting specimen indeed of consummate worldliness, with a very powerfully developed humorous proclivity, which served him better than any suit of armour could in the various vicissitudes of his life. An excellent substitute even for a *shamanizing* faculty, and enabling its possessor to escape the inconveniences and conventional disgrace of being feminine—at the same time it provides him with most of the social advantages of the woman. The sense of humour is from that point of view the masterpiece of worldly duplicity and strategy. On the field of battle at Tewkesbury, Falstaff avails himself of it in a famous scene, and gives us a classical exhibition of its many advantages, and the graceful operation of its deceit. It does not cut off its practitioner from "men" of the rough "hero type," but on the contrary endears him to them. So it becomes even a substitute for courage. There is no lack that it does not cover. With it Falstaff is as safe on the battlefield as the shamanized noble noticed by Percy Hotspur.

So if Falstaff is the embodiment of a mass of worldly expedient, this is of course all directed to defeating the reality as much as Don Quixote's. He is a walking disease, but his disease is used to evade the results of that absence of a sense of humour which is so conspicuous a characteristic of nature and natural phenomena. The sense of humour is woven into a magic carpet; with it he progresses through his turbulent career, bearing a charmed life. This "sense" performs for Falstaff the office of a psychological liberator; it is of magic potency, turning the field of Tewkesbury into a field of play, and cheating death wherever they meet.

The man would indeed be a coward who, possessed of this magic, was seriously timid. Falstaff was evidently not that: yet Morgan thought it necessary to write a book defending his "honour" in this respect. "He had from nature," he said, "as I presume to say, a spirit of boldness and enterprise."

Being a humorous figure *par excellence,* it was not possible for him to be brave in the hero's way, any more than it would be proper for the circus clown to be an obviously accomplished athlete. Gaucherie and laughable failure is, in both cases, of the essence of their rôle. But boldness and enterprise—as far as that was compatible with the necessity of advertising a lack of courage—he possessed to a great degree.

Morgan begins his defence of Falstaff's courage by appealing to the fact that *actions* (by which people usually judge character) are a very misleading key: "The understanding seems for the most part to take cognizance of *actions* only, and from these to infer *motives* and *characters*; but the sense we have been speaking of proceeds in a contrary direction."

So he appeals for the actions that were not there—and in the nature of things could not have been there—in his conventional pleading.

As to Falstaff being "a constitutional coward" (like Parolles or Bobadil) he says:

"The reader, I believe, would wonder extremely to find either Parolles or Bobadil possess himself in danger. What then can be the cause that we are not at all surprised at the gaiety and case of Falstaff under the most trying circumstances; and that we never think of charging *Shakespeare* with departing, on that account, from the truth and coherence of character? Perhaps, after all, the real character of Falstaff may be different from his apparent one; and possibly this difference between reality and appearance, whilst it accounts at once for our liking and our censure, may be the true point of humour in the character, and the source of all our laughter and delight. We may chance to find, if we will but examine a little into the nature of those circumstances which have accidentally involved him, that he was intended to be drawn as a character of much natural courage and resolution; and be obliged thereupon to repeal these decisions," etc.

Morgan's affected defence (of Falstaff's physical courage) is successfully achieved—but at the expense of every psychologic requirement of the case.

Morgan makes a point of Falstaff's freedom from malice:

"He [Falstaff] seems by nature to have had a mind free of malice or any evil principle; but he never took the trouble of acquiring any good one. He found himself (from the start) esteemed and loved with all his faults, nay *for* his faults, which were all connected with humour, and for the most part grew out of it." So "laughter and approbation attend his greatest excesses."

This is of course the "man of the world" in Falstaff—the *anti-Machiavel* of the type of Frederick the Great. But the "good fellow" in Falstaff, as it is in anybody almost, was no more innocent than, actually not as innocent as, Machiavelli's "bad fellow" or *male persona*. There is, in short, much method in such sanity.

Morgan piles up his understandings of the plan of this character:

"We all like *Old Jack*; yet, by some strange perverse fate, we all abuse him, and deny him the possession of any one single good or respectable quality. There is something extraordinary in this; it must be a strange art in Shakespeare which can draw our liking and good will towards so offensive an object. He has wit, it will be said: cheerfulness and humour of the most characteristic and captivating sort. And is this enough? Is the humour and gaiety of vice so very captivating? Is the wit, characteristic of baseness and every ill quality, capable of attaching the heart or winning the affections! Or does not the apparency of such humour, and the flashes of such wit, by more strongly disclosing the deformity of character but the more strongly excite our hatred and contempt for the man?"

The nonsense into which the moralist critic leads the amiable eighteenth-century writer at least becomes palpable here—even if worthlessness does not become more palpable when associated with wit. That it is not good qualities, any more than great qualities, that "attach the heart" it is not necessary to say.

Falstaff is a "man of wit and pleasure," and could generally be described as a very good specimen of a "man of the world." But the same thing applies to him as to Iago: the "man of the world" is never so dramatically and openly cynical as Falstaff, any more than he is so candid as Machiavelli. He is not dramatic at all. To come to one of the necessary conclusions in this connexion, if the *Machiavel* were an Englishman he would be like Falstaff. This laziness, rascality and "good fellow" quality, crafty in the brainless animal way, is the english way of being a "deep-brained Machiavel."

But Falstaff is a "child," too, a "*naif*," as Ulrici says. A worldly mixture of any strength is never without that ingredient. The vast compendium of worldly bluff that is Falstaff would have to contain that. It was like "any christom child" that he "went away," Mistress Quickly says.

He is armed from head to foot with sly feminine inferiorities, lovable weaknesses and instinctively cultivated charm. He is a big helpless bag of guts, exposing himself boldly to every risk on the child's, or the woman's, terms. When he runs away or lies down he is more adorable than any hero "facing fearful odds."

His immense girth and stature lends the greatest point, even, to his character. He is a hero run hugely to seed: he is actually heavier and bigger than the heaviest and biggest true colossus or hero. He is in that respect, physically, a mock-hero. Then this childishness is enhanced by his great physical scale, so much the opposite of the child's perquisite of smallness. And because of this meaningless, unmasculine immensity he always occupies the centre of the stage, he is the great landmark in any scene where he is. It all means nothing, and is a physical sham and trick put on the eye. And so he becomes the embodiment of bluff and worldly practice, the colossus of the *little*.

MURIEL C. BRADBROOK

"Venus and Adonis";
"The Rape of Lucrece"

In 1593, the same year in which Marlowe's poem [*Hero and Leander*] was 'entered'—five years before it appeared in print—Shakespeare published *Venus and Adonis*. Like Lodge's poem, and perhaps like Marlowe's, this was evidently a 'persuasion' to love. The likeness of Adonis to the young man of the Sonnets and the close parallels between the poem and the sonnets in respect of imagery and theme, make it certain that the connexion exists. From Lodge, Shakespeare adopted melodic variety, an interest in the pastoral setting; from Marlowe a more human treatment of the characters. The story is adapted from *Metamorphoses*, Book X: but Ovid's Adonis, unlike the young man of the sonnets, was not reluctant. The story is therefore conflated with that of Salmacis and Hermaphroditus, in the fourth book, to fit its special purpose.

The pace is slower than Marlowe's, for the stanza form is not so nimble as the couplet: the ornament is more elaborated, and the comedy not so sustained. There is indeed a lively enjoyment of the monstrosity of love; its power to breed self-deception and to cloud the judgment is treated as a jest.

> . . . lovers houres are long, though seeming short,
> If pleasd themselves, others they thinke delight,
> In such like circumstance, with such like sport:
> Their copious stories oftentimes begunne
> End without audience, and are never donne.
>
> (842–6)

From *Shakespeare and Elizabethan Poetry*. Copyright © 1952 by Oxford University Press.

So Venus checks the writhing Adonis, at the end of her very long speech:

> Lye quietly, and heare a litle more,
> Nay do not struggle, for thou shalt not rise . . .
> (709–10)

The delightful *bravura* of Marlowe's mocking wit was all-pervasive: but Shakespeare still had some heavy provincial Warwickshire loam sticking to his boots. Indeed, the reminiscences of the countryside, especially the hunting of the hare, have often been praised as the most 'natural' parts of the poem, though in fact they are most carefully worked into the general symbolic design.

The poem is divided into two contrasted halves: the wooing and the hunt. Each has its characteristic images, and each is elaborately contrasted with the other. The commonest imagery is that of animals. The long accounts of the horse and the jennet, and of the hunted hare, repeat within the animal kingdom the themes of the wooing and the hunt. Adonis is compared with a snared bird, a dabchick, a deer and a hunted roe: Venus is an eagle, a vulture, a wild bird and a falcon. She is the beast of prey and Adonis the hunted quarry; this again links up the two halves of the poem. She had hunted Adonis, and to escape he hunts the boar. When the boar kills him, it seems only to be repeating Venus's insensate possessiveness:

> Had I bin tooth'd like him I must confesse,
> With kissing him I should have kild him first.
> (1117–18)

Freshly and naturally observed as it is, this pastoral background also gives humanity to the story. The detail—the small snail shrinking backwards in his shelly cave with pain, the trees and sprays of the wood which come to life and try to keep Venus from knowledge of Adonis's death are both decorative and closely observed.

> And as she runnes, the bushes in the way,
> Some catch her by the necke, some kisse her face,
> Some twin'd about her thigh to make her stay,
> She wildly breaketh from their strict imbrace.
> (871–74)

Venus and Adonis are both presented as lovely but purely instinctive creatures: their arguments are all conventional, and their life is given in terms of the senses. The early part of the poem is full of feeling presented in terms of flesh: its moistness, its texture, Adonis's sweating palm, his rose cheeks, his panting breath upon Venus's skin. The alteration of colour is particularly noticeable: it suggests the 'going hot and cold' of intense nervous excitement, and the coursing of blood beneath the skin. Venus will kiss Adonis until his lips are 'red, and pale, with fresh varietie'; but while she is 'red, and hot, as coles of glowing fire' he is 'red for shame, but frostie in desier'. Later he is

> Twixt crimson shame, and anger ashie pale,
> Being red she loves him best, and being white,
> His best is betterd with a more delight.
>
> (76–78)

Sometimes in violent contrast Shakespeare will adopt the heraldic manner for relief. An example is the much discussed stanza:

> Full gently now she takes him by the hand,
> A lillie prison'd in a gaile of snow,
> Or Ivorie in an allablaster band,
> So white a friend, ingirts so white a fo.
>
> (361–64)

The lily, the snow, the ivory and the alabaster are all chosen for their chilly whiteness, which has nothing in common with that of flesh. They are all symbols of chastity: alabaster was used for the effigies on tombs and hence was opposed to blood, the symbol of life:

> Why should a man whose blood is warm
> Sit like his grandsire cut in allablaster?

asks Bassanio. Lilies were the emblem of virginity: snow was an ancient symbol of chastity and its coldness suggests death.

The ideas of death and chastity are precisely the opposite to those suggested in this passage. Again there is a direct contrast to the warm flexuous restraint of Venus's melting palm in the *hardness* of the ivory and alabaster which *binds* it, in the idea of *imprisonment* in a *gaol*, and the besieging force *engirting* the enemy. This passage is built on sensuous opposites: it is a definition by exclusion.

Often some cool generalization will interrupt the story at its most exciting point. Feelings which cannot be reduced to their sensuous embodiment are not given at all. Perhaps the most perfect example of implied emotion in the poem is the description of Venus hurrying to save Adonis, driven by purely animal instinct.

> Like a milch Doe, whose swelling dugs do ake,
> Hasting to feed her fawne, hid in some brake.
>
> (875–76)

Though a goddess, Venus has no supernatural powers: she is as helpless as any country lass to save Adonis or even to reach him quickly. She is not responsible for his metamorphosis into a hyacinth: it seems to be spontaneous. Shakespeare abandoned the supernatural: his gods are identified with Nature, physically one with it, enmeshed in its toils even more firmly than Marlowe's. Venus's cajolery of death, a pitiable echo of her cajolery of Adonis, is followed by a string of inappropriate conceits: her grief dazzles her eyes with tears till she sees double, and she tries to convey the grief by fantastic elaborations. Yet the horror of the blank glazed stare of the corpse is physically realized.

> She lookes upon his lips, and they are pale,
> She takes him by the hand, and that is cold,
> She whispers in his eares a heavie tale,
> As if they heard the wofull words she told:
> She lifts the coffer-lids that close his eyes,
> Where lo, two lamps burnt out in darknesse lies.
> (1123–28)

The sensuous beauty of Shakespeare's poem gave it a popularity equal to Marlowe's. It was frequently reprinted: the young gallants kept it under their pillows and used it as a model for their courtship. There are, I think, sufficient likenesses between the two to make it probable that Shakespeare knew Marlowe's poem before he composed his own. Similes which are perhaps commonplaces, like the terrified lover compared with a soldier awaiting capture (*Hero and Leander*, I. 121–122: *Venus and Adonis*, 893–894) can be found, but there is more in Marlowe's image of the 'hot proud steed', implying Leander's intractability:

> For as a hot proud horse highly disdains
> To have his head controlled, but breaks the reins
> Spits forth the ringed bit, and with his hooves
> Checks the submissive ground: so he that loves
> The more he is restrain'd, the worse he fares.

This is precisely the quality in Adonis's horse that is illustrated by his action, when he sees the jennet:

> The strong-neckt steed being tied unto a tree,
> Breaketh his raine, and to her straight goes hee . . .
> The yron bit he crushes tweene his teeth,
> Controlling what he was controlled with.
> (263–64, 269–70)

Venus uses his behaviour to point the moral to Adonis, thus making the relationship explicit:

> How like a jade he stood tied to the tree,
> Servilly massterd with a leatherne raine,
> But when he saw his love, his youths faire fee,
> He held such pettie bondage in disdaine:
> (391–94)

The unmanageable horse, symbol of the conquest of reason by passion, is the adopted 'impresa' of both poets . . . .

II

The *Rape of Lucrece* is even more heraldic than *Titus Andronicus*. The combat between Lucrece and Tarquin, saint and devil (as they are called) is introduced by a passage in which the heraldry of Lucrece's face is set forth in a manner derived from the thirteenth sonnet of *Astrophel and Stella*, where Cupid wins the contest of arms from Jove and Mars:

> . . . on his crest there lies
> Stella's faire haire, her face he makes his shield,
> Where roses gules are borne in silver field.

In Lucrece's face there is a contest between the red and white of beauty and virtue:

> But Beautie in that white entituled,
> From Venus doves doth challenge that faire field,
> Then Vertue claimes from Beautie, Beauties red,
> Which Vertue gave the golden age, to guild
> Their silver cheekes, and calld it then their shield:
> Teaching them thus to use it in the fight,
> When shame assaild, the red should fence the white.
> (57–63)

Tarquin, caught between these two armies, yields himself as many a Petrarchan lover had done. He sees clearly the result of his action: 'O shame to knighthood and to shining Armes'. The heralds will contrive some mark of abatement for his coat, but

> Affection is my Captaine and he leadeth
> And when his gaudie banner is displaide,
> The coward fights, and will not be dismaide.
> (271–73)

The long account of Tarquin's assault goes into minute detail of his 'drumming heart', his 'Burning eye', Lucrece's 'ranks of blew vains' which run pale when his hand like a 'Rude Ram' batters the 'Ivorie wall' of the 'sweet Citty'. Later his soul is compared with a 'sacked temple' and her body at the end to a 'late-sacked island'. Her shame is an abatement on Collatine's arms.

> O unfelt sore, crest-wounding, private scare!
> Reproch is stampt in Collatinus' face,
> And Tarquin's eye maie read the mot a farre.

All this imagery is centred in the great lament of Lucrece before the tapestry depicting the Sack of Troy, in which she sees an emblem of her own state. In the figure of Hecuba she sees a mirror image of her grief and in the deceitful Sinon a mirror of Tarquin. The whole passage—it begins by describing the 'life' of the piece which seemed to 'scorn nature' —embodies the violence of war, and confirms the theme implicit in the metaphors describing Tarquin and Lucrece. The lament of the bereaved, the dignity of the commanders, the terror of cowards, are all depicted in little, and what is not depicted is implied by 'conceit deceitful, so compact, so kind' that a part was left to represent the whole which was 'left unseen, save to the eye of mind'. This insistence upon natural representation, within an artificial tapestry, set as an illustration to an artificially-devised poem has a strange recessional effect, comparable in some ways to the play-within-the-play.

The main body of the poem consists of the speeches of Tarquin and of Lucrece: his debate with himself, the debate between them both, the lament, testament and final speech of Lucrece. More than a third of the whole poem consists of her complaints, in which she 'rails' at Time, Night and Opportunity, the authors of her woe. Tarquin's debate with himself is more dramatic, since there is a conflict is his mind between conscience and will. As *Titus* in a simplified and distorted form presents some of the elements of *King Lear,* so the soliloquies of Tarquin are like a first cartoon for the study of *Macbeth.* Here, too, there is an expense of spirit in a waste of shame, a figure of conscious guilt calling in night and the creatures of night for aid, an act of physical violence followed by as quick a repentance. Tarquin, like Macbeth, tries to pray in the very act of committing the act and is startled to find he cannot do it. The atmosphere of Rome is that of Inverness:

> Now stole uppon the time the dead of night,
> When heavie sleep had closed up mortall eyes,
> No comfortable starre did lend his light,
> No noise but Owles and wolves' death-boding cries
> Now serves the season that they may surprise

> The sillie Lambes, pure thoughts are dead and still,
> While Lust and Murder wakes to staine and kill.
>   (162–68)

> Now o'er the one half world
> Nature seems dead and wicked dreams abuse
> The curtain'd sleep: Witchcraft celebrates
> Pale Hecate's offerings; and withered Murther,
> Alarum'd by his sentinel, the Wolf,
> Whose howl's his watch thus with his stealthy pace,
> With Tarquin's ravishing strides, towards his designs
> Moves like a ghost.
>   (2. 1. 49–56)

This figure of 'a creeping creature with a flaming light' remained with Shakespeare as late as *Cymbeline* where Iachimo, stealing towards the sleeping Imogen, says

> Our Tarquin thus
> Did softly press the rushes ere he wakened
> The chastity he wounded.
>   (2. 1. 12–14)

Imogen had been reading the tale of Tereus: Lucrece compares herself, as Lavinia had so often done, to Philomel, and the Ovidian story was evidently at the back of Shakespeare's mind on all three occasions. It may indeed have inspired the expository use of the tapestry of Troy.

Unlike Macbeth, however, Tarquin knows the emptiness of his satisfaction before he ventures on his act of violence, whereas Macbeth does not fully understand it till afterwards. Tarquin's debate with himself is carried out with a clear sense of the issues; too clear to be dramatically plausible. His comments none the less would apply exactly to the later story.

> Those that much covet are with gaine so fond,
> That what they have not, that which they possesse
> They scatter and unloose it from their bond,
> And so by hoping more, they have but lesse. . . .
> So that in ventring ill, we leave to be
> The things we are, for that which we expect:
> And this ambitious foule infirmitie,
> In having much torments us with defect
> Of that we have: so then we doe neglect
> The thing we have, and all for want of wit,
> Make something nothing, by augmenting it.
>   (133–53)

Sententious and explicit posing of the moral question is continued in the laments of Lucrece, in which she indicts the agents of her wrongs: first the allegorical 'Causes' and then the criminal person. Her formal and highly patterned apostrophes are the most artificial part of the poem. 'The well-tuned warble of her nightly sorrow' is copied in T.M.'s *Ghost of Lucrece,* a pure Complaint:

> O comfort-killing night, image of Hell,
> Dim register, and notarie of shame,
> Blacke stage for tragedies and murthers fell,
> Vast sin-concealing Chaos, nourse of blame,
> Blinde muffled bawd, dark harber for defame
> Grim cave of death, whispring conspirator,
> With close-tongd treason and the ravisher:
>   (764–70)

This recalls at once the laments over Juliet, and the absurd Pyramus:

> O grim-lookt night, O night with hue so blacke.
> O night, which ever art when day is not:
> O night, O night, alacke, alacke, alacke,
> I fear my Thisby's promise is forgot.
>   (5. 1. 172–75)

but even such parody cannot be taken as guarantee that by the time he wrote it, Shakespeare had rejected the style of *Lucrece.* Her long apostrophe to Time looks forward to the soliloquy of Richard II in his prison cell: the mental confusion and bewilderment which in the midst of all their speeches can strike the characters dumb prefigure those more dramatic moments when Romeo and Juliet see their hope destroyed.

> Well, thou hast comforted me marvailous much.
> Is it even so? then I defie you, starres.

On the other hand *Romeo and Juliet* is not without those set pictures or icons of the older fashion, such as the description of Lucrece as she lies in her bed, or the description of how she and her maid weep together:

> A prettie while these prettie creatures stand,
> Like Ivorie conduites corall cisterns filling
>   (1233–34)

These deliberate similes help to give Lucrece her emblematic character of Chastity personified. The Elizabethans saw her as a kind of pagan saint: in *Bonduca* the Queen speaks scornfully to the Romans of 'your great saint Lucrece':

> Tarquin tupped her well,
> And mad she could not hold him, bled.

This blasphemy—for as such it is intended—is a measure of Lucrece's significance. The particular crime was so shocking that it allowed Shakespeare to leave a blank at the centre of the picture. In this poem and *Titus Andronicus* he seems to be trying to indicate the blind senseless horror of purely physical outrage, which constituted for the moment his idea of tragedy. Some atrocity that stuns its victim falls upon Lavinia, Titus, Lucrece, and also on the victims of Richard III. They come up against a stone. Titus kneels and pleads with the stones, Lucrece pleads with the 'remorseless' Tarquin, in *Romeo and Juliet* the lovers are literally brought up against a stone wall: that of the orchard, and that of the grave. Tragedy is something that slaps you in the face: it is tragedy in the newspaper sense. Lucrece

> . . . the picture of pure pietie,
> Like a white Hinde under the grypes sharpe clawes.
> Pleades in a wildernesse where are no lawes.
>
> (542–44)

Violence inexplicable and shattering overwhelms her.

The Rape of Lucrece is an ambitious poem. It is more than a third as long again as *Venus and Adonis*, and while *Venus and Adonis* was put out in an unimpressive little quarto, *The Rape of Lucrece* is a handsome and much more costly piece of book-production. It has altogether the air of being more studied and deliberate: yet in the very centre of the poem there is a link with the most personal of the sonnets. The description of Tarquin's revulsion after his crime (693–714) is an expansion of Sonnet cxxix. The self-knowledge which Tarquin had is also present there:

> All this the world well knows: yet none knows well
> To shun the heaven that leads men to this hell.

C. S. LEWIS

Shakespeare's Poems

We must now turn back to the important year 1593 and attempt to see Shakespeare's *Venus and Adonis* as an epyllion among epyllions, a successor to *Scylla* and *Hero and Leander*. We notice at once that it has abandoned Lodge's medieval preliminaries and that it does not, like Marlowe's poem, begin with long descriptions. The characters are in action by line 3. This is promising. We get, too, but not so soon nor so often as we might wish, lines of the deliciousness which was expected in this type of poem; 'leading him prisoner in a red-rose chain', 'a lily prisoned in a gaol of snow'. But in that direction Shakespeare does not rival Marlowe. We get, with surprised pleasure, glimpses of real work-day nature, in the spirited courtship of Adonis's horse or the famous stanza about the hare. The account of Venus's growing uneasiness during the hunt and her meeting with the wounded hounds gives us a fairly strong hint that the poet has powers quite beyond the range which the epyllion requires. What is not so certain is that he has the powers it does require. For as we read on we become more and more doubtful how the work ought to be taken. Is it a poem by a young moralist, a poem against lust? There is a speech given to Adonis (769 et seq.) which might lend some colour to the idea. But the story does not point the moral at all well, and Shakespeare's Venus is a very ill-conceived temptress. She is made so much larger than her victim that she can throw his horse's reins over one arm and tuck him under the other, and knows her own art so badly that she threatens, almost in her first words, to 'smother' him with kisses. Certain horrible interviews with voluminous female relatives in

From *English Literature in the Sixteenth Century Excluding Drama.* Copyright © 1954 by Oxford University Press.

one's early childhood inevitably recur to the mind. If, on the other hand, the poem is meant to be anything other than a 'cooling card', it fails egregiously. Words and images which, for any other purpose, ought to have been avoided keep on coming in and almost determine the dominant mood of the reader—'satiety', 'sweating', 'leaden appetite', 'gorge', 'stuff'd', 'glutton', 'gluttonlike'. Venus's 'face doth reek and smoke, her blood doth boil', and the wretched 'boy' (that word too was dangerous) only gets away 'hot, faint and weary with her hard embracing'. And this flushed, panting, perspiring, suffocating, loquacious creature is supposed to be the goddess of love herself, the golden Aphrodite. It will not do. If the poem is not meant to arouse disgust it was very foolishly written: if it is, then disgust (that barbarian mercenary) is not, either aesthetically or morally, the feeling on which a poet should rely in a moral poem. But of course Shakespeare may well have failed because he was embarrassed by powers, essential for drama, which he could not suspend while writing an epyllion. Perhaps even then he could not help knowing what the wooing of Adonis by Venus, supposing it to be a real event, would have looked like to a spectator.

Venus and Adonis, if it were his only work, might not now be highly praised; but his next poem might stand higher if it stood alone and were compared solely with other Elizabethan products, not with his own masterpieces. *The Rape of Lucrece* (1594) presumably discharges the promise made in the Epistle to Venus and Adonis of 'some graver labour'. It is heroic poetry as the heroic was understood before Virgil had been sufficiently distinguished from Lucan and Ovid; and it differs from its predecessor in merit as much as in kind. The theme would at that time have tempted almost any other poet to one more 'tragedy' modelled on the *Mirror for Magistrates,* and only those who have read many such 'tragedies' can adequately thank Shakespeare for rejecting that form. It is, however, very much a work of its own age. It contains prettinesses and puerilities which the later Shakespeare would have seen to be unsuitable to his heartrending subject. The conceit which makes Lucrece's pillow 'angrie' at 388 would have been tolerable in *Hero and Leander* but is here repellent; and so is the aetiological myth at 1747, or the competitive laments of the husband and the father at Lucrece's death. There is some of Kyd's fustian in the apostrophe to Night (764–77). It is hard not to smile when Lucrece invites the nightingale to use her hair as a grove (1129), but Edward Lear may be partly to blame. The passage in which she becomes preoccupied, like Troilus or a lover in the *Arcadia,* about the style of her letter to her husband is more difficult to judge: perhaps it is not impossible that a woman of the nineties, brought up by a humanist tutor, might, even at such a moment, have remembered the claims of *eloquentia*. These are merely local imperfections. But there is also, whether we reckon it an imperfection or not, something in the structure of the whole poem which is not quite congenial to our taste. It starts indeed with twenty-one lines of purposeful narration, not rivalled in that age outside the *Faerie Queene*: then our sails flap in three stanzas of digression. And we must be prepared for this throughout. Shakespeare's version of the story is about twelve times as long as Ovid's in the *Fasti* and, even so, omits the earlier stages. Much of this length is accounted for by digression (131–54 or 1237–53), *exclamatio* (701–14), *sententiae* (131–54), and *descriptio* (1366–1526). The technique is in fact that of the medieval rhetoricians. Even in those passages which, taken as a whole, are narrative, a great deal of gnomic amplification is brought in. We have 'theme and variations'. Thus at 211 ('What win I if I gain the thing I seek?') Tarquin states the theme of the game not being worth the candle in two lines: it is then varied for five. At 1002 Lucrece states her theme *(noblesse oblige)* in two lines and then varies it for twelve. At 1107 we have theme in two lines and again twelve lines of variation. Minor instances occur throughout. We must not put this down too exclusively to the Age, for Shakespeare was in fact fonder of amplification than many other Elizabethans and used it, sometimes rather grossly, in his earlier plays. There is nothing in *Lucrece* quite so crude as Gaunt's successive variations on the theme 'His rash fierce blaze of riot cannot last' in *Richard II* (II. 3. 33 et seq.). There is a free use of simple one-for-one parallelism, as in the Psalms;

> The shame that from them no device can take,
> The blemish that will never be forgot,

or

> Bearing away the wound that nothing healeth,
> The scarre that will despite of cure remaine.

Whether the method shall prove tedious or delightful depends on style, in the narrowest sense of the word: that is, on the volubility of phrase which makes the variant seem effortless, and on phonetic qualities. Thus in *shame, device,* and *blemish* we have long monosyllable, disyllable in rising rhythm, disyllable in falling rhythm. In the second example we have the alliteration of *away* and *wound* and the very subtle consonantal pattern of *scarre, despite,* and *cure.* The first consonant group *(sk)* is not repeated, but one of its elements recurs in *-spite* and the other in *cure.*

Another example is:

> To stamp the seal of time in aged things
> (941)

No one reads such a line without pleasure. Yet its emotional content is weak and its intellectual weaker still; to say that time stamps the seal of time on things that have existed a long time is near tautology. The charm depends partly, as before, on the distribution of a consonant group between the simple consonants of two later words *(st, s, t)*, and partly on the fact that all the stressed syllables are long and all have different vowels.

But *Lucrece* has more than formal beauties to offer us. If not continuously, yet again and again, our sympathies are fully engaged. The rape itself, from the moment at which Tarquin strikes his falchion on the flint to the moment when he 'creeps sadly thence' is presented with a terror and horror unequalled in Elizabethan narrative verse. And here, certainly, the digression on 'drunken desire' before and after its 'vomit' is fully justified. 'The spotted princess' (Tarquin's soul) is admirable: still a princess, unable to abdicate, and there's the tragedy. Lucrece, too rhetorical in her agonies, is not quite so good as Tarquin, but she has her great moments: 'I sue for exil'd majestie's repeal', pleading 'in a wilderness where are no laws'. And of all the good things that Shakespeare said about Time he puts perhaps the best into her mouth:

> Why work'st thou mischief in thy pilgrimage
> Unless thou couldst returne to make amendes?

She should not have gone on (good though the line is) to add 'Thou ceaslesse lackeye to eternitie'. It matters nothing that the historical Lucretia would have known neither Plato nor Boethius: the Elizabethan Lucrece ought not to have displayed her learning at that moment. For of course the characters are to be judged as Elizabethans throughout: even Christianity creeps in at 624 and 1156–8.

This poem contains what is rare, though not unique, in Shakespeare, a sort of Simpsonian rhyme at 352–4. To make 352 a decasyllable you must make *resolution* (as the Elizabethans often did) five syllables, and the rhyming syllable should then be -*on*. But in 354 you must make the third of *absolution* your last accented syllable: to which you could get a non-Simpsonian rhyme only by turning 352 into an octosyllabic.

Shakespeare would be a considerable non-dramatic poet if he had written only the *Lucrece*: but it sinks almost to nothing in comparison with his sonnets. The sonnets are the very heart of the Golden Age, the highest and purest achievement of the Golden way of writing. We do not know when they were composed. They were published in 1609 'by G. Eld for T. T.' together with 'A Lover's Complaint' (a still-born *chanson d'aventure* in rhyme royal, corrupt in text, poetically inconsiderable, and dialectally unlike Shakespeare). But at least two of them (CXXXVIII and CXLIV) existed as early as 1599, for these two were included in the poetical miscellany which William Jaggard published in that year under the title of *The Passionate Pilgrim*. A year earlier, in 1598, Meres had referred to 'sugred sonnets' by Shakespeare: how far these coincided with the sonnets we now have can only be conjectured. External evidence thus failing us, we look for internal, and find ourselves in a world of doubts. Even if an individual sonnet can be dated (and I think it much more likely that CVII refers to the queen's death or her climacteric than to the Spanish Armada) this would not enable us to date the collection as a whole. Many sonnets, such as LXVI, LXXI, XCVII, and CVI, would be appropriate to any lover at any time and might, so far as their matter goes, be divided by years from other sonnets in the same collection. The evidence from style produces strong convictions in all readers, but not always the same convictions. On my own view it helps us much more to a *terminus post quem* than to a *terminus ante quem*: that is, I can hardly conceive a poet moving from the style of the best sonnets (which means in effect nearly all the sonnets) to that of *Venus and Adonis*, but can easily conceive one who had achieved Shakespeare's mature dramatic technique still writing some of the sonnets we have. For in all ages, and especially in that, form affects style. If Shakespeare had taken an hour off from the composition of *Lear* to write a sonnet, the sonnet might not have been in the style of *Lear*. We cannot even be certain that Shakespeare wrote his sonnets when sonneteering was the vogue: there are expressions in XXXII, LXXVI, and LXXXII which can (though they need not) be interpreted to mean that he knew he was adopting a form no longer fashionable. But I am not arguing that the sonnets were later than is usually supposed. I am arguing for agnosticism. We do not know when, or at what different times, they were written.

Shakespeare's sequence differs in character as well as in excellence from those of the other Elizabethans. It is indeed the peculiarity of these sonnets which has led to a misreading of all the rest. For here at last we have a sequence which really hints a story, and so odd a story that we find a difficulty in regarding it as fiction. It is the story of a man torn between passionate affection for another man and reluctant passion for a woman whom he neither trusts nor respects. No reading of the sonnets can obscure that amount of 'plot' or 'situation'. Yet even this sequence is far from offering us the pleasure we expect from a good novel or a good autobiography. Treated that way, it becomes a mass of problems. I do not mean those problems which (rightly) attract students of Shakespeare's life. With those the literary historian has no concern; he would not give a farthing to know the identity of the 'man right fair' or the 'woman colour'd ill'. The difficulty which faces us if we try to read the sequence like a novel is that the precise mode of love which the poet declares for the Man remains obscure. His language is too lover-like for that of ordinary male friendship; and though the claims of friendship are some- times put very high in, say, the *Arcadia,* I have found no real parallel to such language between friends in sixteenth-century literature. Yet, on the other hand, this does not seem to be the poetry of full-blown pederasty. Shakespeare, and indeed Shakespeare's age, did nothing by halves. If he had intended in these sonnets to be the poet of pederasty, I think he would have left us in no doubt; the lovely παιδικά, attended by a whole train of mythological perversities, would have blazed across the pages. The incessant demand that the Man should marry and found a family would seem to be inconsistent (or so I suppose—it is a question for psychologists) with a real homosexual passion. It is not even very obviously consistent with normal friendship. It is indeed hard to think of any real situation in which it would be natural. What man in the whole world, except a father or a potential father-in-law, cares whether any other man gets married? Thus the emotion expressed in the *Sonnets* refuses to fit into our pigeon- holes. And this, for two reasons, makes singularly little difference to our delight.

In the first place many individual sonnets, and some of the most prized, are very lightly attached to the theme of the sequence as a whole. CXLVI ('Poor soul, the centre of my sinful earth') is not attached at all; it is concerned with the tension between the temporal and the eternal and would be appropriate in the mouth of any Christian at any moment. XXX ('When to the sessions of sweet silent thought'), LXVI ('Tired with all these, for restful death I cry'), LXXIII ('That time of year thou mayst in me behold') are meditations respectively on bereavement, *taedium vitae,* and age, hooked on to the theme of love only by their concluding couplets. The effect of this 'hook' is twofold. On the one hand it makes richer and more poignant the emotion expressed in the preceding twelve lines, but not until that emotion has been allowed to develop itself fully; it converts retrospectively into a mode of love what nevertheless could be felt (and has been felt until we reach the couplet) on its own account. And, on the other hand, there is a formal or structural pleasure in watching each sonnet wind back through unexpected ways to its ap- pointed goal, as if it said at the end *vos plaudite.* Even where the theme of love reaches farther back into the body of the sonnet it is often as universal, as suitable to every lover, as in a sonnet by Daniel or Lodge. Thus XXV ('Let those who are in favour with their stars') or XXIX ('When in disgrace with fortune and men's eyes') are poems that any man can walk into and make his own. And those must be few and fortunate who cannot do the same with XXXIII ('Full many a glorious morning have I seen') and XXXIV ('Why didst thou promise such a beauteous day').

Such is the effect of many individual sonnets. But when we read the whole sequence through at a sitting (as we ought sometimes to do) we have a different experience. From its total plot, however ambiguous, however particular, there emerges something not indeed common or general like the love expressed in many individual sonnets but yet, in a higher way, universal. The main contrast in the *Sonnets* is between the two loves, that 'of comfort' and that 'of despair'. The love 'of despair' demands all: the love 'of comfort' asks, and perhaps receives, nothing. Thus the whole sequence becomes an expanded version of Blake's 'The Clod and the Pebble'. And so it comes about that, however the thing began—in perversion, in convention, even (who knows?) in fiction—Shakespeare, celebrating the 'Clod' as no man has celebrated it before or since, ends by expressing simply love, the quintessence of all loves whether erotic, parental, filial, amicable, or feudal. Thus from extreme particularity there is a road to the highest universality. The love is, in the end, so simply and entirely love that our *cadres* are thrown away and we cease to ask what kind. However it may have been with Shakespeare in his daily life, the greatest of the sonnets are written from a region in which love abandons all claims and flowers into charity: after that it makes little odds what the root was like. They open a new world of love poetry; as new as Dante's and Petrarch's had been in their day. These had of course expressed humility, but it had been the humility of Eros, hungry to receive: kneeling, but kneeling to ask. They and their great successor Patmore sing a dutiful and submissive, but hardly a giving, love. They could have written, almost too easily, 'Being your slave, what should I do but tend?': they could hardly have written, 'I may not evermore acknowledge thee', or 'No longer mourn' or 'Although thou steal thee all my poverty'. The self-abnegation, the 'naughting', in the *Sonnets* never rings false. This patience, this anxiety (more like a parent's than a lover's) to find excuses for the beloved, this clear-sighted and wholly unembittered resignation, this transference of the whole self into another self without the demand for a return, have hardly a precedent in profane literature. In certain senses of the word 'love', Shakespeare is not so much our best as our only love poet.

This content is mediated to us through a masterpiece of Golden technique. On the metrical side all those wide departures from the norm which make the life of Donne's or Milton's work, or of Shakespeare's own later blank verse, are excluded. That sacrifice was essential to his *cantabile*. He has to avoid the stunning regularity of Drab, yet to avoid it only by a hair's breadth. There is a high percentage of lines in which every second syllable is not merely stressed but also long: 'So I, for fear of trust, forget to say', 'So you in Grecian tires are painted new', 'When beauty lived and died as flowers do now'. Most of the rhymes are strong and many of them rest on monosyllables. There is a great use of alliteration both in its obvious and its less obtrusive forms. Thus in XV we have plain alliteration, 'Cheered and check'd' (6) and 'Sets' and 'sight' (10); gentler alliteration on unstressed syllables in 11 ('debateth with decay'); consonant groups linked with simple consonants, where one is unstressed (as 'perceive' and 'plants' in 5, or both as 'perfection' and 'presenteth', 2, 3). In XII we have the heavy alliteration 'Born', 'bier', 'bristly', 'beard' side by side with the much more artful pattern *s, gr, g, sh* in the previous line—groups linked with simples and arranged chiasmically. CXVI opens with a wonderful fantasia on the consonant *m*: full alliteration of initial stressed syllables in 'marriage' and 'minds', a stressed but not initial syllable in 'admit', and the unstressed 'me' and 'ments' in 'impediments'. Then follow 'love' and 'love', no less an alliteration to the ear because they are the same word, and in the next line, a device Shakespeare used well, the play upon kindred words, 'alters' and 'alteration' (compare 'beauty making beautiful' in CVI, 'the wardrobe which the robe doth hide' in LII). Most of these devices are as sweet to us as they were to our ancestors. But Shakespeare does not share our modern dislike of sibilants (he will 'summon' remembrance to 'sessions of sweet silent thought') and in XLV we find the Simpsonian rhyme of 'to thée' with 'melanchóly'.

In most of the sonnets there is a frank and innocent reliance on words which invite emotion and sensuous imagination. Thus in XII we have *time, day, night, violet, sable, silver, trees, leaves, summer, green, bier, wastes*: in XVIII, *summer* again, *day* again, *buds, winds, sun, gold, death, shades*; in XXI, *heaven, sun* again, *moon, earth, sea, gems, April, flowers, mother*; in XXX, *remembrance, past, waste* again, *death* again, *night* again, *moan*; in LXVIII *cheek, flowers* again, *brow, golden* again, *sepulchres, fleece, hours, summer* again, *green* again, and *Nature*. This differentia of the Golden style becomes tolerably clear if we notice, for contrast, the keywords in the first stanza of Herbert's 'Confession'; *quest, grief, heart, closets, chest, trade, boxes, a till*.

The rhetorical structure is often that of theme and variations, as in *Lucrece*. The variations more often than not precede the theme, and there is usually an application which connects the theme of the particular sonnet with what may be called the 'running' theme of that part of the sequence to which it belongs. There are exceptions to this. In CXLIV, for example, we have something like a continuous progression in which each line adds to the thought. CXXIX ('The expense of spirit') starts as if it were going to develop in that way, but progression almost ends with line 5, 'Enjoy'd no sooner but despised straight'. The next seven lines are largely, though not entirely, variations on the fifth. To see the typical Shakespearian structure at its simplest we may turn to LXVI ('Tired with all these'). The theme occupies the first line, the application, the final couplet: in between we have eleven instances of the things which produce weariness of life. This numerical equality between the different variations is very uncommon, and chosen, no doubt, to give a special effect of cumulative bitterness. More often it is contrived that the variations should be either unequal simply, or, if they begin by being equal, that they should presently grow longer. Thus XII ('When I do count the clock') is built on the pattern variations—theme—application. The theme ('You too will pass') occupies the four lines beginning 'then of thy beauty do I question make', and the application is in the final couplet. The preceding variations have the numerical pattern 1, 1, 1, 1, 2, 2; a line each for the clock, the nightfall, the violet, and the curls, then two lines each for the trees and the harvest. The effect on the reader is one of liberation just at the moment when the one-line *exempla* were about to produce a feeling of constraint. In XXXIII ('Full many a glorious morning') we have only one variation in the form of a continuous simile filling the first eight lines. But then this simile contains its own pattern: one line announcing the morning, three which catch each one aspect of its beauty, and four to tell the sequel. XVIII ('Shall I compare thee to a summer's day?') is exquisitely elaborated. As often, the theme begins at line 9 ('But thy eternal summer shall not fade'), occupying four lines, and the application is in the couplet. Line 1 proposes a simile. Line 2 corrects it. Then we have two one-line *exempla* justifying the correction: then a two-line *exemplum* about the sun: then two more lines ('And every fair') which do not, as we had expected, add a fourth *exemplum* but generalize. Equality of length in the two last variations is thus played off against difference of function. The same transition from variation by examples to variation by generalizing is found in LXIV ('When I have seen by Time's fell hand defaced'); theme in line 1–2, first *exemplum* in line 3, second *exemplum* in line 4, the third *exemplum* triumphantly expanding to fill lines 5–8, generalization (9–10) passing into Application which occupies the last four lines. To some, I am afraid, such analysis will seem trifling, and it is not contended that no man can enjoy the *Sonnets* without it any more than that no man can enjoy a tune without knowing its musical grammar. But unless we are content to talk simply about the 'magic' of Shakespeare's poetry (forgetting that magic was a highly formal art) something of the kind is inevitable. It serves at least to remind us what sort of excellence, and how different from some other poetic excellences, the *Sonnets* possess. They very seldom present or even feign to present passionate thought growing and changing in the heat of a situation; they are not dramatic. The end of each is clearly in view from the beginning, the theme already chosen. Instead of a single developing thought we get what musicians call an 'arrangement', what we might call a pattern or minuet, of thoughts and images. There are arithmetical elements in the beauty of this pattern as in all formal beauty, and its basic principle is *idem in alio.* Of course it affects those who have no notion what is affecting them. It is partly responsible for that immense pleasurableness which we find in the *Sonnets* even where their matter is most painful: and also for their curious stillness or tranquillity. Shakespeare is always standing back a little from the emotions he treats. He left it to his created persons, his Lears and Othellos, to pour out raw experience, scalding hot. In his own person he does not do so. He sings (always sings, never talks) of shame and degradation and the divided will, but it is as if he sang from above, moved and yet not moved; a Golden, Olympian poet.

The most secret of his poems remains. In 1601 there came out *Love's Martyr* by Robert Chester, a long, mysterious allegory about a male Turtle-dove and a female Phoenix, halting in metre, defective in rhyme, and almost to be classed with Copley's *Fig for Fortune* as Late Medieval. To this are appended 'diverse poeticall Essaies' on the same subject, signed by *Vatum Chorus, Ignoto,* William Shakespeare, John Marston, George Chapman, and Ben Jonson. Shakespeare's piece is, of course, what we call 'The Phoenix and the Turtle', though it appears without title. Whatever the external occasion may have been, Shakespeare uses his poem to expound a philosophy of love; the last word, presumably, that he has given us in his own person on that subject. Its doctrine consummates that of the *Sonnets.* In them the 'naughting' had been one sided. He had lost himself in another but that other had not lost himself in Shakespeare. Now Shakespeare celebrates the exchanged death, and life, of a fully mutual love. He is not writing 'metaphysical poetry' in the technical sense critics give to that term, but he is writing in the true sense, a metaphysical poem. Such a task leads some poets (Browning, for example) into a loose form and a style *sermoni proprior.* Shakespeare, on the other hand, gives us formality within formality, the *threnos* within the funeral poem, the conduct of his work ritualistic, his metres rigid, deliberately, hypnotically, monotonous. His supreme invention was the introduction of Reason as the principal speaker. The words which sum up Shakespeare's doctrine, 'Love hath reason, reason none' owe all their importance to the fact that it is Reason who utters them. In the mouth of a passionate lover or a passionate mourner they would be the stalest claptrap; one more expression of 'will' revolting against 'wit', one more confirmation of the assumption, traditional since Chrétien, that Love and Reason are adversaries. But it is Reason who here exalts love above reason. It is Reason who has seen rational categories overthrown: 'distincts' becoming indivisible, propriety (*proprium*) 'appalled' by the discovery that the self-same is yet not the same (for of course *the self* in 38 does not mean 'the ego'), and something brought into existence which cannot be called two or one. It is Reason who confesses that neither truth (which is Reason's natural goal) nor beauty is the highest good. For beauty is only a brag or a bravery, a sign or hint, of the true good: and truth 'cannot be', it is not being, but only 'about' being. Reason, in fact, rationally recognizes what is beyond reason. We could not have guessed, I think, from internal evidence that this poem was by Shakespeare. As an anonymous work it would command our highest admiration. The oracular, which of all styles is most contemptible when it fails, is here completely successful; the illusion that we have been in another world and heard the voices of gods is achieved. Approached, as we usually approach it, after long familiarity with the plays, 'The Phoenix and the Turtle' has, in addition, another interest. We feel that we have been admitted to the *natura naturans* from which the *natura naturata* of the plays proceeded: as though we had reached the garden of Adonis and seen where Imogens and Cordelias are made.

C. L. BARBER

Rule and Misrule
in "Henry IV"

If all the year were playing holidays,
To sport would be as tedious as to work . . .
—SHAKESPEARE

The two parts of *Henry IV*, written pro-
bably in 1597 and 1598, are an astonishing development of drama in the
direction of inclusiveness, a development possible because of the range of
the traditional culture and the popular theater, but realized only because
Shakespeare's genius for construction matched his receptivity. We have
noticed briefly in the introductory chapter how, early in his career,
Shakespeare made brilliant use of the long standing tradition of comic
accompaniment and counterstatement by the clown. Now suddenly he
takes the diverse elements in the potpourri of the popular chronicle play
and composes a structure in which they draw each other out. The Falstaff
comedy, far from being forced into an alien environment of historical
drama, is begotten by that environment, giving and taking meaning as it
grows. The implications of the saturnalian attitude are more drastically
and inclusively expressed here than anywhere else, because here misrule is
presented along with rule and along with the tensions that challenge rule.
Shakespeare dramatizes not only holiday but also the need for holiday and
the need to limit holiday.

It is in the Henry IV plays that we can consider most fruitfully

---

From *Shakespeare's Festive Comedy*. Copyright © 1959 by Princeton University Press.

general questions concerning the relation of comedy to analogous forms of symbolic action in folk rituals: not only the likenesses of comedy to ritual, but the differences, the features of comic form which make it comedy and not ritual. Such analogies, I think, prove to be useful critical tools: they lead us to see structure in the drama. And they also raise fascinating historical and theoretical questions about the relation of drama to other products of culture. One way in which our time has been seeing the universal in literature has been to find in complex literary works patterns which are analogous to myths and rituals and which can be regarded as archetypes, in some sense primitive or fundamental. I have found this approach very exciting indeed. But at the same time, such analysis can be misleading if it results in equating the literary form with primitive analogues. When we are dealing with so developed an art as Shakespeare's, in so complex an epoch as the Renaissance, primitive patterns may be seen in literature mainly because literary imagination, exploiting the heritage of literary form, disengages them from the suggestions of a complex culture. And the primitive levels are articulated in the course of reunderstanding their nature—indeed, the primitive can be fully expressed only on condition that the artist can deal with it in a most civilized way. Shakespeare presents patterns analogous to magic and ritual in the process of redefining magic as imagination, ritual as social action.

Shakespeare was the opposite of primitivistic, for in his culture what we search out and call primitive was in the blood and bone as a matter of course; the problem was to deal with it, to master it. The Renaissance, moreover, was a moment when educated men were modifying a ceremonial conception of human life to create a historical conception. The ceremonial view, which assumed that names and meanings are fixed and final, expressed experience as pageant and ritual—pageant where the right names could march in proper order, or ritual where names could be changed in the right, the proper way. The historical view expresses life as drama. People in drama are not identical with their names, for they gain and lose their names, their status and meaning—and not by settled ritual: the gaining and losing of names, of meaning, is beyond the control of any set ritual sequence. Shakespeare's plays are full of pageantry and of action patterned in a ritualistic way. But the pageants are regularly interrupted; the rituals are abortive or perverted; or if they succeed, they succeed against odds or in an unexpected fashion. The people in the plays try to organize their lives by pageant and ritual, but the plays are dramatic precisely because the effort fails. This failure drama presents as history and personality; in the largest perspective, as destiny.

At the heart of the plays there is, I think, a fascination with the individualistic use or abuse of ritual—with magic. There is an intoxication with the possibility of an omnipotence of mind by which words might become things, by which a man might "gain a deity," might achieve, by making his own ritual, an unlimited power to incarnate meaning. This fascination is expressed in the poetry by which Shakespeare's people envisage their ideal selves. But his drama also expresses an equal and complementary awareness that magic is delusory, that words can become things or lead to deeds only within a social group, by virtue of a historical, social situation beyond the mind and discourse of any one man. This awareness of limitations is expressed by the ironies, whether comic or tragic, which Shakespeare embodies in the dramatic situations of his speakers, the ironies which bring down the meanings which fly high in winged words.

In using an analogy with temporary king and scapegoat to bring out patterns of symbolic action in Falstaff's role, it will be important to keep it clear that the analogy is one we make now, that it is not Shakespeare's analogy; otherwise we falsify his relation to tradition. He did not need to discriminate consciously, in our way, underlying configurations which came to him with his themes and materials. His way of extending consciousness of such patterns was the drama. In creating the Falstaff comedy, he fused two main saturnalian traditions, the clowning customary on the stage and the folly customary on holiday, and produced something unprecedented. He was working out attitudes towards chivalry, the state and crown in history, in response to the challenge posed by the fate he had dramatized in *Richard II*. The fact that we find analogies to the ritual interregnum relevant to what Shakespeare produced is not the consequence of a direct influence; his power of dramatic statement, in developing saturnalian comedy, reached to modes of organizing experience which primitive cultures have developed with a clarity of outline comparable to that of his drama. The large and profound relations he expressed were developed from the relatively simple dramatic method of composing with statement and counterstatement, elevated action and burlesque. The Henry IV plays are masterpieces of the popular theater whose plays were, in Sidney's words, "neither right tragedies nor right comedies, mingling kings and clowns."

MINGLING KINGS AND CLOWNS

The fascination of Falstaff as a dramatic figure has led criticism, from Morgan's essay onward, to center *1 Henry IV* on him, and to treat the rest of the play merely as a setting for him. But despite his predominating imaginative significance, the play is centered on Prince Hal, developing in such a way as to exhibit in the prince an inclusive, sovereign nature fitted for kingship. The relation of the Prince to Falstaff can be summarized fairly adequately in terms of the relation of holiday to everyday. As the non-historical material came to Shakespeare in *The Famous Victories of Henry the Fifth*, the prince was cast in the traditional role of the prodigal son, while his disreputable companions functioned as tempters in the same general fashion as the Vice of the morality plays. At one level Shakespeare keeps this pattern, but he shifts the emphasis away from simple moral terms. The issue, in his hands, is not whether Hal will be good or bad but whether he will be noble or degenerate, whether his holiday will become his everyday. The interregnum of a Lord of Misrule, delightful in its moment, might develop into the anarchic reign of a favorite dominating a dissolute king. Hal's secret, which he confides early to the audience, is that for him Falstaff is merely a pastime, to be dismissed in due course:

> If all the year were playing holidays,
> To sport would be as tedious as to work;
> But when they seldom come, they wish'd-for come . . .
> (I.ii.228–230)

The prince's sports, accordingly, express not dissoluteness but a fine excess of vitality—"as full of spirit as the month of May"—together with a capacity for occasionally looking at the world as though it were upside down. His energy is controlled by an inclusive awareness of the rhythm in which he is living: despite appearances, he will not make the mistake which undid Richard II, who played at saturnalia until it caught up with him in earnest. During the battle of Shrewsbury (when, in Hotspur's phrase, "Doomsday is near"), Hal dismisses Falstaff with "What! is it a time to jest and dally now?" (V.iii.57) This sense of timing, of the relation of holiday to everyday and doomsday, contributes to establishing the prince as a sovereign nature.

But the way Hal sees the relations is not the way other people see them, nor indeed the way the audience sees them until the end. The holiday-everyday antithesis is his resource for control, and in the end he makes it stick. But before that, the only clear-cut definition of relations in these terms is in his single soliloquy, after his first appearance with Falstaff. Indeed, it is remarkable how little satisfactory formulation there is of the relationships which the play explores dramatically. It is essential to the play that the prince should be misconstrued, that the king should see "riot and dishonor stain" (I.i.85) his brow, that Percy should patronize him as a "nimble-footed madcap" (IV.ii.95) who might easily be poisoned with a pot of ale if it were worth the trouble. But the absence of adequate summary also reflects the fact that Shakespeare was doing something which he could not summarize, which only the whole resources of his dramatic art could convey.

It is an open question, throughout *Part One*, as to just who or what Falstaff is. At the very end, when Prince John observes "This is the strangest tale that ever I heard," Hal responds with "This is the strangest fellow, brother John" (V.iv.158–159). From the beginning, Falstaff is constantly renaming himself:

> Marry, then, sweet wag, when thou art king, let not us that are squires of the night's body be called thieves of the day's beauty. Let us be Diana's Foresters, Gentlemen of the Shade, Minions of the Moon; and let men say we be men of good government . . .
>
> (I.ii.26–31)

Here Misrule is asking to be called Good Government, as it is his role to do—though he does so with a wink which sets real good government at naught, concluding with "steal":

> . . . men of good government, being governed as the sea is, by our noble and chase mistress the moon, under whose countenance we steal.
>
> (I.ii.31–33)

I have considered in an earlier chapter how the witty equivocation Falstaff practices, like that of Nashe's Bacchus and other apologists for folly and vice, alludes to the very morality it is flouting. Such "damnable iteration" is a sport that implies a rolling-eyed awareness of both sides of the moral medal; the Prince summarizes it in saying that Sir John "was never yet a breaker of proverbs. He will give the devil his due" (I.ii.131–133). It is also a game to be played with cards close to the chest. A Lord of Misrule naturally does not call himself Lord of Misrule in setting out to reign, but takes some title with the life of pretense in it. Falstaff's pretensions, moreover, are not limited to one occasion, for he is not properly a holiday lord, but a *de facto* buffoon who makes his way by continually seizing, catch as catch can, on what names and meanings the moment offers. He is not a professed buffoon—few buffoons, in life, are apt to be. In Renaissance courts, the role of buffoon was recognized but not necessarily formalized, not necessarily altogether distinct from the role of favorite. And he is a highwayman: Shakespeare draws on the euphemistic, mock-chivalric cant by which "the profession" grace themselves. Falstaff in *Part One* plays it that he is Hal's friend, a gentleman, a "gentleman of the shade," and a soldier; he even enjoys turning the tables with "Thou hast done much harm upon me, Hal . . . I must give over this life, and I will give it over . . . I'll be damn'd for never a king's son in Christendom" (I.ii.102–109). It is the essence of his character, and his role, in *Part One*, that he never comes to rest where we can see him for what he "is." He is always in motion, always adopting postures, assuming characters.

That he does indeed care for Hal can be conveyed in performance without imposing sentimental tableaux on the action, provided that actors and producer recognize that he cares for the prince after his own fashion. It is from the prince that he chiefly gets his meaning, as it is from real kings that mock kings always get their meaning. We can believe it when we hear in *Henry V* that banishment has "killed his heart" (II.i.92). But to make much of a personal affection for the prince is a misconceived way to find meaning in Falstaff. His extraordinary meaningfulness comes from the way he manages to live "out of all order, out of all compass" by his wit and his wits; and from the way he keeps reflecting on the rest of the action, at first indirectly by the mock roles that he plays, at the end directly by his comments at the battle. Through this burlesque and mockery an intelligence of the highest order is expressed. It is not always clear whether the intelligence is Falstaff's or the dramatist's; often the question need not arise. Romantic criticism went the limit in ascribing a God-like superiority to the character, to the point of insisting that he tells the lies about the multiplying men in buckram merely to amuse, that he knew all the time at Gadshill that it was with Hal and Poins that he fought. To go so far in that direction obviously destroys the drama—spoils the joke in the case of the 'incomprehensible lies," a joke which, as E. E. Stoll abundantly demonstrates, must be a joke *on* Falstaff. On the other hand, I see no reason why actor and producer should not do all they can to make us enjoy the intellectual mastery involved in Falstaff's comic resource and power of humorous redefinition. It is crucial that he should not be made so superior that he is never in predicaments, for his genius is expressed in getting out of them. But he does have genius, as Maurice Morgan rightly insisted though in a misconceived way. Through his part Shakespeare expressed attitudes towards experience which, grounded in a saturnalian reversal of values, went beyond that to include a radical challenge to received ideas.

Throughout the first three acts of *Part One*, the Falstaff comedy is continuously responsive to the serious action. There are constant parallels and contrasts with what happens at court or with the rebels. And yet these parallels are not explicitly noticed; the relations are presented, not formulated. So the first scene ends in a mood of urgency, with the tired king urging haste: "come yourself with speed to us again." The second scene opens with Hal asking Falstaff "What a devil hast thou to do with the time of day?" The prose in which he explains why time is nothing to Sir John is wonderfully leisurely and abundant, an elegant sort of talk that has all the time in the world to enjoy the completion of its schematized patterns:

> Unless hours were cups of sack, and minutes capons, and clocks the tongues of bawds, and dials the signs of leaping houses, and the blessed sun himself a fair hot wench in flame-colored taffeta, I see no reason why thou shouldst be so superfluous to demand the time of day.
>
> (I.ii.7–13)

The same difference in the attitude towards time runs throughout and goes with the difference between verse and prose mediums. A similar contrast obtains about lese majesty. Thus at their first appearance Falstaff insults Hal's majesty with casual, off-hand wit which the prince tolerates (while getting his own back by jibing at Falstaff's girth):

> And I prithee, sweet wag, when thou art king, as God save thy Grace—
> Majesty I should say, for grace thou wilt have none—
> PRINCE: What, none?
> FALSTAFF: No, by my troth; not so much as will serve to be prologue
>   to an egg and butter.
> PRINCE: Well, how then? Come, roundly, roundly.
>
> (I.ii.17–25)

In the next scene, we see Worcester calling into question the grace of Bolingbroke, "that same greatness to which our own hands / Have holp to make so portly" (I.iii.12–13). The King's response is immediate and drastic, and his lines point a moral that Hal seems to be ignoring:

> Worcester, get thee gone; for I do see
> Danger and disobedience in thine eye.
> O, sir, your presence is too bold and peremptory,
> And majesty might never yet endure
> The moody frontier of a servant brow.
>
> (I.iii.15–19)

Similar parallels run between Hotspur's heroics and Falstaff's mock-heroics. In the third scene we hear Hotspur talking of "an easy leap / To pluck bright honor from the pale-face'd moon" (I.iii.201–202). Then in the robbery, Falstaff is complaining that "Eight yards of uneven ground is threescore and ten miles afoot for me," and asking "Have you any levers to lift me up again, being down?" (II.ii.25–28, 36) After Hotspur enters exclaiming against the cowardly lord who has written that he will not join the rebellion, we have Falstaff's entrance to the tune of "A plague of all cowards" (II.iv.127). And so on, and so on. Shakespeare's art has reached the point where he makes everything foil to everything else. Hal's imagery, in his soliloquy, shows the dramatist thinking about such relations: "like bright metal on a sullen ground, / My reformation, glitt'ring o'er my fault" (I.ii.236–237).

Now it is not true that Falstaff's impudence about Hal's grace undercuts Bolingbroke's majesty, nor that Sir John's posturing as a hero among cowards invalidates the heroic commitment Hotspur expresses when he says "but I tell you, my lord fool, out of this nettle, danger, we pluck this flower, safety" (II.iii.11–12). The relationship is not one of a mocking echo. Instead, there is a certain distance between the comic and serious strains which leaves room for a complex interaction, organized by the crucial role of the prince. We are invited, by the King's unfavorable comparison in the opening scene, to see the Prince in relation to Hotspur. And Hal himself, in the midst of his Boars Head revel, compares himself with Hotspur. In telling Poins of his encounter with the drawers among the hogsheads of the wine-cellar, he says "I have sounded the very bass-string of humility," goes on to note what he has gained by it, "I can drink with any tinker in his own language during my life," and concludes with "I tell thee, Ned, thou hast lost much honour that thou wert not with me in this action" (II.iv.5, 20–24). His mock-heroic way of talking about "this action" shows how well he knows how to value it from a princely vantage. But the remark cuts two ways. For running the gamut of society *is* an important action: after their experiment with Francis and his "Anon, anon, sir," the Prince exclaims

> That ever this fellow should have fewer words than a parrot, and yet the son of a woman! . . . I am not yet of Percy's mind, the Hotspur of the North; he that kills me some six or seven dozen of Scots at a breakfast, washes his hands, and says to his wife, "Fie upon this quiet life! I want work." "O my sweet Harry," says she, "how many hast thou kill'd to-day?" "Give my roan horse a drench," says he, and answers "Some fourteen," an hour after, "a trifle, a trifle." I prithee call in Falstaff. I'll play Percy, and that damn'd brawn shall play Dame Mortimer his wife.
>
> (II.iv.110–124)

It is the narrowness and obliviousness of the martial hero that Hal's mockery brings out; here his awareness explicitly spans the distance between the separate strains of the action; indeed, the distance is made the measure of the kingliness of his nature. His "I am not *yet* of Percy's mind" implies what he later promises his father (the commericial image he employs reflects his ability to use, after his father's fashion, the politician's calculation and indirection):

> Percy is but my factor, good my lord,
> To engross up glorious deeds on my behalf . . .
> (III.ii.147–148)

In the Boars Head Tavern scene, Hal never carries out the plan of playing Percy to Falstaff's Dame Mortimer; in effect he has played both their parts already in his snatch of mimicry. But Falstaff provides him with a continuous exercise in the consciousness that comes from playing at being what one is not, and from seeing through such playing.

Even here, where one world does comment on another explicitly, Hotspur's quality is not invalidated; rather, his achievement is *placed.* It is included within a wider field which contains also the drawers, mine host, Mistress Quickly, and by implication, not only "all the good lads of Eastcheap" but all the estates of England. When we saw Hotspur and his Lady, he was not foolish, but delightful in his headlong, spontaneous way. His Lady has a certain pathos in the complaints which serve to convey how all absorbing his battle passion is. But the joke is with him as he mocks her:

> Love? I love thee not;
> I care not for thee, Kate. This is no world
> To play with mammets and to tilt with lips.
> We must have bloody noses and crack'd crowns,
> And pass them current, too. Gods me, my horse!
> (II.iii.93–97)

One could make some very broad fun of Hotspur's preference for his horse over his wife. But there is nothing of the kind in Shakespeare: here and later, his treatment values the conversion of love into war as one of the important human powers. Hotspur has the fullness of life and the unforced integrity of the great aristocrat who has never known what it is to cramp his own style. His style shows it; he speaks the richest, freshest poetry of the play, in lines that take all the scope they need to fulfill feeling and perception:

> . . . oft the teeming earth
> Is with a kind of colic pinch'd and vex'd
> By the imprisoning of unruly wind
> Within her womb, which, for enlargement striving,
> Shakes the old beldame earth and topples down
> Steeples and mossgrown towers. At your birth
> Our grandam earth, having this distemp'rature,
> In passion shook.

> GLENDOWER: Cousin, of many men
> I do not bear these crossings. Give me leave
> To tell you once again that at my birth
> The front of heaven was full of fiery shapes,
> The goats ran from the mountains, and the herds
> Were strangely clamorous to the frighted fields.
>   (III.i.28–40)

The established life of moss-grown towers is in Percy's poetic speech, as the grazed-over Welsh mountains are in Glendower's. They are both strong; everybody in this play is strong in his own way. Hotspur's humor is untrammeled, like his verse, based on the heedless empiricism of an active, secure nobleman:

> GLENDOWER: I can call spirits from the vasty deep.
> HOTSPUR: Why, so can I, or so can any man;
> But will they come when you do call for them?
>   (III.i.53–55)

His unconsciousness makes him, at other moments, a comic if winning figure, as the limitations of his feudal virtues are brought out: his want of tact and judgment, his choleric man's forgetfulness, his sudden boyish habit of leaping to conclusions, the noble but also comical way he can be carried away by "imagination of some great exploit" (I.iii.199), or by indignation at "this vile politician, Bolingbroke" (I.iii.241). Professor Lily B. Campbell has demonstrated that the rebellion of the Northern Earls in 1570 was present for Shakespeare's audience in watching the Percy family in the play. The remoteness of this rough north country life from the London world of his audience, as well as its aristocratic charm, are conveyed when Hotspur tells his wife that she swears "like a comfit-maker's wife,"

> As if thou ne'er walk'st further than Finsbury.
> Swear me, Kate, like a lady as thou art,
> A good mouth-filling oath; and leave 'in sooth'
> And such protest of pepper gingerbread
> To velvet guards and Sunday citizens.
>   (III.i.255–259)

It is the various strengths of a stirring world, not deficiencies, which make the conflict in *1 Henry IV*. Even the humble carriers, and the professional thieves, are full of themselves and their business:

> I am joined with no foot land-rakers, no long-staff sixpenny strikers, none of these mad mustachio purple-hued maltworms; but with nobility and tranquillity, burgomasters and great oneyers, such as can hold in,

such as will strike sooner than speak, and speak sooner than drink, and
drink sooner than pray; and yet, zounds, I lie; for they pray continually
to their saint, the commonwealth, or rather, not pray to her, but prey on
her, for they ride up and down on her and make her their boots.

(II.i.81–91)

In his early history play, *2 Henry VI,* as we have noticed, Shakespeare
used his clowns to present the Jack Cade rebellion as a saturnalia ignorantly undertaken in earnest, a highly-stylized piece of dramaturgy, which
he brings off triumphantly. In this more complex play the underworld is
presented as endemic disorder alongside the crisis of noble rebellion: the
king's lines are apposite when he says that insurrection can always mobilize

> . . . moody beggars, starving for a time
> Of pell-mell havoc and confusion.
> (V.i.81–82)

Falstaff places himself in saying "Well, God be thanked for these rebels.
They offend none but the virtuous. I laud them, I praise them."

The whole effect, in the opening acts, when there is little commentary on the spectacle as a whole, is of life overflowing its bounds by
sheer vitality. Thieves and rebels and honest men—"one that hath abundance of charge too, God knows what" (II.i.64)—ride up and down on the
commonwealth, pray to her and prey on her. Hotspur exults that "That
roan shall be my throne" (II.iii.73). Falstaff exclaims, "Shall I? Content.
This chair shall be my state" (II.iv.415). Hal summarizes the effect, after
Hotspur is dead, with

> When that this body did contain a spirit,
> A kingdom for it was too small a bound.
> (V.iv.89–90)

The stillness when he says this, at the close of the battle, is the moment
when his royalty is made manifest. When he stands poised above the
prostrate bodies of Hotspur and Falstaff, his position on the stage and his
lines about the two heroes express a nature which includes within a larger
order the now subordinated parts of life which are represented in those
two: in Hotspur, honor, the social obligation to courage and self-sacrifice,
a value which has been isolated in this magnificently anarchical feudal
lord to become almost everything; and in Falstaff, the complementary *joie
de vivre* which rejects all social obligations with "I like not such grinning
honour as Sir Walter hath. Give me life" (V.iii.61).

GETTING RID OF BAD LUCK BY COMEDY

But Falstaff does not stay dead. He jumps up in a triumph which, like Bottom coming alive after Pyramus is dead, reminds one of the comic resurrections in the St. George plays. He comes back to life because he is still relevant. His apology for counterfeiting cuts deeply indeed, because it does not apply merely to himself; we can relate it, as William Empson has shown, to the counterfeiting of the king. Bolingbroke too knows when it is time to counterfeit, both in this battle, where he survives because he has many marching in his coats, and throughout a political career where, as he acknowledges to Hal, he manipulates the symbols of majesty with a calculating concern for ulterior results. L. C. Knights, noticing this relation and the burlesque, elsewhere in Falstaff's part, of the attitudes of chivalry, concluded with nineteenth-century critics like Ulrici and Victor Hugo that the comedy should be taken as a devastating satire on war and government. But this is obviously an impossible, anachronistic view, based on the assumption of the age of individualism that politics and war are unnatural activities that can be done without. Mr. Knights would have it that the audience should feel a jeering response when Henry sonorously declares, after Shrewsbury: "Thus ever did rebellion find rebuke." This interpretation makes a shambles of the heroic moments of the play—makes them clearly impossible to act. My own view, as will be clear, is that the dynamic relation of comedy and serious action is saturnalian rather than satiric, that the misrule works, through the whole dramatic rhythm, to consolidate rule. But it is also true, as Mr. Empson remarks, that "the double plot is carrying a fearful strain here." Shakespeare is putting an enormous pressure on the comedy to resolve the challenge posed by the ironic perceptions presented in his historical action.

The process at work, here and earlier in the play, can be made clearer, I hope, by reference now to the carrying off of bad luck by the scapegoat of saturnalian ritual. We do not need to assume that Shakespeare had any such ritual patterns consciously in mind; whatever his conscious intention, it seems to me that these analogues illuminate patterns which his poetic drama presents concretely and dramatically. After such figures as the Mardi Gras or Carnival have presided over a revel, they are frequently turned on by their followers, tried in some sort of court, convicted of sins notorious in the village during the last year, and burned or buried in effigy to signify a new start. In other ceremonies described in *The Golden Bough*, mockery kings appear as recognizable substitutes for real kings, stand trial in their stead, and carry away the evils of their

realms into exile or death. One such scapegoat figure, as remote historically as could be from Shakespeare, is the Tibetan King of the Years, who
enjoyed ten days' misrule during the annual holiday of Buddhist monks at
Lhasa. At the climax of his ceremony, after doing what he liked while
collecting bad luck by shaking a black yak's tail over the people, he
mounted the temple steps and ridiculed the representative of the Grand
Llama, proclaiming heresies like "What we perceive through the five
senses is no illusion. All you teach is untrue." A few minutes later,
discredited by a cast of loaded dice, he was chased off to exile and possible
death in the mountains. One cannot help thinking of Falstaff's catechism
on honor, spoken just before another valuation of honor is expressed in
the elevated blank verse of a hero confronting death: "Can honour . . .
take away the grief of a wound? No. . . . What is honour? a word. What is
that word, honour? Air." Hal's final expulsion of Falstaff appears in the
light of these analogies to carry out an impersonal pattern, not merely
political but ritual in character. After the guilty reign of Bolingbroke, the
prince is making a fresh start as the new king. At a level beneath the
moral notions of a personal reform, we can see a nonlogical process of
purification by sacrifice—the sacrifice of Falstaff. The career of the old
king, a successful usurper whose conduct of affairs has been sceptical and
opportunistic, has cast doubt on the validity of the whole conception of a
divinely-ordained and chivalrous kingship to which Shakespeare and his
society were committed. And before Bolingbroke, Richard II had given
occasion for doubts about the rituals of kingship in an opposite way, by
trying to use them magically. Shakespeare had shown Richard assuming
that the symbols of majesty should be absolutes, that the names of
legitimate power should be transcendently effective regardless of social
forces. Now both these attitudes have been projected also in Falstaff; he
carries to comically delightful and degraded extremes both a magical use of
moral sanctions and the complementary opportunistic manipulation and
scepticism. So the ritual analogy suggests that by turning on Falstaff as a
scapegoat, as the villagers turned on their Mardi Gras, the prince can free
himself from the sins, the "bad luck," of Richard's reign and of his father's
reign, to become a king in whom chivalry and a sense of divine ordination
are restored.

But this process of carrying off bad luck, if it is to be made
dramatically cogent, as a symbolic action accomplished in and by dramatic
form, cannot take place magically in Shakespeare's play. When it happens
magically in the play, we have, I think, a failure to transform ritual into
comedy. In dealing with fully successful comedy, the magical analogy is
only a useful way of organizing our awareness of a complex symbolic

action. The expulsion of evil works as dramatic form only in so far as it is realized in a movement from participation to rejection which happens, moment by moment, in our response to Falstaff's clowning misrule. We watch Falstaff adopt one posture after another, in the effort to give himself meaning at no cost; and moment by moment we see that the meaning is specious. So our participation is repeatedly diverted to laughter. The laughter, disbursing energy originally mobilized to respond to a valid meaning, signalizes our mastery by understanding of the tendency which has been misapplied or carried to an extreme.

Consider, for example, the use of magical notions of royal power in the most famous of all Falstaff's burlesques:

> By the Lord, I knew ye as well as he that made ye. . . . Was it for me to kill the heir apparent? Should I turn upon the true prince? Why, thou knowest I am as valiant as Hercules; but beware instinct. The lion will not touch the true prince. Instinct is a great matter. I was now a coward on instinct. I shall think the better of myself, and thee, during my life—I for a valiant lion, and thou for a true prince. But, by the Lord, lads, I am glad you have the money. Hostess, clap to the doors: watch to-night, pray to-morrow.
>
> (II.iv.295–306)

Here Falstaff has recourse to the brave conception that legitimate kingship has a magical potency. This is the sort of absolutist appeal to sanctions which Richard II keeps falling back on in his desperate "conjuration" (*R. II* III.ii.23) by hyperbole:

> So when this thief, this traitor, Bolingbroke, . . .
> Shall see us rising in our throne, the East,
> His treasons will sit blushing in his face,
> Not able to endure the sight of day . . .
> The breath of worldly men cannot depose
> The deputy elected by the Lord.
> For every man that Bolingbroke hath press'd
> To lift shrewd steel against our golden crown,
> God for his Richard hath in heavenly pay
> A glorious angel.
>
> (*R. II* III.ii.47–61)

In Richard's case, a tragic irony enforces the fact that heavenly angels are of no avail if one's coffers are empty of golden angels and the Welsh army have dispersed. In Falstaff's case, the irony is comically obvious, the "lies are like the father that begets them; gross as a mountain, open, palpable" (II.iv.249–250). Hal stands for the judgment side of our response, while Falstaff embodies the enthusiastic, irrepressible conviction of fantasy's omnipotence. The Prince keeps returning to Falstaff's bogus "instinct"; "Now, sirs . . . You are lions too, you ran away upon instinct, you will not touch the true prince; no—fie!" (II.iv.29–34) After enjoying the experience of seeing through such notions of magical majesty, he is never apt to make the mistake of assuming that, just because he is king, lions like Northumberland will not touch him. King Richard's bad luck came precisely from such an assumption—unexamined, of course, as fatal assumptions always are. Freud's account of bad luck, in *The Psychopathology of Everyday Life,* sees it as the expression of unconscious motives which resist the conscious goals of the personality. This view helps to explain how the acting out of disruptive motives in saturnalia or in comedy can serve to master potential aberration by revaluing it in relation to the whole of experience. So Falstaff, in acting out his absolutist aberration, is taking away what might have been Hal's bad luck, taking it away not in a magical way, but by extending the sphere of conscious control. The comedy is a civilized equivalent of the primitive rite. A similar mastery of potential aberration is promoted by the experience of seeing through Falstaff's burlesque of the sort of headlong chivalry presented seriously in Hotspur.

In order to put the symbolic action of the comedy in larger perspective, it will be worth while to consider further, for a moment, the relation of language to stage action and dramatic situation in *Richard II.* That play is a pioneering exploration of the semantics of royalty, shot through with talk about the potency and impotence of language. In the first part, we see a Richard who is possessor of an apparently magical omnipotence: for example, when he commutes Bolingbroke's banishment from ten to six years, Bolingbroke exclaims:

> How long a time lies in one little word!
> Four lagging winters and four wanton springs
> End in a word: such is the breath of kings.
> (*R.II* I.iii.213–215)

Richard assumes he has such magic breath inevitably, regardless of "the breath of worldly men." When he shouts things like "Is not the king's name twenty thousand names? / Arm, arm, my name!" he carries the absolutist assumption to the giddiest verge of absurdity. When we analyze the magical substitution of words for things in such lines, looking at them from outside the rhythm of feeling in which they occur, it seems scarcely plausible that a drama should be built around the impulse to adopt such an assumption. It seems especially implausible in our own age, when we are so conscious, on an abstract level, of the dependence of verbal efficacy on the social group. The analytical situation involves a misleading perspective, however; for, whatever your assumptions about semantics, when you have to *act*, to *be* somebody or become somebody, there is a moment when you have to have faith that the unknown world beyond will respond to the names you commit yourself to as right names. The Elizabethan mind, moreover, generally assumed that one played one's part in a divinely ordained pageant where each man *was* his name and the role his name implied. The expression of this faith, and of the outrage of it, is particularly drastic in the Elizabethan drama, which can be regarded, from this vantage, as an art form developed to express the shock and exhilaration of the discovery that life is not pageantry. As Professor Tillyard has pointed out, *Richard II* is the most ceremonial of all Shakespeare's plays, and the ceremony all comes to nothing. In Richard's deposition scene, one way in which anguish at his fall is expressed is by a focus on his loss of names: he responds to Northumberland's "My Lord—" by flinging out

> No lord of thine, thou haught insulting man,
> Nor no man's lord. I have no name, no title—
> No, not that name was given me at the font—
> But 'tis usurp'd. Alack the heavy day,
> That I have worn so many winters out
> And know not now what name to call myself!
> O that I were a mockery king of snow,
> Standing before the sun of Bolingbroke
> To melt myself away in water-drops!
>   (*R. II* IV.i.253–262)

His next move is to call for the looking glass in which he stares at his face to look for the meaning the face has lost. To lose one's meaning, one's social role, is to be reduced to mere body.

Here again the tragedy can be used to illuminate the comedy. Since the Elizabethan drama was a double medium of words and of physical gestures, it frequently expressed the pathos of the loss of meaning by emphasizing moments when word and gesture, name and body, no longer go together, just as it presented the excitement of a gain of meaning by showing a body seizing on names when a hero creates his identity. In the deposition scene, Richard says "mark me how I will undo myself" (IV.i.203). Then he gives away by physical gestures the symbolic meanings which have constituted that self. When at last he has no name, the anguish is that the face, the body, remain when the meaning is gone. There is also something in Richard's line which, beneath the surface of his self-pity, relishes such undoing, a self-love which looks towards fulfillment in that final reduction of all to the body which is death. This narcissistic need for the physical is the other side of the attitude that the magic of the crown should altogether transcend the physical—and the human:

> Cover your heads, and mock not flesh and blood
> With solemn reverence. Throw away respect,
> Tradition, form, and ceremonious duty;
> For you have but mistook me all this while.
> I live with bread like you, feel want, taste grief,
> Need friends. Subjected thus,
> How can you say to me I am a king?
> (*R. II* III.ii.171–177)

In expressing the disappointment of Richard's magical expectations, as well as their sweeping magnificence, the lines make manifest the aberration which is mastered in the play by tragic form.

The same sort of impulse is expressed and mastered by comic form in the Henry IV comedy. When Richard wishes he were a mockery king of snow, to melt before the sun of Bolingbroke, the image expresses on one side the wish to escape from the body with which he is left when his meaning has gone—to weep himself away in water drops. But the lines also look wistfully towards games of mock royalty where, since the whole thing is based on snow, the collapse of meaning need not hurt. Falstaff is such a mockery king. To be sure, he is flesh and blood, of a kind: he is tallow, anyway. He "sweats to death / And lards the lean earth as he walks along." Of course he is not just a mockery, not just his role, not just bombast. Shakespeare, as always, makes the symbolic role the product of a life which includes contradictions of it, such as the morning-after regrets when Falstaff thinks of the inside of a church and notices that his skin hangs about him like an old lady's loose gown. Falstaff is human enough so that "Were't not for laughing, . . . [we] should pity him." But we do laugh, because when Falstaff's meanings collapse, little but make-believe has been lost:

> PRINCE: Thy state is taken for a join'd-stool, thy golden sceptre for a leaden dagger, and thy precious rich crown for a pitiful bald crown.
> (II.iv.418–420)

Falstaff's effort to make his body and furnishings mean sovereignty is doomed from the start; he must work with a leaden dagger, the equivalent of a Vice's dagger of lath. But Falstaff does have golden words, and an inexhaustible vitality in using them. He can name himself nobly, reordering the world by words so as to do himself credit:

> No, my good lord. Banish Peto, banish Bardolph, banish Poins; but for sweet Jack Falstaff, kind Jack Falstaff, true Jack Falstaff, valiant Jack

> Falstaff, and therefore more valiant being, as he is, old Jack Falstaff, banish not him thy Harry's company, banish not him thy Harry's company. Banish plump Jack, and banish all the world!
>
> (II.iv.519–527)

I quote such familiar lines to recall their effect of incantation: they embody an effort at a kind of magical naming. Each repetition of "sweet Jack Falstaff, kind Jack Falstaff" aggrandizes an identity which the serial clauses caress and cherish. At the very end, in "plump Jack," the disreputable belly is glorified.

In valid heroic and majestic action, the bodies of the personages are constantly being elevated by becoming the vehicles of social meanings; in the comedy, such elevation becomes burlesque, and in the repeated failures to achieve a fusion of body and symbol, abstract meanings keep falling back into the physical. "A plague of sighing and grief! it blows a man up like a bladder" (II.iv.365–366). The repetition of such joking about Falstaff's belly makes it meaningful in a very special way, as a symbol of the process of inflation and collapse of meaning. So it represents the power of the individual life to continue despite the collapse of social roles. This continuing on beyond definitions is after all what we call "the body" in one main meaning of the term: Falstaff's belly is thus the essence of body—an essence which can be defined only dynamically, by failures of meaning. The effect of indestructible vitality is reinforced by the association of Falstaff's figure with the gay eating and drinking of Shrove Tuesday and Carnival. Whereas, in the tragedy, the reduction is to a body which can only die, here reduction is to a body which typifies our power to eat and drink our way through a shambles of intellectual and moral contradictions.

So we cannot resist sharing Falstaff's genial self-love when he commands his vision of plump Jack to the Prince, just as we share the ingenuous self-love of a little child. But the dramatist is ever on the alert to enforce the ironies that dog the tendency of fantasy to equate the self with "all the world." So a most monstrous watch comes beating at the doors which have been clapped to against care; everyday breaks in on holiday.

THE TRIAL OF CARNIVAL IN "PART TWO"

In *Part One*, Falstaff reigns, within his sphere, as Carnival; *Part Two* is very largely taken up with his trial. To put Carnival on trial, run him out of town, and burn or bury him is in folk custom a way of limiting, by ritual, the attitudes and impulses set loose by ritual. Such a trial, though conducted with gay hoots and jeers, serves to swing the mind round to a new vantage, where it sees misrule no longer as a benign release for the individual, but as a source of destructive consequences for society. This sort of reckoning is what *Part Two* brings to Falstaff.

But Falstaff proves extremely difficult to bring to book—more difficult than an ordinary mummery king—because his burlesque and mockery are developed to a point where the mood of a moment crystallizes as a settled attitude of scepticism. As we have observed before, in a static, monolithic society, a Lord of Misrule can be put back in his place after the revel with relative ease. The festive burlesque of solemn sanctities does not seriously threaten social values in a monolithic culture, because the license depends utterly upon what it mocks: liberty is unable to envisage any alternative to the accepted order except the standing of it on its head. But Shakespeare's culture was not monolithic: though its moralists assumed a single order, scepticism was beginning to have ground to stand on and look about—especially in and around London. So a Lord of Misrule figure, brought up, so to speak, from the country to the city, or from the traditional past into the changing present, could become on the Bankside the mouthpiece not merely for the dependent holiday scepticism which is endemic in a traditional society, but also for a dangerously self-sufficient everyday scepticism. When such a figure is set in an environment of sober-blooded great men behaving as opportunistically as he, the effect is to raise radical questions about social sanctities. At the end of *Part Two*, the expulsion of Falstaff is presented by the dramatist as getting rid of this threat; Shakespeare has recourse to a primitive procedure to meet a modern challenge. We shall find reason to question whether this use of ritual entirely succeeds.

But the main body of *Part Two*, what I am seeing as the trial, as against the expulsion, is wonderfully effective drama. The first step in trying Carnival, the first step in ceasing to be his subjects, would be to stop calling him "My Lord" and call him instead by his right name, Misrule. Now this is just the step which Falstaff himself takes for us at the outset of *Part Two*; when we first see him, he is setting himself up as an institution, congratulating himself on his powers *as* buffoon and wit. He glories in his role with what Dover Wilson has aptly called "comic hubris." In the saturnalian scenes of *Part One*, we saw that it is impossible to say just who he is; but in *Part Two*, Falstaff sets himself up at the outset as Falstaff:

> I am not only witty in myself, but the cause that wit is in other men. . . .

> A pox of this gout! or, a gout of this pox! for one or the other plays the rogue with my great toe. 'Tis no matter if I do halt. I have the wars for my colour, and my pension shall seem the more reasonable. A good wit will make use of anything. I will turn diseases to commodity.
>
> (I.ii.11–12, 273–278)

In the early portion of *Part One* he never spoke in asides, but now he constantly confides his schemes and his sense of himself to the audience. We do not have to see through him, but watch instead from inside his façades as he imposes them on others. Instead of warm amplifications centered on himself, his talk now consists chiefly of bland impudence or dry, denigrating comments on the way of the world. Much of the comedy is an almost Jonsonian spectacle where we relish a witty knave gulling fools.

It is this self-conscious Falstaff, confident of setting up his holiday license on an everyday basis, who at once encounters, of all awkward people, the Lord Chief Justice. From there on, during the first two acts, he is constantly put in the position of answering for his way of life; in effect he is repeatedly called to trial and keeps eluding it only by a "more than impudent sauciness" (II.i.123) and the privilege of his official employment in the wars. Mistress Quickly's attempt to arrest him is wonderfully ineffectual; but he notably fails to thrust the Lord Chief Justice from a level consideration. Hal and Poins then disguise themselves, not this time for the sake of the incomprehensible lies that Falstaff will tell, but in order to try him, to see him "bestow himself . . . in his true colours" (II.ii.186). So during the first two acts we are again and again put in the position of judging him, although we continue to laugh with him. A vantage is thus established from which we watch him in action in Gloucestershire, where the Justice he has to deal with is so shallow that Falstaff's progress is a triumph. The comedy is still delightful; Falstaff is still the greatest of wits; but we are constantly shown fun that involves fraud. Falstaff himself tells us about his game, with proud relish. Towards the end of the play, Hal's reconciliation with his father and then with the Lord Chief Justice reemphasizes the detached vantage of judgment. So no leading remarks are necessary to assure our noting and marking when we hear Falstaff shouting, "Let us take any man's horses; the laws of England are at my commandment. Blessed are they that have been my friends, and woe unto my lord chief justice!" (V.iii.140–144) The next moment we watch Doll and the Hostess being hauled off by Beadles because "the man is dead that you and Pistol beat among you" (V.iv.18).

Many of the basic structures in this action no doubt were shaped by morality-play encounters between Virtues and Vices, encounters which from my vantage here can be seen as cognate to the festive and scapegoat pattern. The trial of Falstaff is so effective *as drama* because no one conducts it—it happens. Falstaff, being a dramatic character, not a mummery, does not know when he has had his day. And he does not even recognize the authority who will finally sentence him: he mistakes Hal for a bastard son of the king's (II.iv.307). The result of the trial is to make us see perfectly the necessity for the rejection of Falstaff as a man, as a favorite for a king, as the leader of an interest at court.

But I do not think that the dramatist is equally successful in justifying the rejection of Falstaff as a mode of awareness. The problem is not in justifying rejection morally but in making the process cogent *dramatically*, as in *Part One* we reject magical majesty or intransigent chivalry. The bad luck which in *Part Two* Falstaff goes about collecting, by shaking the black yak's tail of his wit over people's heads, is the impulse to assume that nothing is sacred. In a play concerned with ruthless political maneuver, much of it conducted by impersonal state functionaries, Falstaff turns up as a functionary too, with his own version of maneuver and impersonality: "If the young dace be a bait for the old pike, I see no reason in the law of nature but I may snap at him" (III.ii.356–359). Now this attitude is a most appropriate response to the behavior of the high factions beneath whose struggles Falstaff plies his retail trade. In the Gaultree parleys, Lord John rebukes the Archbishop for his use of the counterfeited zeal of God—and then himself uses a counterfeited zeal of gentlemanly friendship to trick the rebels into disbanding their forces. The difference between his behavior and Falstaff's is of course that Lancaster has reasons of state on his side, a sanction supported, if not by legitimacy, at least by the desperate need for social order. This is a real difference, but a bare and harsh one. After all, Falstaff's little commonwealth of man has its pragmatic needs too: as he explains blandly to the Justice, he needs great infamy, because "he that buckles him in my belt cannot live in less" (I.iii.159–160).

The trouble with trying to get rid of this attitude merely by getting rid of Falstaff is that the attitude is too pervasive in the whole society of the play, whether public or private. It is too obviously *not* just a saturnalian mood, the extravagance of a moment: it is presented instead as in grain, as the way of the world. Shakespeare might have let the play end with this attitude dominant, a harsh recognition that life is a nasty business where the big fishes eat the little fishes, with the single redeeming consideration that political order is better than anarchy, so that there is a pragmatic virtue in loyalty to the power of the state. But instead the dramatist undertakes, in the last part of the play, to expel this view of the world and to dramatize the creation of legitimacy and sanctified social power. Although the final scenes are fascinating, with all sorts of illumi-nations, it seems to me that at this level they partly fail.

We have seen that Shakespeare typically uses ritual patterns of behavior and thought precisely in the course of making clear, by tragic or comic irony, that rituals have no *magical* efficacy. The reason for his failure at the close of *Part Two* is that at this point he himself uses ritual, not ironically transformed into drama, but magically. To do this involves a restriction instead of an extension of awareness. An extension of control and awareness is consummated in the epiphany of Hal's majesty while he is standing over Hotspur and Falstaff at the end of *Part One*. But *Part Two* ends with drastic restriction of awareness which goes with the embracing of magical modes of thought, not humorously but sentimentally.

It is true that the latter half of *Part Two* very effectively builds up to its finale by recurrent expression of a laboring need to be rid of a growth or humor. King Henry talks of the body of his kingdom as foul with rank diseases (III.i.39), and recalls Richard's prophecy that "foul sin gathering head / Shall break into corruption" (III.i.76–77). There are a number of other images of expulsion, such as the striking case where the rebels speak of the need to "purge th' obstructions which begin to stop / Our very veins of life" (IV.i.65–66). Henry himself is sick, in the last half of the play, and there are repeated suggestions that his sickness is the consequence both of his sinful usurpation and of the struggle to defend it. Since his usurpation was almost a public duty, and his defense of order clearly for England's sake as well as his own advantage, he becomes in these last scenes almost a sacrificial figure, a king who sins for the sake of society, suffers for society in suffering for his sin, and carries his sin off into death. Hal speaks of the crown having "fed upon the body of my father" (IV.v.160). Henry, in his last long speech, summarizes this pat-tern in saying:

> God knows, my son,
> By what bypaths and indirect crook'd ways
> I met this crown; and I myself know well
> How troublesome it sat upon my head.
> To thee it shall descend with better quiet,
> Better opinion, better confirmation;
> For all the soil of the achievement goes
> With me into the earth.
> (IV.v.184–191)

The same image of burying sin occurs in some curious lines with which Hal reassures his brothers:

> My father is gone wild into his grave;
> For in his tomb lie my affections . . .
>   (V.ii.123–124)

This conceit not only suggests an expulsion of evil, but hints at the patricidal motive which is referred to explicitly elsewhere in these final scenes and is the complement of the father-son atonement.

Now this sacrificial imagery, where used by and about the old king, is effectively dramatic, because it does not ask the audience to abandon any part of the awareness of a human, social situation which the play as a whole has expressed. But the case is altered when Hal turns on "that father ruffian" Falstaff. The new king's whip-lash lines stress Falstaff's age and glance at his death:

> I know thee not, old man. Fall to thy prayers.
> How ill white hairs become a fool and jester!
> I have long dreamt of such a kind of man,
> So surfeit-swell'd, so old, and so profane;
> But being awak'd, I do despise my dream.
> Make less thy body, hence, and more thy grace;
> Leave gormandising. Know the grave doth gape
> For thee thrice wider than for other men.
>   (V.v.51–58)

The priggish tone, to which so many have objected, can be explained at one level as appropriate to the solemn occasion of a coronation. But it goes with a drastic narrowing of awareness. There are of course occasions in life when people close off parts of their minds—a coronation is a case in point: Shakespeare, it can be argued, is simply putting such an occasion into his play. But even his genius could not get around the fact that to block off awareness of irony is contradictory to the very nature of drama, which has as one of its functions the extension of such awareness. Hal's lines, redefining his holiday with Falstaff as a dream, and then despising the dream, seek to invalidate that holiday pole of life, instead of including it, as his lines on his old acquaintance did at the end of *Part One*. (Elsewhere in Shakespeare, to dismiss dreams categorically is foolhardy.) And those lines about the thrice-wide grave: are they a threat or a joke? We cannot tell, because the sort of consciousness that would confirm a joke is being damped out: "Reply not to me with a fool-born jest" (V.v.59). If ironies about Hal were expressed by the context, we could take the scene as the representation of his becoming a prig. But there is simply a blur in the tone, a blur which results, I think, from a retreat into magic by the *dramatist,* as distinct from his characters. Magically, the line about burying the belly is exactly the appropriate threat. It goes with the other images of burying sin and wildness and conveys the idea that the grave can swallow what Falstaff's belly stands for. To assume that one can cope with a pervasive attitude of mind by dealing physically with its most prominent symbol—what is this but magic-mongering? It is the same sort of juggling which we get in Henry IV's sentimental lines taking literally the name of the Jerusalem chamber in the palace:

> Laud be to God! Even there my life must end.
> It hath been prophesied to me many years,
> I should not die but in Jerusalem . . .
> (IV.v.236–238) .

One can imagine making a mockery of Henry's pious ejaculation by catcalling a version of his final lines at the close of *Richard II* (V.vi.49–50):

> Is this that voyage to the Holy Land
> To wash the blood from off your guilty hand?

An inhibition of irony goes here with Henry's making the symbol do for the thing, just as it does with Hal's expulsion of Falstaff. A return to an official view of the sanctity of state is achieved by sentimental use of magical relations.

We can now suggest a few tentative conclusions of a general sort about the relation of comedy to ritual. It appears that comedy uses ritual in the process of redefining ritual as the expression of particular personalities in particular circumstances. The heritage of ritual gives universality and depth. The persons of the drama make the customary gestures developed in ritual observance, and, in doing so, they project in a whole-hearted way attitudes which are not normally articulated at large. At the same time, the dramatization of such gestures involves being aware of their relation to the whole of experience in a way which is not necessary for the celebrants of a ritual proper. In the actual observance of customary misrule, the control of the disruptive motives which the festivity expresses is achieved by the group's recognition of the place of the whole business within the larger rhythm of their continuing social life. No one need decide, therefore, whether the identifications involved in the ceremony are magically valid or merely expressive. But in the drama, perspective and control depend on presenting, along with the ritual gestures, an expression of a social situation out of which they grow. So the drama must control magic by reunderstanding it as imagination: dramatic irony must constantly dog the wish that the mock king be real, that the self be all the world or set all the world at naught. When, through a failure of irony, the dramatist presents ritual as magically valid, the result is sentimental, since drama lacks the kind of control which in ritual comes from the auditors' being participants. Sentimental "drama," that which succeeds in being neither comedy nor tragedy, can be regarded from this vantage as theater used as a substitute for ritual, without the commitment to participation and discipline proper to ritual nor the commitment to the fullest under-standing proper to comedy or tragedy.

Historically, Shakespeare's drama can be seen as part of the process by which our culture has moved from absolutist modes of thought towards a historical and psychological view of man. But though the Renaissance moment made the tension between a magical and an empirical view of man particularly acute, this pull is of course always present: it is the tension between the heart and the world. By incarnating ritual as plot and character, the dramatist finds an embodiment for the heart's drastic ges-tures while recognizing how the world keeps comically and tragically giving them the lie.

A . P . ROSSITER

Angel with Horns:
The Unity of "Richard III"

'Let's write "good angel" on the devil's horn.'
—MEASURE FOR MEASURE, II.iv. 16

In the Second Part of *Henry IV* (III. i.) the King and Warwick are talking away the midnight, or the King's insomnia; and the King remembers how Richard spoke like a prophet of the future treachery of the Percies. Warwick replies that those who look for rotations in history can indeed appear to be prophets:

> There is a history in all men's lives,
> Figuring the nature of the times deceas'd;
> The which observ'd, a man may prophesy,
> With a near aim, of the main chance of things
> As yet not come to life, who in their seeds
> And weak beginnings lie intreasured.
> Such things become the hatch and brood of time.

Richard, he explains, had observed 'the necessary form' of the events he had seen happen; and from that he could 'create a perfect guess' of some that were to ensue as 'the hatch and brood of time'.

Men have always looked for such a predictability in history: it gives the illusion of a comfortably ordered world. They have also often read—and written—historical records to show that the course of events has been

---

From *Angel with Horns*. Copyright © 1961 by Longmans Group, Ltd.

guided by a simple process of divine justice, dispensing rewards and punishments here on earth and seeing to it that the wicked do *not* thrive like the green bay-tree (as the Psalmist thought), and that virtue is not 'triumphant only in theatrical performances' (as the humane Mikado put it: being a Gilbertian Japanese, not an Elizabethan Christian). The storymatter of the Henry VI plays and of *Richard III* accepted both of these comforting and comfortable principles.

When I say 'story-matter' I mean what the Chronicles gave the author (or authors) of these four plays, and I wish to remain uncommitted as to whether their *plots* (and especially that of *Richard III*) work entirely within those reassuring limitations.

I am averse to source-study, as material for lectures. Yet sad experience of human nature (and perhaps of historians) leads me to remind you how the Richard III myth ('*story*') came to reach Shakespeare. In the play, you remember, the Bishop of Ely, Morton, plots with Buckingham and runs away to join Richmond (Henry Tudor). He duly became one of Henry's ministers; and Thomas More grew up in his household—and later wrote the life of Richard III. It would only be human if Morton recounted all the worst that was ever said of the master he had betrayed: it is not surprising that Edward Halle should accept More's account, in writing his vast book on the 'noble and illustre families of Lancastre and York'; and still more human that Raphael Holinshed (whom no one could call a historian) should copy extensively from Halle—and so leave room for all those since Horace Walpole who have had doubts about the historical character of this terrible monarch and the events of his times.

To think that we are seeing anything like sober history in this play is derisible naïvety. What we are offered is a formally patterned sequence presenting two things: on the one hand, a rigid Tudor *schema* of retributive justice (a sort of analogy to Newton's Third Law in the field of moral dynamics: 'Action and reaction are equal and *apposite*'); and, on the other, a huge triumphant stage-personality, an early old masterpiece of the art of rhetorical stage-writing, a monstrous being incredible in any sober, historical scheme of things—Richard himself.

I will talk about the first, first. The basic pattern of retributive justice (or God's vengeance) is well enough illustrated in Holinshed, in the passage telling how Prince Edward (Henry VI's son and Margaret's) was murdered at the Battle of Tewkesbury. The Prince was handed over to Edward IV on the proclamation of a promise that he would not be harmed; he was brought before the King, asked why he 'durst so presumptuously enter into his realm' and replied courageously 'To recover my father's kingdom and heritage' (and more to that purpose)—but let Holinshed say the rest:

> At which words king Edward said nothing, but with his hand thrust him from him, or (as some saie) stroke him with his gantlet; whom incontinentlie, George duke of Clarence, Richard duke of Glocester, Thomas Greie marquesse Dorcet, and William lord Hastings, that stood by, suddenlie murthered; for the which cruell act, the more part of the dooers in their latter daies dranke of the like cup, by the righteous justice and due punishment of God.

There you have the notional pattern, in little, of the whole framework of *Richard III*: Clarence—'false, fleeting, perjur'd Clarence' (who took the sacrament to remain true to Henry VI of Lancaster and deserted him); Gray—one of the group of Queen Elizabeth Woodeville's relations, who fall to Richard and Buckingham next after Clarence; Hastings, who says he will see 'this crown of mine hewn from its shoulders/ Before I see the crown so foul misplaced' (on Richard's head)—and *does* (if a man can be said to see his own decapitation). Holinshed really understates the matter in writing 'the more part of the dooers . . . dranke of the like cup'; for of those he names, everyone did. On the one hand, that is what *Richard III* is about: what it is composed of. A heavy-handed justice commends the ingredients of a poisoned [cup].

This notional pattern of historic events rigidly determined by a mechanical necessity is partly paralleled by, partly modified by, the formal patterns of the episodes (or scenes) and the language. By 'formal patterns' I mean the unmistakably iterated goings-on in scenes so exactly parallel that if the first *is* passable on a modern stage as quasi-realistic costume-play stuff, the second (repeating it always *more* unrealistically) cannot be. The two wooing-scenes (Richard with Anne and Elizabeth) are the simplest case; but in the lamentation-scenes—where a collection of bereft females comes together and goes through a dismal catalogue of *Who was Who* and *Who has lost Whom* (like a gathering of historical Mrs. Gummidges, each 'thinking of the old 'un' with shattering simultaneity)—there, even editors have found the proceedings absurd; and readers difficult. When Queen Margaret, for example, says:

> I had an Edward, till a Richard kill'd him;
> I had a husband, till a Richard kill'd him:
> Thou hadst an Edward, till a Richard kill'd him;
> Thou hadst a Richard, till a Richard kill'd him.
>
> (IV. iv. 40–43)

a reader may *just* keep up (and realize that the last two are the Princes in the Tower, so that Queen Elizabeth is being addressed); but when the Duchess of York takes up with

> I had a Richard too, and thou didst kill him;
> I had a Rutland too, thou holp'st to kill him,

it is likely that you are lost, unless your recollection of *3 Henry VI* and the ends of Richard, Duke of York and his young son (Edmund) is unusually clear.

It is not only the iteration of scene that is stylized: the stiffly formal manipulation of echoing phrase and sequence of words within the scenes is even more unrealistic. A closely related parallelism exists in the repeated occurrence of a sort of 'single line traffic' in sentences: the classicist's *stichomythia*. One speaker takes from the other exactly the same ration of syllables, and rejoins as if under contract to repeat the form of the given sentence as exactly as possible, using the maximum number of the same words or their logical opposites, or (failing that) words closely associated with them. I describe the game pedantically, because it *is* an exact and scientific game with language, and one of the graces and beauties of the play Shakespeare wrote. If we cannot accept the 'patterned speech' of *Richard III*, its quality must remain unknown to us. 'Early work' is an evasive, criticism-dodging term. Early it may be; but the play is a triumphant contrivance in a manner which cannot properly be compared with that of any other tragedy—nor of any history, except *3 Henry VI* (where the manner takes shape, and particularly in III. ii.) and *King John* (which is not half so well built or integrated as this).

I have emphasized the stylization of verbal patterning (with its neatly over-exact adjustments of stroke to stroke, as in royal tennis), because the sequence of most of the important events offers very much the same pattern. I might remark, in passing, that these verbal devices were offering to the Elizabethans an accomplished English equivalent to the neat dexterities they admired in Seneca (a point made by T. S. Eliot years ago; though he did not examine how the dramatic ironies of the action run in parallel with these counter-stroke reversals of verbal meaning, and form a kind of harmony). But we miss something more than Shakespeare's rhetorical game of tennis if merely irritated by, e.g.:

> ANNE: I would I knew thy heart.
> RICHARD: 'Tis figured in my tongue.
> ANNE: I fear me, both are false.
> RICHARD: Then never man was true.

Those reversals of intention (*heart-tongue; false-true*) are on precisely the pattern of the repeated reversals of human expectation, the reversals of events, the anticipated reversals (foreseen only by the audience), which make 'dramatic irony'. The patterned speech of the dialogue—the wit that demonstrates that a sentence is but a cheveril glove, quickly turned the other way—is fundamentally one with the ironic patterns of the plot. 'Dramatic irony' here is verbal *peripeteia*.

You will see that simply exemplified if you read Buckingham's speech at the beginning of Act II, where he calls a curse on himself if ever he goes back on his reconciliation with the Queen (and is quite specific about it); then turn straight to his last lines in V. i., when he is on the way to execution: 'That high All-seer, which I dallied with.' He has got exactly what he asked for. He did not mean the words he used, but they have been reversed into actuality, in exactly the same way as verbal terms are reversed in the tennis-court game of rhetoric.

The same irony plays all over *Richard III*. It lurks like a shadow behind the naïvely self-confident Hastings; it hovers a moment over Buckingham when Margaret warns him against 'yonder dog' (Richard), and, on Richard's asking what she said, he replies, 'Nothing that I respect, my gracious lord' (I. iii. 296)—and this at a time when Buckingham is under no threat whatsoever.

Its cumulative effect is to present the personages as existing in a state of total and terrible uncertainty. This is enhanced if we know the details of what comes into the play from *3 Henry VI*, but is there even if we know only a few bare essentials of what has gone before. We need to know who Margaret is; how Lancaster has been utterly defeated, and King Henry and his son murdered; how Clarence betrayed his King and returned to the Yorkists; and how Richard, his younger brother, has already marked him as his immediate obstruction on his intended way to the crown. We need to know too that the Duchess of York is mother to that unrewarding trio, Edward IV, Clarence, Gloucester; that Edward IV has married an aspiring commoner, Elizabeth Grey (*née* Woodeville); and that she has jacked up her relations into nobility. Beyond those half-dozen facts we do not need back-reference to *3 Henry VI* for any but the finer points—so far as the essential ironies of the plot go.

Far more important than these details is the simple overriding principle derived from the Tudor historians: that England rests under a chronic curse—the curse of faction, civil dissension and fundamental anarchy, resulting from the deposition and murder of the Lord's Anointed (Richard II) and the usurpation of the House of Lancaster. The savageries of the Wars of the Roses follow logically (almost theologically) from that;

and Elizabeth's 'All-seeing heaven, what a world is this!' says but half. It is a world of absolute and hereditary moral ill, in which *everyone* (till the appearance of Richmond-Tudor in Act V) is tainted with the treacheries, the blood and the barbarities of civil strife, and internally blasted with the curse of a moral anarchy which leaves but three human *genera*: the strong in evil, the feebly wicked and the helplessly guilt-tainted (such as the Princes, Anne—all those despairing, lamenting women, whose choric wailings are a penitentional psalm of guilt and sorrow: England's guilt, the individual's sorrow). The 'poor painted Queen's' 'What a world' needs supplementing with the words of the pessimistically clear-sighted Third Citizen:

> All may be well; but, if God sort it so,
> 'Tis more than we deserve or I expect.
> (II. iii. 36)

I have in effect described the meaning of the framework of the play: presented it as 'moral history', to be interpreted in abstract terms. But the play itself is also a symphonic structure which I can only describe in terms of music: a rhetorical symphony of five movements, with first and second subjects and some Wagnerian *Leitmotifs*. The play-making framework is Senecan revenge, the characterization largely Marlovian; but the orchestration is not only original, but unique. It can be sketched like this.

The first movement employs five 'subjects': Richard himself, his own overture; the wooing-theme (to be repeated in the fourth movement); Richard among his enemies (repeating the duplicity with which he has fooled Clarence); Margaret's curse; and the long dying fall of Clarence. It occupies the whole of Act I.

The second movement includes Act II. and scenes i.-iv. of Act III. It begins with the King's feeble peace-making—in which Buckingham invites his curse—and its other subjects are: a lamentation after the King's death (repeated in the fourth movement); the fall of the curse on Rivers, Grey and Vaughan (when the curse is remembered), and on Hastings (the curse briefly recalled again). The future subject of Richard's moves against the Princes is introduced between-whiles.

The third movement cuts across the Act-divisions and runs from III. v. to IV. iii. Its main subject is the Gloucester-Buckingham plot for the crown, with the magnificently sardonic fooling of the London *bourgeoisie* with a crisis-scare, a brace of bishops, and the headline-story that here is a highly respectable unlibidinous monarch for decent England. On its success, Anne is called to be Queen, and thus to meet the curse she herself called on Richard's wife before he wooed her in that humour and won her (the first movement is here caught up). Buckingham now makes himself one of Richard's future victims by showing reluctance for the plot against the Princes, and Richard throws him off with a snub. The Princes are dealt with (the account of Forrest and Deighton echoing that of the murderers of Clarence, one of whom had a temporary conscience); and Richard concludes with a brisk summary and prospectus:

> The sons of Edward sleep in Abraham's bosom,
> And Anne my wife hath bid this world good night;

and so, since Richmond plans to marry 'young Elizabeth, my brother's daughter,' 'To her go I, a jolly thriving wooer'. (Richard's last jocularity). The movement ends with the first murmurs of Richmond. Previously there has been slipped in the trivial-sounding prophecy about 'Rugemount', besides Henry VI's prophecy (IV. ii. 90 f.). The flight of the Bishop of Ely (Morton) really troubles Richard.

The fourth movement brings down the curse on Buckingham (v.i. is obviously misplaced, so the movement runs from IV. iv. to v.i. inclusive). Mainly it repeats themes heard before: with a long lamentation-scene (the Blake-like weeping Queens); a repetition of Margaret's curse with the curse of Richard's mother added; the second wooing-scene; the subject of Nemesis repeated by Buckingham. In it the sound of Richmond's advance has become clearer; and Richard's self-command and certainty begin to waver.

The fifth movement is all at Bosworth: the fall of the curse on Richard himself. There is the dream-prologue of the procession of contra-puntal Ghosts (including all those so qualified from the four previous movements) and, like all ghosts, they are reminiscent and repetitive. The play ends with the epilogue to the Wars of the Roses—spoken by Queen Elizabeth's grandfather—calling a blessing on the English future, and inverting the opening lines of Richard's prologue:

> Now is the winter of our discontent
> Made glorious summer . . .

The deliberateness of this highly controlled workmanship needs but little comment. I shall take up a single musical phrase: one that intertwines its plangent undertones throughout the whole symphony, a true *Leitmotif*.

At first sight, Clarence's dream (I. iv. 9 f.) appears to contribute little to the play, nothing to the plot; and it may seem a rhetorical indulgence, even if we accept Mr. Eliot's judgement that it shows 'a real approximation in English to the magnificence of Senecan Latin at its best. . . . The best of Seneca has here been absorbed into English.' But first recollect the setting. Clarence has been sent to the Tower, by the machinations of the Queen's party (so he thinks), and he is confident that his brother Richard will stand good friend to him. He believes Richard's worried 'We are not safe, Clarence; we are not safe'; cannot possibly see the ironical joke Richard is cracking with himself; has no idea that he has been first on Richard's list since that moment in 3 Henry VI (v. vi. 84) when his brother muttered, 'Clarence, beware; thou keep'st me from the light'. (A line that follows a passage predetermining the gulling of both Clarence and Anne to follow:

> I have no brother, I am like no brother;
> And this word 'love', which greybeards call divine,
> Be resident in men like one another,
> And not in me! I am myself alone).

Clarence had not been there to hear that: knows nothing of the typically sharp reversal of Richard's solemnly hypocritical fooling now with:

> Go tread the path that thou shalt ne'er return.
> Simple, plain Clarence, I do love thee so
> That I will shortly send thy soul to heaven,
> If heaven will take the present at our hands.
>   (I. i. 117–20)

Clarence has his nightmare in the Tower: a vision prophetic of doom, and thick with curdled guilt. He dreams that Richard blunderingly knocks him overboard from a vessel; he drowns; goes to hell; and his guilt-sick mind spews up its own evil:

> KEEPER: Awak'd you not in this sore agony?
> CLARENCE: No, no, my dream was lenthen'd after life.
>   Oh, then began the tempest to my soul!
>   I pass'd, methought, the melancholy flood
>   With that sour ferryman which poets write of,
>   Unto the kingdom of perpetual night.
>   The first that there did greet my stranger soul
>   Was my great father-in-law, renowned Warwick,
>   Who spake aloud 'What scourge for perjury
>   Can this dark monarchy afford false Clarence?'
>   And so he vanish'd. Then came wand'ring by
>   A shadow like an angel, with bright hair
>   Dabbled in blood, and he shriek'd out aloud
>   'Clarence is come—false, fleeting, perjur'd Clarence,
>   That stabb'd me in the field by Tewkesbury.
>   Seize on him, Furies, take him unto torment!'
>   (I. iv. 42–57)

It is as fine a passage in that style as English can offer: calculated to leave
its solemn music in even half-attentive ears. In the second movement of
the play (II. ii. 43 f.), Queen Elizabeth announces the King's death:

> If you will live, lament; if die, be brief,
> That our swift-winged souls may catch the King's,
> Or like obedient subjects follow him
> To his new kingdom of ne'er-changing night.

It is scarcely a proper-wifely expectation of the fate of her husband's spirit:
but the echo of 'Unto the kingdom of perpetual night' is the effect
intended, not Elizabeth's notions. The actors who put together the Q.
text of 1597 showed that they appreciated, if clumsily, the author's
intention. They made it 'To his new kingdom of perpetuall rest': catching
the echo rightly, while missing the point.

The same 'dark monarchy' awaits all these people: they are the
living damned. That is the translation of this echo-technique of *Leitmotifs*;
and why I call the play's anatomy 'musical'. Nor is that all: the phrase
returns again. But before I come to that, remark how Hastings philoso-
phizes on his fall at the end of the second movement:

> O momentary grace of mortal men,
> Which we more hunt for than the grace of God!
> Who builds his hope in air of your good looks
> Lives like a drunken sailor on a mast,
> Ready with every nod to tumble down
> Into the fatal bowels of the deep.
>   (XIII. iv. 98–103)

We have heard that surging rhythm before. And with it the feeling of
being aloft, in air, unbalanced: the rhythm of Clarence dreaming:

> As we pac'd along
> Upon the giddy footing of the hatches,
> Methought that Gloucester stumbled, and in falling
> Struck me, that thought to stay him, overboard
> Into the tumbling billows of the main.
>   (I. iv. 16–20)

Pattern repeats pattern with remarkable exactitude. 'Into the fatal bowels
of the deep' is where the giddy Hastings also goes. 'O Lord, methought
what pain it was to drown' might be extended to all these desperate
swimmers in the tide of pomp and history. The elaboration of the dream is
no mere exercise in fine phrase on Latin models: it offers a symbol of
choking suspense above black depths (the ocean, and perpetual night)

which epitomizes the 'momentary grace' of all these 'mortal men' and women. And the sea as figure of 'the destructive element' appears again in Elizabeth's lines in the second wooing-scene:

> But that still use of grief makes wild grief tame,
> My tongue should to thy ears not name my boys
> Till that my nails were anchor'd in thine eyes;
> And I, in such a desp'rate bay of death,
> Like a poor bark, of sails and tackling reft,
> Rush all to pieces on thy rocky bosom.
>
> (IV. iv. 229–34)

'Bay' of death suggests also an animal at bay; just plausibly relevant, since Richard (the boar) would be at bay when she *could* scratch his eyes out. But the repetition of the rather too emphatic anchors and the eyes from Clarence's dream is much more striking.

You will find a further echo of the 'night-motif' in the last movement. Richard suspects Stanley (confusingly also called Derby), and reasonably so: for he was husband to the Countess of Richmond, Henry Tudor's mother, the famous Lady Margaret Beaufort; and therefore keeps his son, George Stanley, as hostage. Before Bosworth, he sends a brisk message to warn the father of the black depths beneath the son; and again Shakespeare sounds his doom-music from the Clarence sequence:

> . . . bid him bring his power
> Before sunrising, lest his son George fall
> Into the blind cave of eternal night.
>
> (V. iii. 60–2)

Need I remark that Clarence was 'George' too, and lightly called that by Richard when he was afraid that King Edward might die before he signed his brother's death-warrant?

> He cannot live, I hope, and must not die
> Till George be packed with post-horse up to heaven.
>
> (I. ii. 145)

I could further exemplify the play's tight-woven artistry by taking up that very remarkable prose-speech on 'conscience' by Clarence's Second Murderer (I. iv. 133 f.), and following the word into Richard's troubled mind in Act V. before Margaret's curse attains its last fulfilment. But to reduce attention to Richard himself in his own play, beyond what I am already committed to by my insistence on taking the play as a *whole* (as a dramatic pattern, not an exposition of 'character'), would be to do it—and Shakespeare—an injustice.

Richard Plantagenet is alone with Macbeth as the Shakespearian version of the thoroughly bad man in the role of monarch and hero; he is unique in combining with that role that of the diabolic humorist. It is this quality which makes it an inadequate account to say that the play is 'moral history', or that the protagonists are the personality of Richard and the curse of Margaret (or what it stood for in orthodox Tudor thinking about retributive justice in history)—for all that these opposed 'forces' *are* central throughout. The first movement establishes both, and emphatically. First, Richard, stumping down the stage on his unequal legs, forcing his hitched-up left shoulder and his withered arm on us, till we realize that *this* is what the 'winter of our discontent' in *3 Henry VI* has produced, *this* the proper 'hatch and brood of time'; and then, Richard established, his cruel and sardonic effectiveness demonstrated on Clarence and Anne, there arises against his brazen Carl Orff-like music the one voice he quails before (if but slightly): the sub-dominant notes of Margaret and her prophecy of doom, to which the ghosts will walk in the visionary night before Bosworth. It is a conflict between a spirit and a ghost: between Richard, the spirit of ruthless will, of daemonic pride, energy and self-sufficiency, of devilish gusto and *Schadenfreude* (he *enjoys* wickedness even when it is of no practical advantage to his ambitions or to securing himself by murder: it may be only wickedness in *words*, but the spirit revealed is no less evilly exultant for that); and the ghost, as I call her—for what else is Margaret, Reignier's daughter picked up on a battlefield by Suffolk and married to that most etiolated of Shakespeare's husbands, Henry VI, but the living ghost of Lancaster, the walking dead, memorializing the long, cruel, treacherous, bloody conflict of the years of civil strife and pitiless butchery?

You can, of course, see more there if you will. Make her the last stage or age of woman-in-politics: she who has been beautiful, fiercely passionate, queenly, dominating, master of armies, *generalissima*; now old, defeated, empty of everything but fierce bitterness, the illimitable bitterness and rancour of political zeal. What did Yeats write of *his* equivalent symbol? It is in *A Prayer for my Daughter*. For her he prays:

> An intellectual hatred is the worst,
> So let her think opinions are accursed.
> Have I not seen the loveliest woman born
> Out of the mouth of Plenty's horn,
> Because of her opinionated mind
> Barter that horn and every good
> By quiet natures understood
> For an old bellows full of angry wind?

Margaret is that, if you like; but, not to go beyond Shakespeare, I cannot but think that when the old Duchess of York sits down upon the ground for the second lamentation-scene (to tell 'sad stories of the death of kings'), the *author's* mind ran more upon Margaret as he wrote:

> Dead life, blind sight, poor mortal living ghost, . . .
> Brief abstract and record of tedious days,
> Rest thy unrest on England's lawful earth,
> Unlawfully made drunk with innocent blood.
> (IV. iv. 26, 28–30)

Here Shakespeare devises a new variation on the Senecan visitant from another world howling for revenge, by making the spectre nominal flesh and blood; the tune of the Dance of Death to which all dance to damnation is played by Margaret; and one aspect of the play is our watching the rats go into the Weser, compelled by that fatal tune.

But Richard himself is not simply the last and most important (and worst) of the victims—if those justly destroyed can be called 'victims'. That is just where the label 'moral history' is inadequate. For Richard has grown a new dimension since his abrupt and remarkable development in *3 Henry VI*: he has become a wit, a mocking comedian, a 'vice of kings' —but with a clear inheritance from the old Vice of the Moralities: part symbol of evil, part comic devil, and chiefly, on the stage, the generator of roars of laughter at wickednesses (whether of deed or word) which the audience would immediately condemn in real life. On the one hand, his literary relations with the Senecan 'Tyrant' (author of 'In regna mea Mors impetratur', etc.) are clear enough; as they are with the Elizabethan myth of 'the murderous Machiavel' ('feared am I more than loved/Let me be feared,' etc.): enough has been written on them. But only the medieval heritage—from the comic devils with their *Schadenfreude,* and the Vice as comic inverter of order and decency—can fully explain the new Richard of this apparent sequel to the *Henry VI* series.

I have said that the Christian pattern imposed on history gives the simple plot of a cast accursed, where all are evil beings, all deserve punishment. Look, then, with a believing Tudor eye, and ought you not to *approve* Richard's doings? *Per se*, they are the judgment of God on the wicked; and he

> *Ein Teil von jener Kraft*
> *Die stets das Böse will, und stets das Gute schafft.*

A part of that Power which always wills evil and yet always brings about good.

(Goethe's *Faust*)

But that is not all. Richard's sense of humour, his function as clown, his comic irreverences and sarcastic or sardonic appropriations of things to (at any rate) *his* occasions: all those act as underminers of our assumed naïve and proper Tudor principles; and we are on his side much rather because he makes us (as the Second Murderer put it) 'take the devil in [our] mind', than for any 'historical-philosophical-Christian-retributional' sort of motive. In this respect a good third of the play is a kind of grisly *comedy*; in which we meet the fools to be taken in on Richard's terms, see them with his mind, and rejoice with him in their stultification (in which execution is the ultimate and unanswerable practical joke, the absolutely final laugh this side of the Day of Judgment). Here, Richard is a middle-term between Barabas, the Jew of Malta (*c.* 1590) and Volpone (1606). He inhabits a world where everyone deserves everything he can do to them; and in his murderous practical joking he is *inclusively* the comic exposer of the mental shortcomings (the intellectual and moral deformities) of this world of beings depraved and besotted. If we forget to pity them awhile (and he does his best to help us), then his impish spirit urges us towards a positive reversal of 'Christian charity' until the play's fourth movement (which is when the Elizabethan spectator began to back out, I take it)—or even beyond that point.

An aspect of Richard's appeal, which has, I fancy, passed relatively unexamined, is one that we can be confident that William Shakespeare felt and reflected on. I mean the appeal of the actor: the talented being who can assume every mood and passion at will, at all events to the extent of making others believe in it. Beyond question, all our great actors have regarded the part as a fine opportunity. The extent to which the histrionic art (as Shakespeare thought and felt about it) contributed to the making of this great stage-figure is to me more interesting.

The specific interest here is the *power* that would be in the hands of an actor consummate enough to make (quite literally) 'all the world a stage' and to work on humanity by the perfect simulation of every feeling: the appropriate delivery of every word and phrase that will serve his immediate purpose; together with the complete dissimulation of everything that might betray him (whether it be his intentions, or such obstructive feelings as compunction, pity or uncertainty of mind). This appears at once when Gloucester first takes shape as the man self-made to be King, in the long soliloquy in *3 Henry VI* (III. ii. 124 f.). The closing lines are specifically on histrionic genius:

> Why, I can smile, and murder whiles I smile,
> And cry 'Content!' to that which grieves my heart,

> And wet my cheeks with artificial tears,
> And frame my face to all occasions.
>   (ibid. 182–5)

And then, after a little bragging prospectus on his intended deadliness, he ends:

> I can add colours to the chameleon,
> Change shapes with Protheus for advantages,
> And set the murderous Machiavel to school.
> Can I do this, and cannot get a crown?
> Tut, were it farther off, I'll pluck it down.
>   (ibid. 191–5)

M. R. Ridley notes here that 'Machiavelli . . . seems to have been to the Elizabethans a type of one who advocated murder as a method of cold-blooded policy.' It is true that that marks off one point of difference between the 'Senecan' tyrant-villainy (which is primarily for revenge) and the 'Machiavellian' (which is for power, or self-aggrandizement: 'We that are great, our own self-good still moves us'): though I do not think that the distinction can be maintained, if you read Seneca. But surely Ridley's note misses the point, in its context? What the 'Machiavel' allusion represents is, I believe, Shakespeare's recognition that the programme set before the Prince in *Il Principe* is one that demands exactly those histrionic qualities I have just described: a lifelong, unremitting vigilance in relentless simulation and impenetrable deception. There, precisely, lies the super-humanity of the Superman. The will-to-power is shorn of its effective power without it. He is an *artist* in evil.

Now Richard in his own play shows this power—these powers—to perfection. Except to the audience, he is invisible; but the audience he keeps reminded not only of his real intentions, but equally of his actor's artistries. The bluff plain Englishman, shocked at ambitious go-getters and grievingly misunderstood, is perfectly 'done' before the Queen's relations:

> Because I cannot flatter and look fair,
> Smile in men's faces, smooth, deceive, and cog,
> Duck with French nods and apish courtesy,
> I must be held a rancorous enemy.
> Cannot a plain man live and think no harm
> But thus his simple truth must be abus'd
> With silken, sly, insinuating Jacks?
>   (I. iii. 47–53)

A little later, it is: 'I am too childish-foolish for this world,' (ibid., 142); and even: 'I thank my God for my humility'. (II. i. 72).

Then, left to himself and the audience, after egging on all their quarrels:

> But then I sigh and, with a piece of Scripture,
> Tell them that God bids us do good for evil.
> And thus I clothe my naked villainy
> With odd old ends stol'n forth of holy writ,
> And seem a saint when most I play the devil.
>   (I. iii. 334–8)

The stage-direction, *'Enter two Murderers'*, caps this nicely. It is not simply that Richard is a hypocrite and (like other stage-villains) tells us so. The actor's technique of 'asides' is the essence of his chuckling private jokes—made to 'myself alone'. (You might say that Shakespeare is giving not merely 'the acting of drama', but also 'the drama of consummate *acting*').

The same reminders, nudging the audience's attention, appear in his swift-switched actual asides: e.g., his thoroughly unholy reception of his mother's blessing, spoken as he gets up off his dutiful knees:

> Amen! And make me die a good old man!
> That is the butt end of a mother's blessing;
> I marvel that her Grace did leave it out.
>   (II. ii. 109–11)

Or, again, we have Richard's insinuating equivocations in talking to the prattling little Princes; in one of which he acknowledges his theatrical-historical legacy from the Moralities: 'Thus, like the formal vice, Iniquity,/I moralize two meanings in one word.' (III. i. 82–3). Over and above this there is that striking passage (III. v. 1–11) where he and Buckingham are working up a crisis (appearing ill-dressed in old rusty armour, as if they had armed in desperate haste), when Richard specifically inquires whether Buckingham can 'do the stage-tragedian':

> RICHARD: Come, cousin, canst thou quake and change thy colour,
>   Murder thy breath in middle of a word,
>   And then again begin, and stop again,
>   As if thou wert distraught and mad with terror?
> BUCKINGHAM: Tut, I can counterfeit the deep tragedian;
>   Speak and look back, and pry on every side,
>   Tremble and start at wagging of a straw,
>   Intending deep suspicion. Ghastly looks
>   Are at my service, like enforced smiles;
>   And both are ready in their offices
>   At any time to grace my stratagems.

It is all sardonically jocular; but nothing shows more clearly the artist's delight in his craft: call it illusion or deception, it makes no odds. It is this dexterity that his other rapid reversals of tone keep us aware of; whether he is half-amazedly rejoicing in his conquest of Anne, or poking unfilial fun at his mother (a performance more shocking to Elizabethans than to our more child-foolish days).

Yet again, there is that admirable moment when the Londoners are being fooled into believing that he must be persuaded to be king; when Buckingham pretends to lose patience, with 'Zounds, I'll entreat no more.' And Richard, bracketed aloft with two Bishops, is distressed: 'O, do not swear, my lord of Buckingham.' (III. vii. 220). (It is like the moment in *Eric or Little by Little* (ch. 8) when Eric refers to the usher as a 'surly devil'; and the virtuous Russell exclaims: 'O Eric, that is the first time that I have heard you swear.') It is this unholy jocularity, the readiness of sarcastic, sardonic, profane and sometimes blasphemous wit, the demonic gusto of it all, which not only wins the audience over to accepting the Devil as hero, but also points us towards the central paradox of the play. And, through that, to a full critical awareness of its unity: with a few remarks on which I shall conclude.

To begin with Richard. On the face of it, he is the demon-Prince, the cacodemon born of hell, the misshapen toad, etc. (all things ugly and ill). But through his prowess as actor and his embodiment of the comic Vice and impish-to-fiendish humour, he offers the false as more attractive than the true (the actor's function), and the ugly and evil as admirable and amusing (the clown's game of value-reversals). You can say, 'We don't take him seriously.' I reply, 'That is exactly what gets most of his acquaintances into Hell: just what the devil-clown relies on.' But he is not only his demon incarnate, he is in effect God's agent in a predetermined plan of divine retribution: the 'scourge of God'. Now by Tudor-Christian historical principles, this plan is *right*. Thus, in a real sense, Richard is a King who 'can do no wrong'; for in the pattern of the justice of divine retribution on the wicked, he functions as an avenging angel. Hence my paradoxical title, 'Angel with Horns.'

The paradox is sharpened by what I have mainly passed by: the repulsiveness, humanely speaking, of the 'justice'. God's will it may be, but it sickens us: it is as pitiless as the Devil's (who is called in to execute it). The contrast with Marlowe's painless, dehumanized slaughterings in *Tamburlaine* is patent.

This overall system of *paradox* is the play's unity. It is revealed as a constant displaying of inversions, or reversals of meaning: whether we consider the verbal patterns (the *peripeteias* or reversals of act and intention or expectation); the antithesis of false and true in the histrionic character; or the constant inversions of irony. Those verbal capsizings I began by talking about, with their deliberate reversals to the opposite meaning in equivocal terms, are the exact correlatives of both the nature of man (or man in power: Richard) and of the nature of events (history); and of language too, in which all is conveyed.

But, start where you will, you come back to history; or to the pattern made out of the conflict of two 'historical myths'. The orthodox Tudor myth made history God-controlled, divinely prescribed and dispensed, to move things towards a God-ordained perfection: Tudor England. Such was the *frame* that Shakespeare took. But the total effect of Shakespeare's 'plot' has quite a different effect from Halle: a very different meaning. Dr. Duthie may write, 'But there is no doubt that Shakespeare saw history in the same light as Halle saw it.' I say there *is* doubt. Dover Wilson has nothing to offer but what he summarizes from Moulton, but his last sentence points my doubting way: 'it appears, to me at least, unlikely that Shakespeare's "main end" in *Richard III* was "to show the working out of God's will in English history".' (The quotation he is discussing is from Tillyard's *Shakespeare's History Plays*, 1944.) He can go no further because his own limitations on *Henry IV* inhibit his ever observing that the comic Richard has no more place in Halle's scheme than Falstaff has.

The other myth is that of Richard the Devil-King: the Crookback *monstrum informe, ingens* whom Shakespeare *found* as a ready-made Senecan tyrant and converted into a quite different inverter of moral order: a ruthless, demonic comedian with a most un-Senecan sense of humour and the seductive appeal of an irresistible gusto, besides his volcanic Renaissance energies. They are themselves demoralizing: *Tapfer sein ist gut* (To be bold is good.) is the antithesis of a Christian sentiment.

The outcome of this conflict of myths was Shakespeare's display of constant inversions of meaning; in all of which, two systems of meaning impinge and go over to their opposites, like the two 'ways' of the cheveril glove. This applies equally to words and word-patterns; to the actor-nature; to dramatic ironies; and to events, as the hatch and brood of time, contrasted with opposite expectations.

As a result of the paradoxical ironic structure built from these inversions of meaning—built above all by Richard's demonic appeal—the naïve, optimistic, 'Christian' principle of history, consoling and comfortable, modulates into its opposite. The 'Christian' system of retribution is undermined, counter-balanced, by historic irony. (Do I need to insist that the coupling of 'Christian' and 'retribution' itself is a paradox? That the God of vengeance is *not* a Christian God; that his opposite is a God of mercy who has no representation in this play. If I do, I had better add that the so-called 'Christian' frame is indistinguishable from a pagan one of Nemesis in which the 'High all-seer' is a Fate with a cruel sense of humour.)

But do not suppose I am saying that the play is a 'debunking of Tudor myth', or that Shakespeare is disproving it. He is not 'proving' anything: not even that 'Blind belief is sure to err/And scan his works in vain' (though I think that is *shown*, nevertheless). Contemporary 'order'-thought spoke as if naïve faith saw true: God was above 'order'-thought spoke as if naïve faith saw true: God was above God's Englishmen and ruled with justice—which meant summary vengeance. This historic myth offered absolutes, certainties. Shakespeare in the Histories always leaves us with relatives, ambiguities, irony, a process thoroughly dialectical. Had he entirely accepted the Tudor myth, the frame and pattern of order, his way would have led, I suppose, towards writing *moral history* (which is what Dr. Tillyard and Dr. Dover Wilson and Professor Duthie have made *out* of him). Instead, his way led him towards writing *comic history*. The former would never have taken him to tragedy: the latter (paradoxically) did. Look the right way through the cruel-comic side of Richard and you glimpse Iago. Look back at him through his energy presented as evil, and you see Macbeth. And if you look at the irony of men's struggles in the nets of historic circumstance, the ironies of their pride and self-assurance, you will see Coriolanus; and you are past the great tragic phase and back in history again.

STEPHEN BOOTH

Shakespeare's Sonnets

Sonnet 94 is a great and beautiful sonnet, and I mean it no disrespect when I suggest that its current vogue is partly accountable to the qualities in it that make it such a useful example here: it displays the stylistic particulars I have been describing throughout the essay, but it does so more obviously, more crudely, and to that extent less satisfactorily than the other poems I have discussed:

> They that have pow'r to hurt and will do none,
> That do not do the thing they most do show,
> Who, moving others, are themselves as stone.
> Unmoved, cold, and to temptation slow;
> They rightly do inherit heaven's graces
> And husband nature's riches from expense;
> They are the lords and owners of their faces,
> Others but stewards of their excellence.
> The summer's flow'r is to the summer sweet,
> Though to itself it only live and die;
> But if that flow'r with base infection meet,
> The basest weed outbraves his dignity:
>> For sweetest things turn sourest by their deeds;
>> Lilies that fester smell far worse than weeds.

Recent interest in 94 got its start from a lengthy account of the sonnet by William Empson in 1933. All of Empson's comments on the poem are constricted by his assumption of not only the justice but the comprehensiveness of the following précis:

The best people are indifferent to temptation and detached from the world; nor is this state selfish, because they do good by unconscious influence, like the flower. You must be like them; you are quite like them already. But even the best people must be continually on their guard, because they become the worst, just as the pure and detached lily smells worst, once they fall from their perfection.

In 1938 John Crowe Ransom responded to Empson with his own equally just and equally incomplete abstract of sonnet 94. Like Empson, Ransom suppresses or subordinates most of the experience of the first eight lines in the interests of developing a coherent and consistent statement based on his reaction to the last six. Both abstracts make heavy use of conjunctions ("because" and "but" for Empson, "but" for Ransom), which furnish the subordination of idea to idea that Shakespeare pointedly omits to make:

> You have your own free will, to be unchaste or not, and your beauty exposes you to the temptation of women. But consider yourself as sole inheritor from heaven of this beauty, and expected to keep it to yourself; those who share their beauty in sex must regard themselves as but its stewards. There is no reproach upon the flower for being self-contained. But infected flowers smell to heaven.

Both abstractors are trying to make the poem internally consistent in *one* of its own terms. Ransom has noticed that, although the poem Empson wants us to see may be internally consistent, it is inconsistent with its context in the 1609 sequence: whatever the offenses of the beloved may be, sonnets 92 and 93 suggest to the reader that the beloved is anything but cold, aloof, or "detached from the world." On the other hand, although Ransom makes 94 fit for the handmaid of 92, 93, 95, and 96, he ignores Shakespeare's probable awareness of a reader's antipathy to people who are cold as stone.

On no internal evidence whatever, both Empson and Ransom paraphrase the poem as a direct statement to and about the beloved. The assumption is unwarranted, but it is entirely understandable. As more naïve critics have needed to anchor their understanding in Elizabethan politics or society, so Empson and Ransom need to assume a fixed point of reference for the sonnet before they can attempt to line up its elements and make them march single-mindedly in one direction.

Under usual critical conditions, the critic can assume that, when he looks at a poem and likes it, the essential statement of the poem will be capable of reduction into prose. He is probably quicker than his readers to stress the implications of the word *reduction*; nevertheless, experience has taught him to assume that from a coherent poem he will be able to perceive and state a general and inclusive attitude evoked in the reader toward the subject matter of the poem. That is a hard assumption for men who are rational by profession to give up. Empson and Ransom hold on to it with as much difficulty as tenacity. Notice the urgency with which each of them fights down his lurking dislike of those who are *as stone*—Empson: "nor is this state selfish"; Ransom: "There is no reproach upon the flower."

In 1952 Hallett Smith quoted Empson's and Ransom's abstracts and commented on them:

> It might be possible to reconcile the differences between these two versions, and preserve what each of them has of truth, by examining first the structure of the sonnet. The first eight lines constitute a definition of the true and false heirs of "heaven's graces" or "nature's riches"—perhaps not exactly true and false heirs, but heirs who are real owners, lords and masters, as distinguished from mere stewards, managers, or tenants. The inheritance is clearly one of physical beauty, "their faces," and its value is clearly considered to be very great, since it is inherited from heaven. Physical beauty is, however, to be regarded as the wealth of nature, "nature's riches," and this gives rise to the figure of the beautiful as either owners of this wealth or mere stewards of it. Perhaps the class distinction here has something to do with the aristocracy of the supposed addressee of the sonnets, but in any case there is the feeling about the responsible lord, who "husbands" natural wealth from "expense." This last word reminds us of its use in the first line of sonnet 129. "Th' expense of spirit." Whether a beautiful person is a lord-owner or a mere steward depends upon whether he makes use of his powers or refrains from doing so. The cautious vagueness of the first few lines, especially the second, conveys a sense of shame about the wrong to be committed "That do not do the thing they most do show."
>
> The octave of the sonnet, then (for the image structure here is Italian, though the rhyme scheme is English), seems to urge the hoarding or at least husbanding of this beauty: the doctrine is the exact opposite of the argument in the first seventeen sonnets of the cycle. [Empson had tried to reconcile 94 with 1–17.] It needs some justification. This justification is provided by the device of a metaphor: the summer's flower. The self-sufficiency of a flower was of course established or fortified by a sacred text, "Consider the lilies of the field, how they grow; they toil not, neither do they spin," and it may well have been the recollection of this verse which brought into Shakespeare's mind the line . . . which ends the sonnet: "Lilies that fester smell far worse than weeds."

These are remarkable paragraphs, first for introducing the obvious relevance of the Sermon on the Mount into criticism of this sonnet, and secondly for being incoherent. Like his immediate predecessors, Smith assumes an obligation to assign a single fixed meaning to any given word or phrase in the poem; thus, although the repetition of *clearly* suggests some self-doubt, *their faces* in line 7 establishes the fact that back in line 5 the reader's only legitimate reaction to *heaven's graces* was to understand it to mean heaven-sent physical beauty. Most of the time, however, particularly in the first of these paragraphs, Smith sets out firmly to fix the sense of a word or line and then, with admirable honesty, modifies his position until it dwindles away into nothingness. This is not the sort of prose one expects from Hallett Smith, but it is the sort one expects to see evoked by this poem.

Edward Hubler says that " 'They that have power to hurt' is both a great poem and an imperfect one." The bulk of his discussion of the sonnet is devoted to a solid and sober attempt to eke out its imperfections by recourse to the plays and other of the sonnets. When one is faced with an obscure line, one can do no better than go to a writer's other work to see what he is likely to have meant. However, where a line or, as in this case, a whole poem makes sense, one needs to remember that any such search for clarity is posited on the assumption that the writer lacked the skill both to achieve the effect he wanted and to see that he had failed. For Hubler the source of the imperfection he finds in the poem seems to be Shakespeare's inability to articulate a clearcut attack on those who, like Rosencrantz, Guildenstern, and Northumberland, are lords and owners of their faces. As his predecessors tried to ignore the bad qualities of the people described in the octave, Hubler exaggerates them at the expense of the good qualities. He protests too much:

> On first reading the sonnet, we shall, of course, notice the irony of the first eight lines; and everything that we find in the other works will confirm it. It is preposterous on the face of things to proclaim as the inheritors of heaven's graces those who are "as stone." It can be other than ironical only to the cynic, for even the hardhearted man thinks of himself as generous and cherishes an abstract admiration for warmth. In addition, it will be noticed that what Shakespeare says here contradicts everything that he has said elsewhere on the subject. The irony of the octave is Swiftian in both method and force. In specious terms the poet states as true that which he is well known to consider false: those men whose appearance does not square with reality, whose deeds do not fulfill their promise, who move others while remaining cold, are proclaimed the heirs to heaven's graces. They are the owners of themselves, whereas throughout Shakespeare's works self-possession in the sense of living without regard for others is intolerable.

The most extensive commentary on 94 is by Hilton Landry. Although he attempts to harden the meanings of some words and phrases
that resist his efforts, and although he is inclined to overstress a reader's
negative reactions to the unmoved movers, his line-by-line analysis of the
poem is generally sensible and I am grateful for it. He prefaces his
concluding chapter with the following quotation from Coleridge's *Table
Talk,* and in his practical criticism demonstrates an awareness of its
justice:

> In Shakespeare one sentence begets the next naturally; the meaning is
> all inwoven. He goes on kindling like a meteor through the dark
> atmosphere. . . .
>   Shakespeare's intellectual action is wholly unlike that of Ben
> Jonson or Beaumont and Fletcher. The latter see the totality of a sen-
> tence or passage, and then project it entire. Shakespeare goes on creat-
> ing, and evolving B. out of A., and C. out of B., and so on, just as a
> serpent moves, which makes a fulcrum of its own body, and seems
> forever twisting and untwisting its own strength.

I do, however, quibble with some of Landry's general principles
and statements. He says that "interpretation consists of rejecting some
contexts and readings while accepting others, of deciding what a poem
does not mean as well as what it does." That sounds truer than it is. A
major duty of a critic of any noncontemporary literature must be to
acquaint his reader with the background against which a work was written, and conversely, to remove historically irrelevant notions from a
modern reader's mind. In sonnet 127, for example, one cannot have
twentieth-century memories of a children's book about a horse impinging
on *black beauty's successive heir.* Neither, however, can one legitimately
bar some historically probable contexts and set up others as what Landry
calls controlling contexts. At one point, after quoting some earlier critics
of sonnet 94, Landry says, "What the critical labors of these literalists
illustrate is that how one reads this Sonnet is largely a matter of what
contexts are brought to bear on it." No. How one reads this sonnet or any
other work depends on what contexts it invades: within what systems of
relationships does it demand consideration from any reader historically
equipped to recognize the demands?

Landry's governing contexts for sonnet 94 are sonnets 87–93 and
95–96, on the one hand, and sonnet 4 and the parable of the talents, on
the other. Surely for a reader following the 1609 sequence, any echoes of
a sonnet immediately preceding 94 will make that sonnet a relevant
context for this one. Moreover, a clear reminder of a sonnet as far from
this one as sonnet 4 could bring the reader's experience of the distant

poem to bear here. But on what basis can Landry limit relevance to the two contexts to whose terms he would subordinate all others? After objecting to an oversimplification by J. Q. Adams, Landry says, "It is ironic that Mr. Adams should be aware of the relevance of the Parable of the Talents to Sonnet 4 and utterly fail to perceive its bearing on this poem." I don't perfectly see that irony, but if it is there it is surely no greater than that in which Landry sees the parable of the talents and ignores the Sermon on the Mount.

All in all, I don't see how any effort to dismiss or subordinate any historically valid reaction evoked by sonnet 94 or any of the other sonnets can be useful or (considering the ability of the sonnets to spring back into shape after undergoing definitive criticism) possible. The essence of this sonnet will not fit into any neat package except the one it is in. I offer the following loose package in evidence.

They that have pow'r to hurt should not endear themselves to a reader first coming upon them, but *They that have pow'r to hurt and will do none* sound like the stuff of heroes. Having the power to hurt makes them sound bad, or at least dangerous; not using it sounds good. This first line describes a dichotomy in the nature of its subjects. The only two qualities it presents for "them" are irrevocably connected and also antipathetic. The line also begins a process of creating a state of mind in the reader in which contrary but inseparable reactions uneasily coexist. The key word in line 1 is *and,* which connects the mutually contradictory impressions in the line as if the second were a straightforward extension of the first. The use of *but* would have presented the reader with a formally structured antithesis that he could have taken in whole. As it is, the reader's attitude toward the subjects of the line is in active flux as he reads it.

In line 1, *that* appears in a perfectly usual relative construction, but in the parallel construction in line 2, *That* is physically so far separated from the grammatical subject as to accentuate the impersonality implied by Shakespeare's use of "that" rather than "who." The word *That* reintroduces the disapprobation dispelled in the previous line by *and will do none.* The reader's coldness toward "them" increases as their own impersonality becomes more evident: *do not do the thing they most do show. Thing* is ominously mechanical, and *show* adds a suggestion of theatrical distance and detachment which intensifies the threat inherent in the fact that *the thing they most do show* is *the pow'r to hurt.* On the other hand, the substance of this line is a restatement of another fact: they do no hurt. The double response of the reader is comparable and appropriate to the conflict between the internal and external natures of the subjects of the lines.

At the beginning of the next line *Who,* introducing the third relative clause of the quatrain, simultaneously presents change and continuity; it breaks the pattern established by the preceding *that* clauses, but its vowel sound participates in a phonetic pattern established in the repetitions of *do* in the preceding lines and echoed in *moving.* The hint of comparative humanity in *Who* is also present in *moving others,* which suggests some positive relationship between "them" and other people; in the contexts of the sonnet convention in general, this collection, and the particular poem that precedes this one in the 1609 sequence, *moving others* is likely to suggest that "they" move others by their physical beauty. The reader may be expected at this point to be swaying toward the admiration he felt at the end of line 1, but the completed line brings him back more strongly than ever to the antipathy he felt for "them" at the end of line 2: *Who, moving others, are themselves as stone.*

The next line maintains the reader's antipathy in *Unmoved, cold.* Between *stone* and *cold, Unmoved* can only confirm the impression made by those two words, but *to temptation slow* is linked—by another casual *and*—to the series that began with *as stone, Unmoved,* and *cold.* To be slow to temptation is an admirable quality in any context and one that here suggests another way of evaluating *Unmoved.* At the same time, however, *to temptation slow* also reflects the idea of enticement back upon *moving others* in line 3. None of the qualities listed in the first quatrain is inconsistent with any other, but the reader's reactions are inconsistent with one another. Unmoved people who are cold as stone are unfeeling and unadmirable. Unmoved people who are slow to temptation are steadfast and admirable. Shakespeare is not describing the vacillation of a lover, but re-creating a lover's state of mind in the reader by putting him through a miniature but real experience of an attempt to think coherently about people who are both worthy and unworthy objects of admiration.

The syntactical unit begun in line 1 is still incomplete at the end of the first quatrain; the promise of completion is sufficient to push the reader on without pause into quatrain 2. The new quatrain makes a new start on the same statement, repeating the subject and immediately predicating it: *They rightly do inherit heaven's graces.* After evoking such a range of reaction to the subject, the repetition of *They* in line 5 has a forward-thrusting effect comparable to that of the unfinished syntactical unit; in effect, the capability for concrete identification in a pronoun of the people to whom the reader's attitude has been so fluid and unsure gives him a sense of solid grasp on his experience of the poem and gives him the sureness to go on without puzzlement.

It is quite reasonable in this context to expect the reader to hear faint overtones of "as a right" or "as if by right" in *rightly*. Since "they" are so self-controlled, the same is true of the meaning "decorously." Still, the most obvious significance of *rightly do* must be "have a right to," because the usual practice of the language makes a reader expect *rightly* to indicate the speaker's judgment rather than describe the subjects' behavior. Moreover, the reader's understanding of *rightly* as indicative of the speaker's approval is heightened by its position in a line that echoes the beatitudes. Still, the assertion that it is right that "they" prosper carries with it the open admission of possible doubt in the matter, and thus confirms the reader's experience of conflicting evidence in quatrain 1. An effect of *rightly* is thus to do what *but* would have done and *and* did not do in lines 1 and 4: it gives rationally graspable form and substance to the contradictions in quatrain 1. The reader gets that comfort, however, after the fact of the experience of the contradictions.

The echo of the beatitudes in *inherit heaven's graces* is appropriate to *will do none* and to *temptation slow*, but the first quatrain gives no suggestion that "they" are meek or poor in spirit. The strongly religious context created by the juxtaposition of *heaven's* and *graces* suggests grace, unearned and from heaven, but *grace* here is plural, and *graces* has only secular meaning. By Shakespeare's time the metaphoric nature of "grace" in love sonnets was so nearly forgotten that, even juxtaposed to "heaven," its sense is secular. Moreover, the reader is prepared to take *heaven's graces* as an atrophied courtly-love metaphor by the fact that *moving others . . . themselves as stone,/ Unmoved, cold, and to temptation slow* is an excellent description of courtly "daunger."

The reader's sense of the secular nature of the blessedness described here is increased by the next line: *And husband nature's riches from expense.* Although *heaven's graces* and *nature's riches* are sharply distinguished in theology, a reader is likely here to take the second as a gloss for the first, because the phrases are parallel, and because it is natural to assume that what is *husbanded* will be identical with what is *inherited*. When the reader first comes upon it in the preceding line, *inherit* gives the general sense of "possess." Here, as the theme of estate management begins to develop, it brings with it the particular sense which has become the only modern meaning of *inherit*. The idea of the succession of physical property from one mortal generation to another emerges to weigh against the suggestions of stonelike immutability in quatrain 1 at just the moment when they are about to be made explicit: *They are the lords and owners of their faces,/ Others but stewards of their excellence.*

As he was in the first quatrain, the reader is here actively engaged in the experience of contradiction. In the lines quoted above, the contradiction is between the response to *stewards* and *owners* that the poem seems to require and the reader's everyday knowledge of the activities of real stewards and owners. In the poem "They" are definable as *lords and owners* because they *husband nature's riches*. Therefore it follows that *Others* are but stewards because they do not exercise like thrift. One of a steward's duties is likely to be dispensing funds, but the usual connotations of "steward" suggest the conservation and thrifty husbandry he is hired to provide. In the ordinary course of things the verb *husband* goes with *stewards*, not with *lords* and *owners*. The sense these lines demand depends on the distinction between owners who possess the land and stewards who do not. The distinction, however, is presented in two related but not interchangeable systems at once: in terms of ownership it makes sense, and in terms of thrift it does not.

Another kind of contradiction is present in *Others but stewards of their excellence*. In the estate metaphor *their* most reasonably refers to the lords and owners. On the other hand, because of the parallelism of *owners of their faces* and *stewards of their excellence, excellence* presents itself to the reader as a synonym for *faces. Faces* is foreign to the metaphor, and one is either lord or steward of one's *own* face. In addition, Landry points out that " 'faces' is both a reminder of the deceitful looks and face of sonnet 93 and, as the equivalent of physical beauty, a representative of *all* their excellences." In quatrain 1 the reader's attitude vacillated. Here contrary reactions are evoked simultaneously. The reader now cannot really have an opinion of "them." The tone of this quatrain demands that he consider it a virtue to be *lords and owners of their faces*, but the proximity of sonnet 93 suggests that the virtue may be a talent for hypocrisy; the proximity of *heaven's graces* and *nature's riches* suggests that outright possession of one's body is a mortal impossibility; and the presence in this collection of sonnets 1–17 suggests that such hoarding is selfish and unnatural.

One cannot, I think, give a reading, in the usual sense, of the first eight lines. I have given a description of the experiences of reading them. I cannot validly generalize from the description further than to say that the lines exercise the reader's mind within the boundaries of their several artistic patterns. That exercise is possible because, although Shakespeare is constantly and overtly informing the reader of "their" nature, "their" qualities do not all admit of evaluation within a single system of values. Shakespeare invites the reader to judge "them," but the implied standards for judgment change from phrase to phrase and from word to word. The reader's essential experience of the lines is the experience of his own mind in flux.

Line 9 both sharply divides and firmly unites the octave and the last six lines:

> The summer's flow'r is to the summer sweet,
> Though to itself it only live and die;
> But if that flow'r with base infection meet,
> The basest weed outbraves his dignity:
> > For sweetest things turn sourest by their deeds;
> > Lilies that fester smell far worse than weeds.

The new subject of the new sentence is very different from "them." The subject of the first eight lines was animate and plural; *flow'r* is inanimate and singular. "They" are powerful and steadfast; a flower is a traditional emblem of transitory frailty (*no stronger than a flower*, 65.4). "They" are cold, and this is *summer's flow'r*. On the other hand, the flower and "they" have their beauty in common. Moreover, the rhyme between the fourth syllable of line 1 and the fourth syllable of line 9 phonetically makes the equation of "them" and the flower that most readers have taken for granted: *They that have pow'r / The summer's flow'r*. The flower is also a reasonable extension of *nature's riches* in the estate metaphor that precedes it.

Lines 9 and 10 limit the significance of the first eight lines by providing an incomplete but satisfying gloss for them. In effect, these lines say that the octave has made the simple statement that its subjects keep themselves to themselves. The apparent restatement of the octave invites the reader's approbation. One cannot reasonably think of blaming a flower for lack of gregariousness, and so the reader gives "them" the moral benefit both of the limitations imposed on a flower by its physical nature and of his fondness for flowers.

Just when the reader has come to see "them" as flowerlike, the next lines present him with another contradiction of common sense. The first overt statement of the danger of corruption and the responsibility of the potentially corrupt being for maintaining his purity is made not about those *that have pow'r to hurt* but about the frail and inanimate flower. *Meet* in line 11 comes closer to describing physical motion than any previous verb; *outbraves* in line 12 suggests glorious array and chivalric vigor more appropriate to the subjects of the octave than to flowers and weeds. Finally, in the couplet, where the reversion to a plural subject fully equates "them" and the flower, Shakespeare presents his reader with *their deeds;* "they" in the octave who are capable of deeds do none; it is *sweetest things* that are made likely to act.

Throughout the poem the reader has to cope with conflicting

reactions, impressions, and systems of coherence. Still, the reassuring presence of conjunctions in the third quatrain and couplet make them much easier to think about than the octave. The third quatrain offers a clean antithesis hinged on *But;* the couplet begins with *For* and formally presents itself as a neat, simple, explanation in a proverb of the essence of the poem:

> For sweetest things turn sourest by their deeds;
> Lilies that fester smell far worse than weeds.

The couplet talks with the directness and simplicity of a medieval tragedy about the total power of change, about the ease with which the best *things turn* into bad. However, the reader of the firm and rational couplet comes to the direct statement from an actual experience of mutability, in which anything is likely to turn into anything else at any moment.

The experience of reading through a Shakespeare sonnet is like a dream where one accepts improbable transformations without hesitation and where one slips imperceptibly from one frame of reference to another. The couplet is like an awakening in which one knows and still does not know that the experience of the dream was unreal. Intellectually and in miniature, the awakening of the couplet is like the awakening Clarence describes in *Richard III:*

> I trembling waked, and for a season after
> Could not believe but that I was in hell,
> Such terrible impression made the dream.
> (I.4.61–63)

SHAKESPEARE AND THE ESSENCE OF VERSE

An artist usually presents a given object or idea in one relationship to other objects and ideas; if he opens his reader's consciousness to more than one frame of reference, he focuses on the object in one of its relationships and subordinates all other relationships to it. The essential action of the artist in creating the experience of an audience is the one that in grammar is made by indicators of relationship like "although," "but," "after," "because," "however." In literature such indicators of relationship tell the reader that he is not in the borderless world outside art where he himself has always to work upon what he perceives, to arrange it around a focal point chosen and maintained by himself. Syntactic organization tells the reader that he is dealing with what we are likely to label "truth," experience sorted, classed, and rated, rather than with "what is true," the still to be sorted data of "real" experience.

The great distinction between the experience of life and of art is that art, by fixing one or more sets of relationships, gives its audience an experience in which objects *are* as they must be to be thought about, in which the audience can see what I have called "truth" without having to hunt it out and pull it out, in which "what is true" and "truth" can be the same. Art presents the mind with an experience in which it is at home rather than one in which it must make itself at home by focusing, stressing, and subordinating. All works of literary art, from the simplest sentence of the simplest mind to *King Lear,* are alike in that they are fixed orderings that place their audiences in an experience ready fitted to the experiencer's manner and means of experiencing.

Such orderings incline to be self-defeating. What we ask of art is that it allow the mind to comprehend—know, grasp, embrace—more of experience than the mind can comprehend. In that case, art must fail because the impossibility of its task is one of its defining factors. To state it simplemindedly, we demand that the impossible be done and still remain an impossibility. When an artist focuses his audience's mind and distorts what is true into a recognizable, graspable shape to fit that mind, he not only does what his audience asks but what cannot long satisfy audience or artist just because the desired distortion *is* a distortion. Art must distort; if it is to justify its existence, it must be other than the reality whose difficulty necessitates artistic mediation. It must seem as little a distortion as possible, because its audience wants comprehension of incomprehensible reality itself. We do not want so much to live in *a* world organized on human principles as to live in *the* world so organized. Art must seem to reveal a humanly ordered reality rather than replace a random one. Our traditional values in art exhibit its self-contradictory nature; all the following adjectives, for example, regularly say that the works of art to which they are applied are good: "unified," "sublime," "clear," "subtle," "coherent," "natural." In a style we are likely to value both simplicity and complexity; we ask that a character be both consistent and complex. Above all, what we want of art is the chance to believe that the orderliness of art is not artificial but of the essence of the substance described, that things are as they look when they have a circle around them. We don't want to feel that art is orderly. We want to feel that things are orderly. We want to feel that art does not make order but shows it.

There are as many ways of trying for the contradictory effects of art as there are artists. All of them aim at replacing the complexities of reality with controlled complexities that will make the experience of the orderly work of art sufficiently similar to the experience of random nature, so that the comfort of artistic coherence will not be immediately dismissed as irrelevant to the intellectual discomfort of the human condition. No work of art has ever been perfectly satisfactory. That is obvious. No work of art has ever satisfied the human need to hold human existence whole in the mind. If a work of art ever succeeded perfectly, it would presumably be the last of its kind; it would do what the artist as theologian describes as showing the face of God. All works have failed because the experience they are asked for and give is unlike nonartistic experience. Neither reality nor anything less than reality will satisfy the ambitions of the human mind.

Of all literary artists, Shakespeare has been most admired. The reason may be that he comes closest to success in giving us the sense both that we know what cannot be known and what we know is the unknowable thing we want to know and not something else. I have tried to demonstrate that in the sonnets Shakespeare copes with the problem of the conflicting obligations of a work of art by multiplying the number of ordering principles, systems of organization, and frames of reference in the individual sonnets. I have argued that the result of that increase in artificiality is pleasing because the reader's sense of coherences rather than coherence gives him both the simple comfort of order and the comfort that results from the likeness of his ordered experience of the sonnet to the experience of disorderly natural phenomena. In nonartistic experience the mind is constantly shifting its frames of reference. In the experience of the sonnet it makes similar shifts, but from one to another of overlapping frames of reference that are firmly ordered and fixed. The kind and quantity of mental action necessary in nonartistic experience is demanded by the sonnet, but that approximation of real experience is made to occur within mind-formed limits of logic, or subject matter, or form, or sound.

Shakespeare's multiplication of ordering systems is typically Shakespearean in being unusual not in itself but in its degree. The principle of multiple orders is a defining principle of verse in general. Although "verse" and "prose" are not really precise terms, verse is ordinarily distinguishable from prose in that it presents its materials organized in at least two self-assertive systems at once: at least one of meaning and at least one of sound. Here, as an almost random example, are the first lines of Surrey's translation of the *Aeneid,* Book II:

> They whisted all, with fixed face attent,
> When prince Aeneas from the royal seat
> Thus gan to speak: "O Quene! it is thy will
> I should renew a woe cannot be told,

How that the Grekes did spoile and ouerthrow
The Phrygian wealth and wailful realm of Troy.

As the principle of multiple ordering is common to poems at large, so its usual operation is different only in degree from its operation in a Shakespeare sonnet. Where one system tends to pull things together, another tends to separate. In the sample above, the syntax tends to unify and the form to divide. Similarly, in all literature any single system of organization is likely both to unify and to divide. Since not only verse but any literature, any sentence, is a putting together, the very nature of the undertaking evokes an awareness both of unity and of the division that necessitates the unifying. Thus, at the risk of belaboring the evident, the statement *They whisted all, with fixed face attent* is a clear unit of meaning made up of clearly articulated parts. The larger whole of the Surrey passage is similarly a unit made of distinct clauses and phrases. Formal organizations work the same way. The second line looks like the first and rhythmically is pointedly similar, but they are not identical either in appearance or sound. They look and sound as different from one another as they look and sound alike. Inside a line the same unifying and dividing exists. What is on one side of the pause, *They whisted all*, is roughly the same length as *with fixed face attent*, which balances it. Moreover, the fact that they make up a single line is just as active as the fact that they are divided by the pause.

The addition of rhyme to syntactic and metrical organization is the addition of one more independent system of organization. This is Dryden's version of the opening of the *Aeneid,* II:

> All were attentive to the godlike man,
> When from his lofty couch he thus began:
> "Great queen, what you command me to relate
> Renews the sad remembrance of our fate:
> An empire from its old foundations rent,
> And every woe the Trojans underwent

Rhyme also adds another manifestation of the principle of unification and division. Aside from puns, rhyme presents the best possible epitome of the principle. Two rhyming words are pointedly like and unlike in sound, and they pull apart and together with equal force.

Any verse is capable of this kind of analysis. Since what it demonstrates is obvious, there is no need to prolong it. Still, if such analysis is unnecessary in most verse, what it reveals is nonetheless true: verse in general is multiply organized.

SHAKESPEARE AND THE SONNET FORM—SONNET 15

Although Wordsworth's "Scorn not the Sonnet" is not a good advertise-
ment for the justice of its plea, the fact that Wordsworth himself wrote
sonnets, that he wrote them when nobody else was writing sonnets, that
Milton wrote them when almost nobody else was writing sonnets, and
that Shakespeare wrote his well after the Elizabethan sonnet vogue had
passed suggests that there may be something about the sonnet form that
makes it not to be scorned. In an earlier chapter I said that the sonnet
form in any of its varieties is simultaneously unifying and divisive. Those
contradictory coactions result from its unusually high number of systems of
organization. In the limited terms of my thesis that multiplicity of structures is an essence of verse, the sonnet is an especially poetic form. The
first line of an English sonnet participates in a metrical pattern (fourteen
iambic pentameter lines), a rhyme pattern (*abab*), a trio of quatrains
(alike in being quatrains, different in using different rhymes), and an
overall pattern contrasting two different kinds of rhyme scheme (three
quatrains set against one couplet). I suggest that the concentration of
different organizing systems active in the form before any particulars of
substance of syntax are added is such as to attract the kind of mind that is
particularly happy in the multiple organizations of verse: witness Shakespeare, Milton, and Wordsworth. The different patterns inside the sonnet
form pull together and pull apart just as the different patterns do in verse
forms less crowded with coherences. The sonnet does what all verse does;
it just does more of it.

    As the sonnet form extends the basic verse principle of multiple
organization, so Shakespeare's sonnets reflect and magnify the tendencies
of the form itself. In superimposing many more patterns upon the several
organizations inherent in the form, Shakespeare marshals the sonnet the
way that it was going. Having talked at length about the kind, quantity,
and operation of the patterns in which Shakespeare organizes his sonnets,
I propose to pull together what I have said and summarize it, but to do so in
the abstract would not, I think, be meaningful. Instead, I will take one
sonnet, number 15, and use it to make a summary demonstration of the
kinds and interactions of patterns in Shakespeare's sonnets generally:

> When I consider everything that grows
> Holds in perfection but a little moment,
> That this huge stage presenteth nought but shows
> Whereon the stars in secret influence comment;
> When I perceive that men as plants increase,
> Cheerèd and checked even by the selfsame sky,

> Vaunt in their youthful sap, at height decrease,
> And wear their brave state out of memory:
> Then the conceit of this inconstant stay
> Sets you most rich in youth before my sight,
> Where wasteful Time debateth with Decay
> To change your day of youth to sullied night;
>> And, all in war with Time for love of you,
>> As he takes from you, I ingraft you new.

On top of the formal pattern (4, 4, 4, 2) is a logical pattern (8, 6) established in the syntactical construction *when/then.* In the first eight lines, which are formally two quatrains and logically an octave, a 2, 2, 4 pattern arises from the three object clauses: [*that*] *everything . . .* (two lines), *that this huge stage . . .* (two lines), *that men as plants . . .* (four lines).

In addition to these three major structures and structuring principles, the nonformal phonetic patterns that operate in the poem are probably literally innumerable. They tend to interact with the other patterning systems in much the same way that the other systems interact with each other: an informal sound pattern will link elements that are divided, or divide elements that are linked, by the formal or logical or syntactical or rhythmic patterns.

Considering the great many words it takes to talk about sounds, it would not be profitable to talk about them here. Even a token description of sound patterns threatens to imbalance the discussion that contains it. I have therefore relegated a description of the liveliest of the sound patterns in sonnet 15 to the Appendix. It should suffice here to say that informal sound patterns do what I have said the multiple patterns of the sonnets do generally. The mere fact of their presence adds to the reader's sense that he is engaged in an ordered, coherent, nonrandom, humanly geared experience. They help the poem give a sense of the intense and universal relevance of all things to all other things. The companion fact of their great number helps maintain in the reader an accompanying sense that, for all the artistic order of his reading experience, it is not a limited one. No one of the sound patterns dominates the others over the whole length of the poem; similarly, no one pattern of any kind dominates the whole poem. From moment to moment incidental sound patterns keep the reader aware of the orderliness, the rationality, of the experience, but the principal patterning factor does not stay the same from moment to moment. The multiplication of sound patterns, like the multiplication of structures generally, increases the reader's sense of order, while at the same time it diminishes the sense of limitation that a dominant pattern can add to the limitation inherent in the focusing of the reader's attention on particular subjects in particular relationships. In short, by fixing so many phonetic relationships and by putting a single word in so many of those relationships, Shakespeare overcomes the limitation that order entails. The reader is engaged in so many organizations that the experience of the poem is one both of comprehending (for which order, limit, pattern, and reason are necessary) and of having comprehended what remains incomprehensible because it does not seem to have been limited. Nothing in the poem strikes the reader as seen only "in terms of." Everything is presented in multiple terms—more as it is than as it is understood.

SHAKESPEARE AND THE SONNET TRADITION—SONNET 15

I have said that the peculiarly Shakespearean effect of these sonnets arises in part from a bold extension of a principle basic to verse generally and to the sonnet form particularly. The same can be said about an extension of the basic principle of courtly love in general and the sonnet convention in particular.

More than a writer in any other genre, a sonneteer depends for his effects on the conjunction or conflict of what he says with what the reader expects. Like the basic courtly love convention from which it grew, the sonnet convention is one of indecorum. Its essential device is the use of the vocabulary appropriate to one kind of experience to talk about another. The writer talked about his lady and his relation to her as if she were a feudal lord and he a vassal, or as if she were the Virgin Mary and he a supplicant to her. A witty emphasis on the paradoxically simultaneous pertinence and impertinence of the writer's language and stance to his subject matter is of the essence of the convention. The lady was not a deity or a baron, but she was virtuous, powerful, beautiful. In all stages of its development, the courtly love tradition relies upon a reader's sense of the frame of reference in which the writer operates and the writer's apparent deviation from that pattern in a rhetorical action that both fits and violates the expected pattern.

By the time the first Italian and French sonnets were written, the conventions of courtly love were traditional, and a decorum, albeit a decorum of indecorum, was firmly established for aristocratic secular love poetry. Followers of Petrarch wrote to be judged on their success in introducing variations within a narrow and prescribed space, using set vocabulary and subject matter. To be appreciated, the sonneteer presupposed an audience whose presuppositions he could rely on. An audience for a sonnet had to be able to recognize a new surprise in a convention of long established paradoxes.

Perhaps the poems most typical of all the rhetorical actions of courtly love writers are those which exploit the apparently inexhaustible surprise of returning the language of religion to religious subject matter inside the courtly love and sonnet conventions. Dante did it in the thirteenth century; Donne did it in the seventeenth. A good example is this sonnet which George Herbert sent home to his mother from Cambridge:

> My God, where is that ancient heat towards thee,
>> Wherewith whole showls of *Martyrs* once did burn,
>> Besides their other flames? Doth Poetry
> Wear *Venus* Livery? only serve her turn?
> Why are not *Sonnets* made of thee? and layes
>> Upon thine Altar burnt? Cannot thy love
>> Heighten a spirit to sound out thy praise
> As well as any she? Cannot thy *Dove*
> Out-strip their *Cupid* easily in flight?
>> Or, since thy wayes are deep, and still the same,
>> Will not a verse run smooth that bears thy name?
> Why doth that fire, which by thy power and might
>> Each breast does feel, no braver fuel choose
>> Than that, which one day Worms may chance refuse?

Exaggerated predictability and surprise, pertinence and impertinence, are in the nature of the convention; and all the devices I have talked about have a common denominator with the more grossly effective conjunction of frames of reference in the earliest courtly love poetry, in Donne's *Holy Sonnets*, and in such collisions of value systems as that between the last line of this Sidney sonnet and the rest of the poem:

> It is most true, that eyes are form'd to serve
> The inward light: and that the heavenly part
> Ought to be king, from whose rules who do swerve,
> Rebels to Nature, strive for their owne smart.
>> It is most true, what we call *Cupid's* dart,
> An image is, which for our selves we carve;
> And, fooles, adore in temple of our hart,
> Till that good God make Church and Churchman starve.
>> True, that true Beautie Vertue is indeed,
> Whereof this Beautie can be but a shade,
> Which elements with mortall mixture breed:
>> True, that true Beautie Vertue is indeed,
>> And should in soule up to our countrey move:
> True, and yet true that I must *Stella* love.

Sometimes, as in the following sonnet from *Arcadia,* the whole
effect of a poem will depend upon a reader's familiarity with the genre
being so great that for an instant he will hear only the poet's manner and
not his matter:

> What length of verse can serve brave *Mopsa's* good
>   to show,
> Whose vertues strange, and beuties such, as no man them
>   may know?
> Thus shrewdly burdned then, how can my Muse escape?
> The gods must help, and pretious things must serve to
>   shew her shape.
>   Like great god *Saturn* faire, and like faire *Venus*
>   chaste:
> As smooth as *Pan,* as *Juno* milde, like goddesse *Isis* faste.
> With *Cupid* she fore-sees, and goes god *Vulcan's* pace:
> And for a tast of all these gifts, she borowes *Momus'*
>   grace.
>   Her forhead jacinth like, her cheekes of opall hue,
> Her twinkling eies bedeckt with pearle, her lips of Saphir
>   blew:
> Her haire pure Crapal-stone; her mouth O heavenly
>   wyde;
> Her skin like burnisht gold, her hands like silver ure
>   untryde.
>   As for those parts unknowne, which hidden sure are
>   best:
> Happie be they which well beleeve, and never seeke
>   the rest.

Like his predecessors, Shakespeare plays openly on his reader's
expectations about the sonnet convention in poems like sonnet 130 (*My
mistress' eyes are nothing like the sun*) and in the bawdy conclusions of
sonnets 20, 144, and 151. Shakespeare's dark lady is traditionally cited as
contrary to the traditional beloved, but the very impropriety of a techni-
cally unattractive and morally vicious beloved is a consistent enlargement
on the standard rhetorical principle of the convention; and, whatever
other significance there may be, certainly addressing love sonnets to a
man is an all but predictable extreme of courtly love technique. Shakespeare's surprises, like Dante's, Donne's, and George Herbert's, come from
going farther in the direction natural to the convention.

Although Shakespeare exploits the reader's expectations in the
largest elements of the sonnets, similar smaller plays on the reader's
expectations about syntax and idiom are more numerous. Moreover, their
effects are more typical of the general rhetoric of the sonnets. Where both

the traditional clashes of contexts in courtly love poetry, and Sidney's sudden shifts in clearly distinguished systems of value call attention to themselves, the comparable actions in the syntactical fabric of sonnets like number 15 do not fully impinge on the reader's consciousness, and so do not merely describe inconstancy but evoke a real sense of inconstancy from a real experience of it. In sonnet 15 the reader is presented with the subject, verb, and direct object of the potentially complete clause *When I consider everything that grows.* The next line continues the clause and requires an easy but total reconstitution of the reader's conception of the kind of sentence he is reading; he has to understand *When I consider [that] everything that grows / Holds in perfection but a little moment.* The kind of demand on the reader made syntactically in the first two lines is made in lines 11 and 12 by a nonidiomatic use of the common construction "debate with":

> . . . wasteful Time debateth with Decay
> To change your days of youth to sullied night. . . .

Having newly learned to understand *with* as "in the company of," the reader is forced by the couplet to readjust his understanding when essentially the same idiom appears in a variation on its usual sense, "fight against":

> And, all in war with Time for love of you,
> As he takes from you, I ingraft you new.

Just as the reader's mind moves from one to another formal or logical or phonetic structure, it also moves back and forth among metaphoric frames of reference. The terms in which the speaker presents his meaning, the "things" of the poem, are from a variety of ideological frames of reference, and the reader's mind is in constant motion from one context to another. Like all the other stylistic qualities I have talked about, the variation and quick change in the metaphoric focus of the sonnets presents in little the basic quality of courtly love and sonnet convention.

The first active metaphor of the poem, *grows*, carries a vaguely botanical reference over into line 2, whose substance lends itself to overtones of traditional floral expressions of the *carpe diem* theme. The overtones would have been particularly strong for a reader accustomed to *perfection* in its common Renaissance meaning, "ripeness":

> When I consider everything that grows
> Holds in perfection but a little moment

Line 3 begins a new object clause, logically and syntactically parallel with the first. That parallelism helps the reader accept the new theatrical metaphor as an alternative means of simply restating the substance of the first clause. Moreover, the theatrical metaphor continues and reinforces the *watcher-watched* relationship established first in line 1 for the speaker and what he considers, and fully mirrored when line 4 introduces a new metaphor, the secretly influential stars, which are to the world-stage roughly as the powerless speaker was to the mortal world in line 1:

> That this huge stage presenteth nought but shows
> Whereon the stars in secret influence comment

The tone of the quatrain is matter-of-fact as befits a declaration so simple and so obviously justified that it is a subordinate prologue to the statement proper. That the matter-of-fact tone withstands coexistence with three distinct metaphors would be remarkable if each new metaphor were not introduced into the reader's mind as if it were already there.

Parallel syntax and parallel relationships suggest equation between the two object clauses—an equation which gives the reader a sense that what is both new and separate from the first two lines is at the same time neither new nor separate. In short, the physics of the quatrain's substance are the same as those of its rhyme scheme. The three metaphors pull both apart and together. The stars in line 4 are both new to the poem and have been in it covertly from the start. Probably only a mind as pun-ready as Shakespeare's own could hear the echo of Latin *sidus, sider-*, "star," in *consider*, but for any reader the act of imagining *this huge stage* presupposes the vantage point of the stars; the reader is thinking from the heavens, and, when the stars themselves are mentioned, their propriety is immediately further established because the stars comment, like critics at a play.

Just as such an incidental sound pattern as *cheerèd and checked* emerges (from *perceive* and *increase*) into dominance and then submerges again (in *sky* and *decrease*) into the music of the whole, so the substance of the poem slips into and out of metaphoric frames of reference, always in a frame of reference some of whose parts pertain incidentally to one of the other metaphors from which and into which it moves.

> When I perceive that men as plants increase,
> Cheerèd and checked even by the selfsame sky,
> Vaunt in their youthful sap, at height decrease,
> And wear their brave state out of memory

At the beginning of quatrain 2, *plants increase* returns the botanical metaphor to clear prominence. The next line, *Cheerèd and checked even by the selfsame sky*, pertains very well to a growing plant (*Cheerèd*—smiled upon—*and checked*—restrained, held back, by the vagaries of the weather), but the primary syntactical object here is *men*, and *Cheerèd and checked* suggests the theatrical metaphor, particularly in the second half of the line, when the encouragement and rebuke turn out to be given *by the selfsame sky* that has earlier been audience to the shows on the huge stage. In line 7, *Vaunt* confirms the metaphoric dominance of boastful, strutting actors, but in the phrase that follows, *youthful*, which pertains directly to men (actors), is coupled with *sap*, a word from the botanical frame of reference to which *youthful* applies only figuratively, and which itself is only metaphorically descriptive of the humors of men: *Vaunt in their youthful sap, at height decrease*. *At height* is metaphorically applicable to the careers of men and the performances of haughty actors, and it is literally descriptive of a plant at its full growth, but the context to which *height* more usually belongs is astronomy (its context in sonnet 116). The phrase *at height decrease* confirms an earlier suggestion of the sun's passage across the sky or of the waxing moon—a suggestion that does not conform logically to the other use of astronomical metaphor, but that does persist throughout the quatrain. At the end of line 5, *increase* pertained obviously to *plants*. Its noun-meaning "fruit of the harvest," appears prominently in sonnets 1 and 11 which precede this one in the 1609 sequence; here, however, astronomical senses of *increase* also pertain. The *OED* reports Renaissance uses of the noun form of *increase* to mean "the rising of the tide . . . the advance of daylight from sunrise to noon; the waxing of the moon," and cites Renaissance examples in which forms of *decrease* indicate the negative of all three astronomical senses of *increase*. In this context *at height decrease* suggests the waning of the moon (taking *at height* figuratively to mean "fullness"), the descent of the sun (taking *at height* literally, and *decrease* to mean the decline of daylight from noon to sunset), and a tidelike ebbing of once *youthful sap*.

The last line of the quatrain, *And wear their brave state out of memory*, brings back the actors strutting in their finery, but its juxtaposition with *at height decrase* and the vague, cosmic immensity of *out of memory* give the line a majestic fall more appropriate to the descent of the sun than the perseverance of a player king. The reader's experience of this line is a type of his experience of this sonnet and the sonnets in general. The line is easy to understand, but it would be hard to say just what it says or how it says it. *Wear* in combination with *their brave state* says something like "wear their fine clothes." Following on *at height decrease*, *and wear* has reference to movement in space (*OED*, s.v. *Wear*, v. 21), and so, still under the influence of *Vaunt*, the half line says: "continue to advance in their pomp and finery." Thus, when he comes upon *out of,* the reader is likely to take it spatially (as in "out of the country"). On the other hand, *out* is in the same line with *wear* and *brave state,* and so leads the reader's understanding into a context of wearing out clothes, a context that is an excellent metaphor for the larger idea of the decay in time of everything that grows. The syntax of the line presents *memory* as if it were a place, but its sense makes it capable of comprehension only in terms of time. In common idiom "out of memory" refers to the distant, unseen past; but in *wear their brave state out of memory* the reference must be to the unseeable future. The statement of the octave takes in everything that has grown, grows, or will grow, and the multiple reference made by the conflict between standard usage and the use of *out of memory* in this line allows the reader an approximation of actual comprehension of all time and space in one.

The last six lines of the sonnet are more abstract than the first eight, and the three metaphors become more separable from each other, from a new metaphor of warfare, and from the abstract statements that they figure forth. In line 10 the beloved is set before the speaker's sight in a refrain of the theatrical metaphor; in line 12 the astronomical metaphor appears overtly in a commonplace; in the last line *ingraft* brings the botanical metaphor into a final statement otherwise contained entirely in the metaphor of warfare:

> Then the conceit of this inconstant stay
> Sets you most rich in youth before my sight,
> Where wasteful Time debateth with Decay
> To change your day of youth to sullied night;
>   And, all in war with Time for love of you,
>   As he takes from you, I ingraft you new.

After the experience of the octave, the experience of the sestet is a clear awareness of the simplicity hidden in a great—a lifelike—complexity of relationships. The couplet describes a facile and fanciful triumph over time. The reader's experience of it, however, is the justified culmination of a small but real intellectual triumph over the limits of his own understanding.

THE VALUE OF THE SONNETS

A formulated idea—written down, ordered, settled, its elements fixed in permanent relationship to one another as parts of a whole—accentuates its reader's incapacity to cope fully with what is outside the description.

Like a fort, any statement presupposes, and so emphasizes, the frailty of the people it serves. Wordsworth made the point more cheerfully and in specific praise of the sonnet:

> Nuns fret not at their convent's narrow room;
> And hermits are contented with their cells;
> And students with their pensive citadels;
> Maids at the wheel, the weaver at his loom,
> Sit blithe and happy; bees that soar for bloom,
> High as the highest Peak of Furness-fells,
> Will murmur by the hour in foxglove bells:
> In truth the prison, unto which we doom
> Ourselves, no prison is: and hence for me,
> In sundry moods, 'twas pastime to be bound
> Within the Sonnet's scanty plot of ground;
> Pleased if some Souls (for such there needs must be)
> Who have felt the weight of too much liberty,
> Should find brief solace there, as I have found.

The many different patterns that exist in any sonnet by virtue of its form make it seem crowded or, if that word has irremediably derisive connotations, full. Shakespeare's enlargement of the number and kinds of patterns makes his sonnets seem full to bursting not only with the quantity of different actions but with the energy generated from their conflict. The reader has constantly to cope with the multitudinous organizations of a Shakespeare sonnet; he is engaged and active. Nonetheless, the sonnets are above all else artificial, humanly ordered; the reader is always capable of coping. He always has the comfort and security of a frame of reference, but the frames of reference are not constant, and their number seems limitless.

The solace to be found in a Shakespeare sonnet is brief indeed, but it is as great a solace as literature can give—the feeling that the weight of liberty is not too much. That is a remarkable achievement for a reader and for the writer who gives it to him. I think it is that achievement which readers acknowledge when they praise Shakespeare's sonnets.

ALVIN B. KERNAN

"The Henriad":
Shakespeare's Major History Plays

Taken together, Shakespeare's four major history plays, *Richard II*, *1 Henry IV*, *2 Henry IV*, and *Henry V* constitute an epic, *The Henriad*. Obviously these four plays are not an epic in the usual sense—there is no evidence that Shakespeare planned them as a unit—but they do have remarkable coherence and they possess that quality which in our time we take to be the chief characteristic of epic: a large-scale, heroic action, involving many men and many activities, tracing the movement of a nation or people through violent change from one condition to another. In *The Iliad* that action involves the wrath of Achilles and the misfortunes which it brought to the Achaeans before Troy. In *The Aeneid* the action is the transferal of the Empire of Troy to Latium. And in *Paradise Lost* the action is man's first disobedience and the fruit of that forbidden tree.

In *The Henriad*, the action is the passage from the England of Richard II to the England of Henry V. This dynastic shift serves as the supporting framework for a great many cultural and psychological transitions which run parallel to the main action, giving it body and meaning. In historical terms the movement from the world of Richard II to that of Henry V is the passage from the Middle Ages to the Renaissance and the modern world. In political and social terms it is a movement from feudalism and hierarchy to the national state and individualism. In psy-

From *Modern Shakespearean Criticism*, edited by Alvin B. Kernan. Copyright © 1970 by Harcourt Brace Jovanovich. First published in a shorter form in *The Yale Review* 1 (Fall 1969). Copyright © 1969 by *The Yale Review*.

chological terms it is a passage from a situation in which man knows with certainty who he is to an existential condition in which any identity is only a temporary role. In spatial and temporal terms it is a movement from a closed world to an infinite universe. In mythical terms the passage is from a garden world to a fallen world. In the most summary terms it is a movement from ceremony and ritual to history:

> The Renaissance was a moment when educated men were modifying a ceremonial conception of human life to create a historical conception. The ceremonial view, which assumed that names and meanings are fixed and final, expressed experience as pageant and ritual—pageant where the right names could march in proper order, or ritual where names could be changed in the right, the proper way. The historical view expresses life as drama. People in drama are not identical with their names, for they gain and lose their names, their status and meaning—and not by settled ritual: the gaining and losing of names, of meaning, is beyond the control of any set ritual sequence. . . . The people in [Shakespeare's] plays try to organize their lives by pageant and ritual, but the plays are dramatic precisely because the effort fails.

It is by means of ceremony and ritual that the old kingdom is presented in the beginning of *The Henriad*. *Richard II* opens on a scene in which two furious peers, Mowbray and Hereford, confront and accuse one another of treason before their legitimate king. The place of judgment is the court itself, with all its ceremonial forms and symbols: crowns, trumpets, thrones, ranked retainers, robes of state and heraldic arms. This court, in its traditional setting with its ancient emblems and established procedures, repeats the pattern of innumerable former assemblies convoked for the same purpose, to absorb and reorder once again the disorderly elements in man and society.

When this ritual attempt fails, an even more solemn ritual is ordered, trial by combat. The ceremonial elements in I.iii are heavily emphasized: the combatant knights enter in the proper manner and take their assigned places in the lists. They make the expected speeches, and the marshal of the lists puts the formulaic questions to them.

> *The trumpets sound.* Enter BOLINGBROKE, DUKE OF HEREFORD,
> *appellant, in armour, and a* HERALD.
> KING RICHARD: Marshal, ask yonder knight in arms,
>   Both who he is and why he cometh hither
>   Thus plated in habiliments of war;
>   And formally, according to our law,
>   Depose him in the justice of his cause.
> MARSHAL: What is thy name? and wherefore com'st thou hither
>   Before King Richard in his royal lists?

Against whom comest thou? and what's thy quarrel?
Speak like a true knight, so defend thee heaven!
BOLINGBROKE: Harry of Hereford, Lancaster, and Derby,
Am I; who ready here do stand in arms
To prove, by God's grace and my body's valour,
In lists on Thomas Mowbray, Duke of Norfolk,
That he is a traitor, foul and dangerous,
To God of heaven, King Richard, and to me.
And as I truly fight, defend me heaven!

(*Richard II*, I.iii.26–41)

Here, and throughout the early acts of the play, traditional ways of acting and traditional values—the law, the sanctity of a knight's oath, established duty to God and king—reflected in the formulaic phrases, the conventional terms, and the orderly rhythms, control the violent passions, fury, fear, outrage, hatred, the lust for power, at work in Richard's England. The individual is submerged within the role imposed upon him by prescribed ways of thinking, acting, and speaking.

But, even as we admire, this old world is breaking up. The patriarchs of England—the seven sons of Edward II—are, like the twelve sons of Jacob, passing from the land, and with them their world passes. The sense of an ancient, more perfect world, fading from existence into memory is focused in John of Gaunt's comparison of England, as it was only yesterday, to another Eden:

This royal throne of kings, this scept'red isle,
This earth of majesty, this seat of Mars,
This other Eden, demi-paradise,
This fortress built by Nature for herself
Against infection and the hand of war,
This happy breed of men, this little world,
This precious stone set in the silver sea,
Which serves it in the office of a wall,
Or as a moat defensive to a house,
Against the envy of less happier lands;
This blessed plot, this earth, this realm, this England. . . .

(*Richard II*, II.i.40–50)

By III.iv when the "sea-walled garden" appears again, presided over by a gardener in "old Adam's likeness," it is full of weeds, the flowers choked, the trees unpruned, the hedges in ruin, the herbs eaten by caterpillars, and the great tree in its center dead.

What is passing in the course of *Richard II* is innocence, a sense of living in a golden world, and no one is more innocent than Richard himself. When Bolingbroke begins his rebellion, Richard confidently expects that God himself will send down soldiers to defend him and blast the usurper. The order of nature and the laws of men, he believes, guarantee his kingship:

> Not all the water in the rough rude sea
> Can wash the balm off from an anointed king;
> The breath of worldly men cannot depose
> The deputy elected by the Lord.
> For every man that Bolingbroke hath press'd
> To lift shrewd steel against our golden crown,
> God for his Richard hath in heavenly pay
> A glorious angel. Then, if angels fight,
> Weak men must fall; for heaven still guards the right.
> (*Richard II*, III.ii. 54–62)

Richard, here and elsewhere in the play, manifests his belief in the conservative world view which has been variously called "The Great Chain of Being," "The Elizabethan World Picture," and "The Tudor Political Myth." This world view imaged the whole of creation, from God down to the meanest pebble, as being organized hierarchically, as a series of rungs in a ladder or links in a chain. Each category in turn mirrored the systematic arrangement of the whole, and its parts were distributed in descending order of authority, responsibility, and power. To act "naturally," to live in accordance with things as they are, was to accept your assigned place in society, controlled justly by the powers above and controlling justly those below entrusted to your care and authority. When man acted in a disorderly fashion, creating a disturbance within his own "little world" or microcosm, "Nature" quickly acted to right itself: all the other categories of being trembled sympathetically, the ripples spread through all creation, and the great powers began to react to restore order. This world view saw in all areas of life—religion, physics, psychology, government, zoology, and all social organizations—a reflection of the human dream of order, stability, harmony, coherence, and community. Life ideally lived was a dance or music.

Richard takes this great imaginative projection of human values for absolute fact, mistakes metaphor for science, and so believes that God will directly intervene in the coming battle and that the king's appearance in England will cause rebellion to disappear just as the rising of the sun (the "king" of the cosmos) banishes night and darkness. Like a child, he fails to distinguish human desire from actuality and therefore fails to understand that he cannot trust to "Nature" to maintain him as a king, simply because he *is* king. From the outset of the play powerful political and personal forces are at work undermining the social system, making a mockery of ritual and ceremony. Mowbray has been involved in graft and assassination for political purposes. Henry Hereford has been courting popularity with the common people, and he accuses Mowbray of treason knowing that he is innocent. His motive may be to embarrass Richard, who is himself deeply implicated in the murder of his uncle, Duke of Gloucester, the crime of which Mowbray is accused. Richard is violently jealous and suspicious of his cousin Hereford and uses the trial as an occasion for banishing him under the pretense of being merciful. Pressed by the perpetual need for money, Richard sells his right to gather taxes to profiteers. He neglects affairs of state to spend his time reveling with male favorites. Each of these acts indirectly undermines the order which Richard thinks immutable, and when upon John of Gaunt's death he seizes the banished Hereford's lands, he strikes a direct blow, as the Duke of York points out, against the great law of orderly succession on which his kingship rests:

> Take Hereford's rights away, and take from Time
> His charters and his customary rights;
> Let not to-morrow then ensue to-day;
> Be not thyself—for how art thou a king
> But by fair sequence and succession?
> (*Richard II,* II.i.95–99)

In general, Richard treats his kingdom and subjects in an arbitrary manner, and the play realizes his implication in his own destruction in the scene in which he uncrowns himself, names Bolingbroke his successor, and confesses the sins which brought him down. This is, of course, good political strategy for Bolingbroke, who, like modern dictators, realizes that nothing is so valuable to an uneasy ruler as his victim's public confession and admission of the justice of punishment. But the scene has another function. By uncrowning himself visibly, Richard is repeating and making manifest what he did earlier in the play when he worked so busily and blindly to destroy the values and rituals on which his kingship rested.

In *Paradise Lost* the results of the fall, Adam and Eve's disobedience to God, are immediate and spectacular: the earth tilts and the seasons become intemperate, the animals become vicious and prey on one another and on man, and man himself knows fear, anger, lust, and shame. What Milton presents on the scale of the universe, Shakespeare presents on the scale of the kingdom and the individual. Most immediately, Richard's disorders release a variety of other disorders on all levels of life. Richard having rebelled against the order which made and kept him king, Henry Bolingbroke immediately rebels against Richard. By the end of the play there is already another group of plotters planning to overthrow Henry. Throughout the three succeeding plays political scheming, plotting, raids on the commonwealth, and civil wars never cease. As one group of rebels dies, another group is already forming to take its place, each more desperate and violent than the last. Henry IV lives out his days facing one revolt after another, and even Henry V, whose reign in some ways is a restoration of political order, is still forced to deal with treasons which are "like / Another fall of man" (*Henry V*, II.ii.141–42).

As the old political order weakens, simple men like the good old Duke of York become confused and inept. His duty is, he knows, to his king; but who is his king? what to do if that duty now conflicts with other primary duties? The confusion in his mind is reflected in the confusion in his family. His son, the Duke of Aumerle, intrigues against the new king, and the Duchess of York tells her husband that his primary duty lies not to the King but to his own son. But the anguished York goes to the King to accuse his son of treason. This civil war within the family eventuates in an absurd scene in which the King hears York ask him to execute his son, while the Duchess of York asks the King for mercy and pleads against her own husband. The most serious matters have become a kind of mad joke. The disorder in York's family expands to the family of Henry, and by the end of the play we learn that Hal, the Prince of Wales, is already roistering in a tavern, defying his father, and using his power to break the law with impunity.

As the old order breaks up, a profound psychological confusion parallels the political confusion. In that Edenic world which Gaunt described and Richard destroyed, every man knew who he was. His religion, his family, his position in society, his assigned place in processions large and small, his coat of arms, his traditional duties, and even his clothing, which was then prescribed by sumptuary laws, told him who he was and what he should do and even gave him the formal language in which to express this socially-assigned self. But once, under the pressures of political necessity and personal desires, the old system is destroyed, the old identities go with it. Man then finds himself in the situation which Richard acts out in IV.i, the deposition scene. Richard is speaking, and when Northumberland attempts to break in with the exclamation "My lord," he responds with words which reveal how thoroughly shattered is his sense of the power of his name and the immutability of his identity as Richard Plantagenet, King of England:

> No lord of thine, thou haught insulting man,
> Nor no man's lord; I have no name, no title—
> No, not that name was given me at the font—

> But 'tis usurp'd. Alack the heavy day,
> That I have worn so many winters out,
> And know not now what name to call myself!
> (*Richard II*, IV.i.254–59)

Like the great actor he is, Richard cannot pass the opportunity to demonstrate visually the lesson he has learned. He calls for a looking glass, and holding it before his face he muses:

> No deeper wrinkles yet? Hath sorrow struck
> So many blows upon this face of mine
> And made no deeper wounds? O flatt'ring glass,
> Like to my followers in prosperity,
> Thou dost beguile me! Was this face the face
> That every day under his household roof
> Did keep ten thousand men? Was this the face
> That like the sun did make beholders wink?
> Is this the face which fac'd so many follies,
> That was at last out-fac'd by Bolingbroke?
> A brittle glory shineth in this face;
> As brittle as the glory is the face;
> *He breaks the mirror.*
> (*Richard II*, IV.i.277–88)

Having already discovered that one's name can change rapidly in the world, Richard now becomes self-conscious, aware that the unchanged face he views in the glass squares with neither his greatly changed political condition nor his equally changed inner sense of himself.

Richard is not the first man in this play to discover that he no longer knows who he is. He has already forced the question of identity on Bolingbroke by banishing him from England and robbing him of his succession as Duke of Lancaster. Bolingbroke—whose names change rapidly: Hereford, Bolingbroke, Lancaster, and Henry IV—has understood the lesson well. Speaking to Bushy and Green, two of Richard's favorites, the man who had once confidently answered the question "What is thy name?" with the proud words "Harry of Hereford, Lancaster, and Derby / Am I," now tells the bitterness of banishment and the pain that comes from loss of those possessions and symbols which had heretofore guaranteed identity:

> Myself—a prince by fortune of my birth,
> Near to the King in blood, and near in love
> Till you did make him misinterpret me—
> Have stoop'd my neck under your injuries
> And sigh'd my English breath in foreign clouds,

> Eating the bitter bread of banishment,
> Whilst you have fed upon my signories,
> Dispark'd my parks and fell'd my forest woods,
> From my own windows torn my household coat,
> Raz'd out my imprese, leaving me no sign
> Save men's opinions and my living blood
> To show the world I am a gentleman.
>
> (*Richard II*, III.i.16–27)

Man has not merely lost his true identity for a time; he has, once he abandoned the old hierarchies and rituals, broken into a strange, new existence where he is free to slide back and forth along the vast scale of being, coming to rest momentarily at various points, but never knowing for certain just who and what he is. John of Gaunt's awkward punning on his name as he lies dying suggests the pervasiveness of the feeling that names and the identities they carry are no longer real and permanent but only the roles of the moment. This fluctuation in identity is the basic rhythm of the play, and we feel it everywhere, in Richard's ever-changing moods, in Bolingbroke's rising fortunes and changing names, in Richard's decline from King of England to his last appearance on stage, a body borne in by his murderer. The pattern of up-down, of restless change in the self, appears in its most complete form in the great final speech Richard gives, sitting in the dungeon of Pomfret Castle, about to die, and trying desperately to understand himself and this strange world into which he has fallen. Richard began as a great and secure king, seated on a throne, sure of himself, surrounded by pomp, confirmed by ceremony, looking out over a world of light where everything in the universe was open and ordered. At the end of the play he is the isolated individual, solitary, sitting in a small circle of light, surrounded by darkness and by a flinty prison wall, uncertain of any reality or truth. Isolated, like some hero of Kafka, in a mysterious and a containing world, Richard takes the confusing and conflicting evidence which his mind offers him and attempts, by means of reason and the poetic power to construct analogies, to "hammer it out," to give it shape and form, to achieve some new coherence. The results are not comforting. As hard as he hammers, he can discover only endless mutability in the life of man and endless restlessness in his soul. All evidence is now ambiguous: Where the Bible promises innocence an easy salvation in one passage, "come little ones," turn the page and it speaks in tragic tones of the passage to the Kingdom of Heaven being as difficult as a camel's threading the eye of a needle. Man's powers at one moment seem infinite and he feels that he can "tear a passage through the flinty ribs / Of this hard world," but at the next moment he is the most helpless of creatures and can only comfort himself that many others have endured like misery. Fate forces new identities on him, but even in his own mind man can find no stability, and reality becomes theatrical, a playing of many roles in a constantly changing play:

> Thus play I in one person many people,
> And none contented. Sometimes am I king;
> Then treasons make me wish myself a beggar,
> And so I am. Then crushing penury
> Persuades me I was better when a king;
> Then am I king'd again; and by and by
> Think that I am unking'd by Bolingbroke,
> And straight am nothing. But whate'er I be,
> Nor I, nor any man that but man is,
> With nothing shall be pleas'd till he be eas'd
> With being nothing.
> (*Richard II*, V.v.31–41)

To accommodate the newly perceived paradoxical, shifting reality Richard changes from the formal, conventional style of the beginning of the play to a metaphysical style capable of handling irony and a reality in which the parts no longer mesh, capable of carrying deep, intense agitation and the passionate effort of thought.

The world continues to speak ambiguously to Richard in the form of two visitors. The first is a poor groom from his stables who, having seen the King before only from a distance, now risks his life to come to speak of sympathy and duty which alters not when it alteration finds. The second visitor is the murderer Exton, who has come to kill Richard in hopes of reward from Henry. Richard, having tried to define himself by means of poetry and failed, now takes the way of drama, and acts. He seizes a sword from one of Exton's thugs and strikes two of them down before being killed himself. And so he defines himself in a dramatic or historic—not a philosophical—way. He has never solved the question whether he is king or beggar, never found the meaning he hoped to have; but he has stumbled through experience to quite a different answer. He, like the rest of men, has no stable identity certified by the order of things immutable. He is instead tragic man, whose identity fluctuates between hero and victim, king and corpse; whose values are not guaranteed by anything but his own willingness to die for them; whose life is a painful and continuing process of change. Richard traces the way that all other characters in this world must follow in their turn.

Looking back on the lost past, the men of Henry IV's England see the "fall" occurring at that fatal moment when Richard threw down his warder, the symbol of his office and his duty, to stop for political reasons the ritual trial by combat between Bolingbroke and Mowbray. In *Richard II* the effects of that act are focused in the person of Richard and his passage into tragic existence. In the two parts of *Henry IV*, however, the effects are exploded to create an entire dramatic world and the many various characters who inhabit it. Richard's internal disorders and conflicting values grow into the increasingly bitter political and social disorders of a world racked by rebellion, strife, ambition, self-seeking, squabbling, and desperate attempts to hold things together. Richard's growing fear and awareness of the inevitable movement of time into an unknown future expand into polarities: a complete rejection of time (Falstaff) on one hand, and on the other an obsession with the limited amount of time available to man, and the necessity of using it as completely and efficiently as possible, which leads ultimately to a fearful vision of infinity. Richard's loss of certainty and his increasing inability to reconcile the contrary evidence of his own feelings and experiences enlarge into the murky confusion of history, the world of rumor, suspicion, and half-truth, where men making decisions of the utmost importance to themselves and to their country never really know the necessary facts. There may even be no definite answer to such crucial questions as, "Is the King's planned crusade genuine piety or political strategy?" "Is Hal really a riotous youth or is he only pretending to be a wastrel?" "Did Mortimer treasonously surrender his army to Glendower, and does Henry refuse to ransom him because he is a traitor or because he has a legal claim to the throne?" The kind of suspicion raised on suspicion, on which men must risk their lives in this world where truth is impossible to come by, is perfectly conveyed in the Earl of Worcester's lines in which he sketches out the path of reasoning which leads him to rebellion: he helped the King, the King can never forget this and will always fear that his former friends will think themselves not fully rewarded, and therefore they must always fear the king who may fear them:

> For, bear ourselves as even as we can,
> The King will always think him in our debt,
> And think we think ourselves unsatisfied,
> Till he hath found a time to pay us home.
> (*1 Henry IV*, I.iii.285–88)

As Richard's identity crumbles, he begins with increasing frequency to use images of the theater, of acting and role-playing, to reflect the growing gap between appearance and reality, and the instability of character. In the later plays, the impulse to theatricality, the sense of life as play and man as actor breaks into the open in repeated images of the theater, in numerous brief plays-within-the-play, in the conception of character and action. Playing becomes not only an instrument of deceit— Prince John's pretense that he will pardon the rebels if they lay down their arms—but also a means to truth—Hal's parodies of Hotspur's excessive energy and violence. Men in the world of *Henry IV* no longer take their identities as settled but assume that life is a succession of roles, played with skill and style to achieve a desired end. Hal plays the part of the prodigal son and the wastrel in order to appear better when he is settled as king; the Protean Falstaff plays a succession of roles for pleasure and profit.

Richard's discovery that man is a creature of infinite possibilities ranging all the way from dust to god, beggar to king, is also projected in the Henry plays into the wide and varied cast of characters, each of whom seems to be not a whole man but a fragment, some singular power inherent in human nature isolated and carried to its extreme. "Homo," may be, as Gadshill says, "a common name to all men" (*1 Henry IV*, II.i.92–93), but the adjective which should follow is constantly questioned. Does man to realize his humanity properly seek power? pleasure? learning? love? order? glory? Is the truly human setting the place of pleasure and fellowship, the Boar's Head Tavern in Eastcheap? the council table in the palace at Westminster? the desperate battlefields far to the north and west along the Scottish and the Welsh marches? Glendower's castle where old songs of love are played and the vast mysteries of the universe are discussed? These are the principal symbolic places in the Henry plays, the places in which man now works out, in a sudden surge of freedom and released energy, his destiny and his nature. Each of these symbolic places has a resident deity, a genius of the place, whose speeches and actions provide the best understanding of its attitudes and values.

The Glendower world, which focuses the values of magic, science, poetry and love, remains strangely peripheral, as if, despite the high value Shakespeare elsewhere places on these powers, they were not of fundamental importance in the great conflict. There is perhaps even a disqualifying sensitivity here, a tendency to withdraw from the power struggle, for when Hotspur—who also finds love trivial—offends Glendower by laughing at his magic, the Welshman simply withdraws his support and is not heard of again.

Falstaff presides over the tavern world, and when first seen this latter-day Bacchus is waking from a nap on a bench. Sitting up, stretching, he asks the Prince, "What time of day is it, lad?" The Prince, who has a supreme sense of time, realizes that Falstaff is the one character in this play to whom time, the sequence of irrecoverable moments, is totally meaningless.

> PRINCE: Thou art so fat-witted with drinking of old sack, and unbuttoning thee after supper, and sleeping upon benches after noon, that thou hast forgotten to demand that truly which thou wouldest truly know. What a devil hast thou to do with the time of the day? Unless hours were cups of sack, and minutes capons, and clocks the tongues of bawds, and dials the signs of leaping-houses, and the blessed sun himself a fair hot wench in flame-coloured taffeta, I see no reason why thou shouldst be so superfluous to demand the time of the day.
>
> (*1 Henry IV*, I.ii.2–11)

The old knight is enormously fat, a walking version of the roast beef of Old England, given over entirely to epicurean pleasures. He never pays his debts; he is a liar, a thief, a drunkard, the very energy of disorder and lawlessness. For him a true man follows the pleasures of the belly and the bed, avoiding pain and labor whenever possible. He takes what he wants without worrying about property rights or morality. Such abstracts as honor, truth, duty, and honesty, those hard, painful virtues which he is always being exhorted to practice, seem to him patently ridiculous and self-defeating, and he is an adept at sliding around and under such claims. When trapped in some obvious lie or charged with some gross weakness of the flesh, he will, without regard for the restraints of logic, gaily change the subject, take up another pose, or make some such comment as "all's one for that." He is a master at staying alive and comfortable in an extremely difficult, dangerous, and potentially painful world.

Viewed from a sternly moral direction, Falstaff is a vice, a demidevil, a tempter, a mere caterpillar of the commonwealth. When viewed from a more tolerant perspective Falstaff is an amusing and cunning old rogue, but still an obvious, slow-witted glutton and braggart, a victim of his own appetites and a figure of fun. But Falstaff meets these challenges more than halfway by asking continually the eternal comic questions: "What is so important about a well-run state? Why all this strange passion for this 'grinning honor,' this order and honesty, which cost so much pain and suffering?" These questions are usually asked indirectly, by means of parody and wit, and the shrewdness of mind and the style of execution are exquisite at points. For example, when he is urging Hal to join the robbery at Gadshill, and Hal protests that the Prince of Wales cannot become a common thief, Falstaff remarks quickly, "Thou cam'st not of the blood royal, if thou darest not stand for ten shillings." On the face of it he seems merely to be punning on the meaning of "royal," a type of coin. But there is an edge to this remark, which Hal apparently misses, for it remembers that that royal blood of England achieved its present eminence by means of robbery, not a little robbery such as the thieves are planning on Gadshill, but a big robbery in which all of England was taken.

While Falstaff is efficient in use of the rapier thrust of wit, his most masterful attacks are delivered by means of parody. When Hal seems to have bested him in a wit-combat, Falstaff shifts ground and plays the misled youth, the penitent determined to return to the paths of righteousness:

> Thou hast done much harm upon me, Hal—God forgive thee for it! Before I knew thee, Hal, I knew nothing; and now am I, if a man should speak truly, little better than one of the wicked. I must give over this life, and I will give it over. By the Lord, an I do not I am a villain! I'll be damn'd for never a king's son in Christendom.
>
> (*1 Henry IV*, I.ii.87–95)

To his appreciative audience this is no more than another of the Monsieur Remorse's self-beguilements or posturings. Given over entirely to the life of the flesh, he can still fool himself and try to fool others into believing that he is about to repent and care for his soul. But several features of the speech—its style, its obvious exaggeration, and its sly suggestion that true wickedness comes from the palace, not the tavern—combine to create behind the lines an eye-twinkling self-consciousness which is aware at once of how ridiculous is this pretense and yet how good a game it is. The speech is then self-parody, but it goes further, for Falstaff is also acting out the ridiculous pretenses of the rest of the world to holiness. Behind each of his pretenses—the royal king, the brave captain, the innocent child, the loyal knight, the penitent sinner—stands Falstaff himself, the old Adam, fat, red-nosed, slothful, and lecherous, a living low-burlesque of the establishment.

Each of Falstaff's parodies contains both the pretense of virtue (the pose) and what he takes to be human reality (himself), and as the play progresses he stages ever more pointed demonstrations of the gap between appearance and reality. On the eve of the great battle at Shrewsbury, Sir John, acting as draftmaster, has allowed all the healthy and prosperous to buy out and collected instead the poor, the battered, and the inept to assemble a remarkable regiment, "slaves as ragged as Lazarus in the painted cloth where the glutton's dogs licked his sores." As he marches this strange rout toward the battle, he encounters Hal and Westmoreland, banners flying, armor shining, horses snorting, filled with confidence and chivalry. These brave knights are astounded at the sight of such ridiculous soldiers, and Hal exclaims: "I did never see such pitiful rascals." Falstaff's reply contains a grimly realistic view of war and the function of the common soldier:

> Tut, tut; good enough to toss; food for powder, food for powder; they'll fill a pit as well as better: tush, man, mortal men, mortal men.
>
> (1 Henry IV, IV.ii.63–65)

War's reality has been paraded before war's pretenses. Falstaff's view that since the soldier's function is to be blown to pieces and fill a ditch, one man will do as well as another is proven by the events of the battle, in which only three of his men survive, and they so badly wounded that the rest of their lives will be spent begging. Falstaff's most famous use of this parody technique is, of course, his catechism, in which he compares the abstraction, honor, with the reality, the body of the honorable but dead Blunt, and draws some very common-sense conclusions about the durability of honor and its ability to set a leg or take away the pain of a wound.

Falstaff, and the tavern world which he personifies, is a most dangerous antagonist to any moral point of view, to any set of abstractions such as honor, duty, and country. His questions, so pointedly put, so beautifully dramatized, about what honor means, what a king really is, and what a nation does, are never satisfactorily answered in the play. He is always acting out some hilarious and penetrating truth about the establishment, and each time he asserts such a truth, he strengthens his own case for leading a pleasant, harmless life, asleep behind the arras after lunch, drinking a bottle of sack, and laughing and joking with a few witty friends about the foolishness of life as most sober-sided citizens lead it.

In the figure of Henry Percy, Hotspur, Shakespeare has constructed the exact opposite of Falstaff. If the old knight is all earth and water, the heavy elements, then Hotspur is all fire and air, the light and ascending elements. Where Falstaff seems all flesh and bones and body, Hotspur appears to lack a body and be all spirit. Where Falstaff, who always longs for a horse, is always forced by circumstances to walk—Hal steals his horse and later procures for him "a charge of foot"—Hotspur is fully alive only on the back of his horse. Where Falstaff refuses to have anything to do with time, Hotspur is always rushing forward to meet time, to outrun it. Falstaff's natural habitat is in the tavern before the fire; Percy's is on the battlefield. But the contrast between the two characters is best understood in terms of their distinct aims: where Falstaff always seeks pleasure, Hotspur always seeks fame, honor, *gloire*.

Scarcely aware of other people, never aware of their feelings, Hotspur is aimed like an arrow toward that mystical place where absolute honor is to be won. The farther away it is, the more difficult to arrive at, the more honor for the man who achieves it:

> By heaven, methinks it were an easy leap
> To pluck bright honour from the pale-fac'd moon;
> Or dive into the bottom of the deep,
> Where fathom-line could never touch the ground,
> And pluck up drowned honour by the locks;
>   So he that doth redeem her thence might wear
> Without corrival all her dignities.
>   (1 Henry IV, I.iii.201–07)

Honor, as Hotspur understands it, is no longer the honor of the medieval knight, of Roland or Galahad, achieved by humbling one's self and performing the difficult tasks imposed by one's God, one's feudal lord, or one's lady. It is instead the Renaissance thirst for individual fame, for immortality of reputation in a world where all else dies and is forgotten, and it possesses Hotspur utterly. Even his sleep is a restless, impatient dream of battle, which culminates in a breath-taking vision of Fame:

> And in thy face strange motions have appear'd,
> Such as we see when men restrain their breath
> On some great sudden hest.
>   (1 Henry IV, II.iii.57–59)

Hotspur's life is a surging rush onward which endures no obstacles. He has no time for love or poetry or song, for grace or manners or political maneuvering. He prides himself on being honest, direct, bluntly straightforward. What his heart feels his lips speak. In a world of actors, he alone refuses to pretend, and his virtues lead him on to greatness and to death. His bluntness alerts his enemies, his honesty offends his allies, his impetuousness and courage lead him to charge a superior army. The thirst for fame is death-marked even before it dies on Shrewsbury Field. Its republican cry for liberty cries also for blood, "If we live, we live to tread on kings." It tastes the pleasure of the battle, feels the charge like a thunderbolt, is all on fire to hear that victims are coming to be offered to its god, "the fire-ey'd maid of smoky war." Honor covers a sensual delight in the nearness of death, death for the self and death for all others: "Doomsday is near; die all, die merrily" (1 Henry IV, IV.i.134).

A life and values which have so much death in them cannot endure for long, and Hotspur shortly dies at the hands of a more efficient and more durable force, embodied in the greatest of the Lancastrian kings, Prince Hal, later to be Henry V. As Hotspur dies, he glimpses, as Richard had earlier, the vast, infinite reaches of time where men briefly live, die, and are forgotten; where life and fame are but the fools of time; and where in some distant future even time itself gives way to some unthinkable emptiness:

> But thoughts, the slaves of life, and life, time's fool,
> And time, that takes survey of all the world,
> Must have a stop. O, I could prophesy,
> But that the earthly and cold hand of death
> Lies on my tongue. No, Percy, thou art dust
> And food for—
> *Dies.*
>
> (*1 Henry IV*, V.iv.81–86)

Hal's completion of Percy's thought, "for worms," suggests the extent to which he understands and shares this modern vision of the transience of man in the vastness of time and space.

It is the work of the politician to control and adjust such extremes as Hotspur's idealism and Falstaff's sensuality, which threaten civil order in the pursuit of what they take as the good. Superb politician though he may be, it is Henry IV's fate to spend his lifetime trying to order such contraries as these, and it is equally his fate never to succeed in doing so. All his skill and canniness cannot restrain the freedom, the individuality, and the energies he unleashed by usurping the throne and destroying the principle of traditional order that once kept such excesses in bounds. In seizing the throne from the weak and politically inept Richard, Henry sought his own advancement and perhaps even the good of the state (his motivation is never clear, even to himself), but the result is a life of anxiety and travail for him and for England. His life and reign are a great continuing irony: the politically effective king creates a disordered kingdom.

The irony begins to make itself felt from the moment of Henry's assuming the kingship. At the end of *Richard II*, the new king sits on the throne at Windsor Castle with a sense of security bred of his own efficiency and power. Giving Richard the last of his many names, Exton enters and offers his body as Henry's ultimate victory:

> Great King, within this coffin I present
> Thy buried fear. Herein all breathless lies
> The mightiest of thy greatest enemies,
> Richard of Bordeaux, by me hither brought.
> (*Richard II*, V.vi.30–33)

Without the slightest intention of doing so, Exton defines perfectly the problem which the body of Richard is going to constitute when he offers it to the King as "thy buried fear." Buried the body is in the ground; but the fear is also buried deep in the heart of Henry IV. Neither he nor his son will ever forget that their throne was secured by the murder of a king, and throughout their lives, even to the eve of the battle of Agincourt, they continue to make promises of expiation. The ghost of Richard will haunt them in another way as well, for the Lancastrian kings will always remember, will always have buried deep within them, the fear that what they have shown as possible, the murder of a king to seize a throne, abides as a dreadful example for others. The politically necessary act of king-killing is at once a success and a failure.

At what should have been the highest moment of Henry's triumph, this practical, efficient man begins to discover the tragic complexities of his being and his political situation. What are only hints in the closing scene of *Richard II* become obvious facts in the beginning of the first part of *Henry IV*. As the play opens, the King longs to undertake a crusade to the Holy Land to atone for the murder of Richard, but "dear expedience" has forced him to postpone this journey earlier and now is forcing him to delay it once more. Although he hopes that peace has come to England at last, even as he hopes word is brought of new disorders and barbarism on the far edges of the kingdom. The Welsh under the irregular and wild Glendower have defeated Henry's army, and after the battle the Welsh women mutilated the bodies in unspeakable ways. In the north, where Hotspur commands, the battle has been won against the Scot and Douglas, but the bodies were piled in high windrows oozing blood. The winning general, young Harry Hotspur, has now refused to surrender his prisoners to the King, whom he earlier helped to power. While the kingdom trembles and totters, Hal, the Prince of Wales, spends his time drinking in the tavern and rioting in the streets.

Throughout *Part I*, rebellion and disorder intensify, culminating in the battle at Shrewsbury, but even as the sounds of that battle die away, new rebels spring up and new armies march. As these internal disorders continue in *Part II* they become more savage and fierce until Northumberland, crying out in fury over the death of his son Hotspur, calls for chaos and universal death:

> Let heaven kiss earth! Now let not Nature's hand
> Keep the wild flood confin'd! Let order die!
> And let this world no longer be a stage
> To feed contention in a ling'ring act;
> But let one spirit of the first-born Cain
> Reign in all bosoms, that, each heart being set
> On bloody courses, the rude scene may end
> And darkness be the burier of the dead!
> (*2 Henry IV*, I.i.153–60)

As rebellion becomes more savage, so do the opposing political forces. In *Part I* the political maneuvering is adroit and skillful, but in *Part*

II politics becomes a very dirty game indeed, and its full viciousness arrives when Henry's younger son, Prince John, tricks the rebels into dismissing their army by promising them an honest hearing and redress of grievances. But as soon as the rebel army has been disbanded, John orders all the rebellious lords off to execution. His explanation is the Machiavellian one that there is no need to keep faith with traitors, and after his "victory" he remarks piously, "God, and not we, have safely fought today." *The Prince,* not law and established duty, has become the guide to realistic politics.

As their leaders become more savage and more cynical, the ordinary Englishmen become, in the terms of the Archbishop of York, revolting animals, "beastly feeders," never satisfied with any ruler they have, always restlessly seeking change in government, willing to embark on any adventure. Having cheered Bolingbroke and rejoiced in the death of Richard, they are now dissatisfied with Henry and, howling like dogs to find and eat their vomit, go crying to the grave of Richard, which has become a shrine (*2 Henry IV,* I.iii.97–102).

Struggling with endless rebellions and increasing savagery, Henry IV comes at last to the place where Richard and Hotspur have already stood—where Adam and Eve stand in Books 11 and 12 of *Paradise Lost*—looking out on that vast span of time and change which swallows hope and obliterates the meaning of individual life:

> O God! that one might read the book of fate,
> And see the revolution of the times
> Make mountains level, and the continent,
> Weary of solid firmness, melt itself
> Into the sea; and other times to see
> The beachy girdle of the ocean
> Too wide for Neptune's hips; how chances mock,
> And changes fill the cup of alteration
> With divers liquors! O, if this were seen,
> The happiest youth, viewing his progress through,
> What perils past, what crosses to ensue,
> Would shut the book and sit him down and die.
>   (*2 Henry IV,* III.i.45–56)

At the same time that he breaks into the vastness of time and space, the endlessness of change, man also discovers the iron law of historical necessity. Having rejected the old social restrictions of obedience, submission to tradition and ritual, and maintenance of assigned station and rank, having chosen freedom, men now begin to discover that freedom leads ironically, to another kind of necessity, the tragic necessity of history, which forces you to endure the unsuspected consequences of what you are and what you have done. "The main chance of things" to come "in their seeds / And weak beginning lie intreasured," and just as Richard found himself surrounded by the stone walls of Pomfret dungeon, just as Hotspur followed fame to the point where he became food for worms, so Henry can only grimly meet what must be, the rebellion which follows endlessly from rebellion. The only possible virtue is dogged courage: "Are these things then necessities? / Then let us meet them like necessities" (*2 Henry IV,* III.i.92–93).

Near the end of *Part II* Henry at last receives the news he has waited for so long, the defeat of the last rebel army. But even as the news reaches him, he has a stroke and realizes that Fortune never comes "with both hands full," but writes "her fair words still in foulest letters." In the tragic world the past is never done with until you are dead, and even as Henry lies dying, the "polished perturbation" for which he has suffered so much lying beside him, Hal enters and, thinking his father dead, carries the crown away. The act is innocent, perhaps, but it reenacts another crime in which the wish was also father to the thought and the crown was also taken from its rightful possessor before he was dead. That crown which glittered so attractively has become for Henry "a rich armour worn in heat of day, / That scald'st with safety," and so it will also be for the man who now carries it away.

Henry's experience is the experience of his world. If at first men felt an exhilarating release from the restraints of the old traditional order and realized in themselves newly-discovered potentialities of self, they now begin to discover that freedom and the individual life have their terrifying as well as their grander sides. Having confidently relied on themselves to make of life whatever they will it to be, they now begin to discover what it means to live without some of the ultimate comforts provided by the older system: without the grace and mercy of God, without an unchanging nature which continues to circle in its great patterns and manifest an order and meaning in the universe quite independent of the actions of men, without a stable society in which the individual man can achieve permanence and meaning by living the same life his father did and passing that life on to his children.

The continuing turmoil and suffering of the new world are intensified by the will to power and the incompatibility of its dominant energies. The sensualist, the idealist, and the politician, each seeks to be king, to control the kingdom, to become, as it were, the whole world. Each way of life challenges and is challenged by the others. This mutual antagonism is implicit in Percy's belief that he must have preeminent honor, "without co-rival," and in his contempt for the "sword and buckler" Prince of Wales. It is in Hal's and Falstaff's mocking scorn of Percy's bloodthirstiness, his reckless impatience, and his preference of his horse to his wife. It is in Falstaff's cynical awareness of the great world's hypocrisy and his continuing burlesques of its pretenses. It is in the King's contempt for the tavern world and his fear of the northern lords.

Out of these antagonisms rises the plot of the play. The politician seeks social order and stability but runs athwart the headlong search for honor and sensuality's absolute rejection of any kind of restraint. Sensuality and idealism in turn find that the social need for order imposes upon them limits which they cannot endure. At first the conflict is managed in terms of word-combats, such as Hotspur's angry argument with the King about the return of prisoners, and Falstaff's various parodies of the world of honor or of politics. Words issue into actions as the underworld disturbs the peace and ventures into the kingdom to rob and cheat. The desire for fame and honor finds no satisfaction in peaceful life and flares into open rebellion. The conflict intensifies as the play proceeds, and there is an inevitable drawing movement towards the north, where the King marches to encounter the opposing manifestations of will assembled under the banner of Hotspur. Politics and sensuality mix better than either does with idealism and its death-directedness, and Falstaff marches uneasily with the forces of order. Idealism, honor, and raw courage lack the sense and control needed for a world where only the fittest survive, and Hotspur's body, with the strange wound in his thigh, is borne off on the back of Falstaff. Falstaff's quick opportunism, raw common sense, and cat-footed sense of survival; and the politician's hard, clear objectivity, practicality, and ability to control passions are the virtues which survive.

Despite all the disorders of *1 Henry IV*, life there has a saving vitality, exuberance, and even joy—so much so that it is impossible really to regret the loss of the stability and ceremonial order of the older, more peaceful world which lies behind. The release of energy and the exhilarating effects of freedom—the positive side of the transition from the Middle Ages to the Renaissance—are so attractive that disorder seems almost a small price to pay for the wit and pleasure in life of Falstaff, the fiery idealism and high courage of the knight Harry Percy, the political skill and masterful strategy of statesmen like Henry IV and the Earl of Worcester. The vast possibilities of human nature and the mind of man come into view, and men begin to discover what they and their world are really like. As in *Paradise Lost*, the first experience of disobeying God, satisfying appetite, and eating of the tree of knowledge is hot and pleasurable. But as in Milton, so in *2 Henry IV* men soon learn that knowledge is knowledge of good *and* evil. The first joy of power and pleasure soon passes and the previously hidden side of freedom begins to turn into view. Justice Shallow and his cousin Silence sitting talking of the old days that are gone and agreeing that "Death is certain" set the tone of this darkening world. The Boar's Head Tavern, formerly the center of wit and pleasure, now has an ugly quality about it. It is openly a brothel, run by Mistress Quickly, whose name takes on a new significance; and we learn that Pistol and Doll Tearsheet have killed one of the customers. The jokes have lost their cutting edge, and the characters seem to be wearily imitating their successes at wit in *Part I*. True honor and military virtue seem to have died with Hotspur, existing now only in their grotesque forms: in Prince John, who finds it unnecessary for a man of honor to be honorable with rebels, and in the crazed pimp and bully, Pistol, raving about glory and conquest in a jumble of fantastic language picked up in the theater listening to the heroic rant of such figures as Marlowe's Tamburlaine.

The pleasure principle and common sense may be more durable than Hotspur's idealism, but Falstaff also has his fatal necessities, which begin to appear prominently in *Part II*. He appears first reeling drunk, having just voided, and throughout the play his flesh reacts with illnesses and pain, gout and pox, to the excesses of pleasure, food, drink, sex. There are flashes here and there of the old Falstaff, but even his wit is blunted by a growing sense of self-satisfaction and sentimentality. As the old King sickens and Hal nears the throne, Falstaff begins to taste power and his imperial ambitions take open shape. His will to power has always been in the background of such actions as robbing the crown tax money, playing the king, and joking about the office he would hold when Hal assumed the throne; but he now displays an unconcerned insolence towards authority, mocks the Chief Justice in the streets, and cheats openly. As he begins to take himself more and more seriously, Falstaff turns philosopher, carrying his previously unexamined, amoral sense of life as pleasure to its inevitable and unpleasant extreme, a universal rule of dog-eat-dog: "If the young dace be a bait for the old pike, I see no reason in the law of nature but I may snap at [the gullible Justice Shallow]."

His moment comes, as it does to all the others. Upon hearing of the death of King Henry, Falstaff pauses only long enough to borrow a thousand pounds from Justice Shallow before riding hard toward London and his king, shouting the ominous words "The laws of England are at my commandment. Blessed are they that they have been my friends; and woe to my Lord Chief Justice!" In most matters Falstaff is a skeptic, but there remains a fatal innocence in this fascinating old man, who now expects that his old companion, Hal, will greet him with open arms and the tavern and the palace will at last become one. As Falstaff steps out from the crowd towards the coronation train with all its symbols of the power of England, he opens his arms and cries: "God save thy Grace, King Hal; my royal Hal! . . . God save thee, my sweet boy!" The mistake in identity is surprising for a man so adept at playing roles and changing masks to suit the need of the moment. It is not Hal who replies but King Henry V, the mirror of all Christian kings:

> I know thee not, old man. Fall to thy prayers.
> How ill white hairs become a fool and jester!
> I have long dreamt of such a kind of man,
> So surfeit-swell'd, so old, and so profane;
> But, being awak'd, I do despise my dream. . . .
> Presume not that I am the thing I was. . . .
> (2 Henry IV, V.v.48–57)

And so Falstaff, who long ago had been page to Thomas Mowbray, is also banished and comes to that vision of nothingness to which so many have preceded him. His understanding of where he is takes the form of a simple acceptance of a duty he has earlier steadfastly refused to acknowledge, the necessity of paying debts: "Master Shallow, I owe you a thousand pound." We never see the knight again. He retires to the Boar's Head to die early in Henry V with a broken heart, calling for sack, babbling of green fields, and swearing still that women are devils incarnate. Ambition should be made of sterner stuff, as another Shakespearean character says; but while pleasure, wit, and good-natured common sense may lack the restraint and calculation needed in the long struggle for survival and power, their absence impoverishes, as does the death of Hotspur's frankness, courage, and idealism. The England which is made by killing Richard, Hotspur, and Falstaff is a more orderly but a less vital and less honest realm. And yet their deaths were certain, guaranteed by the very excess of their own virtue and by their own narrow interpretation of reality. The banishment of Falstaff and the destruction of wit and pleasure do not teach a moral lesson but present a tragic necessity. Henry V is not here making a wrong choice but simply instrumenting the inevitable triumph of politics over pleasure. If he is Falstaff's executioner, as he was Hotspur's, then both Falstaff and Hotspur made that execution inevitable. If the gain of order achieved by their deaths is at the same time a loss of energy, pleasure, common sense, and selfless dedication to the ideal, that is the nature of existence East of Eden, where every gain is loss and every good an evil.

Politics and statecraft, the passion for order, ultimately triumph in the competition for rule. The genius of the palace and council table is finally not Henry IV but his son Hal, Henry V, and he alone escapes the decline into despair, and death. As others sicken he grows stronger, and as others make fatal mistakes he becomes ever more sure and certain in his actions. Critics have seen Hal as the ideal prince undergoing a process of education. Not a cold and careful schemer like his father, Hal, we are told, moves easily between the world of the flesh in the tavern and the world of honor on the battlefield. He excels in both ways of life and has in addition the ability to act with the temperance, prudence, and good sense necessary to the politician. His position at Shrewsbury Field standing between the body of Hotspur, whom he has killed, and the supposed body of Falstaff, playing dead in order to live, is thus an emblematic presentation of his situation in *The Henriad*. In other words, passing through a series of trials, Hal comes to be not only the ideal king but the ideal man, the only total man in a world where all the rest of the characters are possessed by a single great energy or virtue. As such he becomes the hero-king restoring life to a dying land, removing the curse of Richard's murder from the kingdom.

There is much evidence to support these ethical and mythic readings, but Shakespeare complicates the situation enormously by his realistic portrayal of character. There is from the beginning something cold, withdrawn, and impersonal, even icily calculating, about Hal. He jokes, drinks, and joins in the fun of the tavern world, holds long conversations with the hostess and her servants, but he seems to be *in* not *of*, this lower world. Though he may enjoy the company of Falstaff and his gang, he is fully aware of a very practical, political reason for being here, and he regards his boon companions with a hard awareness of their worth:

> I know you all, and will awhile uphold
> The unyok'd humour of your idleness;
> Yet herein will I imitate the sun,
> Who doth permit the base contagious clouds
> To smother up his beauty from the world,
> That, when he please again to be himself,
> Being wanted, he may be more wond'red at
> By breaking through the foul and ugly mists
> Of vapours that did seem to strangle him.
> If all the year were playing holidays,
> To sport would be as tedious as to work;
> But when they seldom come, they wish'd-for come,
> And nothing pleaseth but rare accidents.
> So, when this loose behaviour I throw off
> And pay the debt I never promised,

> By how much better than my word I am,
> By so much shall I falsify men's hopes;
> And, like bright metal on a sullen ground,
> My reformation, glitt'ring o'er my fault,
> Shall show more goodly and attract more eyes
> Than that which hath no foil to set it off.
> I'll so offend to make offence a skill,
> Redeeming time when men think least I will.
>
> (1 Henry IV, I.ii.188–210)

There is something grim about the phrase "I know you all," and something even grimmer about the adjective "unyok'd," suggesting an ethic in which only those things harnessed and made to draw are worthwhile. Furthermore, Hal has a very modern sense of the people's love of change, the value of a political "image," and the mechanics of constructing one. Henry IV created his political image by appearing only rarely before the people but always acting with the utmost affability and kindness to all. Hal's strategy, however, is to appear like a roisterer and a wastrel in order that expectations will be low and any achievements whatsoever as a ruler will seem magnificent by comparison. His strategy works perfectly, and in Henry V the Archbishop expresses the wonder of the King's knowledge and ability (Henry V, I.i.38–59). Hal never seems to lose sight of the fact that he is preparing to be king of England, and each of his schemes works, each of his predictions is fulfilled. After Falstaff has played the king, Hal surveys him critically and finds that this is no king, and so Falstaff stands down and Hal plays the role with all the sternness, the rhetoric, the authority of true majesty. Falstaff, innocently thinking this is only a merry jape, takes the part of the penitent prince and uses the occasion to put in a good word for himself:

> FALSTAFF: . . . .No, my good lord: banish Peto, banish Bardolph, banish Poins; but, for sweet Jack Falstaff, kind Jack Falstaff, true Jack Falstaff, valiant Jack Falstaff—and therefore more valiant, being, as he is, old Jack Falstaff—banish not him thy Harry's company, banish not him thy Harry's company. Banish plump Jack, and banish all the world.
> PRINCE: I do, I will.
>
> (1 Henry IV, II.iv.521–29)

In that "I do, I will," we hear the voice of the future and see the coronation at Westminster, where a great king proves his ability to rule himself and others by the words addressed to an old rogue standing with open arms: "I know thee not, old man."

Hal's view of honor is equally detached and his calculations for achieving it are as precise as his management of the world of pleasure. He can be the chivalric knight, the man of honor, as well as he can be the tavern roisterer. But his parodies of the kind of honor which kills a dozen Scots before breakfast and complains of the quiet life suggest an objective view; and his completion of Hotspur's dying sentence, "Food for worms," measures the ultimate value of this kind of honor as coolly as the words "I do, I will" sum up Falstaff's future. Hal values honor, however, knows that a king must have it, and he has a plan for acquiring it. When Henry IV berates his son for a wasted life, contrasting him unfavorably with Hotspur, Hal replies that he intends to become the very chief of honor on some battlefield where his features will be covered all in blood—a sign which will, he says, mark him as his father's true son—and where he will tear honor from Hotspur's heart:

> Percy is but my *factor*, good my lord,
> To *engross* up glorious deeds on my behalf;
> And I will call him to *so strict account*
> That he shall *render* every glory up,
> Yea, even the *slightest* worship of his time,
> Or I will tear the *reckoning* from his heart.
> (*1 Henry IV*, III.ii.147–52, italics mine)

The bookkeeping imagery here suggests a view of honor as a negotiable commodity, not the insubstantial ideal of Chaucer's "very, perfect, gentle knight," nor the Renaissance gentleman's honor achieved by a life of unremitting gentleness, of duty, of service, and of manners, nor Hotspur's fame that must be sought steadfastly in hard and difficult places through a lifetime of honesty and courage and dedication. Percy is wrong about honor and Hal is, as usual, precisely correct. He kills Hotspur in battle, acquires his honor, which in time becomes the honor of the king and the pride of the national state he rules. Private virtues become national virtues in *The Henriad*, even as the absolute individuals become Englishmen.

Though the Prince's bent is clearly political, his attitude toward the exercise of power and the rights of succession is remarkably clear-eyed and basic. When the old king on his deathbed tries to explain that the agonizing complexities resulting from his illegal seizure of the throne may continue to haunt his heir, Hal is rather surprised. His right to the crown is, he feels, absolute, and he intends to allow no questioning:

> My gracious liege,
> You won it, wore it, kept it, gave it me;
> Then plain and right must my possession be;

Which I with more than with a common pain
'Gainst all the world will rightfully maintain.
(*2 Henry IV*, IV.v.221–25)

This modern view of succession and kingship, which is as direct and practical as Hal's view of honor, is a world away from that mystical theory of legitimacy and the king's sacred involvement with God and the order of the cosmos which Richard took for granted.

A great production sets the playing style and the interpretation of a play for a generation. The ruling version of *Henry V* in our time has been the Laurence Olivier film with its hearts-of-oak and roast-beef-of-old-England tone. It is the story of bluff and hearty King Hal, swaggering his way across France, wooing in good foursquare English words the shy, but delighted, Princess of France, twirling his crown and tossing it on the back of his throne, roaring defiance to the gift of tennis balls from the degenerate French dauphin, giving great battlefield speeches about St. Crispin's Day, and exhorting the troops to close up the breaches in the wall with their English dead. It is the great swish of the arrows from the longbows of the sturdy English yeomanry—the first national army—which scythe down the gorgeously caparisoned but clumsy chivalry of France— the last feudal army—charging across the field at Agincourt. It is England becoming Britain as the hero-king unites his people and draws into his order the Welshman Fluellen, the Irishman Macmorris, and the Scot Captain Jamy, the violent and cantankerous representatives of those savage border lands where his predecessors fought so many barbarous battles. It is a land united as one man which marshals a democratic modern army to attack and defeat France; it roots out traitors with almost miraculous knowledge of their treason; it hangs thieves and looters without hesitation. It is, as Canterbury describes it, in an epic simile drawn from *The Aeneid*, a kingdom like the beehive where the "singing masons" build "roofs of gold," and the justice delivers "o'er to executors pale / The lazy yawning drone." Such rebellious elements as remain—traitorous peers and a gang of cutthroats and thieves at the Boar's Head who go to France "to suck, to suck, the very blood to suck"—the King handles with remarkable ease.

Henry V has the public virtues of a great king, magnanimity, courage, resourcefulness, energy, efficiency, and a great public presence. At the same time, certain private traits seen in him earlier—flat practicality, hard objectivity, a lack of complexity amounting almost to insensitivity, a sense of the uses of a public image, and a definite coldness—persist and contribute much to his political efficiency, even while raising questions about him as a man.

As *Henry V* opens, the Bishop of Ely and the Archbishop of Canterbury tell us that Parliament has proposed to expropriate church lands, but the King has not yet committed himself on the issue. Canterbury has offered a deal: if Henry will block the bill, the clergy will provide him with a great deal of money to support his proposed expedition to France. Rather than give a direct answer, Henry has asked the Archbishop what he thinks about the English king's rights to the throne of France,

> The severals and unhidden passages
> Of his true titles to some certain dukedoms,
> And generally to the crown and seat of France,
> Deriv'd from Edward, his great-grandfather.
> *(Henry V,* I.i.86–89)

Taking up the hint, the Church is now here, in the persons of Canterbury and Ely, to interpret Henry's French title for him. Before the Archbishop begins to speak Henry charges him most solemnly to speak nothing but certain truth, for a war between great nations and the deaths of many men hang upon his words. Happily for Canterbury, Hal's title to the throne of France is "as clear as is the summer's sun," but the proof he offers is an incredible jumble of ancient geography, the customs of the primitive Germans, the workings of something called the Salic Law prohibiting females from ruling in central Europe, and other obscure pedantries. The King, still not clear about his title, or wishing to declare himself again, asks plainly, "May I with right and conscience make this claim?" When reassured once more, all doubt dies and Henry determines to seize France as his right or obliterate it:

> Now are we well resolv'd; and, by God's help
> And yours, the noble sinews of our power,
> France being ours, we'll bend it to our awe,
> Or break it all to pieces;
> *(Henry V,* I.ii.222–25)

Nothing more is heard about the expropriation of church lands. It would be most interesting to hear either Falstaff or Hotspur comment on these speeches and events, but their voices are no longer heard in Henry V's England. What Hal's thoughts are it is impossible to say—his motives are always as obscure as his father's—but it is also impossible to forget the dying Henry IV's advice to his son, "to busy giddy minds with foreign quarrels."

This is not the only occasion on which there is something puzzling about Hal's motives, on which it is possible to see him acting as both the hero-king and a subtle politician. Hal, in III.iii, has brought his army across the sea to the walls of Harfleur. The town at first resists siege, but the citizens then decide that there is no hope and ask for a parley. As the parley begins, Hal turns on the citizens and storms at them for defending their town so long and putting themselves and their dependents in such danger. Furthermore, if the town continues to resist he will batter it to pieces and burn it to ashes. His soldiers inflamed by battle will break loose into the town "with conscience wide as hell" to murder, rape, and pillage. "What is it to me," the King shouts again and again, if these dreadful things happen? What responsibility do I have if these animals run lusting for blood through your streets, since it is you, the citizens of Harfleur, who by your stubbornness endanger your people? The repeated rhetorical question, "What is it to me," with its implicit answer, "nothing," sounds very strange in this context. Considering the brutalities that he is describing, it should be a great deal, and how does he think this army got across the English Channel and arrived before the walls of Harfleur? Who was it who assembled such cutthroats as Pistol and Nym and brought them to France "to suck, to suck, the very blood to suck"? The very question by which the King disclaims responsibility, ironically forces a more profound consideration of the matter.

I offer one more example of this kind of thing. Shortly after the terrified Harfleur surrenders, the King rides by his army, and Fluellen tells him that no one has been lost in the recent battle except a man executed for looting a church, "one Bardolph, if your Majesty know the man; his face is all bubukles, and whelks, and knobs, and flames o' fire; and his lips blows at his nose, and it is like a coal of fire, sometimes plue and sometimes red." This same Bardolph is the only one of Falstaff's gang who has survived all three Henry plays, and Hal has enjoyed with Falstaff and Poins many a joke about that great red nose in which the fire is at last out. But the King's only response is "We would have all such offenders so cut off." He then goes on to use the occasion to issue general orders to the army prohibiting looting, "for when lenity and cruelty play for a kingdom the gentler gamester is the soonest winner."

Whether Henry's reaction expresses indifference, forgetfulness, or an all-demanding sense of duty, it is impossible to say. His motives again escape us, but we can see that while there seems to be a thinness of personal feeling, there is at the same time a sure political sense of what is required of a king and the leader of a great army engaged in the conquest of a kingdom. This ambivalence emerges again and again, to reach full statement at last on the night before the battle of Agincourt. The King puts aside his public role, covering himself with a dark cloak, and walks in the night among the army. He comes to the campfire, flickering in the darkness like Richard's candlelight in Pomfret dungeon, of three ordinary English soldiers, John Bates, Alexander Court, and Michael Williams. The soldiers are face to face on the eve of the battle with those fundamental questions which so many others have faced in *The Henriad,* and they voice these questions in a most simple way—a way which contrasts powerfully with the pedantic language of the Archbishop of Canterbury which launched this army on the French adventure and with the heroic rhetoric which exhorts the army to go once more into the breach. The soldiers are frightened about dying and worried about their families and their own souls. Is the cause for which they fight a just one? If it is not, what happens to the soul of a man who dies hating and killing other men? How can a man reconcile his duty to his king and his duty as a Christian?

> But if the cause be not good, the King himself hath a heavy reckoning to make when all those legs and arms and heads, chopp'd off in a battle, shall join together at the latter day and cry all "We died at such a place"—some swearing, some crying for a surgeon, some upon their wives left poor behind them, some upon the debts they owe, some upon their children rawly left. I am afeard there are few die well that die in a battle; for how can they charitably dispose of anything when blood is their argument? Now, if these men do not die well, it will be a black matter for the King that led them to it; who to disobey were against all proportion of subjection.
>
> (*Henry V,* IV.i.133–45)

Harry Plantagenet responds as authority must respond: The King's cause *is* just, and his quarrel honorable, and therefore the men are absolved of any responsibility before God for shedding blood. But, almost as if in doubt, he goes on to argue that "the King is not bound to answer the particular endings of his soldiers" because he did not intend their deaths when he brought them to France. Here again, as before Harfleur, he is raising the questions he intends to avoid: Whether he intended death or not, he did bring his subjects to France, where they may die, and surely he bears some responsibility. And he continues to avoid the full question of responsibility by arguing that many of the soldiers carry mortal sins upon their souls and that therefore if they die in battle the King bears no responsibility for their damnation: "Every subject's duty is the king's, but every subject's soul is his own." But this really does not answer Williams' objection that every man who dies in battle dies in sin trying to murder his fellow men, and he is doing so because his king has brought him to this place and ordered him to fight. It is impossible to forget in this discussion of the justice of the cause the doubtful way in which the French war began.

In this brief scene in the middle of darkness on the edge of a great battle, Michael Williams has faced for himself and his king the most fundamental questions about his responsibility as ruler and as man. But Henry does not answer the questions, either because he does not understand them or because no ruler of a state can ever answer such questions.

The actions and the speeches of King Henry V produce a curious ambiguity. On one hand he is the hero-king, the restorer of England's glory, and the efficient manager of the realm; but he is at the same time, it would appear, a cunning Machiavel, a cynical politician, a man lacking in moral depth, perhaps even a limited intelligence. Our difficulties in understanding the King are intensified by the almost total absence from the play of speeches in which Henry speaks as a private man, directly revealing his own feelings. He lives in the full glare of public life, and even those usually private activities such as wooing a wife are carried out on the great stage of the world. Nor does his language yield insights into the depths of self of the kind found in the language of Richard II, Falstaff, Hotspur. Instead, Henry uses a political and heroic rhetoric whose brightly polished surface allows no penetration.

Faced with the absence of motives, critics have resolved the problem by judging Henry according to their particular moral bias and concluding that he is either a good and efficient ruler who sacrifices himself for the good of the state, or a hypocritical and cunning politician who relentlessly seizes every opportunity to extend and consolidate his power. We must, however, take Henry as Shakespeare gives him to us: a man who has no private personal self, but only a public character, a character which is supremely, unerringly political, which chooses without hesitation that course of action which will make the kingdom function efficiently, balance the divisive powers within, and strengthen the ruler's grasp on the body politic. This type of man is not unknown to Shakespeare's or our own time. Historians have been guessing for centuries about Elizabeth I's motives for not marrying—hatred of men because of her father's treatment of her mother? ingrown virginity? pelvic malformation? unhappy love affair in youth?—but whatever Elizabeth's reasons, her constant hesitation was a political masterpiece. To have married a Protestant would have caused her Catholic subjects to despair and set Catholic Europe against her. To have married a Catholic would have driven her Protestant subjects to rebellion and alienated England from the growing Protestant powers in Europe. So long as she remained unmarried, but always considering marriage, she could prevent, even among the proud lords in her own court, that polarization of power which would have meant civil and world war.

Our own age shares with Shakespeare some understanding of political man, and the following description of an American politician is a perfect description, even down to the small details, of Henry V:

> He is a totally political man, clever but not thoughtful, calculating more than reflective. He appears at once sentimental and ruthless, thin-skinned and imperious, remarkably attuned to public moods and utterly expert at the "game" of political maneuver. He is all of a piece, seemingly monolithic, not only completely *in* but totally *of* politics. Upon the devices and costs of political manipulation he is capable of looking with some irony, but toward the idea of the manipulation itself and the kind of life it entails he shows no irony whatever.

No one would agree more completely than Henry V that political man "is the role," that "the person [is] the function." As he turns away from the bitter encounter with his soldiers around the campfire, draws back from the tragic place where Richard, Hotspur, Falstaff, and Henry IV looked and died, Henry pauses alone in the darkness and asks himself the question Richard had so long ago answered so confidently: "What is a king?" Even here his speech is still rhetoric rather than poetry; and rather than revealing a self, it is as if some vague memory of a real self were sadly contemplating its final disappearance into a role, into ceremony:

> No, thou proud dream,
> That play'st so subtly with a king's repose,
> I am a king that find thee; and I know
> 'Tis not the balm, the sceptre, and the ball,
> The sword, the mace, the crown imperial,
> The intertissued robe of gold and pearl,
> The farced title running fore the king,
> The throne he sits on, nor the tide of pomp
> That beats upon the high shore of this world—
> No, not all these, thrice gorgeous ceremony,
> Not all these, laid in bed majestical,
> Can sleep so soundly as the wretched slave
> Who, with a body fill'd and vacant mind,
> Gets him to rest, cramm'd with distressful bread;
> (*Henry V*, IV.i.253–66)

But having seen the person fade into the political function, the King turns away from tragic knowledge and returns to his tent and to his role to become the conqueror of France, the greatest of the English kings, the husband of Katherine, and the father of Henry VI.

Henry reverses the path taken by Richard II, who believed that kingship and rule were his reality but discovered under the battering of circumstances that he was only a mortal man:

> You have but mistook me all this while.
> I live with bread like you, feel want,
> Taste grief, need friends; subjected thus,
> How can you say to me I am a king?
> (*Richard II*, III.ii.174–77)

At the other end of the cycle, the King who has known from the beginning that he is a man playing king—"Yet herein will I *imitate* the sun"—discovers, however briefly, the claims of his humanity, only to turn away and lock himself forever into the role. *The Henriad* traces in its kings a great paradox: Necessity forces man out of role into reality—necessity forces man back out of reality into role. The movement is much like that of *The Aeneid*, where the establishment of New Troy and, eventually, Augustan order requires the absorption of the man Aeneas into the role of the founder of Rome, and the destruction of such turbulent energies as Dido and Turnus. In both the Roman and English epics the even balance of loss and gain creates finally a tone of great sadness inextricably mixed with great triumph.

The world of Henry V with its state rituals and ceremony looks much like a restoration of the English Eden, ordered, prosperous, and united under a hero king. But under the surface all is changed. In Richard's feudal kingdom society was organized and life lived in accordance with the great unchanging patterns of order, mutual support, and hierarchy, which were believed to govern all the created world. In Henry's national state, life is shifting and fluid, and action is taken not because it is morally, unchangeably right, but because it will bring about the desired result. Identity is now no longer God-given but only a role within which an individual is imprisoned by political necessity. The restored English garden, the beehive state, is superimposed on the ruined garden of France, a weed-filled, untilled wildness (*Henry V*, V.ii.30–62). Man no longer confidently expects the future to repeat the past but stands on the edge of great vistas of time and lives in the historical process of endless change. What was small and coherent is now vast and tends to fragmentation, what was unchanging is now in ceaseless flux, what was real is now acted, and what was external and certain is now internalized and ambiguous.

The Henriad is a brief but fairly accurate history of the reigns of Richard II, Henry IV, and Henry V. But the chronicle of the wars of succession between York and Lancaster is only the outward form of an action tracing the great psychological, social, and political shifts from the medieval to the modern world. Below the level of these great cultural shifts, however, a still more fundamental plot exists and gives to the plays much of their energy and perpetual fascination.

In the beginning there is a king, Richard II, and a society which believe like the child that the world is all of a piece, from the clod of earth up to God Himself. Man cannot be distinguished from world, for all parts of the indivisible universe move in sympathy with all other parts. God watches benevolently over this world overseeing the endless operation of justice and right. But man is at the center of this rich and brilliant universe. He trusts the authorities and traditions that he has inherited and assumes that nothing will ever change from the way it is.

Then, the knowledge of death, the conflicting pressures of reality, and the more violent passions—hate, blood-lust, the will to power—erupt and break up the old certainties. When the earthly king calls for help to the heavenly king there is not even the whisper of an answer. Feelings of isolation in great darkness grow. Certainty of identity is lost and the vastnesses of eternity and infinity are glimpsed. Man is driven inward upon himself, becomes self-conscious, as he realizes that there is a world "out there" which does not conform to his will or imagination. Confused, the old innocence dies with Richard II.

Life fragments, new energies are released, and many new possibilities of life appear: pleasure, politics, honor, war, poetry, and magic. The individual is no longer limited to "what he is" but is free to experiment and act out many parts. Prince Hal—shrewd and reality-oriented—now replaces Richard as the central figure in the psychic journey. At first he rejects the authority figures, the king, the father, the law, to live a life of pleasure and self-indulgence in the tavern, taking Falstaff as a father temporarily. He turns from the flesh to the spirit and seeks to find himself on the battlefield and in the search for honor and fame. In both tavern and battlefield, however, he "keeps his wits about him" and avoids the total involvement with these ultimately unrealistic extremes, both of which have death implicit in them.

In the end, the Prince kills wild idealism, Hotspur, and banishes unlimited pleasure, Falstaff, to return to his true father in spirit and person. With the death of the father, the Prince assumes the burdens of rule and takes up the adult role of trying to order and "make the world work." In the process of becoming a ruler his personal self, the essential "I," is lost forever as the man disappears into the role his work demands.

FRANK KERMODE

Shakespeare's Learning: "The Phoenix and the Turtle"

The most direct challenge to people who suppose Shakespeare to have been a 'natural' arises from the poems, above all from 'The Phoenix and the Turtle'. The imagery of this poem, however interpreted, is certainly in some way learned; and to deny Shakespeare this kind of learning you must say he was not the author of the poem. This has indeed often been done; but the external evidence in favour of his authorship happens to be unusually strong. It can also be said, I think, that the learned interests it reflects—and its mode of reflecting them—are Shakespearian.

Let us retreat a few years from 1601, the undoubted date of the poem, to *Richard II*. It would not be difficult to show, with the help of Ernst Kantorowicz, the degree to which Shakespeare was affected by certain ideas on perpetuity having their origin in medieval philosophy and law. I have already commented upon his preoccupation with time; if one wished to place that in the context of the history of ideas one would doubtless label it 'Augustinian'. Time began with the creation and will have a stop. Its course is marked by acts of will, by sin, senescence, and mutability. Against it may be placed for instance, such glory as derives from poetry, if not from honour, as existing not in time but in some perpetual duration. But what of the great *continuities* of earthly life? The most obvious of them is kingship: the king never dies; or rather, he dies in his body natural, not in his body politic. Kantorowicz has shown that the theory was associated with the scholastic concept of *aevum*.

This was originally an angelological concept, a third order between time and eternity. I believe that both Spenser and Shakespeare had a deep and exploratory interest in this concept. In so far as it relates to the kingship, Shakespeare put it into *Richard II*. This aspect of the doctrine is summed up in Kantorowicz's title: the king has a mortal body and also a dignity which does not die, and which is represented by ceremonies. The painful separation of the two bodies is part of Lear's experience also; he gives away the *dignitas* and is left with his natural body, subject, as the lawyers said, to all infirmity. He sees the lost *dignitas* as adhering to the natural body only by means of ceremony and ceremonial clothing. When he curses the robed justice he curses the ironical antithesis between the Dignity and the erring man within the robe—a contrast as great as that between the decaying body in the coffin and the robed effigy of the king that was placed upon it in royal funerals. Lear in the storm is realizing the loss of the *dignitas*, tearing off the last fragments of the clothing that have come to symbolize it, as his daughters have stripped away lands, knights, servants; only in madness is he a mockery king, every inch a king, with his fading regalia of wild flowers. But when Gloster kisses the hand of his body natural 'it smells of mortality'. And throughout *Lear* we are made to share (with Kent and Gloster and Lear) the sense that such dissolution means the end of time, 'the promised end'. But—and this is the strange power of the conclusion—the truth is different. The Dignity falls on Edgar, in all the misery of regal mortality and the death of good men and women, life continues; we see that continuity must be accounted for even in tragedy. Aquinas says that without revelation (and revelation is excluded from *Lear*) we could not know that the world ever had a beginning; without it we should be sure enough of misery, but not of an end. What we have in *Lear* is not an end but a bleak perpetuity of the dignity.

Now kingship, a topic which so preoccupied Shakespeare, is not the only instance of his application of the concept of *aevum* to continuity in human affairs. We have seen that he applied it also to the justice: he dies but his office does not. Above all, perhaps, it applied to the Empire. The Virgilian *imperium sine fine* began with Augustus, sometimes called the first vicar of Christ, and the Empire thenceforward was coeval with the Church. Since the power of *imperium* was held to be conferred by the Roman people, the people also never died; its *maiestas* was continuous, transmitted to the peoples of every kingdom which claimed the rights of the Roman *imperium*. Thus, in England, which had not the Roman law but which under Elizabeth carefully imported the main elements of European imperial mythology, it was held that the Queen wore the *dignitas* of Augustus and of Constantine. In two plays Shakespeare interests himself deeply, but with some obliquity, in the nature of Empire. In *Antony and Cleopatra* we may take the hint from Caesar's prophecy of the 'time of universal peace' (IV. vi. 4) his reign will begin; indeed it brought the birth of Christ and the extinction of pagan time, represented by Antony and Cleopatra in their masks as Isis and Osiris (for Shakespeare knew more Plutarch than the *Lives*). *Cymbeline*, set at the time of the birth of Christ, describes the reception into Britain of Roman civility and establishes as from the earliest possible moment the British share of the Roman *maiestas* now devolving upon the imperial James.

I do not mean to imply that Shakespeare unambiguously celebrates these regal and imperial continuities. In fact, the situation of the incumbent of the *dignitas* strikes him rather as humanly appalling, and no one could say that he tried to make the founder of the imperial dignity humanly attractive; the majesty that *dies* in what we remember from *Antony and Cleopatra*. The point is that these are poetic meditations on a learned theme, a philosophico-legal complex.

Now the twin-natured incumbent of the *dignitas* was held to be unique, in that he was both species and individual. The nearest analogues were in the Trinity, in angelology, and in the bestiary, from which was drawn, as emblem of the doctrine, the Phoenix. This bird was both mortal and immortal, its own father and son. It stood for perpetuity in mortality, and had a long connection with the idea of perpetual dignity. Coins of Valentinian II (375–392) show a phoenix and the legend *Perpetuetas*. The same emblem served the French and English dynasties in Shakespeare's time; it had a special propriety in the case of Elizabeth, since it also stood for virginity. The Phoenix was sexless or hermaphrodite, according to Lactantius, the great source of its lore: 'femina seu mas sit seu neutrum seu sit utrumque'; he also insists on its virginity: 'felix quae Veneris foedera nulla colit'. The use of the Phoenix in the propaganda of the later Elizabeth—'semper eadem'—has been illustrated by Miss Frances Yates. And half a century later the medal struck by English royalists to commemorate the death of Charles I showed the dead king on the obverse, and on the reverse a phoenix rising from its ashes and representing the immortal dignity. Later the bird became the emblem of the British and American insurance house, signifying an *aevum* (sustained by your premiums) in which property, mortal in individual cases, achieves perpetuity as a species. This by no means exhausts the figurative significances of the phoenix; it stood also for 'felix renovatio temporum', as Elizabeth remembered; and it was also the bird of the *saeculum*, the century—Milton's 'secular bird'. It was the king or emperor of all the other birds, and is sometimes, as by Claudian represented as receiving the praise and devotion of the others:

> convenient aquilae cunctaeque ex orbe volucres
> ut Solis mirentur avem.

The Phoenix, then, concentrates clusters of learned themes. What did Shakespeare make of it? He was evidently preoccupied by problems of continuity and *dignitas*, and he alludes rather frequently to the Phoenix, sometimes with glancing familiarity, as when Iachimo calls Imogen 'the Arabian bird', meaning that she is unique, the most chaste of women. Cranmer's speech at the baptism of Elizabeth in *Henry VIII* makes James I the heir who will arise from the queen's virgin ashes; a prophecy by hindsight not only of her virginity but of the unusual transmission of the dignity to a new dynasty. But there is nothing greatly out of the way in that passage, whether or not Shakespeare wrote it; whereas everybody agrees that 'The Phoenix and the Turtle' is out of the way.

I take it we should agree that there is not much to be learned about Shakespeare's poem from the other poems in *Loves Martyr*. Chester, of course, was responsible for introducing the Turtle into what might seem the self-sufficient life of the Phoenix. Nobody has ever succeeded in saying what Chester's poem is about. If he is really talking about the marriage of Sir John Salisbury, it follows, as Chambers observed, that Shakespeare did not read the poem closely, since the marriage was not childless. In Chester the two birds discuss true love, and then, Turtle first, throw themselves on a pyre in the expectation of some even better Phoenix from the ashes. Before this, Nature, before bringing the birds together, offers the Phoenix a survey of English history, and especially of King Arthur's life (King Arthur was a notable Phoenix; he rose again as a Tudor king). At the end of the poem the Pelican confusedly argues that the Phoenix, though unique, is improved by union with a bird symbolizing constancy, which will give the new Phoenix what it surely should not have lacked, 'loue and chastitie'. Chester's poem is obviously one which remains confused about its occasion, and for this reason (and, I suspect, his having cleared out his desk and fitted all the extraneous matter into the long poem) it is likely to remain a kind of Bottom's Dream. But some better poets added verses on the theme. The first, Ignoto, ignores the Turtle and stresses only the uniqueness and self-perpetuation of the Phoenix ('Her rare-dead ashes fill a rare-line urn'). The second is Shakespeare. Marston, following him, briefly mentions the turtle, but then embarks on a crabbed celebration of the new Phoenix, 'God, Man, nor Woman', (recalling the passage of Lactantius already quoted). Chapman, though celebrating 'the male Turtle', dwells only on the perfection of his beloved 'Whome no prowd flockes of other Foules could moue, But in her selfe all companie concluded'. Jonson lengthily celebrates voluntary chastity, and the constancy of 'a person like our *Doue*' to his phoenix. None of them needed more than the title and a hazy idea of the contents of Chester's poem. Some of Marston's hyperbole suggests that he must be thinking of the queen, though one cannot be certain of that in the age of Donne's *Anniversaries*; and if one wanted to develop the point one would have to use the Pelican's speech, since the Pelican was another of Elizabeth's birds. I doubt, indeed, whether all the contempt poured on Grosart's theory, that the poem has to do with the queen and Essex, is justified; Chester could just have been talking about the death of Essex and the almost mortal grief of the queen, and the other poets could have had it in mind.

But we had better not depend on the other contributors. It seems likely enough, of course, that writing at the end of a reign (and the end of a century) the poets, invited to reflect for whatever occasion on the Phoenix, would remember the old queen, her body natural in decay, her dignity seeming all too mortal in the uncertainty of the succession (she would hardly, like Shakespeare's Cranmer, think of James of Scotland in that way). Yet the only one of these learned men who really did meditate the Phoenix emblem, consider all its deep meanings, was Shakespeare.

> Here the Antheme doth commence:
>   Loue and Constancie is dead;
>   *Phoenix* and the *Turtle* fled
> In a mutuall flame from hence.
>
> So they loued, as loue in twaine,
>   Had the essence but in one;
>   Two distinct, Diusion none;
> Number there in loue was slaine.
>
> Hearts remote, yet not asunder;
>   Distance, and no space was seene,
>   'Twixt the *Turtle* and his Queene:
> But in them it were a wonder.
>
> So betweene them Loue did shine,
>   That the *Turtle* saw his right,
>   Flaming in the *Phoenix* sight;
> Either was the other's mine.

> Propertie was thus appalled,
>   That the selfe was not the same:
>   Single Natures double name
> Neither two nor one was called.
>
> Reason in it selfe confounded,
>   Saw Diuision grow together,
>   To themselues yet either neither,
> Simple were so well compounded,
>
> That it cried, how true a twaine
>   Seemeth this concordant one,
>   Loue hath Reason, Reason none,
> If what parts, can so remaine.

How did he go about it? He must have known Lactantius, as T. W. Baldwin argues, and he would also remember the parrot in Ovid (*Amores*, II. 6). Baldwin says that the poem is about married chastity, and a charming variation, in the Lactantian vein, on Ovid's parrot and the sparrow of Catullus. And certainly the old phoenix is there, with its 'wondrous voice,' inimitable even by the nightingale or the dying swan; its lack of sex, its chorus of birds. Above all, Lactantius is present, in the poem, when it says that 'the selfe was not the same'; 'ipse quidem sed non eadem est, eademque nec ipsa est'. Translating this, Shakespeare rather characteristically plays on the two parts of the English word *selfsame*, achieving by a sort of pun what Lactantius does by profuse repetition. On these words of Lactantius, quoted by Shakespeare, depends most of the traditional emblematic quality of the phoenix as continuity in the *aevum*.

So we are here very close to a large and difficult body of learning, one in which, as we have seen, Shakespeare elsewhere showed some interest. And his language in the poem is obviously learned. No one has written about it so well as J. V. Cunningham; indeed, his is the best essay ever written on this poem. He shows that the terminology is borrowed from scholastic enquiries into the Trinity, where you have to go to find 'distinct persons' with only one essence. 'Two distincts, Diuision none'—as Aquinas observes, 'to avoid the Arian heresy . . . we must avoid the terms *diversity* and *difference* so as not to take away the unit of essence; we can, however, use the term *distinction* . . . we must [also] avoid the terms *separation* and *division*, which apply to parts of a whole . . .' (*S.T.*, I, 31.2). 'Number' is 'slain' because plurality is a consequence of division; as the mathematicians said, 'One is no number'. 'Distance and no space' is from the argument for the co-eternality of the Persons of the Trinity. 'Property' (the *proprium*) is the quality that distinguishes separate persons; it is 'appalled' in Shakespeare because what ought to characterize only one person here characterizes two. But the English word can hardly be used purely in this sense, and the less technical reference to matters of *meum* and *tuum* is here also present, outraged because of this ideal commonwealth ('either was the other's mine'). 'Reason' is confounded because it has to work by division, and in these 'distincts' there is no 'division'. Love has achieved what Reason cannot.

So St. Thomas is also behind the poem. Cunningham refers to the *Summa Theologica*, I. 31, 'de his quae ad unitatem vel pluralitatem pertinent in divinis'. The Thomist paradoxes and distinctions become strained, even tragic, because of the difficulty of making such points in English. Aquinas can develop distinctions between *alium* and *alienum*, *alius* and *aliud*, the first relating to a difference *secundum personas*, the second to a difference *secundum essentiam* (I. 21. 2). For the momentary establishment of such distinctions Shakespeare torments English terminology; it is a learned and sombrely witty torture.

Yet even granting that, we may be reluctant to think of Shakespeare as working with the *Summa* open before him. How, then, did he know about this? The answer is that this scholastic terminology persisted and was in common enough use. To speak of the Father and Son as distinct Persons with but one essence was familiar theology—Hooker, as Cunningham reports, even says that 'their distinction cannot admit separation'. And when Bacon wanted for a legal purpose to argue that 'it is one thing to make things distinct, another to make them separable', he clinches the point with a scholastic tag: 'aliud est distinctio, aliud separatio.'

Bacon's argument occurred in a plea of 1608. The question was whether natives of either Scotland or England, born after the accession of James I, should be naturalized in both kingdoms. The King's natural body, reasons Bacon, operates upon his body politic, so that although his bodies politic as King of England and King of Scotland 'be several and distinct, yet nevertheless his natural person, which is one . . . createth a privity between them'. Because of this privity, a Scots subject of the king's natural person must also be a subject of his English body politic. His person and crown are 'inseparable though distinct', like the persons of the Trinity. The language which a contemplation of the Phoenix educes from Shakespeare is, in short, a language based upon certain paradoxes still indispensable to theology and constitutional law. Spenser, as I have argued elsewhere, was interested in them; and now it seems clear that Shakespeare, invited to dwell upon the Phoenix, related it to precisely this complex of paradoxes concerning continuity, number, property, and so forth. They derive from scholastic thought, but are variously associated with the figure of the Phoenix, which makes them available in many contexts: dynastic, imperial, legal, constitutional. They can suggest the Tudor renovation, the virginity of the last Tudor, the end of a century and a dynasty. Who can say whether some particular aspect of all this was in Shakespeare's mind? It seems almost impossible that he shut out from his mind all the broader implications of the theme: the end of the century, for which the secular bird could stand; the decay of the Phoenix Elizabeth, with no certainty, in 1601, of the survival of her Dignity. Perhaps he uses the strange intrusive dove, as a figure for the hermaphroditic relation of the Queen's two bodies.

And yet for our present purposes it is enough to say that he gave in this poem a rather strict metaphysical expression to concepts—the *aevum*, the dignity, the double name of natural beings—which had long interested him. Perhaps he *was*, after all, as the editions say, thinking of a chastely married pair, and that from such a point of departure all the rest was made to follow. But this sequel is what concerns us. It is learned, but not so learned that only a scholar could possess the materials of which it is made; its language, though wrought from a technical vocabulary, is freestanding, the language of a poet and not of a scholar, the language of a man whose craft is learned but not scholarly.

I have gone a long way about to make this point, which is the centre of my argument. We do not need to think of a very learned Shakespeare, but we do need to think of a Shakespeare who was capable of an intense interest—intense, yet sometimes at the same time wanton or even perverse—in the formulae of learning: a strong-minded, wilful, private, reading man. This is at any rate a way out of the old dilemma; if you measure his learning or his mind by some entirely inappropriate calculus, he emerges as a natural, all wit and no art, or, on the other hand, as the slave of familiar text books and homiletic commonplaces, all art and no wits. What we shall have instead is a plausible representation of a great poet: a speculative, interested man, a man of great intellectual force, who employs that force in poetry.

ANNE BARTON

The King Disguised: Shakespeare's "Henry V" and the Comical History

In the worst moment of the French campaign, when the night before Agincourt finds the English army re-duced, dispirited, and ailing, "even as men wrack'd upon a sand, that look to be wash'd off the next tide" (IV.i.97–98), Henry V pays two quite different visits to his despondent troops. Although the first of them, made in his own person as king, is not enacted, the Chorus testifies eloquently to its success:

> . . . every wretch, pining and pale before,
> Beholding him, plucks comfort from his looks.
> A largess universal like the sun
> His liberal eye doth give to every one,
> Thawing cold fear, that mean and gentle all,
> Behold, as may unworthiness define,
> A little touch of Harry in the night.
> (IV.41–47)

Later, in the first scene of act IV, Henry borrows a cloak from Sir Thomas Erpingham, conceals his royal identity, and ventures alone among soldiers no longer able to recognize him as their king. His fortunes in this second sally are altogether less prosperous. Thorny and disquieting from the start, his conversation with Williams, Court, and Bates ends in an open quarrel. Moreover, it provokes Henry's only soliloquy in the play: a bitter examination of kingship itself and of the irremovable barriers isolating the monarch from a world of private men.

Shakespeare may well have remembered from Holinshed, or from *The First English Life of Henry V*, that the historical Henry "daylie and nightlie in his owne person visited the watches, orders and stacions of everie part of his hoast." Nowhere, however, is it suggested that he ever did so incognito. Geoffrey Bullough has argued that when Shakespeare made Henry muffle himself in Erpingham's cloak he was thinking of a passage from Tacitus's *Annals* in which Germanicus disguises himself on the eve of a battle in order to assess the morale of the Roman legions. Germanicus, however, lurks outside his soldiers' tents as a mere eaves-dropper; he never attempts a personal encounter. Although the passage cannot be discounted entirely as a source for Henry's disguise, its impor-tance has surely been overestimated. For those Elizabethans who watched *Henry V* in the new Globe theatre in 1599, the king's behavior before Agincourt would have had analogues far more striking and immediate. There is a surprising number of disguised kings to be found in those English history plays which have survived from the period 1587–1600. A few of these princes are driven to dissemble their identity for a time out of political necessity, as Marlowe's Edward II does after the triumph of Young Mortimer and Queen Isabella, or Shakespeare's Henry VI in the last part of the trilogy, when he rashly steals across the border into England "disguised, with a prayerbook," only to be recognized despite this precau-tion by the two Keepers and haled away to the Tower. A larger and more interesting group is composed of kings who, like Shakespeare's Henry V, adopt disguise as a caprice, for reasons that are fundamentally exploratory and quixotic.

Toward the end of *George a Greene, the Pinner of Wakefield* (?Rob-ert Greene, c. 1590), an unspecified King Edward of England decides to "make a merrie journey for a moneth" along with his friend King James of Scotland, for the purpose of meeting the folk hero George a Greene, a loyal pinner in the north country who has been instrumental in putting down a rebellion against the Crown. The two monarchs travel on foot and in disguise. At the town of Bradford they yield meekly to the insolent demands of the locals, trailing their staves in order to pass without argument through the town. George a Greene, disgusted by such pusilla-nimity, berates the two kings soundly for cowardice and forces them to hold up their staves. King Edward gains a vivid and somewhat disconcert-ing idea of the character and temper of his subject before the revelation of his royal identity puts an end to the game. All is forgiven. George is offered a knighthood, which he politely refuses, preferring to remain an

English yeoman. Edward unites him with Bettris, his love, over-riding the snobbish objections of her father, and the play ends harmoniously with a feast at which King Edward, King James, George a Greene, Robin Hood and Maid Marian, and all the shoemakers of Bradford sit side by side as friends and good companions.

Peele's *Edward I* (c. 1591) also associates the king in disguise with the Robin Hood stories. Lluellen, the rebellious Prince of Wales, his mistress Elinor, and his friend Rice ap Meredith have taken to the greenwood in the company of a friar, "to live and die together like Chamber-Britaines, Robin Hood, Little John, Frier Tucke, and Maide Marrian." King Edward, intrigued to learn of this little society, decides to pay it a secret visit, disguised, and accompanied only by Lluellen's brother, Sir David of Brecknock:

> . . . as I am a Gentleman,
> Ile have one merrie flirt with little John,
> And Robin Hood, and his Maide Marian.
> Be thou my counsell and my companie,
> And thou maist Englands resolution see.
>   (x. 1548–52)

In the forest, Edward adjudicates in a dispute between two rogues who have tried to cozen one another, agrees with Lluellen that his purse will belong to whichever man can overcome the other in a fair fight, and (exactly as his prototype Richard Coeur de Lion had done in the ballads) sends "Robin Hood" sprawling. The exigencies of Peele's plot made it impossible for this forest scene to end with reconciliation and pardon in the ballad tradition. Lluellen, rebellious to the end, is killed in battle later in the play. It is remarkable, however, how close this personal encounter between the outlaw and the king he cannot recognize—in both senses of that word—has come to healing the breach between them. When "Longshanks" has gone, his identity disclosed, Lluellen admits ruefully that "his courage is like to the Lion, and were it not that rule and soveraigntie set us at jarre, I could love and honour the man for his valour" (xii. 1917–19).

The two anonymous plays *Fair Em* (c. 1590) and *The True Chronicle History of King Leir* (c. 1590) both present kings who disguise themselves in the cause of love. William the Conqueror, in *Fair Em*, falls in love with a picture of Blanch, Princess of Denmark, and travels to see her in her father's court under the name of Sir Robert of Windsor. Finding the lady less glamorous in reality than she seemed in her portrait, he tries to elope with Mariana, a lady promised to his friend and traveling companion, the Marquis of Lubeck. Mariana, however, not only surmounts the temptation to abandon Lubeck for a crown but contrives to substitute a masked and lovesick Blanch for herself at the rendezvous appointed. William, who discovers the fraud on arrival in England, is understandably put out but decides that although Blanch is not Mariana she is nonetheless tolerable, and certainly preferable to war with Denmark. At the end of the play, William marries Blanch and, at the same time, restores Godard the supposed miller to his rightful place in society and bestows his daughter Em upon Valingford, the suitor who best deserves her.

In *King Leir*, the Gallian king comes to England disguised as a pilgrim, in order to determine which is the best and most marriageable of Leir's three daughters. He meets Cordella after her disgrace, finds her fair and good, and pretends that he has been sent as an ambassador by his royal master to make her the Gallian queen. Cordella, who has most perspicaciously fallen in love with the humble palmer himself, spurns this splendid offer and bids him "cease for thy King, seeke for thy selfe to woo." After this gratifying proof that Cordella loves the man and not the monarch, the palmer reveals his identity and the two are married immediately and return to France. Disguise, however, remains a feature of their court. In scene xxiv, the Gallian king and queen mingle with their subjects in the guise of country folk and, thus obscured, discover and are reconciled with the wretched Leir and his counsellor Perillus on the seacoast of Brittany.

Finally, *The First Part of King Edward IV*, a play written by Thomas Heywood before 1599, presents two quite separate royal disguises. Edward conceals his identity when he goes into Lombard Street for the first time to lay amorous siege to Mistress Shore. More relevant to *Henry V*, however, is his encounter with John Hobs the tanner. The king, hunting incognito at Drayton Basset, becomes separated from his queen and courtiers. Hobs, meeting him in the forest, suspects him at first for a thief ("How these roysters swarm in the country, now the King is so near"), but is persuaded at length that Edward is a minor hanger-on at court; in fact, the king's butler. Under this delusion, he prattles on merrily about the two kings of England, Edward at court and the deposed Henry VI in the Tower. Edward, slyly anxious to know how he is regarded by this outspoken subject, receives some disconcertingly frank answers to the questions he puts. The commons of England, according to Hobs, love King Edward

as poor folk love holidays, glad to have them now and then; but to have them come too often will undo them. So, to see the King now and then 'tis comfort; but every day would beggar us; and I may say to thee, we fear we shall be troubled to lend him money; for we doubt he's but needy.

Even more improbable in its light-hearted political inconsequence is Edward's amused acceptance of the tanner's shifting loyalties. "Shall I say my conscience?" he inquires cunningly. "I think Harry is the true king."

> HOBS: Art advised of that? Harry's of the old house of Lancaster; and that progeny do I love.
> KING: And thou dost not hate the house of York?
> HOBS: Why, no; for I am just akin to Sutton Windmill; I can grind which way soe'er the wind blow. If it be Harry, I can say, "Well fare, Lancaster." If it be Edward, I can sing, "York, York, for my money."

Basically, as it turns out, Hobs approves of King Edward for reasons that have nothing to do with his government of the realm: "He's a frank franion, a merry companion, and loves a wench well." To his way of thinking, the king ought not to encourage patents and monopolies, but Hobs is willing to believe that Edward does so out of ignorance, because he has been misled by greedy counsellors and because he cannot see for himself how the system operates. As subject and king converse, Edward's respect for this "honest true tanner" and for his powers of observation grows. Hobs, for his part, comes to like the supposed butler so well that he invites him home to his cottage for dinner and the night. The tanner has a pretty daughter and there is even some talk of a match, although Hobs would like his prospective son-in-law to have a steadier profession, not one of these fly-by-night court posts. Not until daybreak does Edward tear himself away from the tanner's hospitality to return to London and the troubles of a kingdom in revolt. Again, the meeting between subject and king in disguise has generated harmony, good fellowship, and mutual understanding.

In all these English histories—and there must have been many more plays like them, now lost—the king's disguise demands to be seen as a romantic gesture. Edward IV, William the Conqueror, Edward I, the Gallian king, or the brace of monarchs in *George a Greene*, all conceal their identities in much the spirit of Haroun al Raschid, the caliph of *The Arabian Nights* who liked to walk the streets of Baghdad incognito, in search of the marvellous and the strange. Moreover, the people they meet come from the world of balladry and legend. Robin Hood and Maid Marian, the folk-hero George a Greene, the miller and his daughter, thieves and outlaws, the beggar-maid destined to become a queen, or the tanner of Tamworth: all were characters nurtured in the popular imagination. Maurice Keen, in *The Outlaws of Medieval Legend*, describes the informal meeting of commoner and king as the wish-dream of a peasantry harried and perplexed by a new class of officials, an impersonal bureaucracy against which the ordinary man seemed to have no redress:

> They only knew that the King was the ultimate repository of a law whose justice they acknowledged, and they saw treason against him as a betrayal of their allegiance to God himself. If they could only get past his corrupt officers, whose abuse of the trust reposed in them amounted to treason in itself, and bring their case before the King, they believed that right would be done. Their unshakeable faith in the King's own justice was the most tragic of the misconceptions of the medieval peasantry, and the ballad-makers and their audiences shared it to the full.

In the ballads, king and unsuspecting subject meet time after time and discover unanimity of opinion and mutual respect. Richard Coeur de Lion banquets in Sherwood Forest on stolen venison, forgives Robin Hood and his men, and confounds the sheriff of Nottingham. Henry II so enjoys the rough but generous hospitality of the miller of Mansfield that he makes him a knight and gives him a royal license to keep the forest of Sherwood. Other ballads describe the meeting of Edward I and the reeve, King Alfred and the shepherd, Edward IV and the tanner, Henry VIII and the cobbler, James I and the tinker, William III and the forester, and many similar encounters.

That conversations of this sort represent a fantasy, the "misconception," as Keen terms it, of a victimized agrarian class, is obvious. They derive from attitudes far removed from anything which the hard-headed citizens of Elizabeth's London actually believed. Yet the old roots ran deep. This type of ballad not only survived through Jacobean and Caroline times: the idea behind it remained oddly resonant and haunting. Real Tudor monarchs sometimes played at enacting it. Henry VIII, as Hall tells us, graciously allowed himself to be "waylaid" and dragged off to a reconstruction of Coeur de Lion's feast with Robin Hood, Maid Marian, and their fellows. Queen Elizabeth, walking in Wanstead gardens, suddenly found herself confronting a group of supposed country folk: "Though they knew not her estate, yet something there was which made them startle aside and gaze upon her." Cunningly, Philip Sidney proceeded to involve the queen in a dispute between a shepherd and a forester for possession of the Lady of May, requesting her, after she had heard the rustic arguments of both sides, to award the lady to the suitor she considered most deserving. Traces of this kind of situation can be seen as well in some of the masques at court, but it was in the drama proper that the idea of the king's personal engagement with his subjects and their problems flowered and was most fully exploited.

There are a few Elizabethan plays in which the king manages to mingle with his subjects freely and dispense justice without resorting to disguise. At the end of Dekker's *The Shoemaker's Holiday*, Henry V in his own person sweeps away the snobbery of his officers and nobles:

> Dost thou not know that love respects no blood,
> Cares not for difference of birth or state?
> The maid is young, well born, fair, virtuous,
> A worthy bride for any gentleman.

As benevolent *deus ex machina*, he joins the hands of Rose, the citizen's daughter, and Lacy, nephew to the Earl of Lincoln. Annihilating objections based upon wealth or class, he acts from principles of perfect equity as soon as he examines the case himself, just as the medieval minstrels had always believed he would. Yet even Dekker's Henry, in a play which could scarcely be described as realistic, worries about the constraints and inhibitions which his declared royal presence may impose on London's madcap mayor, Simon Eyre, at the Shrove Tuesday banquet where these events take place. Most Elizabethan dramatists seem to have accepted the idea that disguise was an essential prerequisite for the ease and success of the meeting between private man and king. Only if the King's identity was concealed could there be natural conversation, frankness, and a sense of rapport. It is the fundamental premise of all these plays that the king, rightly considered, is but a man, and a remarkably understanding man at that. If only, they seem to suggest, king and commoner could talk together in this way, without formality or embarrassment, how many problems would be solved, how many popular grievances redressed. Humanity and humor, an easy cameraderie: these qualities, usually obscured by ceremony, distance, and that hierarchy of officials standing between the monarch and his people, emerge clearly as soon as he steps down from his throne to speak, for a little while, as a private man.

When Shakespeare sent Henry V to converse incognito with Williams, Court, and Bates on the night before Agincourt, he was surely influenced by plays like these far more than by any distant memory of how Germanicus had behaved in the war against Arminius. Generically, Shakespeare's disguised king belongs with Peele's Edward I, Heywood's Edward IV, or the accommodating monarchs of *George a Greene*. Yet the *Henry V* episode is unique. By 1599, the king who freely chooses disguise had become the hallmark of a particular kind of play. Polonius almost certainly would have defined the mode (quite shrewdly) as the "comical-historical." *Henry V*, however, is not a comical history. Far more ironic and complicated than the plays which belong properly to that genre, it introduces the timeworn and popular dramatic motif of the king disguised into its fourth act in order to question, not to celebrate, a folk convention. In itself, the gesture could be relied upon to generate certain clearly defined emotional expectations in an Elizabethan audience powerfully conditioned by both a ballad and a stage tradition. Shakespeare built upon this fact. He used Henry's disguise to summon up the memory of a wistful, naive attitude toward history and the relationship of subject and king which this play rejects as attractive but untrue: a nostalgic but false romanticism.

As the royal captain of a ruined band, a sun-god radiating his beams indiscriminately upon the soldiers among whom he walks, Henry is effective, as the Chorus makes plain. Throughout this play, the relation between the Chorus's unequivocal celebration of Henry and his war in France and the complicated, ambiguous, and sometimes flatly contradictory scenes which these speeches are made to introduce is productive of irony and double focus. This duality of attitude is particularly striking in act IV, where the Chorus's epic account of the king dispensing comfort to his troops in his own person leads directly into that altogether more dubious scene in which Henry visits the army a second time, disguised, in the manner of a ballad king. Once he has obliterated his identity, Henry falls into a series of nonencounters, meetings in which the difficulty of establishing understanding between subject and king is stressed, not the encouraging effect of "a little touch of Harry in the night" (IV.47).

It is true that Ancient Pistol, the first man Henry faces, is scarcely capable of rational discourse. Pistol lives in a wholly private world, a heightened and extravagant realm where everything appears twice life size. His overcharged style of speech, filled with contempt for Fortune, exotic geography, and resounding proper names, derives from Marlowe and from those lesser dramatists who imitated Marlowe. Pistol's language is a tissue of play scraps. In his own mind, as Leslie Hotson has pointed out, he is Tamburlaine. "As good a gentleman as the emperor" (IV.i.42), he appears blatantly literary, a mere stage king, as soon as he confronts Henry. Linguistically, Shakespeare's early histories had been intermittently Marlovian. Here, at the end of his Elizabethan cycle, he effectively laid the ghost of Tamburlaine as a hero, making it impossible for him to be taken seriously again until the Restoration. By deliberately weighing Pistol's egotism, his histrionics, against the workaday prose of the true king, he indicated the distance between one kind of theatrical fantasy and fact.

Perhaps because he fears recognition by his captains, Henry makes no attempt to speak to Fluellen and Gower. He waits in silence until the entry of Williams, Court, and Bates: three ordinary soldiers for whom the king has always been an unapproachable and distant figure. This encounter is, of course, the mirror image of all those scenes in plays like *George a Greene* or *Edward IV* in which the king and his humble subject reach a frank and mutual accord. Here, nothing of the kind occurs. Instead, Henry finds himself embroiled in a tough and increasingly embarrassing argument. He is rhetorically dexterous, and he succeeds in convincing the soldiers that the king cannot be held responsible for the particular state of soul of those individuals who die in his wars. The other question raised by Williams, that of the goodness of the king's cause in itself, his heavy reckoning at that latter day when he must confront the subjects who have been mutilated and have died for him in a war that perhaps was unjust, Henry simply evades. Here, as in the play as a whole, it is left standing, unresolved.

Even worse, Henry discovers with a sense of shock that his soothing account of the king as "but a man, as I am" (IV.i.101–2), sensitive to the disapprobation or approval of his humblest subject, is treated as flatly absurd. For Williams, the gulf between commoner and king is unbridgeable. A man "may as well go about to turn the sun to ice with fanning in his face with a peacock's feather" as expect his "poor and private displeasure" to influence the behavior of a monarch (IV.i.194–99). This shaft strikes home, exposing the speciousness of Henry's pretense that he can really be the friend and brother of these soldiers, as well as their king. The conversation ends in a quarrel, a failure to arrive at understanding which contradicts the romantic, ballad tradition. Left alone, Henry meditates acrimoniously on the pains of sovereignty, the doubtful worth of the "ceremony" that divides the king from a world of private men without providing him with any adequate compensation for his isolation and his crippling weight of responsibility.

Subsequently, after Agincourt has been won, Williams learns that it was the king himself whom he offended and with whom he has promised to fight. Like the outlaws of medieval legend, Williams meets not only with pardon but with royal largesse. He receives his glove again filled with golden crowns by Henry's bounty. Yet this gift, unlike its archetypes in the ballads and in Elizabethan comical histories, seems strangely irrelevant. Consciously anachronistic, it provides not the ghost of an answer to the questions raised during this particular encounter between common man and king disguised. Is the king's cause just? if not, what measure of guilt does he incur for requiring men to die for anything but the strict necessity of their country? Can the opinions and judgments of private men influence the sovereign on his throne? Henry is generous to Williams, but it is a dismissive generosity which places the subject firmly in an inferior position and silences his voice. The two men do not sit down at table together to any common feast, in the manner of Dekker's Henry V or Heywood's Edward IV. Indeed, Williams himself seems to be aware that the answer represented by the glove full of crowns is inadequate. He never thanks Henry for the present, accepting it without a word and turning, in the next instant, to repudiate the shilling offered him by Fluellen: "I will none of your money" (IV.viii.70). That gift he can dare to refuse. Even his plea for pardon is filled with suppressed anger and resentment:

> Your majesty came not like yourself: you appeared to me but as a common man; witness the night, your garments, your lowliness; and what your highness suffered under that shape, I beseech you, take it for your own fault, and not mine.
>
> (IV.viii.51–56)

Henry V is a play concerned to force upon its audience a creative participation far more active than usual. The Chorus urges an unceasing visualization, bright pictures in the mind, of horses, ships under sail, silken banners, or the engines of siege warfare. Within the play itself, Shakespeare suggests without indicating priority a multiplicity of possible responses to every character and event. Celebration and denigration, heroism and irony exist uneasily side by side. The Chorus may regard England's despoliation of France as a species of sacred obligation. Elsewhere, the attitude is far less clear-cut. Always in the background there hovers a disconcerting memory of Canterbury and Ely in the opening scene, busily fomenting the war in France to divert attention from the temporal wealth of the Church. Behind that lurks Henry IV's deathbed advice to his son to "busy giddy minds with foreign quarrels" (2 Henry IV, IV.v.213–14) in the hope that the shaky legitimacy of Lancastrian rule might thus escape scrutiny. Among Shakespeare's other histories, only Henry VIII is so deliberately ambiguous, so overtly a puzzle in which the audience is left to forge its own interpretation of action and characters with only minimal guidance from a dramatist apparently determined to stress the equivalence of mutually exclusive views of a particular complex of historical event.

In both Henry V and Henry VIII, the fact that the mind and heart of the king are essentially opaque, that his true thoughts and feelings remain veiled behind a series of royal poses—as those of Richard II, Richard III, King John, Henry VI, or even Henry IV do not—contributes to the difficulty of assessment. Even Henry's soliloquy before Agincourt is strangely externalized and formal, in no sense a revelation of the private workings of a mind. Neither here nor anywhere else in the play is the whole truth about the king's personal decision to invade France disclosed. This reticence is not accidental. Henry is, by secular standards, an extraordinarily successful example of the God-man incarnate. The conception of kingship in this play derives not from the relaxed and essentially personal tradition of the ballads but from a complicated, inherently tragic Tudor doctrine of the king's two bodies. Shakespeare had previously dealt with the violence of divorce or incompatibility between the twin natures of the king. Henry V, by contrast, has achieved a union of body natural and body politic difficult to flaw. Yet the price he pays for his subordination of the individual to the office is heavy, in personal terms. There is loss as well as gain in the gulf that now divides Henry from his old associates Bardolph and Pistol, from a world of private men in which he alone speaks out of a double nature. Hal's sudden unavailability as a person, his retreat into an oddly declamatory series of stances, reflects neither his own nor Shakespeare's weakness. It is simply a measure of the signal effectiveness of this man's incarnation as king.

In many respects *Henry V* is a success story. Agincourt, at least from one angle, is a splendor. Within its own limited sphere the rhetoric of the Chorus rings true. Henry himself can be described as an "ideal" sovereign, God's gift to an England weary of rebellion, usurpation, and civil war. At the same time, it is not easy for any mere mortal to support the psychological and moral burden of a double self. At a number of points in the play, particularly in situations which seem to demand an essentially personal response, the strain involved in maintaining such a constant ventriloquism becomes obvious. Even when Henry tries temporarily to obliterate one half of his identity, as he does in the scene with Williams, Court, and Bates, he finds it impossible to produce a natural and unforced imitation of a private man. Richard II, ironically enough, had experienced similar difficulties after his deposition. In Henry's case, the suppression of one side of his nature is only momentary, the product of whim rather than political defeat. Nevertheless, his awkwardness with the soldiers points to the irrevocability of that mystic marriage of king and man accomplished in the ceremony of coronation. Only death can dissolve this union.

Meanwhile, the king must contrive to deal with a world of single-natured individuals from which he himself stands conspicuously apart. Henry cannot have personal friends as other men do. There is a sense in which the rejection of Falstaff at the end of *2 Henry IV* leads directly on to the rejection of the traitor Scroop in the Second act of *Henry V.* Precisely because Scroop is someone Henry has imagined was bound to him as a man by private ties of affection and liking, his treason is far more painful than the more neutral betrayal of Cambridge and Grey. With the latter he deals in an efficient, almost perfunctory fashion. Only Scroop evokes a long and suddenly emotional remonstrance in which Henry effectively bids farewell to the possibility of personal relationship. Significantly, this scene at Southampton is placed between the two episodes in London dealing with the death of Falstaff. The epic voyage to France is thus preceded by three scenes dealing not merely with the death of former friends but with the final severance of the new king's remaining personal ties. Thereafter in the play, he will use the term "friend" in a special sense.

Not by accident, Henry abruptly abandons the royal "we" when he turns to accuse Scroop. In act I he had spoken almost entirely from this corporate position, allowing himself only infrequently to be jolted into an adventurer's "I." The Southampton scene is also one which insists throughout upon the double nature of the king and makes that nature grammatically clear through his habitual use of a plural first person. Cambridge and Grey, it seems, have conspired to kill "us" (II.ii.85–91): "But O, / What shall I say to thee, Lord Scroop?" (II.ii.93–94). In his long, passionate speech to this false friend "that knew'st the very bottom of my soul" (II.ii.97), Henry grieves more as man than as king. Not until the moment comes for sentencing all three conspirators does he regain his balance, discriminating calmly between the offense intended to his body natural and his body politic:

> Touching our person seek we no revenge;
> But we our kingdom's safety must so tender,
> Whose ruin you have sought, that to her laws
> We do deliver you. Get you therefore hence,
> Poor miserable wretches, to your death.
>   (II.ii.174–78)

The voice here is impersonal, speaking from behind the mask of kingship, deliberately avoiding the first person singular of individual response.

Once arrived in France, Henry refers to himself far more often as "I" or "me" than he does as "we" or "us," at least up to the council of Troyes in the fifth act. As leader of an English host stranded in a foreign country and in a position of increasing danger, Henry finds it not only possible but necessary to simplify his royalty to some extent. After much painful marching in the rain-drenched field, he can describe himself as a soldier, "a name that in my thoughts becomes me best" (III.iii.5–6). In this role he achieves a measure of escape from the royal impersonality demanded under more ordinary and formal circumstances. When he warns the governor of Harfleur of the horrors that lie in store for his city if it fails to capitulate, when he exchanges badinage with Fluellen, or celebrates honor in the Crispin day speech in terms that Hotspur would have understood, he is playing a part—much as Prince Hal had done in the tavern scenes of the *Henry IV* plays or among the alien but imitable chivalries of Shrewsbury. In this context, the infrequent appearances of the royal "we" in acts III and IV become purposeful and striking reminders of the ineluctable reality of the king's twin nature—a nature temporarily obscured by the adventurer's pose appropriate to the French campaign.

Gravely, Henry reminds Williams that "it was ourself thou didst abuse," before he dismisses him with pardon and reward (IV.viii.48). When his old associate Bardolph is summarily executed for robbing a church, Fluellen informs the king and, describing the dead man's face in terms so vivid that there can be no possible mistake, inquires somewhat tactlessly: "If your majesty know the man" (III.vi.96–101). Henry's stiff reply to this appeal to his memory of a time before his coronation is more than a politic evasion: "We would have all such offenders so cut off." His sudden use here of the first person plural of majesty, occurring as it does in a scene where even the French herald Montjoy is addressed by Henry as "I," constitutes the real answer to Fluellen's question. As a twin-natured being, the king is stripped not only of personal friends but also of a private past. To recognize Bardolph, let alone to regret him, is impossible.

The war in France provides Henry with "friends" of a rhetorical and special kind. It also allows him an ambiguous use of the pronoun "we" which momentarily clothes the abstract doctrine of the king's two bodies with flesh. Before Harfleur, Henry rallies "dear friends" to the breach, or urges them "to close the wall up with our English dead" (III.i.1–2). The good yeomen whose limbs were made in England are asked to "show us here the mettle of your pasture" (III.i.26–27). Later, before Agincourt, he will tell his cousin Westmoreland that "if we are mark'd to die, we are enow / To do our country loss" and speak of "we few, we happy few, we band of brothers" (IV.iii.20–21, 60). His encounter with Williams, Court, and Bates in act IV is prefaced by a speech addressed to Bedford and Gloucester in which the pronouns "we" and "our" are by implication both royal and collective:

> Gloucester, 'tis true that we are in great danger;
> The greater therefore should our courage be.
> Good morrow, brother Bedford. God Almighty!
> There is some soul of goodness in things evil,
> Would men observingly distil it out;

> For our bad neighbour makes us early stirrers,
> Which is both healthful and good husbandry:
> Besides, they are our outward consciences,
> And preachers to us all; admonishing
> That we should dress us fairly for our end.
> Thus may we gather honey from the weed,
> And make a moral of the devil himself.
>
> (IV.i.1–12)

In passages like these, where Henry's "we" and "our" seem to refer both to himself as king and to the nobles and soldiers around him as a group, a community in which he participates, the idea of the king's two bodies acquires a meaning that is concrete and emotionally resonant. Rightly considered, Henry's soldiers are part of his body politic and thus extensions of his own identity. But it is only in moments of stress and mutual dependence that the doctrine articulates itself naturally, allowing the king an easy jocularity which is familiar without being intimate, essentially distant at the same time that it creates an illusion of warmth and spontaneity. As the peril of the situation in France grows, so does Henry's sense of fellowship. It is almost as though he extracts from danger a kind of substitute for the genuinely personal relationships abandoned with Falstaff and Scroop.

Ironically, Henry's dazzling victory at Agincourt necessarily spells the end of this special accord. The king who speaks in the council chamber at Troyes in act V is once again firmly entrenched behind a royal "we" that is a diagram rather than a three-dimensional fact. Somewhat disconcertingly, he insists upon using the first person plural even in his request that the girl he intends to marry should remain in the room with him when the peers of France and England depart to discuss terms of peace:

> Yet leave our cousin Katharine here with us:
> She is our capital demand, compris'd
> Within the fore-rank of our articles.
>
> (V.ii.95–97)

For all its political realism, this seems a desperately awkward beginning to a declaration of love. In the wooing scene that follows, Henry falls back upon his soldier's persona. He resurrects this "I" to deal with a situation of peculiar difficulty. How should a king, encumbered by twin natures, embark upon what is necessarily the most personal of all relationships, that of love? Henry's particular compromise is witty, and yet the problems of communication in this scene do not spring entirely from the fact that the king's French is even more rudimentary than the lady's English. Most of Henry's blunders, his various solecisms, derive from his uncertainty as to whether at a given instant he is speaking as Harry or as England, and whether the girl he addresses is the delectable Kate or the kingdom of France. Certainly the princess, when informed that her suitor loves France so well that "I will not part with a village of it; I will have it all mine: and Kate, when France is mine and I am yours, then yours is France and you are mine," might well be excused for complaining that "I cannot tell wat is dat," even if her linguistic skills were considerably greater than they are (V.ii.178–83). The loving monarchs of *Fair Em* and *King Leir* recognized no such problems of expression. Whatever this wooing scene was like in the lost, original text of *The Famous Victories of Henry V*, it has been made in Shakespeare's play to serve the theme of the king's two bodies: the dilemma of the man placed at a disadvantage in the sphere of personal relations by the fact of a corporate self.

The first part of *Sir John Oldcastle*, a play belonging to the Lord Chamberlain's rivals, the Admiral's Men, was staged by 1600. Its four authors, Michael Drayton, Anthony Munday, Richard Hathway, and Robert Wilson, were certainly painfully conscious of Shakespeare's Henry IV plays and probably of *Henry V* as well. In the absence of any Elizabethan equivalent to Vasari, a writer who would have relished and also recorded the whole imbroglio, there seems no way of knowing precisely what steps the Brooke family took to try and dissociate their ancestor Sir John Oldcastle, the Lollard martyr, from Shakespeare's Falstaff. That Shakespeare had originally christened his fat knight Oldcastle is clear from surviving allusions within *1 Henry IV*, from the public apology in the epilogue to the second part—"For Oldcastle died a martyr, and this is not the man"—and from the malicious references of contemporaries as anxious to press the connection as Sir Henry Brooke was to repudiate it. Whether Shakespeare was forced to remove Falstaff from *Henry V* because of the protests of the Brookes and then permitted to display him at full length in *The Merry Wives of Windsor* at the direct request of Queen Elizabeth remains conjectural. It seems likely, however, that the Brooke family eventually realized that their repressive tactics were only serving to make them ridiculous and, in desperation, decided to fight fire with fire: to appeal to the stage itself to counteract the slanders of the stage.

There is no positive evidence that the mysterious sum of money received by Philip Henslowe "as a gefte" to the four authors of *Sir John Oldcastle* came from Sir Henry Brooke. On the other hand, everything about the first and only surviving part of their history suggests a work especially commissioned as an answer to the Falstaff plays:

> The doubtfull Title (Gentlemen) prefixt
> Upon the Argument we have in hand,

May breed suspence, and wrongfully disturbe
The peacefull quiet of your setled thoughts.
To stop which scruple, let this briefe suffise:
It is no pampered glutton we present,
Nor aged Councellor to youthfull sinne,
But one, whose vertue shone above the rest,
A valiant Martyr and a vertuous peere;
In whose true faith and loyaltie exprest
Unto his soveraigne, and his countries weale,
We strive to pay that tribute of our Love,
Your favours merite. Let faire Truthe be grac'te,
Since forg'de invention former time defac'te.

That the "pamperd glutton," the "aged Councellor to youthfull sinne" referred to in this prologue in Shakespeare's Falstaff admits of no doubt. Drayton, Munday, Wilson, and Hathway were out to soothe the Brooke family by presenting their ancestor as a hero, claiming in the process that they spoke truth where Shakespeare had lied. Furthermore, they had to construct an effective dramatic entertainment: a play which could support inevitable comparison with the popular Henry IV and V plays offered by the rival Lord Chamberlain's Men at The Globe. The result is curious. The first part of Sir John Oldcastle is, in effect, a detailed demonstration of how to turn a tragical into a comical history.

The four Sir John Oldcastle authors faced from the beginning a problem even more difficult than that of rivaling Shakespeare's invention. The historical Sir John Oldcastle, a follower of Wicliffe, had eventually given his life for the Protestant faith. As such, he was entirely eligible for the status of Elizabethan hero. Unfortunately, he happened to live in the reign of Henry V, a king who not only was not a Protestant himself, but one who firmly put down any outbreaks of this heresy that came to his attention. In writing his own Henry V play, Shakespeare had been able to ignore the inconvenient fact of the Henrician persecutions. The Oldcastle authors, on the other hand, could scarcely evade the religious issue, given a hero who was remembered solely because of it. Neither could they ask an Elizabethan audience to accept Henry V, the hero-king of the Agincourt ballad, the conqueror of France, as a villain. Because the second part of Sir John Oldcastle has been lost, it is impossible to know how they treated the awkward fact of the martyrdom itself. Part I, however, is remarkable for the consistency with which it romanticizes and obscures political and religious issues that were potentially dangerous. Carefully, and unhistorically, the four dramatists dissociated Oldcastle from a Lollard uprising aimed against the king as well as the pope. The rabble in the play is confused about its religious motives and activated chiefly by the hope of plunder.

With this irresponsible and seditious mob the character Oldcastle is shown to have no connection. It is only the bishops, and certain nobles jealous of his popularity, who pretend that he leads the rebels. Henry himself is in no way distressed by Oldcastle's Protestantism, so long as it remains unconnected with the elements of political disorder in the state. It is almost suggested that Henry yearns to become a Protestant himself, except that the time is somehow not right. (There were, after all, limits to the liberties Elizabethan dramatists could take with history.)

That the Oldcastle authors were perfectly familiar with Shakespeare's histories is obvious. Indeed, they seem to have spent a good deal of their time wondering how to convert the fine things in the possession of the Lord Chamberlain's Men to their own uses. Like *Henry V*, *Sir John Oldcastle* opens just before the expedition to France. Here too, the clergy are scheming to divert attention from the wealth and rich livings of the church through the judicious dispensation of a portion of their gold: some is destined to help finance the war; some is offered to the Earl of Suffolk as a bribe to persuade him to speak against the troublesome Oldcastle—the most articulate opponent of ecclesiastical wealth and ceremonies—to the king. At the beginning of act II, a summoner engaged by the wicked Bishop of Rochester arrives before Oldcastle's house in Kent to serve a summons upon its master. Unluckily for him, he meets Harpoole, Oldcastle's brusque but loyal steward, first. Harpoole examines the legal document carefully:

> HARP.: Is this process parchment?
> SUM.: Yes, mary.
> HARP.: And this seale waxe?
> SUM.: It is so.
> HARP.: If this be parchment, & this waxe, eate you this parchment and
> this waxe, or I will make parchment of your skinne, and beate your
> brains into waxe: Sirra Sumner, dispatch; devoure, sirra, devoure.
> (II.i.56–65)

After a comic struggle, in the course of which the wretched summoner is threatened with a beating and administered a cup of sack with which to wash down the last scraps, he duly eats the summons including the seal. "Wax," as Harpoole opines, is wholesome: "the purest of the hony."

This episode has its obvious parallel in *Henry V*. In act V, Fluellen invokes the aid of a cudgel to force a reluctant and histrionic Ancient Pistol to eat the leek he had previously mocked. The New Arden editor regards the similarity here as part of the evidence that the Oldcastle authors were familiar with *Henry V* as well as the two parts of *Henry IV* when they wrote their own play. He is probably right. Yet it is surely important to note that there is a third scene of this kind, earlier than either *Henry V* or *Sir John Oldcastle*, which should be taken into account. In *George a Greene*, Sir Nicholas Mannering arrives at the town of Wakefield bearing a commission from the rebellious Earl of Kendall for the requisition of victuals for his soldiers. George a Greene himself, outraged both by the request and by Mannering's insolence in urging it, first tears the parchment and then compels this traitor to King Edward's throne to eat the seals that were attached to it:

> MAN.: Well, and there be no remedie, so, George:
> *Swallows one of the seals.*
> One is gone: I pray thee, no more nowe.
> GEORGE: O sir,
> ' If one be good, the others cannot hurt.
> So, sir;
> *Mannering swallows the other two seals.*
> Nowe you may goe tell the Earle of Kendall,
> Although I haue rent his large Commission,
> Yet of curtesie I haue sent all his seales
> Back againe by you.
>
> (144–53)

The episode involving Harpoole and the Summoner in *Sir John Oldcastle* may well have been inspired by Pistol's encounter with Fluellen; it is nevertheless with this older scene from *George a Greene* that its real affinities lie. Like the pinner of Wakefield, Harpoole is a man of the people, someone who clings to a vanishing world of immediate feudal loyalties. His aggression stems not, like Fluellen's, from the need to avenge a personal affront but from the desire to defend his master from traitors who obscure simple right and wrong with the aid of a new and suspect legalism. The spice of the incident lies in the audacity of the underdog: the simple, honest man converting rotten parchment bonds into matter-of-fact fodder. It reflects one of the wish-dreams of a lower class victimized by legislation forced upon it from above, by a sea of paper which it could not understand. In both *George a Greene* and *Sir John Oldcastle*, the plain old loyalties of master and servant, subject and king, achieve a triumph in the moment that the parchment (or the seals) slides down the officer's unwilling throat. When Shakespeare converted the original legal document into a vegetable, the dapper courtier worsted by the pinner into an entirely personal matter involving Fluellen's Welsh pride and Pistol's unconsidered boasting, he was moving away from traditional forms in response both to the spirit of the time and to the shape of his own history play. By 1599, the comical history was a consciously reactionary, an outdated dramatic mode. That cycle of Shakespearean plays which begins with *Richard II* and ends with *Henry V* had helped to make it so. Yet Elizabethans could still be made to respond emotionally to the ballad and folk material upon which the genre depended, while withholding actual belief in such distant and half-legendary types of social protest.

Harpoole himself has nothing but praise for the constable who enters immediately after the discomfited summoner has crept away. This functionary has been sent to make hue and cry after a thief who has robbed two clothiers. He means to search the ale-house for the culprit, but because that building stands in Oldcastle's "libertie" he refuses to exercise his function "except I had some of his servants, which are for my warrant" (II.i.140–41). In effect, the constable of his own free will recognizes and honors an older order of jurisdiction and responsibility based on the autonomy of the great house and its demesne. That the inviolability of Oldcastle's "libertie" from outside interference is no longer something taken for granted is apparent in Harpoole's cry of relief: "An honest Constable! an honest Constable!" The steward is old-fashioned, a believer in relationships and prerogatives which, in his time, were beginning to be questioned and superseded. Later in the play, he will engineer his master's escape from the Tower and loyally, without hope of reward, accompany Oldcastle and his Lady in their flight. His taste in literature reflects his attitudes toward society and the proper relationship of vassal and overlord. When the Bishop of Rochester orders the "heretical" books in Cobham's house to be burned, Harpoole makes a heated defense of his own personal library: "for I have there English bookes, my lord, that ile not part with for your Bishoppricke: Bevis of Hampton, Owleglasse, the Frier and the Boy, Ellenor Rumming, Robin Hood, and other such godly stories" (IV.iii.166–69).

Harpoole and his library are by no means the play's only links with the ballad and romance tradition. The cast of characters includes another Sir John besides the hero: Sir John the parson of Wrotham. This cleric is a hanger-on of precisely those covetous bishops who cause Oldcastle so much trouble. He follows them, however, purely to serve his own ends:

> Me thinkes the purse of gold the Bishop gave
> Made a good shew; it had a tempting looke.
> Beshrew me, but my fingers ends do itch
> To be upon those rudduks. Well, 'tis thus:
> I am not as the worlde does take me for;
> If ever woolfe were cloathed in sheepes coate,
> Then I am he,—olde huddle and twang, yfaith,

> A priest in shew, but in plain termes a theefe.
> Yet, let me tell you too, an honest theefe,
> One that will take it where it may be sparde,
> And spend it freely in good fellowship.
> I have as many shapes as *Proteus* had,
> That still, when any villainy is done,
> There may be none suspect it was sir John.
> Besides, to comfort me,—for whats this life,
> Except the crabbed bitternes thereof
> Be sweetened now and then with lechery?—
> I have my Doll, my concubine, as t'were,
> To frollicke with, a lusty bounsing gerle.
>   (I.ii.155–73)

As an example of Shakespearean influence, this speech would be hard to surpass. It is perfectly evident that Sir John of Wrotham represents an attempt on the part of the *Oldcastle* authors to make use of precisely the character their play was designed to discredit and obliterate from the memory of Elizabethan audiences: Sir John Falstaff. Somehow, Drayton, Munday, Hathway, and Wilson were going to contrive to introduce the Gad's Hill robbery into their work too. Doll, the parson's paramour, is sister to Falstaff's Doll Tearsheet and, in the course of the play, will display the same mixture of tenderness and fury as her prototype. The line about Proteus has been stolen from one of the speeches of the future Richard III, in *3 Henry VI* (III.iii.192). Otherwise, the speech appears on the surface to be all fake Falstaff. Yet something about the tone is alien. Falstaff, after all, was scarcely "an honest theefe," concerned to "take it where it may be sparde." A purse was a purse for him, whether it belonged to a wealthy traveler or was to be extracted from poor Mistress Quickly at the cost of all her plate. It is in the outlaw ballads of the late Middle Ages, particularly those centered upon Robin Hood, that the source of this Sir John's attitude may be found. What the *Oldcastle* authors have done is to reach back through Falstaff to resurrect the far older figure of Friar Tuck.

When Shakespeare's Henry V adopted disguise, the night before Agincourt, he found himself confronting men who inquired into the nature of the king's responsibility with uncomfortable particularity. The *Oldcastle* Henry V also resorts to disguise, perhaps in imitation of Shakespeare's play. At the end of act III, the king sets off to Westminster alone and incognito to gather news about the rebellion. On Blackheath he encounters Sir John disguised in green, the color traditionally worn by the followers of Robin Hood. Courteously and wittily the thief relieves his unknown sovereign of a purse containing one hundred pounds in gold.

This Henry V, unlike his Shakespearean counterpart, evinces no hesitation in speaking about his disreputable past and old associates:

> Wel, if thou wilt needs have it, there 'tis: just
> the proverb, one thief robs another. Where the
> divil are all my old theeves, that were wont to
> keepe this walke? Falstaffe, the villaine, is
> so fat, he cannot get on's horse, but me thinkes
> Poines and Peto should be stirring here aboute.
>   (III.iv.59–65)

Sir John, informed that his victim is a gentleman of the King's chamber, professes himself doubly pleased: this traveler can spare his money without hardship and may also be useful in future to "get a poor thiefe his pardon" (III.iv.82). With this latter contingency in mind, the concealed parson breaks a golden angel between them so that they may know each other again. Sir John swears that this token, when produced, will forestall any second robbery. Henry, in return, is to remember his promise of a pardon. In high good spirits, and without the least animosity on either side, the two men shake hands and separate.

Henry, now quite penniless, but delighted by this irregular encounter, proceeds on his way and joins his army in a field near London after dark. His lords greet their king ceremoniously, but find him strangely reluctant to abandon his disguise. "Peace, no more of that," he tells Suffolk, who has addressed him formally as "your Highnesse":

> The King's asleepe; wake not his majestie
> With termes nor titles; hee's at rest in bed.
> Kings do not use to watch themselves; they sleepe,
> And let rebellion and conspiracie
> Revel and havocke in the common wealth. . . .
>   . . . this long cold winter's night

> How can we spend? King Harry is a sleepe
> And al his Lords, these garments tel us so;
> Al friends at footebal, fellowes al in field,
> Harry, and Dicke, and George. Bring us a drumme;
> Give us square dice, weele keepe this court of guard
> For al good fellowes companies that come.
>   (IV.i.6–10, 29–35)

Predictably, Sir John is the first good fellow to wander in. In the gaming that ensues, the disguised king wins back his hundred pounds. When the parson produces his half of the broken coin as a final stake, Henry matches it, and challenges the thief to a combat. The two take up their positions and are about to engage when a horrified noble intervenes and reveals the identity of the king. Without this interruption, the episode would fairly clearly have terminated in the manner sanctioned by the Robin Hood ballads and actually demonstrated in Peele's *Edward I*: with a victory for the king that vindicated his strength and manly prowess.

In *Sir John Oldcastle*, Henry amuses himself for a few moments by adopting a pose of mock severity toward this Friar Tuck. Reminded, however, by the culprit that "the best may goe astray, and if the world say true, your selfe (my liege) have bin a thiefe" (IV.i.182–84), the king freely admits the fact and contents himself with urging upon the parson a repentance and reclamation like his own. He makes him a free present of the stolen gold, a gift which Sir John receives with an unfeigned gratitude and delight that is worlds away from Williams's taciturn acceptance of the glove filled with crowns in Shakespeare's play: "*Vivat Rex & currat lex!* My liege, if ye have cause of battell, ye shal see sir John of Wrootham bestirre himself in your quarrel" (IV.i.197–99). One may well suspect the parson's ability to forswear cards and wine and become an honest man— indeed, on his next appearance, in act V, he is confessing to Doll that drink, dice, and the devil have consumed the hundred pounds and preparing to recoup his fortunes by way of another robbery—but not the sincerity of his admiration for King Henry as a man.

Consistently, in borrowing from Shakespeare, the *Oldcastle* authors turned their material back in the direction of balladry and romance. That doctrine of the king's two bodies which underlies all of Shakespeare's histories from *Richard II* to *Henry V* is nowhere visible in their play, any more than it is in *George a Greene, James IV*, or the old *Famous Victories of Henry V*. The *Oldcastle* Henry shifts from the first person singular to the plural form much as he might put on a furred cloak for a state occasion: to mark the momentary appropriateness of formality. This king is first and foremost a man, an understanding good companion, happy to try conclusions with a thief, prevented only by lack of time and the necessary affairs of state from engaging more often in the kind of light-hearted, picaresque adventure he so clearly loves. Not even his confrontation with the traitors Cambridge, Scroop, and Grey in act V can shake his confidence in the possibility of personal relations. The whole idea of kingship in this play is uncomplicated, stripped of sacramental overtones, and essentially gay. It is also deliberately unreal, a fiction deriving from a distant and half-legendary past. *Henry V* may seem, by comparison with Shakespeare's other histories, to be optimistic and celebratory, a simplified and epic account of certain events in the Hundred Years' War. To set it for an instant beside *Sir John Oldcastle* is to realize, not only that Shakespeare was an incomparably finer dramatist than his four rivals put together, but that his conception of history, even when he was chronicling one of England's moments of glory, was fundamentally tragic.

In the absence of any formal dramatic theory which could be said to connect with the productions of the public stage, Elizabethan drama seems to have developed to a large extent through a curious kind of dialogue among specific plays. The world of the London playhouses was small and intimate: everyone, as it seemed, knew everyone else. Kyd once shared a room with Marlowe, and lived to regret it; Ben Jonson loved Shakespeare but prided himself on being able to beat Marston and take his pistol from him; Shakespeare suffered from the animosity of Greene and was defended by Chettle; the so-called War of the Theatres sent a number of poets into battle with each other for reasons that must have been aesthetic and personal in about equal measure. The true history of the hostilities and allegiances, the jealousies and discipleships among the dramatists writing between 1587 and 1600 can never be recovered now. Yet the plays that have survived from this period are in a sense projections and records of these long vanished relationships and artistic controversies. Because the history play was a relatively new genre, without the classical sanction possessed by comedy and tragedy, and also because its brief flowering was effectively bounded by the reign of Elizabeth, it can provide a particularly rewarding study of the way writers tended to articulate their own dramatic ideas by reference to pre-existing plays. No Puttenham or Abraham Fraunce, no Sidney or Ben Jonson ever troubled to distinguish between the comical and the tragical history as dramatic forms. It is only from the plays themselves that these categories emerge as something more real and consequential than the private lunacy of a Polonius, or the rodomontade of Elizbethan printers concerned to imp out a title-page with words.

The roots of the tragical history lie, fairly obviously, in those Tudor entertainments which A.P. Rossiter called "the interludes of church and state." The consequential dialogue between plays begins, however, in 1587 when Marlowe used the memory of Preston's *Cambises* (1561) and plays like it to launch his own counterstatement in the form of *Tamburlaine the Great.* Plays like the anonymous *Locrine* (1591) or *Selimus* (1592) reveal much about the impact of Marlowe upon his contemporaries: the need to assimilate and learn from *Tamburlaine* but also to domesticate and render it harmless. In *Edward II* (1592), on the other hand, Marlowe himself seems to have felt impelled to imitate Shakespeare's new style of history play, much in the way that Raphael, painting in the Vatican Stanza della Segnatura, suddenly was led to create figures patently Michaelangelesque after he had been shown the unfinished Sistine ceiling. Because Vasari thought such things important, the details of how and when Raphael managed to see the tormented grandeurs of the Sistine Chapel are known, even as the long hours Michaelangelo himself had spent absorbing the figure style of Masaccio in the Brancacci Chapel are known. Without the testimony of Vasari, there would only be certain stylistic features from which to construct a hypothesis that Raphael's experience of the Sistine ceiling was so unexpectedly intense that for a time it altered the character of his own work, or that Michaelangelo learned from Masaccio. The problem of identifying reaction and specific indebtedness would, in fact, strongly resemble the one which confronts the Elizabethan scholar trying to make sense of the development of dramatic forms during the crucial years 1587–1600.

As it was defined by Shakespeare, the tragical history became a serious, and politically a somewhat incendiary, examination into the nature of kingship. At the heart of the form lay the Tudor doctrine of the king's two bodies, which, in the fullness of time, was to provide the Puritans with justification for the execution of Charles I. Shakespeare himself, absorbed by the difficulties of royal incarnation, never wrote a comical history, unlike Peele, Greene, Heywood, Dekker, and a host of other contemporary dramatists. Yet he must have been aware of it as an alternative form, stemming originally from ballads and romances, made dramatic at least as early as 1560, and still wistfully alive in his own time. Certainly he introduced its most characteristic motif, that of the king disguised, into *Henry V* because he expected to gain, by his atypical handling of it, a calculated and powerful emotional effect. For Shakespeare, *Henry V* seems to have marked the end of his personal interest in the tragical history. He had virtually exhausted the form, at least in its English version, and not only (as it turned out) for himself. When the four *Oldcastle* authors accepted the doubtful task of competing with Shakespeare's Henry IV and V plays, it cannot have been only the religious difficulties posed by their subject matter which led them to turn tragical history so completely into comical. *Sir John Oldcastle* is a tribute to Shakespeare not only because it is haunted everywhere by characters, episodes, and turns of phrase taken from his own cycle, but also because its entire style and anachronistic ethos as a play stand as silent witness to the fact that in the English tragical history, the more consequential form Shakespeare had made peculiarly his own, little or nothing now remained for anyone else to do.

JOHN BLANPIED

Stalking "Strong Possession" in "King John"

K*ing John* is the "morning-after" play
—cautious, suspicious, coldly analytical. It opens vigorously enough—
nothing like Richard's boldly knowing wink at the audience, but still,
with John speaking in a naturally strong public voice that, say, York
would admire in a king. But in private John suffers the nagging of his
mother. Then he must adjudicate a quarrel between brothers, and while
he waxes magisterial, one of those brothers—the Bastard—begins to swell
and fill the stage with mocking, charismatic presence. The upshot is that
though John acquires a loyal lieutenant to defend his "strong possession"
of the crown, he has been upstaged. He exits, but the Bastard remains
behind to expand in his new role of resident satirist. John's swift momen-
tum, his bid to impose a shaping power upon the play, has been fatally
interrupted.

The effect thereafter is of dissipated strength, a division of power
into two centers, neither of which can last. John's force splatters against its
opposition in Angiers; the Bastard maintains his antic vigor for two more
acts, but then succumbs to the general collapse that overtakes virtually all
aspects of the play. It is a play in which nothing seems able to take root.
There are erratic patches of passion that have, indeed, made it occasionally attractive in the theater: the pathos of young Arthur, the histrionic
grief of Constance, the feverish death of John, the patriotic fervor of the
Bastard's late speeches. But these are strained or gratuitous; they do not

From *Time and the Artist in Shakespeare's History Plays.* Copyright © 1983 by University
of Delaware Press.

feed into the unreceptive body of the play nor grow out of it. Even most of the play's violence—and it is more fundamentally preoccupied with violence than *Richard III*—seems frozen under glass. Perhaps it is this sense of obstinacy, of Shakespeare's refusal to do what we know he could do with this material, that is so frustrating. Consider this burst of nostalgia that a nineteenth-century critic, Edward Rose, permitted himself after a patient demonstration of Shakespeare's improvement upon his source play, *The Troublesome Raigne of John:*

> Shakespeare has no doubt kept so closely to the lines of the older play because it was a favourite with his audience, and they had grown to accept its history as absolute fact; but one can hardly help thinking that, had he boldly thrown aside these trammels and taken John as his hero, his great central figure; had he analyzed and built up before us the mass of power, craft, passion, and devilry which made up the worst of the Plantagenets; had he dramatized the grand scene of the signing of the Charter, and shown vividly the gloom and horror which overhung the excommunicated land; had he painted John's last despairing struggles against rebels and invaders, as he has given us the fiery end of Macbeth's life—we might have had another Macbeth, another Richard, who would by his terrible personality have welded the play together, and carried us along breathless through his scenes of successive victory and defeat.

Rose's frustration is understandable. After *Richard III*'s confident, swaggering assertiveness, the brilliant clarity of its presentation, *King John* may indeed seem to suffer from a failure of nerve. Yet the diagnosis will not hold up. Rose, like many other critics, is surely wrong in assuming that Shakespeare would have felt fettered either by the old play, by "history," or by his audience's presumed tastes. He attributes too much authority to the reputation of TR (as *The Troublesome Raigne* is commonly known), forgets or did not know that Shakespeare had other sources for the life of John (which, however, he used only sparingly) and assumes, wrongly, that a monolithic view of John prevailed among Shakespeare's contemporaries. In other words, Shakespeare surely had at least as much freedom with the John material as with that of the first tetralogy, and probably more. Indeed, as Rose reminds us, *King John* might easily have been another *Richard III* (though Rose in fact seems to take *Mabeth* as his real model). It may even seem remarkable that Shakespeare either neglected or refused this obvious opportunity, especially given the great popular success of *Richard III*. The fact is that in no other play does Shakespeare bind himself with such a dogged closeness to a source that is itself a play. That he *chose* such a course is clear; therefore, the question must be why? What did he find in TR to answer to his needs of the moment?

The "moment," in retrospect, is the void between the two sets of historical tetralogies. The question is how to cross it, and the answer—in retrospect—turns out to be *King John.* Here, I think, is the trouble. In *Richard III* Shakespeare was beguiled by the sheer formal mastery that a strongly centralized king made possible. Through Richard he lights up the night of *Henry VI,* bringing the relief of form to the murky impulses and conflicts of those plays. But he gains the control by anesthetizing a desire for a deeper engagement of the audience—by fabricating a personality coherent only as an antitype of the providentialism it opposes. To use a term from *King John:* the relationship between play and audience, centered in Richard, is based upon a principle of mutual "commodity"—we feign engagement to keep from being truly engaged. Through Richard Shakespeare maintains a control that keeps us comfortably at a distance. What he finds he needs, the morning after the *Richard III* blowout, is a strongly centered play that, paradoxically, does not refuse to relinquish control. He needs to find or contrive a center where an authentic encounter between audience and play may be risked.

TR is the model Shakespeare clings to in order to cross the void without a relapse. Stoically, he accepts it as a grim substitute for the allure of *Richard III,* the temptation to resort to the hair of the dog that bit him. In holding to the old play Shakespeare thwarts his own manipulative tendencies, his natural impulse to overbear his limp material with exuberant reconstruction. In *Richard III* he had asserted "strong possession" by imposing a strongly theatrical personality. Now he deliberately splits the central power, not into contending halves like York and Henry VI, but into coordinate halves. In other words, he seizes upon TR's rather murky lack of a central figure as a positive opportunity to analyze the relationship between those powers that in Richard were overwhelmingly combined: the machiavellian and the antic, political power and dramatic power, power of will and power of consciousness, power of "land" and power of "presence."

In TR John's claim to heroism lies in his resistance to the Church, his weakness lies in his submission, and in the end he supposedly gains stature through his denunciations. Shakespeare neutralizes the antipapal material, leaving John without a polemical base from which to borrow his authority. Shakespeare also depolemicizes the issue of regal legitimacy, the question being not a legal one between "right" and "strong possession," but a dramatic one of what constitutes strong possession. John's initial thunder to the French ambassador, asserting a shaping power that flows directly from his office, is quite new in the histories. But John lacks York's and Richard's special dramatic consciousness, their ability to stand apart and look upon experience playfully. John's is the power of the land; yet he has no consciousness to inform that power, to quicken and transform it into a power that we in the theater can share. Consequently when he goes to prove his claim, his "strong possession" dissipates like smoke. Unable to convey it, like an actor cut off from the part and from the audience, he has nothing but will to exert, exerts it with double vehemence, and so underscores his helplessness.

The Bastard, on the other hand, possesses just that dramatic self-consciousness that John pointedly lacks. The expansion of the Bastard's character is Shakespeare's most marked departure from TR. The expansion is formalized in the first scene when the Bastard, though winning the legal dispute with his brother, is offered the chance to forgo it all, acknowledge his Plantagenet blood, and rise "Lord of thy presence and no land beside" (1. 1. 37). Thereafter, besides endowing him with the antic mediator's self-delighting wit and dramatic consciousness, Shakespeare carefully generalizes his function, detaching him from specific historical situations and muting or eliminating personal motivations. And unlike his counterpart in TR, he is not obsessed with his namesake, Richard I—neither overly impressed nor distressed by his bastardy, nor envious of his lost inheritance. Rather, his bastardy frees him to be "lord of thy presence" only, "and no land beside." To rise as Plantagenet *means* to be derived from outside the "times" he satirizes—that is, from the mythical offstage figure of Coeur-de-lion—but derived powerlessly, blessedly unimplicated in the contents of history and all the more at home on the stage itself. For nearly three acts he maintains this role, enjoying and conveying something of Richard III's exuberant freedom, but with little of Richard's thrusting aggressiveness, and none of the shaping power of a dispossessed machiavellian plotter.

From this split of the power center all else follows. Shakespeare seizes upon TR's tedious episodic sequence and sculpts the material into a distinctively two-part structure responsive to our perceptions. In the first part (acts 1–3) the action moves from England to the arena of international political gamesmanship in Angiers. Here the Bastard stands forth as the improviser. He soliloquizes, satirizes, comments chorically upon the mercilessly formal public proceedings. He humanizes the play by eliciting our more private and critical responses to this action, and helps us to penetrate its highly polished exterior. The second part of the play (acts 4 and 5) returns to England. The tone is private, nervous, confused. Formally, or in the collapse of form, this part presents the chaotic interior of the glassy postures assumed in the first part. Our perceptions and perspective have been disturbingly shifted inward; we see John in private as a writhing hysteric, and like the Bastard, who has conducted us into this strange inner domain, we may lose our way. The Bastard is desperate to locate a center in a formless world. But the illusion and facile comforts of a sturdy center are just what this play refuses. The "indigest" that he strives valiantly to set some form upon is too profound.

In TR the "indigest" is inadvertent. But then TR takes its own polemical plot at face value and expects its audience to do so, too. Shakespeare, on the other hand, does everything to make us see plot as a kind of screen upon which shadows of real motivations, real issues, are projected. This is a matter of style. For although Shakespeare follows TR's sequence of incidents very closely, in fact he lifts only one line verbatim from the older play. This careful transformation of the verbal texture serves to heighten the discontinuities between form and feeling and between public and private experience. In the first half of the play, the most extravagantly polished public style becomes increasingly helpless to shape or disguise the chaos—or the lust for chaos—that sits inside all the public postures like some vicious animal inside a cage, biding its inevitable release. Indeed, the most artful style can do nothing but bring on the moment of its release. Late in the day King Philip appeals to Cardinal Pandulph to "devise, ordain, impose / Some gentle order" upon the mess he has helped make (3. 1. 250–51). In other words, he begs the Cardinal to *perform* a way out of the cynically solemn oath of alliance he has just grandly sworn with John (and by which he had forsworn his earlier oath to Arthur and Constance). Pandulph's superbly impenetrable casuistry easily does the trick—but the point is, it is a stylistic trick before it is a philosophical one. And it is precisely the powder-dry sophistication of his argument (253–97) that licenses the savagery of the war that follows Philip's new oath-breaking. But then, by this late point in the long Angiers day, it has become clear that the most formal pretensions of language are not so much a covering as a version of the bloodlust they strain to express. "France," pants John,

> I am burned up with inflaming wrath,
> A rage whose heat hath this condition,
> That nothing can allay, nothing but blood,
> The blood, and dearest-valued blood, of France.
>   (3. 1. 340–43)

And Blanch, new-made bride, fresh from her sacrificial political wedding, solemnized by heartfelt vows and the best Petrarchan conceits, can only gasp to her new husband: "Upon thy wedding-day? / Against the blood that thou hast married?" (300–301).

> The sun's o'ercast with blood. Fair day, adieu!
> Which is the side that I must go withal?
> I am with both. Each army hath a hand,
> And in their rage, I having hold of both,
> They whirl asunder and dismember me.
>
> (326–30)

No one but Blanch laments or even notices her dismemberment. Her little fate is swallowed by the large and indiscriminating war lust that smokes behind the formal confrontations at Angiers. John had warned the Ambassador that his "strong possession" would be voiced by his cannon. Indeed, his voice *is* his cannonshot. There is no language by which to assert and gain "strong possession" except that of cannon. John comes literally to speak destruction. Whose does not really matter, it is the self-assertive act that matters. To possess is to destroy.

Not surprisingly, the language of possession and destruction is that of rape. The object of the rape is not important since what one possesses through sexual self-assertion is ultimately oneself; but Renaissance psychology understood very well what a waste of spirit, how self-defeating, such a pursuit of selfhood is. The rival kings' language of cannonshot and rape expresses a lust, but it does not express or distinguish the kings themselves. Take John's appeal to the Citizen of Angiers, where the city is cast as a maiden threatened by the savage French, and John as her protector. The French, he says,

> Have hither marched to your endamagement.
> The cannons have *their bowels* full of wrath,
> And ready mounted are *they* to spit forth
> *Their iron indignation* 'gainst your walls.
> All preparation for a bloody seige
> And merciless proceeding *by these French*
> Comforts *your city's eyes, your winking gates,*
> And but for our approach *those sleeping stones,*
> That *as a waist* doth girdle you about,
> By the compulsion of *their ordinance*
> By this time from their fixed *beds of lime*
> Had been *dishabited,* and wide havoc made
> For *bloody power* to rush upon *your peace.*
>
> (2. 1. 209–21, my italics)

The slippery personification continues with the "city's threat'ned cheeks," "a shaking fever in your walls," and "calm words folded up in smoke, / To make a faithless error in your ears." John's speech makes Angiers a maiden, but one already jumbled and dismembered. Is the violence here

John's, or an accident of the conventional style he employs? The rhetorical strategy is to threaten while offering safety, but how "playfully" is it used? Where does the libidinal desire for destruction lodge—in the speaker or in the social code he speaks in? The effect is of menace loosed, unrooted in personality. Philip's more sanctimonious speech is less sinister only because it is less playful, its libidinal appetite expressed through a simpler mechanism of displacement:

> And then our arms, like to a muzzled bear,
> Save in aspect, hath all offense sealed up.
> Our cannons' malice vainly shall be spent
> Against th' invulnerable clouds of heaven,
> And with a blessèd and unvexed retire,
> With unhacked swords and helmets all unbruised,
> We will bear home that lusty blood again
> Which here we come to spout against your town,
> And leave your children, wives, and you, in peace.
> (2. 1. 249–57)

Despite the difference in style, what we hear beneath the highly polished rhetoric—and hear it doubled—is a persistent grating lust for violence and blood. But no consciousness bridges the lust and the language: it is not John's will, nor Philip's, that is expressed, but something far more general and impersonal that possesses *them* as they manipulate the verbal conventions of sex and war. When language is a version of cannonshot—and both words and shot are regularly said to be discharged from "mouths" in this scene—it fails to distinguish the speaker. And indeed, aloofly overlooking his suitors, the Citizen finds nothing to choose between the two rival claimants to "strong possession":

> Blood hath brought blood, and blows have answered blows,
> Strength matched with strength, and power confronted power.
> Both are alike, and both alike we like.
> (2. 1. 329–31)

The setting intensifies the dream-dissociations of the action. The Angiers day drones on and on beneath the Angiers sun. "Angiers" is really a formal space, like the stage itself, and the struggle to possess this space is fraught with menacing ambiguities and reversals. On one hand the surreal clarity of the Angiers action serves to heighten the contrasts, bringing forth shadowed intentions vividly. On the other hand, the studied formality of opposition, the intense artificiality, produces a hypnotic effect. Both the heightening and the hypnosis are effects potential in any drama, but here our attention is channeled in these conflicting directions by two onstage mediators. The Bastard has maintained a drum-beat of satire varying from outright scorn for Austria to mocking admira-tion of the kings, including John:

> Ha, majesty! How high thy glory towers
> When the rich blood of kings is set on fire!
> (2. 1. 350–51)

Opposite the Bastard stands the Citizen of Angiers, equally detached, certainly neutral, seemingly passive in his stance, and respectful of the proceedings. The Bastard pulls us back from the debate, urging us to observe the style of kings. But the Citizen is soberly attentive, absorbed in the issues, peering into the debate for its intrinsic significance. He mirrors that part of our attention hypnotized by the conflict; the Bastard mirrors our critical faculties. Both are detached, but one is anonymous, respectful of the conventions of public rhetoric, the other, though loyal to his king, a maverick and cynic.

Given that balance—rather comfortable to us as theater-goers—consider the effect one of our onstage surrogates turns on the other. The Citizen has refused to distinguish between the kings; stymied, smoking with frustration, they can only think of returning to combat. We laugh in our detachment: the kings are trapped in the absurd frame of the onstage fiction they have created. Then the Bastard steps forward:

> By heaven, these scroyles of Angiers flout you, kings,
> And stand securely on their battlements
> As in a theatre, whence they gape and point
> At your industrious scenes and acts of death.
> (2. 1. 373–76)

Suddenly the Citizen-judge looks naked, his solemn robes collapsed about his ankles. Heads turn toward him darkly, with new awareness. Why (continues the Bastard) should the kings not join forces to "brawl down" the "flinty ribs of this contemptuous city"—and then afterwards fight it out for mastery? He spells out the kings' aggression, releases it from its conventional trappings and aims it at the city, the maidenly city, directly. Indeed, what *do* they really care whom they rape and dismember? In the Bastard's words they hear their underlying wills legitimized as "something of the policy," the invitation to violent release as a game: "I'd play incessantly upon these jades, / Even till unfencèd desolation / Leave them as naked as the vulgar air" (385–87). The kings are like children, delighted: they will "lay this Angiers even with the ground, / Then after fight who shall be king of it" (399–400).

At the bottom of "policy" lies this vortex of self-consuming energy. This is the historical will, possessing those who would possess it. It makes puppets of heroes, helpless boys of strongest men; but here, the Bastard half-inadvertently exposes a demented cackling child inside a war machine. And yet, the moment of exposure itself is exhilarating, as is any moment when the theater suddenly discovers itself. The Citizen has been flushed out of his spurious idealism; the wrath of the royal actors, trapped in their vicious cycle of "industrious scenes and acts of death," spills over to threaten the detached observer; the field of play is abruptly widened. The Bastard beams: he sees the battle to come, the more anarchic the better, as a fresh resolution of diplomatic hypocrisies.

But in his aggression upon the Citizen, the Bastard also attacks *us* in our security and detachment, our passive credulity, our sedated attention to the glossy surface of the formal action of Angiers. Now, within the onstage fiction, the Citizen responds to this aggression by a kind of diplomatic violence of his own: in place of attack, he proposes a cynical wedding match, which is cynically accepted. But how can we, as offstage audience, respond to this new kind of violence by the Bastard? Only, I think, by growing sharper, less passive in our attention; only by refusing to credit the stage image, the fiction of kings contending over issues of honor and legitimacy. We respond through a quickened perceptiveness, a coming-alive in the theater. We break our attention away from the hypnotic formal surface; returned, we thrust, we penetrate, forcing what lies inarticulate behind the smooth-faced rhetorical surface to show itself; to speak to us. Through the awakened sharpness of our attention we demand to know what is going on *inside*.

In other words, we repudiate the Citizen's share in us, and with his neutrality goes our comfortably balanced perspectives of credulity and detachment. We become now openly dependent on the Bastard, just when he himself is thrown off-balance and into consternation by the giddy dismembering events that follow. In his famous soliloquy ("Mad world! Mad kings! Mad composition!" 2. 1. 561 ff), taking a breather, groping for balance, the Bastard finds a name for the spirit of Angiers; lovingly, gratefully he mouths the word that, because it is discovered *outside* the general parlance, temporarily keeps him free and poised as a shaper and satirist. "Commodity" is a solid word for a swiftly widening whirlwind, and the Bastard invokes it magically. But its inadequacy is forgone. The soliloquy, at midday, movingly demonstrates his deepened character, just because he knows he is losing his easy independence, even as he grabs for a cynical role by which to assert it. By the end of the day—after the wedding, after Constance's implacable hysteria of betrayal, after Pandulph's ruthless sophistry and Philip's second pious treachery, after the whole atrocious day at last dissolves into its orgy of blood-letting—"A wicked day, and not a holy day! / What hath this day deserved?" (3. 1. 83–84)—in the end, the Bastard is pulled into the centripetal center of chaos. "Now, by my life, this day grows wondrous hot. / Some airy devil hovers in the sky / And pours down mischief" (3. 2. 1–3). We have had the last of the antic satirist, securely centered in his own strong "presence." We are on our own.

By every public standard we have been offered, John's victory, the result of a speed and force that even his enemies acknowledge with awe (3. 4. 11–14), establishes his strong possession. But precisely in the flush of triumph Shakespeare conducts our gaze right through it. The Bastard is dispatched to England to ransack monasteries. In TR this mission becomes the burden of the scene, and indeed we follow him into a long comic action where he uproots a nun and a monk from each other's closets. In Shakespeare, the focus (which is to say our gaze) settles on John; the antipapist business is so much public image-mongering, carried on remote from the center of feeling. Shakespeare, indeed, finds the focus in response to our critical attention. The sudden revelation of John comes as if a rock had been sharply cracked open by the pressure of our gaze. It is our first revenge upon the smooth hypnotic surface of Angiers. Quite suddenly, all the public issues with which the play seemed so concerned up to now have become superficial, as if conducted all this while by a dummy-king, the real king only now coming into view in his secretive seduction of Hubert. John wants Arthur dead; the boy is a political threat. What comes through in the seduction, however, is not machiavellian policy, but something in excess of political needs, discontinuous with public plotting. John employs a sidewise lover's language. Crafty-shy of speaking, he presses his desires upon Hubert with a heavy-sighing wordy wordlessness. As a machiavellian he tries to convey and conceal his intentions simultaneously. But there is something else at work not nearly so well controlled—a leaking of personality. John seems on the edge of hysteria, full of nervous energy, first overextending himself, then seeking to cancel intimacy even as he utters it—to circumscribe the self, hold it back from discovery. What causes this strange behavior? The pressure of our attention feeds John's nervousness and elicits both this lurid exposure and the reflex attempt to cover it up. The emotional energy spent here exceeds its original motivation; motivation must be found to contain the energy. It is therefore improvised in the form of a seduction to murder a harmless child.

The play's second part opens out from that scene. John returns to England, publically strong, but the real action is interior; we are aware of being in touch with the increasingly chaotic personality in the center of that public edifice. The sense of collapse extends outward from John to the play itself, as if time, held so archly at bay in Part 1, were taking its revenge upon the false formalities of the Angiers action. In another sense we are the aggressors, taking our revenge in Part 2 for the intolerable mode of drama in Part 1. There we endured as public theater-goers, our perspective arrested through five long public scenes (with breaks provided by the Bastard's monologues). The action in Part 2 is distributed over ten restless and irregular scenes: the settings shift rapidly, the rhetorical level fluctuates wildly, the business becomes increasingly frantic and futile. Rather than sit as spectators to a public show, we wander within the public domain, which we discover rotting from the inside out. We over-hear private confessions and desperate strategies; hear reports of incursions upon the ramparts; witness distracted efforts to publish an official image of vigor to the world. When the Bastard returns to the play in 4. 2 it is already in shambles and he feels himself a stranger within a collapsing body politic. "Commodity" is too robust an explanation for the kind of feverish self-destruction he encounters now, and he almost yields to despair. Yet he agrees to be John's public relations man, to represent him to peers and to enemy invaders as "strong."

But before he returns, the crucial scene of the play occurs. Young Arthur persuades Hubert, his one friend in the world, not to torture and murder him (4. 1). This is the play's central scene because it is the most private, the most naked one. Shakespeare has utterly depoliticized it. Arthur is a boy with no interest in the crown, rather than a young man posing a real threat as in TR, and he dissuades Hubert, not through logical argument, but strictly by an appeal to his sense of horror and pity. In other words, the intimacy is a further stage in the emotional penetra-tion begun in the seduction scene. There John's political motives seemed only distantly related to the seduction. But here those motives are wholly dissociated. The full emphasis falls upon the sheer gratuitous attempt to blind the boy with red-hot irons; even the intent to follow up with murder fades from view.

All the play's generalized violence condenses here into the all-too-particular form of a virtual rape. Arthur piteously pleads his love of Hubert; the fierce hot irons are repeatedly invoked against the boyish innocence and vulnerability, the delicacy, of Arthur's eyes. Here the reified images from Angiers—the cannons' "iron indignation" and the "winking eyes" of the maidenly city's gates—have become excruciatingly literal. And Arthur struggles in the only way available to him, by talking as much and as fast as he can, to waken Hubert's pity. The point is that

Hubert is unable to do the deed not because Arthur's arguments carry weight as arguments, but precisely because they force him to see the deed as simply too heinous, too physical, too real. And Hubert's recoil is our own. The apparatus of fire, poker, chair, and Hubert's repeated thrustings, only to be thwarted by the sight and sound of Arthur, all make the scene, though bordering on melodrama, pathetic and potent. And if not played sentimentally—that is, histrionically—and if Arthur's speech is uttered not decoratively, but as a life- and eye-saving strategy, then the scene in the theater will have us squirming. We might remember how *Richard III* maneuvers to distance us from the pathetic murder of the boys by framing it in a twice-removed and mannered monologue by a minor character. *Richard III* refuses to offer or risk such an intimacy. Here, in *King John*, we find ourselves looking on at the most nakedly private encounter of the play, and unless our presence here is justified by our sympathy, we will be here either as voyeurs or as mockers. Both we and the play (its actors) are on the line here, joined in a complex moment. This is the rape, the outrage that underlies the diplomatic diffusions and reifications of the earlier scenes. Our revenge on those scenes has been to elicit this view of the interior. The violence is located because we have come to understand it, and partly because it *is* located it can, for the one time in the play, be refused.

The refusal is the rub. I said earlier that the patches of passion in *King John*, and preeminently in this scene, found no rooting in the play's general ground, and in turn were unable to nourish such a ground. We are likely then to be embarrassed by these self-declaring shows of feeling. But such embarrassment may accurately reflect the internal chaos we have uncovered. For Hubert's humane refusal of violence not only seems to count for nothing in the play—Arthur goes on to kill himself in a pathetic attempt to run away—but in his attempt to integrate his action into the weave of John's dodges and deceits Hubert only contributes to the tangle. What is more, the impulse vanishes in the confusion—it bears no consequence, even in terms of a sweetening or deepening of Hubert's character. At most we are aware of something lost, as the Bastard is in seeing Hubert lift the body of Arthur: "How easy dost thou take all England up!" (4. 3. 142). Arthur has never remotely been "all England," but nothing else fits the Bastard's strong but obscure pain of loss. From uncertain sources (indeed, from us, if he could only know) an incursion has been made into this "England"; from the breach lifeblood, vitality, flood out like chaos.

"History" in *Henry VI* is a tide of time swallowing even the most assertive of characters, those who would shape it in their own image. In *Richard III* Richard himself controls this time: he is Mercury speeding the king's execution order upon Clarence, and he is the cripple bearing the countermand tardily. Sequence is that of *his* plot, the materialization of his wishes. He energetically imposes his temporal ordering upon the wider world of the city and the realm, and thence upon that of his audience. But then his decline is manifested as a dissociation of time from himself. Henry Tudor, the fixed future, approaches like a clock striking (4. 1) and the play begins running to its conclusions impatiently, without waiting for Richard to resolve things. The sense of headlong impatience, of mechanical plot taking over, is the image of *our* impatience; the play reflects us. Time, dissociated from Richard, becomes "history" since without Richard there is nothing else for it to be. And "history" turns out to be the triumph of the very providential structure of time whose debunking Richard has thrived on.

King John refuses the providential structure of time, the prefabricated system whose negation might serve as the play's dramatic structure. Shakespeare allows his public material to collapse in order to probe in its rubble for a means of transformation from the inside out. He seeks an internal rhythm of time, rooted in sentience, that might offer some authentic dramatic resistance. Following the privacy of the torture scene we feel waves of disintegration breaking outward into the public domain of the play. The "lily-gilding" scene (4. 2)—the longest, busiest, most superbly wrought—comes at once: here, as Honigmann observes, "practically the whole span of John's reign [is] crammed into one scene and made to appear simultaneous, for the dramatic advantage of heaping up John's troubles and omens of misfortune." Everything here happens in frantic excess. John is crowned for a second time, to strengthen his "possession," though as his fretful peers point out in gilded-lily speeches, the act only makes any claim to authority seem arbitrary. Hubert enters twice and is dispatched twice; there are two reports of rumors and disquiet over the news of Arthur's death; that news is both reported and rescinded; there is news of Lewis's invasion and of the deaths of both Constance and John's mother. Through all this John's moods and reactions vacillate wildly as he seeks out a "policy" through which to recenter himself. But it is plain that policy is self-defeating now; the harder he tries, the more swiftly he undermines himself.

When he hears that "the copy of your speed is learned" by Lewis, and that his mother is dead, John cries out:

> Withhold thy speed, dreadful occasion!
> O make a league with me, till I have pleased
> My discontented peers.
>
> (4. 2. 125–27)

Time is no longer his to command; indeed, having been squandered in the Angiers action, it now turns on him savagely. "Five moons were seen to-night" (182)—all is out of order; above all, *sequence* is undone. There is no stately mechanical tolling of the clock of Providential reprisal as in *Richard III*. Rather, it is as if some central dispatching system had broken down and John finds himself in the middle of a ludicrous pileup of rush-hour traffic. The scene is a frenzied action of comings-and-goings, only John on stage throughout. And it is, strangely enough, his best scene. It fulfills the earlier hints of a morbidly interesting character beneath the crush of conventional heroic posturing. In his seduction of Hubert he gave off a strong whiff of excessive nervous energy, as of a character rotting away, without sufficient motive for the spending-off: the order to blind the boy before killing him was an arbitrary attempt to give form to this motiveless energy of decomposition. Likewise, in the lily-gilding scene John is charismatic as a comic victim because under the absurdly uneven odds he simply breaks apart, fails to cohere, to show himself as anything other than a bundle of commodity-driven reactions to the assaults of "dreadful occasion." While he disintegrates in his frenzied dodges, twists, and turns, his rapid succession of postures and voices, his attempts at machiavellian manipulation, accommodation, assertions of "policy," he glows with a terrific nervous energy. An hysterical antic, he runs through his actorly arsenal of effects at top speed, discarding them with each new assault, finding none to sustain him, none with which to resist the implacable tide.

The scene gives splendid form to a cascade of disintegration similar to that in the *Henry VI* plays, but with more compressed and rousing energy. We must feel that John reveals and exhausts himself completely; that he has physically performed his way through every effect at his disposal without finding an answering form, a center of self-knowing sentience to resist the wild undoing of form. Thus, the suddenness of his decline and death in act 5 really follows with wonderful logic from this scene. Shakespeare is often criticized for failing to motivate the poisoning, whereas in TR it is elaborately staged and explained in the context of the anti-Rome material. But in Shakespeare the point is surely the leaking of vitality itself. An organism fails to find the means, in its actions, to recreate itself: it wastes away. Fever has been in John's blood from the beginning; he has not been able to arrest or shape its course through the play of consciousness. Clearly the fever is time itself, located, for the first time in the histories, literally as an internal organic process.

After this scene, if anywhere, Shakespeare might have intervened with an answering form, like the resurgent providential structure in

Richard III. He does not; the very plot and movement decline into a giddy "indigest" before a form is set on it in the end. The emphasis meanwhile falls on the sense of a loss too dire for a credible recovery. The collapse of specious form—specious presence—in Angiers yields above all negative form and negative presence. By this I mean that we experience centerlessness in Part 2, as does the Bastard, giddy and amazed, when he tries to locate the sense of loss in Arthur's corpse:

> I am amazed, methinks, and lose my way
> Among the thorns and dangers of this world.
> How easy dost thou take all England up!
> From forth this morsel of dead royalty
> The life, the right and truth of all this realm
> Is fled to heaven, and England now is left
> To tug and scramble and to part by th' teeth
> The unowed interest of proud swelling state.
> (4. 3. 140–47)

All of the second part of the play is marked by what is not there: the Bastard's antic wit, Arthur, all the women. This last omission is a curious feature. The two mothers die, Blanch simply vanishes. To be sure, the play is quite barren of women or of the feminine from the first—self-denying Blanch is just the obverse of the overbearing mothers—but even these traces are washed away by the time Part 2 emerges from Part 1. Constance's last tirade has been a curse on every male around for cowardice, brutality, treachery, and (by implication) the obscene expenditure of manhood. Lewis, his bride "dismembered" by the war, bleakly sums up the exhaustion following the expense of spirit in this waste of shame:

> There's nothing in this world can make me joy.
> Life is as tedious as a twice-told tale,
> Vexing the dull ear of a drowsy man,
> And bitter shame hath spoiled the sweet world's taste,
> That it yields nought but shame and bitterness.
> (3. 4. 107–11)

The rape of Arthur would have been a natural extension of this mood: easier to do it than not to (and there *is* no good machiavellian reason) until Hubert's pity is aroused.

But neither Arthur nor the women are central to the play. The betrayal, dismemberment, and rape are better realized than are the victims themselves. Arthur speaks a uniquely moving language in the torture scene, and yet in the play at large it is allowed to count for very little. Like Blanch, Arthur is self-ciphering—he wishes, early on, that he were "low laid in my grave. / I am not worth this coil that's made for me" (2. 1. 164–65)—and of course he fulfills that wish soon enough. Like Blanch he suggests, but with a meekness, a ghostliness that flirts with the ludicrous, his own alternative to the "bias" of a giddy centerless world, that all-changing commodity.

What *is* sacrificed in Arthur is an opportunity to value something ineffable, someone uniquely *not* self-serving, self-interested; an opportunity to commit oneself with no guarantee or even likelihood of a profitable return. Through such a hazardous commitment, the willingness to exchange oneself with an object not in itself obviously valuable, comes the possibility of a quickening. Hubert provides the paradigm, coming alive through his compassionate valuing of Arthur, even in the sacrifice of his "interests." But in the chaos of the play the real sacrifice is just this exchange itself, this quickening, this possibility of renewal. Hubert's act, though inadequate, declares the need and desire for a sacrifice that *is* adequate. Later, when the Bastard tries to transform Arthur's body into the symbolic center of an enlarged idea of "England," the effort itself, however expressive, dulls the Bastard's character. He loses the advantage of antic-equipoise, skeptical detachment, without gaining a clear or functional new character. He loses lordship of his "presence" without taking up potent residence as lord of the "land." Thereafter he can really only play, without much sense of commitment, the vague official voice of an officially reconstituted realm.

But between his "brave" of Lewis in 5. 2 and his submission to Prince Henry in the end, the Bastard is thrust forward in a quirky little scene where Shakespeare seems to focus precisely on the moment of self-diffusion. The scene (5. 6) is preternaturally still, catching the Bastard as if by surprise in a private moment laden with the possibility of revelation. It all recalls the "dark glass" that A. P. Rossiter sees as the history plays generally: "The mystery beneath the surface of the magic mirror with its shows of kings is chill and deeply saddening." Hubert has found the Bastard wandering "in the black brow of night," "half my power . . . taken by the tide." In groping recognition he is asked who he is and replies, "Who thou wilt"—and only then rather bitterly proceeds to claim his known, public identity. The scene is marked in this play by the plainness of its language and the pained reluctance of its approach to the public world. It catches the momentary sense of a nameless loss and a revulsion from the mechanisms of Providence and Order that are to be endorsed the next morning. Told by Hubert that "the lords are all come back" and that someone called "Prince Henry" has materialized, the Bastard's only acknowledgement is oblique. "Withhold thine indignation, mighty heaven, / And tempt us not to bear above our power!" (37–38). Something else preoccupies him, almost wonderfully, as if he had been on the edge of a vision:

> I'll tell thee, Hubert, half my power this night,
> Passing these flats, are taken by the tide.
> These Lincoln Washes have devourèd them.
> Myself, well mounted, hardly have escaped.
>
> (5. 6. 39–42)

For a moment he stares, as if to pierce the dark and arrive there at the meaning of these intimations. He must stare at us, without seeing us but perhaps feeling the intense return of our attention. He is feeling his own nakedness reflected by the stage and is darkly urged toward the relinquishing of himself to an unseen presence. He had assumed the stage in act 1 as its resident satirist, confiding in and guiding us with effortless éclat. But he had lost his detachment, become immersed (as *Lord Jim*'s Stein would say) in the dream of reality, the fiction of the play. And now in the heart of that fiction he stands on the edge of the void, sensing a theatrical intimacy far beyond that which binds a satirist to his audience. But he turns back. He has no choice—there is nothing left in him with which to make the leap in the void—and in this play there is no time to follow up these obscure promptings. "Away before," he bids Hubert, "conduct me to the king."

This ends the bright hopes—ours and perhaps Shakespeare's—roused by the character of the Bastard. New-made, nonhistorical, he was Shakespeare's most carefully poised and lovingly articulated mediator-figure yet—a parodist without heavy armor against involvement, a vigorous shaper of the historical matter, without the lust to possess it. He is the chance—the desire—to transform this mean and sodden stuff, and he fails. It overwhelms him. And so he must fail, given the conditions of his genesis. Shakespeare brutally flays his material in this play, and neither John as a character nor the storystuff of *The Troublesome Raigne* can sustain the abuse, absorb it, and return it recreated. The Bastard can neither maintain John himself, nor join the assault by seizing John's power. For he is not ambitious for power, only for life and life-allowing form. He *is* the antic element split off from the machiavellian love of power, and it is only the machiavel who is able to sustain a plot long and complex enough to admit the possibility of gratifying form. The Bastard can crack open a deadly structure, as he does with his "wild counsel" in Angiers, or he can impose a temporary form upon incoherent materials, as he does in the end, but he cannot possess the center of the play and positively reform it.

I assume that after *Richard III* Shakespeare turned aside, for a short while, from his histories, to concentrate on other, less starkly ironic forms: sonnets and narrative poems, *Romeo and Juliet, Love's Labor's Lost,* maybe *A midsummer Night's Dream,* and possibly other early comedies. In this period he gains the craft, the knowledge, the supple ways and marvelous intuitions that make for generative drama, occasions of trans-formative theatrical power. His desire to transform his intransigent histori-cal materials reasserts itself. It also reawakens his revulsion, and so in turn underscores the need to find a way to deliver over this besotted material, truly, as generative theater. Surely the "way" is not to recapitulate *Richard III:* no longer can he be content to exuberantly expose the passive violence of the historical will, to mock it down through parody. Parody, of course, is a vital *part* of the way: *King John* is, first of all, a parody of TR. But the Bastard, in the ambiguity of his status, expresses the ambigu-ities of feeling and form that Shakespeare does not seem eager to suppress—a strong theatrical force where Shakespeare distrusts such force, a loyal partisan where Shakespeare distrusts such feelings: a strong character, but incomplete, and in the late acts uncentered, floundering—above all, ex-pressing the downright need for vulnerability and sacrifice.

Shakespeare knows by now that if he is to elicit new life from the materials of history he must engage a dramatic mode radically different from the manipulative, self-protective mode of the history plays up to this moment. *King John* is therefore a "holding action," the necessary middle of a process, incomplete and destined to be wasted in the process. The need it expresses cannot be summed up in the choral pieties of the last scene. It is not a need for national integrity, much less the need that an ideal ("right") prevail over a reality ("strong possession") as the basis for such integrity. Rather, the play expresses the need for transforming the meaning of "strong possession" from its narrow political significance to an embracing theatrical significance. The question, in other words, is how to "possess" the theatrical occasion and all of us that make it up, "strongly." The political idea of "strong possession" depends upon the stifling of circulation, the dissociation of blood from consciousness, in which case the blood remains brute and ruling, running in ever-tightening circles toward self-exhaustion, while consciousness remains decorative, or at best merely satirical. We have witnessed this pattern of dissociation repeatedly in the *Henry VI* plays and have seen the cul-de-sac it comes to in *Richard III.* But the theatrical idea of "strong possession" depends on the integration of the vital elements. Consciousness quickens blood, blood embodies consciousness, the circulation widens to include the audience in the enlarged and lively field of play.

King John is unable to make this transformation, but the play makes it possible and clearly foreshadows it. The tone of the ending registers quite a delicate awareness of the audience. In the last scene the Bastard arrives grim and breathless with the news of his forces lost in the Lincoln Washes and Lewis raging at his heels. He finds John dying, Pandulph "within at rest," having already arranged a peace with Lewis, and all the doubly forsworn rebel peers, their lilies thrice gilded, rallied around the young Prince Henry (the child-figure resurrected from Arthur, according to Honigmann) who, we are told, is "born / To set a form upon that indigest / Which [John] hath left so shapeless and so rude" (5. 7. 25–27). Miraculous legitimacy: a form of sorts is indeed "set" upon the indigest, rather than growing out of it. The Bastard kneels, leads the company in an oath of fealty to the new king, and closes out the whole with the choric speech often cited as the showcase of Shakespeare's patriotic poetry:

> This England never did, nor never shall,
> Lie at the proud foot of a conqueror
> But when it first did help to wound itself. . . .
> (112–14)

Considering how mercilessly this play has dealt with the public postures this ending so blandly assumes, it is remarkably persuasive. Shakespeare knew how over-eager we are to participate in a ritual of resolution, a show of healing harmony. A play, especially one so bleakly angry, is an exhausting experience. Even in the comedies that offer recreative enlargements of experience, festive resolutions grown authentically out of the woods of the play, Shakespeare chooses to remind us in the end of the costs of such resolution. Always he appeals to our memory of the play's experience, as against a too-easy desire to participate in an ending. This in the comedies; how much more necessary in *King John*?

Bitter as the play is, its ending is only gently sardonic. As with the endings of the "problem comedies"—*The Merchant of Venice, Measure for Measure, All's Well That Ends Well*—*King John*'s allows us to believe in it if we must. Audiences and readers have done so for centuries, it seems. The point is that Shakespeare does not force an attitude. Already I think he is looking ahead, having given us a kind of voucher for another kind of play, one derived from the insights and debris of *King John*. The ending is an incomplete imaginative act, its feeling suspended, its form perfunctory, its language worked up for the occasion. Yet we come to it by way of a penetrating theatrical experience, one that has enlarged the play with our own empathetic presence. Therefore, in the incompleteness of the end, we can discern access to a new kind of acting, one that taps regenerative energies through a bold eagerness to spend, risk, waste the constituted self.

Chronology

1564	Birth of William Shakespeare at Stratford-upon-Avon; christened April 26.
1582	Marries Anne Hathaway in late November.
1583	Birth of daughter Susanna.
1585	Birth of twins, Judith and Hamnet.
1588–89	Shakespeare's first plays are performed in London.
1590–92	*Henry VI*.
1593–95	Publication of *Venus and Adonis* and *The Rape of Lucrece*, both dedicated to the Earl of Southampton. *Richard III*.
1594	Helps to establish the Lord Chamberlain's company of actors.
1595–97	*Richard II; King John*.
1596	Death of his son, Hamnet.
1597–98	Purchases New Place in Stratford. *Henry IV*.
1599	*Henry V*; construction of the Globe Playhouse.
1601	*Hamlet*; Shakespeare's father dies.
1603	Death of Queen Elizabeth I; James VI of Scotland becomes James I of England. Shakespeare's company becomes the King's Men.
1608–13	Publication of the sonnets; Shakespeare's company purchases Blackfriars Playhouse; *Henry VIII*; Shakespeare retires to Stratford.
1616	Death of Shakespeare at Stratford, April 23.
1623	Publication of Folio edition of Shakespeare's plays.

Contributors

HAROLD BLOOM, Sterling Professor of the Humanities at Yale University, is the author of *The Anxiety of Influence, Poetry and Repression* and many other volumes of literary criticism. His forthcoming study, *Freud: Transference and Authority*, attempts a full-scale reading of all of Freud's major writings. He is the general editor of *The Chelsea House Library of Literary Criticism*.

WILLIAM EMPSON was a distinguished poet and literary critic. His other books include *The Structure of Complex Words* and *Milton's God*.

E. M. W. TILLYARD was Master of Jesus College, Cambridge. His books include *The English Epic and its Background* and *The Elizabethan World Picture*.

HAROLD C. GODDARD was Head of the Department of English at Swarthmore College from 1909 to 1946.

WYNDHAM LEWIS was a novelist, poet and critic associated with Ezra Pound and the Vorticist Revolution. He is best remembered as the author of *Tarr* and *The Apes of God*.

M. C. BRADBROOK has been a Fellow at Girton College, Cambridge, since 1932, and Professor Emeritus of Cambridge University since 1976.

C. S. LEWIS was Professor of Medieval and Renaissance Literature at Cambridge. His works include *The Allegory of Love, Studies in Words* and *Spenser's Images of Life*.

C. L. BARBER was Professor of Literature at the University of California, Santa Cruz. At the time of his death, he was completing a book on Shakespeare.

A. P. ROSSITER was Lecturer at Durham and Cambridge, and the author of *English Drama* and *Angel with Horns*.

STEPHEN BOOTH is Professor of English at the University of California, Berkeley. He has edited an edition of Shakespeare's sonnets.

ALVIN B. KERNAN was Professor of English and Dean of the Graduate School at Princeton University, 1973–77, and has been Andrew Mellon Professor of

Humanities since 1977. His writings include *The Cankered Muse* and *The Imaginary Library*.

FRANK KERMODE was King Edward VII Professor of English Literature, Cambridge University, and is now Professor of English at Columbia University. His books include *The Classic, The Sense of an Ending* and *The Genesis of Secrecy.*.

ANNE BARTON is Fellow of New College and University Lecturer in English, University of Oxford. She is the author of *Shakespeare and the Idea of the Play*.

JOHN BLANPIED is Professor of English at the University of Rochester.

Bibliography

HISTORIES

Altick, Richard D. "Symphonic Imagery in Richard II." *PMLA* 62 (1947): 399–65.

Bethell, Samuel L. "The Comic Element in Shakespeare's Histories." *Anglia* 71 (1952): 82–101.

Bullough, Geoffrey, ed. *Narrative and Dramatic Sources of Shakespeare*. New York: Columbia University Press, 1957.

Calderwood, James. *Metadrama in Shakespeare's Henriad*. Berkeley: Univ. of Ca. Press, 1979.

Campbell, Lily, B. *Shakespeare's "Histories": Mirrors of Elizabethan Policy*. San Marino, Ca.: Huntington Library, 1947.

Chambers, Edmund K. *The Elizabethan Stage*. Oxford: Clarendon Press, 1923.

Charlton, Henry B. *Shakespeare: Politics and Politicians*. Oxford: Oxford Univ. Press, 1929.

Dorius, Raymond J. *Discussions of Shakespeare's Histories*. Boston: Heath, 1964.

Ellis-Fermor, Una. *The Frontiers of Drama*. London: Methuen, 1945.

Empson, William. "Falstaff and Mr. Dover Wilson." *Kenyon Review* 2, vol. 15 (Spring 1953): 213–62.

Frey, David L. *The First Tetrology: Shakespeare's Scrutiny of the Tudor Myth*. Paris: Mouton, 1976.

Harbage, Alfred. *Shakespeare and the Rival Traditions*. New York: Macmillan, 1952.

Hunter, G. K. "Shakespeare's Politics and the Rejection of Falstaff." *Critical Quarterly* 1, (1955): 299–36.

Jenkins, Harold. "Shakespeare's History Plays: 1900–1951." *Shakespeare Survey* 6 (1953): 1–15.

Kantorowicz, Ernst H. *The King's Two Bodies*. Princeton: Princeton Univ. Press, 1957.

Knights, L. C. "Time's Subjects: The Sonnets and *King Henry IV*, Part II." In *Some Shakespearean Themes*. London: Chatto & Windus, 1959.

Mack, Maynard Jr. *Killing the King: Three Studies in Shakespeare's Tragic Structure*. New Haven: Yale Univ. Press, 1973.

Ornstein, Robert. *A Kingdom for a Stage: The Achievement of Shakespeare's History Plays*. Cambridge Mass: Harvard Univ. Press, 1972.

Palmer, John L. *Political Characters of Shakespeare*. London: Macmillan, 1945.

Prior, Moody E. *The Drama of Power: Studies in Shakespeare's History Plays*. Evanston, Ill.: Northwestern Univ. Press, 1973.

Ribner, Irving. *The English History Play in the Age of Shakespeare*. Princeton: Princeton Univ. Press, 1957.

Righter, Anne. *Shakespeare and the Idea of the Play*. London: Chatto and Windus, 1967.

Saccio, Peter. *Shakespeare's English Kings*. London: Oxford Univ. Press, 1977.

Smidt, Kritian. *Unconformities in Shakespeare's History Plays*. London: Macmillan, 1982.

Tillyard. E. M. W. *Shakespeare's History Plays*. London: Chatto and Windus, 1944.

Traversi, Derek A. *Shakespeare from "Richard II" to "Henry IV"*. Stanford, Ca.: Stanford Univ. Press, 1957.

Wilders, John. *The Lost Garden: A View of Shakespeare's English and Roman History Plays*. London: Macmillan, 1978.

Wilson, J. Dover. *The Fortunes of Falstaff*. New York: Macmillan, 1944.

Wilson, J. Dover, and Worsley, T. C. Shakespeare's Histories at Stratford. London: M. Reinhardt, 1952.

POEMS

Alpers, Paul J., ed. *Elizabethan Poetry: Modern Essays in Criticism*. New York: Oxford Univ. Press, 1967.

Alvarez, Alfred. "How to Read a Poem (III), Shakespeare's 'The Phoenix and the Turtle'." *Mandrake* II (1955–56): 395–408.

Auden, W. H. *Introduction to the Sonnets*. New York: New American Library, 1964.

Barber, C. L. "An Essay on the Sonnets." In *The Sonnets*. New York: Dell Publishers, 1962.

Bradbrook, M. C. "The Phoenix and the Turtle." *Shakespeare Quarterly* VI (1955): 356–58.

Cunningham, J. V. *Tradition and Poetic Structure*. Denver: Alan Swallow, 1951.

Empson, William. "The Phoenix and the Turtle." *Essays in Criticism* XVI (1966): 147–53.

Ferry, Anne. *All in War With Time*. Cambridge, Mass.: Harvard Univ. Press, 1975.

Fiedler, Leslie. "Some Contexts of Shakespeare's Sonnets." In *The Riddle of Shakespeare's Sonnets*, edited by Edward Hubler. New York: Basic Books, 1962.

Grundy, Joan. "Shakespeare's Sonnets and the Elizabethan Sonneteers." *Shakespeare Survey* 15 (1962).

Herrnstein, Barbara, ed. *Discussions of Shakespeare's Sonnets*. Boston: D. C. Heath and Co., 1964.

Hubler, Edward. *The Sense of Shakespeare's Sonnets*. New York: Hill and Wang, 1952.

John, Lisle C. *The Elizabethan Sonnet Sequences*. New York: Russell & Russell, 1964.

Keach, William. *Elizabethan Erotic Narratives*. New Brunswick, N.J.: Rutgers Univ. Press, 1977.

Knight, G. Wilson. *The Mutual Flame*. London: Methuen, 1955.

Lever, J. W. *The Elizabethan Love Sonnet*. London: Methuen, 1956.

———. "Shakespeare's Narrative Poems." In *A New Companion to Shakespeare Studies*, edited by Kenneth Muir and S. Schoenbaum. Cambridge: Cambridge Univ. Press, 1971.

Peterson, Douglas L. *The English Lyric from Wyatt to Donne: A History of Plain and Eloquent Styles*. Princeton, N.J.: Princeton Univ. Press, 1967.

Price, Hereward T. "The Function of Imagery in Venus and Adonis." *Papers of the Michigan Academy* 31 (1945).

Ransom, John Crowe. *The World's Body*. Baton Rouge: Louisiana State Univ. Press, 1968.

Richards, I. A. "The Sense of Poetry: Shakespeare's 'The Phoenix and the Turtle'." *Daedalus* 87 (1958): 86–94.

Smith, Hallett. *Elizabethan Poetry: A Study in Conventions, Meaning and Expression*. Cambridge, Mass.: Harvard Univ. Press, 1952.

Tuve, Rosamund. *Elizabethan and Metaphysical Imagery*. Chicago: Univ. of Chicago Press, 1961.

Walley, Harold R. "The Rape of Lucrece and Shakespearean Tragedy." *PMLA* vol. 76 (1961).

Winny, James. *The Master-Mistress: A Study of Shakespeare's Sonnets*. London: Chatto & Windus, 1968.

Acknowledgments

"Some Types of Ambiguity in Shakespeare's Sonnets" by William Empson from *Seven Types of Ambiguity* by William Empson, copyright © 1930 by Chatto & Windus, Ltd. Reprinted by permission.

"They That Have Power" by William Empson from *Some Versions of Pastoral* by William Empson, copyright © 1974 by William Empson. Reprinted by permission.

"*Richard II*" by E. M. W. Tillyard from *Shakespeare's History Plays* by E. M. W. Tillyard, copyright © 1944, 1956 by Chatto & Windus, Ltd. Reprinted by permission.

"*Henry IV*" by Harold C. Goddard from *The Meaning of Shakespeare* by Harold C. Goddard, copyright © 1951 by The University of Chicago Press. Reprinted by permission.

"Falstaff and Don Quixote" by Wyndham Lewis from *The Lion and the Fox* by Wyndham Lewis, copyright © 1951, 1955 by Methuen & Co. Reprinted by permission.

"*Venus and Adonis; The Rape of Lucrece*" by Muriel C. Bradbrook from *Shakespeare and Elizabethan Poetry*, copyright © 1952 by Oxford University Press. Reprinted by permission.

"Shakespeare's Poems" by C. S. Lewis from *English Literature in the Sixteenth Century Excluding Drama* by C. S. Lewis, copyright © 1954 by Oxford University Press. Reprinted by permission.

"Rule and Misrule in *Henry VI*" by C. L. Barber from *Shakespeare's Festive Comedy* by C. L. Barber, copyright © 1959 by Princeton University Press. Reprinted by permission.

"Angel with Horns: The Unity of *Richard III*" by A. P. Rossiter from *Angel with Horns* edited by Graham Storey, copyright © 1961 by Longmans Group, Ltd. Reprinted by permission.

"Shakespeare's Sonnets" by Stephen Booth from *An Essay on Shakespeare's Sonnets* by Stephen Booth, copyright © 1969 by Yale University Press. Reprinted by permission.

"*The Henriad*: Shakespeare's Major History Plays" by Alvin B. Kernan from *Modern Shakespearean Criticism* edited by Alvin B. Kernan, copyright © 1970 by Harcourt Brace Jovanovich. Reprinted by permission.

"Shakespeare's Learning: 'The Phoenix and the Turtle' " by Frank Kermode from *Shakespeare, Spenser, Donne* by Frank Kermode, copyright © 1971 by Frank Kermode. Reprinted by permission.

"The King Disguised: Shakespeare's *Henry V* and the Comical History" by Anne Barton from *The Triple Bond* by Anne Barton, copyright © 1975 by Pennsylvania State University Press. Reprinted by permission.

"Stalking 'Strong Possession' in *King John*" by John Blanpied from *Time and the Artist in Shakespeare's History Plays* by John Blanpied, copyright © 1983 by University of Delaware Press. Reprinted by permission.

Index